# The Land and Its Kings

*A People and a Land*

VOLUME 3

# The Land and Its Kings

## 1–2 KINGS

Johanna W. H. van Wijk-Bos

WILLIAM B. EERDMANS PUBLISHING COMPANY

GRAND RAPIDS, MICHIGAN

Wm. B. Eerdmans Publishing Co.
4035 Park East Court SE, Grand Rapids, Michigan 49546
www.eerdmans.com

26  25  24  23  22  21  20        1  2  3  4  5  6  7

ISBN 978-0-8028-7745-1


**Library of Congress Cataloging-in-Publication Data**

A catalog record for this book is available from the Library of Congress.

*For my students*
*Louisville Presbyterian Theological Seminary*
*1977–2017*

# Contents

# *Preface*

The Former Prophets of the Hebrew Bible are a part of the great arc of biblical narrative that begins with the creation of the world and ends with the Babylonian exile. The framework of entry and exile encloses the four books of Joshua, Judges, Samuel, and Kings, texts that include some of the most familiar and some of the least known material in the Bible. In Christian circles, where there is a certain amount of acquaintance with the Bible, the outlines of the David and Goliath story will be remembered, as well as the story of Solomon and the two prostitutes. Few, however, will recall the tricky Gibeonites or the prophet killed by a lion on his way home after dining at the house of one of his colleagues. The names of the prophets Elijah and Isaiah we recognize, but Deborah and Huldah are unlikely to have importance in the collective memory even of those who attend church or synagogue.

One purpose of this writing is to offer a close reading of the Hebrew text in translation to reacquaint us with the path taken by the people called Israel as they cross the Jordan into the land of the promise, live there—first under loosely organized tribal leadership but eventually embracing a form of monarchy—and finally lose the land and go into exile. In studying these books, we traverse more than six hundred years of history, much of it periods of great turbulence for the people of the Bible as well as the surrounding nations. The land the Israelites believed to be granted to them as a gift from God is a reality into which they cross, where they learn to live together, become divided from one another, and which they eventually lose. This land is not only the place where they live but it betokens for them the presence of God, a utopian ideal concentrated in the

city of God, Jerusalem/Zion, and most of all in the temple. In the
end, ironically, it is not land or city or temple, even less kingship,
that guarantees for this people their ongoing identity, orientation,
and self-definition. Rather, the words spoken, written, and read—
deposited in documents—became the lodestar for the community
out of which Rabbinic Judaism and Christianity were born.

Some of the stories we find here may move us; some may appall;
all will speak to the imagination if we let them. The histories were
written for education, edification, and also entertainment. This is
the way the people went; this is the way God went with them as they
saw it and described it. It is a remarkable collection describing an
ancient people in an ancient world—far removed from ours, that at
the same time invokes contemporary situations and questions. In
considering these accounts, we also look in a mirror. We engage in
our own quandaries regarding our communities and the God of our
faith. The people who wrote the narratives, the ones who collected
and edited them, believed that God was involved in their story—in
the way they went, with all its ups and downs. By getting closer to
their story, we may find a guiding hand in our own lives as individuals and communities. There is no boilerplate here, no script to
copy, but in it and through our reading, we too may encounter the
presence of the Holy One and derive a moral compass for our lives.

As always, I have written as a scholar of the Bible with deep
commitments to feminism and issues of gender and to analysis of
patriarchal structures and ideologies. Women's voices and the roles
they play in the various accounts have received special attention.
I also write as a child of World War II who absorbed in mind and
heart the sights and sounds of atrocious violence and inhumanity
that infested communities and individuals when entire groups were
defined as outsiders, deprived of the basic claim to have a share in
the human race. My awareness as a writer and interpreter of Scripture is attentive to the historical Christian dishonoring and victim-
ization of the Jewish people, and it has been my aim to be respectful
toward a part of Scripture that describes a history of which Jews are
the direct descendants. The history we find here may not be history
as it would be written today in the modern world. It is nevertheless
history in the sense of a people writing about its past. The name in

the Jewish community for what Christians call the Old Testament is "Tanakh," or "Miqra." Because Christian communities are unfamiliar with these terms, I have for the most part chosen "Hebrew Bible" to refer to the first part of Christian Scripture. The sacred Name of God, called the Tetragrammaton for its four consonants, is often presented as "Lord" in translations but is here rendered "Adonai," which is how it is read in Reform Jewish congregations.[1]

All translations of biblical texts are my own, based on the accepted Hebrew text of the Bible. For biblical quotations, set on the page as inserts, I use short, so-called colo-metric lines, giving the appearance of poetry.[2] Setting the biblical text on the page in short lines was advocated by Martin Buber and Franz Rosenzweig in their translation of the Hebrew Bible into German.[3] Their method was adopted and explained in the United States by Everett Fox in his translation of the Torah and the Former Prophets.[4] More recently, Susan Niditch has advocated the method and discussed it in her commentary on Judges.[5] The short lines emphasize the structure of a

---

1. For an extensive discussion of responsible Christian references to the sacred Name, see Johanna W. H. van Wijk-Bos, "Writing on the Water: The Ineffable Name of God," in *Jews, Christians, and the Theology of the Hebrew Scriptures*, ed. Alice Ogden Bellis and Joel S. Kaminsky (Atlanta: Society of Biblical Literature, 2000), 45–59.

2. Hebrew poetry distinguishes itself from prose mainly by a sequence of clauses in which the second one corresponds to the first, a phenomenon usually called parallelism, although the dividing line between prose and poetry in the Bible is to my understanding often not sharp. For insight into issues of poetry and prose, see Robert Alter, *The Art of Biblical Poetry* (New York: Basic Books, 1985); Robert Alter, *The Book of Psalms* (New York: Norton, 2007), xx–xxviii; and James L. Kugel, *The Idea of Biblical Poetry: Parallelism and Its History* (New Haven: Yale University Press, 1981).

3. Martin Buber and Franz Rosenzweig, *Scripture and Translation*, trans. Lawrence Rosenwald with Everett Fox (Bloomington, IN: Indiana University Press, 1994); trans. of *Die Schrift und ihre Verdeutschung* (Berlin: Schocken, 1936).

4. Everett Fox, *The Five Books of Moses* (New York: Schocken, 1995); Everett Fox, *The Early Prophets: Joshua, Judges, Samuel and Kings: A New Translation with Introductions, Commentary, and Notes* (New York: Schocken, 2014).

5. Susan Niditch, *Judges*, OTL (Louisville: Westminster John Knox, 2008),

unit, reveal the parts that create the whole and emphasize key words that serve the interpretation of a passage. Translators who follow in Buber's footsteps also focus more on being as faithful as possible to the word order and word choice of the Hebrew original and less on the accessibility of the translation in the receiving language. The purpose of my translations and of this book is to draw the reader/ listener "into the world of the Hebrew Bible." To paraphrase the German scholar Franz Rosenzweig, we "need to hear its alien tone in all its alienness . . . its cast of mind, its heartbeat." For Rosenzweig, the translator becomes "a mouthpiece for the alien voice that transmits it across the chasm of space and time."[6]

In the books of the Former Prophets, this alien world unfolds itself before us in all its variety, its different sights and sounds, its foreign nature and texture, and especially its multiple voices. The multivoiced character of the text is on full display in these books of the Bible. In the books of Samuel the hesitancy with which charismatic leaders embrace the notion of kingship is palpable and the road to a hereditary monarchy is a rocky one. David, appointed by God and anointed by Samuel, succeeds in establishing his hold on the throne, but at the end of 2 Samuel it remains to be seen if his achievement will result in dynastic kingship. Consequently, Kings opens with a question mark surrounding the issue of David's heir. Once the issue of succession is settled, his son Solomon ostensibly has the reins of rule firmly in his hand and manages to establish Jerusalem as a center of religious as well as political leadership through the building of the Temple. But the voice that is critical of kingship and holds it accountable for the dissolution of bonds of kinship and the eventual loss of the land, already present in the description of Solomon's reign, becomes dominant in the chapters that follow.

---

19–26. See Phyllis Trible, *God and the Rhetoric of Sexuality* (Philadelphia: Fortress, 1978); Phyllis Trible, *Rhetorical Criticism: Context, Method and the Book of Jonah* (Philadelphia: Fortress, 1994); J. P. Fokkelman, *King David*, vol. 1 of *Narrative Art and Poetry in the Books of Samuel* (Assen: Van Gorcum, 1981), 1–20.

6. Franz Rosenzweig, "On the Scriptures and Their Language," in *Franz Rosenzweig: His Life and Thought*, ed. Nahum L. Glatzer, 2nd ed. (New York: Schocken, 1961), 253.

The writing and shaping of the book took place in the absence of my primary conversation partner of more than forty years, my beloved husband, A. David Bos, of blessed memory. Our son, Martin, is an example of one who had the courage to traverse his own boundaries, stepping forward into unknown territory to embrace life while daily confronting giants in this new land.

Other important conversation partners were present. They patiently listened to my enthusiastic ramblings and responded with interest and insight. I acknowledge with gratitude my colleague and friend Heather Thiessen, who is always ready to address issues vital to writing on the Bible, and my assistant Christiaan Faul, who checked the manuscript for accuracy of biblical citations and who eased my transition from full-time professor to full-time writer in many ways. My special thanks go to my friend Aaron Guldenschuh Gatten, whose presence supported me through the grievous loss of my beloved only sister, who made my garden a place not only of beauty but also of rest and tranquility, and who was always ready to exchange thoughts about the latest Scriptural adventure. My friends at Saturday morning Torah study not only gave me a place for weekly intense concentration on Scripture but made this stranger in the house of Israel feel welcome and loved. Rabbi David Ariel Joel of Temple Adath Israel Brith Sholom in Louisville, Kentucky, has a special place in this list. I am deeply indebted to his outstanding teaching and his meticulous, unfailing attention to the biblical text and the rabbis and sages who comment on it. I am profoundly appreciative of his patience and readiness to respond to my inquiries.

I am grateful to Louisville Presbyterian Theological Seminary, its board of trustees, and its faculty for allowing me to articulate the first outlines of this book and begin my work during a sabbatical leave. To my first editor at Eerdmans, Allen Myers, and my present editor, Andrew Knapp, go my thanks for their patience with this "slow professor" and their meticulous oversight of the project. The copyeditor, Samuel Kelly, also has my gratitude for his judicious work on this volume. I dedicate the book to my students at Louisville Seminary, who provided the stimulus and the sounding board for all my writing during my forty years of teaching.

The texts under consideration in this book do not have a happy ending; the adventure that begins in great expectation and hope with the crossing of the Jordan River ends in loss and exile. Yet out of ruin and destruction, a new way was found toward life as a community that discerned guidance and divine presence in the words it preserved and guarded. The Teaching enjoined upon Joshua at the beginning of the Former Prophets, authorized by the prophet Huldah in a document at the end, endured in time.

> *When Torah entered the world, freedom entered it.*
> *The whole Torah exists only to establish peace.*
> . . .
> *Let us learn then in order to teach.*
> *Let us learn in order to do!*[7]

---

7. *Mishkan T'filah: A Reform Siddur* (New York: Central Conference of American Rabbis, 5767/2007), 257.

# Introduction

## The Power of Story

*A fact is like a sack—it won't stand up till you've put something into it.*[1]

The Historical Books of the Bible, also called the Former Prophets, tell the history of the people from the time they first entered the land until it was lost to them in the Babylonian conquest. The books are historical because they tell of the people's past; prophetic because they contain teachings and warning for the future. They cover more than five hundred years and move along a fairly straightforward timeline, although not always as ordered and schematic as might be done today. They contain the facts of history available in memory and document, arranged according to what a generation recovering from the loss of land and exile considered important and instructive. The devastation of war creates ongoing trauma and the trauma of war gives birth to story. My own formative years are marked by the power of story, as my community too sought recovery from the devastation of war.

One of my stories: I am four years old, lodged on a farm in the countryside, together with my parents and two siblings. We are there because our country is under German occupation and our house was requisitioned by the German army. The occupying authorities forced us to leave and ordered another family to take us in. The term for this mandatory move is "evacuation." The word comes

---

1. E. H. Carr, *What Is History?* 40th anniversary edition (London: Palgrave, 1986), 5.

from a Latin root, a combination of "out" and "empty," and the verb is used for excretion. I am very little and know nothing of Latin, but in my small vocabulary this word has a place and a meaning. Our family has been removed from our house, emptied like waste matter from the body and put somewhere else. In dangerous times people may be evacuated to move to a safer place. Our removal is not to put us out of harm's way in a safe place. Everywhere is harm's way. Nowhere is safe. I am little and very afraid. I know it is war and I know there is danger everywhere, but at this moment my mother seems more unsettled than usual. I see her standing at the window, staring out to the street where trucks are rumbling by. I see her tense body and white-knuckled hands, I hear her gasp of horror at something she sees outside. What I cannot see but what she sees is a man running down the driveway from the house to the street, trying to catch up to one of the open flatbed trucks, a truck that has stopped to pick up able-bodied men from houses nearby. What she sees is my father, who was supposed to be hiding behind one of the haystacks on the property so he would not have to be transported to a labor camp in Germany. What she sees is her husband, the father of her three small children, running into the street, waving and shouting and drawing attention to himself while he should be hiding his able body behind the house.

I do not have any recollection of this event; I only know the story. The tale is a favorite one told by family members other than my father during our family get-togethers after the war. It is told over and over again and no doubt embellished in the telling, but the core elements are the same. My father, then in his early forties, was liable to be one of the workers rounded up from occupied countries to be deported for work in one of the German labor camps at a time when Germany ran short of workers. Although these were not concentration camps, the conditions of these camps were abominable and it was far from certain that men deported for forced labor would return.[2]

2. Nazi Germany employed an estimated fifteen million people from twenty European countries during World War II. Most were mistreated in some manner, with starvation and torture among the causes of death.

During one such roundup in the village of our forced residence, word had gone out about the impending event ahead of time and my parents decided that my father would hide. We were lodged on a farm that had the usual sprawl of barns, sheds, and farm implements behind it, and at certain times of the year large haystacks. They figured my father would be safe enough behind one of the stacks until the coast was clear, counting on no one searching the premises too carefully. The story goes that my father, peering out from his hiding place, saw an acquaintance on the back of one of the trucks and spontaneously ran out, down the driveway to the street, hollering and waving to his friend, inquiring about his welfare and that of his wife and children. There is no doubt that my mother, witnessing this, stood frozen in horror. What on earth was my father thinking?

The truck driver, however, paid no attention to my father and drove on, perhaps speeding up a bit. One significant fact of this story is that it was wartime and life was beset by dangers. Another important fact is that my father suffered from a cleft palate. An operation to repair the cleft had been only minimally successful and his speech was severely damaged. Only his intimates and family understood everything he said. When friends from school in later years visited they would remark how my conversations with him impressed them as being conducted from one side in a foreign language. My father lived his entire life in a small town where people did not always treat him kindly; he was mocked behind his back, and at times to his face, for the incomprehensible sounds he made. My father was a gregarious person who engaged fully in his work and social life. He chaired many committees and gave public speeches when the occasion arose, judging people's incomprehension to be their problem rather than his burden. As he ran from his hiding place, this attitude put his life in serious danger and at the same time bore fruit. The Germans driving the truck clearly believed a madman was trying to join the ranks of the workers they had already collected and showed no interest in getting hold of my father. They rode on and my father returned to the house to join his horrified wife and the rest of his family.

The historical facts of the last world war and the roundups of workers for German labor camps, together with my father's disability, constitute the sack to which the quotation from Carr refers. The story that makes the facts stand is the way the facts are arranged and no doubt embellished. My father was an unlikely hero. Apart from his disability he was impulsive and dramatic, qualities not admired in a man in our stolid farming communities. The details of the haystack story may not all have been true. Its power lay in the irony that my father, so often mocked for the foolish sounds he made, was not the fool in this event. Rather he made a fool of the German occupier who missed the chance of adding another able-bodied man to their collection. The fool, flawed as he was, became the hero of the story. It was only a small gesture. But at a time when the most natural tendency was for everyone to look after their own interests, my father kept alive his interest in the welfare of others. At a time when multitudes were annihilated because they did not belong to the approved group of people, my father put himself outside his safety zone and entered another reality: the reality in which neighbors show care for one another's well-being. After the traumatic events of the war, my community engaged in much storytelling. The stories had heroes and villains. All of them were meant to help us find a way of going forward after what had happened to us. We needed "a story to see in the dark."[3]

The people who put their final stamp on the texts we call the Historical Books of the Bible also told their stories in the aftermath of great trauma, the decimation of their people and land, the loss of their holy city and sanctuary, when they were under threat of disappearing entirely from the sack that holds the facts of history. In the course of their existence they tried various forms of leadership with various results, until they decided on the centralized hierarchical form of monarchical government. Each period had its heroes and villains, but often main characters exhibit characteristics of both. Even a perfect hero like King David is shown to descend to

3. Peter Schaffer, *Equus* (New York: Samuel French, 1973) as cited in John Westerhoff III, *A Pilgrim People. Learning through the Church Year* (Minneapolis: Seabury, 1984), 3–4.

great depths of human depravity. A remarkable feature of Israelite history writing is the complexity assigned to major characters. The best hero is a flawed hero.

Compared to what came before, the rulers in Kings are portrayed in a more monochromatic fashion. Following King Solomon most of them receive not only a negative evaluation but scathing indictment and censure. With few exceptions, they fall short of the standard for loyalty to Adonai set in Deuteronomy. But kings are not the only major characters in the drama. Even during David and Solomon's time the role of the prophet as critic and intermediary between the divine and the human realm has great importance. After the Solomonic era the prophets are the ones to issue divine guidance, condemnation, and, rarely, approval. Many of them dot the landscape of Kings, named and unnamed, and it is in their company that we look for the more nuanced portrayal of protagonists. Two who stand out from the crowd, Elijah and Elisha, take up more than a third of the text. With their arrival we are once again in the company of flamboyant protagonists who appeal to the imagination of past and present readers. These "men of God" give evidence of all too human characteristics, sometimes going overboard in their zeal or ignoring divine directives, and other human beings are put more vividly on the page in their wake.

Once we consent to embrace biblical heroes in all their humanity, the story becomes more interesting. There is solace in this feature of the literature for those who intend to learn from it. This world, these people, with whom the God of Israel chose to engage in a particular way, are not so far removed from today's readers when they recognize themselves in the events. The realistic manner of portraying communal and individual character sets biblical literature apart from that of the rest of the ancient world, and it became an important factor in safeguarding the continued existence of the community that created the histories. For the communities that inherited this text and consider it sacred it is not so much the story's historical truth that illuminates a way forward. Its power resides rather in the way it is told, the questions it raises, and the multivoiced truths it unfolds.

## Content and Historical Setting

*At the close of the day, the ups and downs of Israel's history under its kings seem to have gone nowhere, except down and out.*[4]

Unlike Samuel, Kings covers a large sweep of history, approximately 400 years, from the last days of King David in the first half of the tenth century BCE until the fall of Jerusalem in the first quarter of the sixth. The text is framed by the notation on David's advanced age at the beginning (1 Kgs 1:1) and the description of the last king, Jehoiachin, in exile in Babylon eating at the table of the Babylonian ruler (2 Kgs 25:27–30). While the monarchy appears firmly established at the time of David's death, remaining intact throughout the reign of King Solomon, the always fragile unity among the tribes breaks apart under his successor in 928. Henceforth there will be two kingdoms: the larger, the people called "Israel" in Kings, with nine dynasties and nineteen kings until it is overrun by Assyria in 722; the smaller, Judah, ruled continuously by the house of David until Jerusalem is captured by the Babylonians in 586. Murder and mayhem mark the downfall of one royal house and the rise of another in the North. Yet it is not for abundant bloodshed that the kings of Israel are condemned. Rather, they are judged negatively on account of their idolatrous worship practices. They "did what was evil in the eyes of Adonai" because they "walked in the ways of Jeroboam and in his sins that he caused Israel to sin." This phrase, or a variation on it, punctuates the judgment of the kings in the North.[5] Such behavior did not remain confined to the monarchs, however, but infected the entire people. The verdict is elaborately stated in 2 Kings 17 after the fall of Israel and the capture of its capital, Samaria:

---

4. Terence E. Fretheim, *First and Second Kings*, Westminster Bible Companion (Louisville: Westminster John Knox, 1999), 2.

5. See, for example, 1 Kgs 15:26, 34; 16:2, 19; 22:53[52]; 2 Kgs 8:27; 13:2, 6, 11; 14:24; 15:9, 18, 24, 28; 17:2.

2 Kings 17:7–8, 12

7  This was because the Israelites sinned
against Adonai their God,
who brought them up from the land of Egypt,
from under the hand of Pharaoh, the king of Egypt,
and they were in awe of other gods.
8  They walked according to the rules
of the peoples whom Adonai dispossessed before Israel,
and those the kings of Israel made.
. . .
12  They served idols
of which Adonai had said to them
they should not do this.

This condemnation does not refer to an individual because the nation has become caught up in the wrongdoing of its rulers: *"they* sinned," *"they* walked," *"they* served idols."

After the extensive review of King Solomon in the first eleven chapters, the content presents a strict timeline reviewing one king after another, with a synchronistic listing of the kings in each kingdom.[6] The end of a king's rule is ordinarily accompanied by a reference to scrolls containing annals of the details of his government—"the scroll of the times of the kings of Israel" or "of Judah," as the case may be (e.g., 1 Kgs 14:19, 29; 15:7, 31), referring to records now lost to us. Since the completed text takes the reader into the experience of the Babylonian exile in the last chapters of 2 Kings,

6. The synchronized listings are often difficult to follow for the modern reader, who may lose track in the forest of alien names and references. Also, the dates of the kings are not always reconcilable, which makes precise dating of certain reigns complicated. In what follows, precise dating will not be a major concern, as the periods in question are generally clear enough. For detailed information on the kings and the terms of their reign, see John H. Hayes and Paul K. Hooker, *A New Chronology for the Kings of Israel and Judah and Its Implications for Biblical History and Literature* (Atlanta: John Knox, 1988); and J. Maxwell Miller and John H. Hayes, *A History of Ancient Israel and Judah*, 2nd ed. (Louisville: Westminster John Knox, 2006), 222–477.

the collection was necessarily completed after the exile in the first decades of the sixth century BCE. I assume the final shaping of the text to have taken place in the period of Judah's restoration, perhaps the fifth century BCE.[7]

Kings does not pretend to offer all the detail necessary for a complete historical review but provides the overview the compilers considered necessary for the remnant that remained of Israel after the Babylonian exile to come to an understanding of itself in view of its past and to find a way forward. In this sense, the editors of the material in Kings share the function of all historians, for whom history is "an unending dialogue between the present and the past."[8] The theological voice in Kings leans heavily on Deuteronomy: There is only one sanctuary for true worship, the Temple in Jerusalem; a proliferation of sanctuaries involves the worship of gods other than the Holy One of Israel. Idolatry is the major issue by which king and people are measured and found wanting and because of which national disasters befall them. The land is considered lost as a consequence of disloyalty to the God of Israel. There is most likely no way that the small kingdoms of Israel and Judah could have survived the voracious appetites of the large, aggressive empires that surrounded them; the loss of their land was probably inevitable given their tenuous grasp of it. Yet the book of Kings does not ascribe the eventual demise of Israel and Judah to size or weakness in the face of an overpowering enemy. Rather, it holds the rulers, with the people following their lead, accountable for the debacle.

Prophets play a major role in this material. Their announcements and activities dot the landscape from beginning to end. They speak on God's behalf to sovereigns as advisors and critics, making clear that major movements and events are guided by a divine hand.

---

7. Since the main endeavor of this commentary is to offer a close reading of the biblical text of the Historical Books, questions of specific historical layers in the composition of Kings will be addressed in passing rather than in detail. Throughout the discussion, however, I assume a postexilic perspective on the history of people and land and a consistent attempt to provide insight for the postexilic community from a review of the past.

8. E. H. Carr, *What Is History?* 40th anniv. ed. (Basingstoke, UK: Palgrave, 2001), 24.

The prophets are deeply involved in the political scene and actively engage with administrative concerns, including the succession to the throne. The period described in Kings, particularly the eighth and seventh centuries, is also the time of the great prophets known from the Bible by the books named after them: Isaiah, Micah, Amos, Hosea, and Jeremiah. Although Isaiah makes an appearance in 2 Kings 19 and 20, the book provides a parade of other prophetic personalities at times only identified as a "man of God" or a "prophet" (e.g., 1 Kgs 13:1–31). Some are familiar, many unfamiliar. Their presence in these records is a witness to the growing importance of prophets in ancient Israel not only as forecasters and seers but as those who represent God to individuals and communities in the biblical world. Direct exchange between Deity and human becomes rare in these texts after the Solomon narrative and is most often mediated through a prophet. Some of the liveliest narratives are devoted to the prophets, possible testimony to preexisting legends about these larger-than-life figures. Common people come into view as their existence intersects with those who govern them or who come to them as God's representatives. Where prophets and people connect, there is a word of judgment but also of hope and new life arising in the midst of deprivation and loss.

The world outside the borders of Israel is frequently present in Kings as the nation and its rulers wield whatever power they have in an international arena, or as hostilities arise; international negotiations and trade agreements take place as well as military campaigns.[9] Under Solomon, Israel becomes a part of the international commercial world. Witness the records of Solomon's trade with Tyre and southern Arabia (1 Kgs 5:15–25[1–11]; 9:10–14; 10:1–13).[10] Royal marriages are made to consolidate alliances (1 Kgs 3:1; 11:1), and mil-

9. For an overview of major peoples and their regions around Israel during this period, identified by archaeologists as the mid-centuries of the Iron Age, see Miller and Hayes, *A History of Ancient Israel and Judah*, 224–39, "The International Scene during the Mid-Centuries of the Iron Age."

10. Major trade routes ran along the coast and both the west and east of the Jordan between Egypt and Mesopotamia. Even if the stories in 1 Kings 1–11 suffer from exaggeration in all respects, very likely at least a modest beginning was made in the area of trade under Solomon.

itary campaigns are waged to fend off attackers or pursue enemies. The final chapters of 1 Kings record continued altercations with Aram/Syria to the northeast (1 Kgs 20:1–22:36). Caught as they are between the large and stable Egyptian Empire in the southwest and the aggressive territories of the Assyrians and Babylonians in Mesopotamia, Israel and Judah perforce position themselves in relation to these powers, for whom their land provided natural trade routes. While the necessity of trade does not originate with the establishment of the monarchy in Israel, the institution of royalty and its attendant court required luxury goods, such as fabrics, well-crafted receptacles made of glass or pottery, and perfumes and spices.[11] The construction of palaces and central sanctuaries contributed to the need for precious metals and wood.[12]

## Approach to the Text

Kings presents an uneven collection of records about individual kings and prophets. For some, a few lines suffice to characterize their presence and significance, while others receive a disproportionate amount of attention. After the kingdoms divide, Northern rulers get major notice, all of them condemned under the rubric of *walking in the ways of Jeroboam* and *sinning in the ways he caused Israel to sin.* David is the model by which the kings of Judah are measured, because David *did what was right in the eyes of Adonai* (1 Kgs 15:5, 11; 2 Kgs 18:3; 22:2).[13] While Judah's kings and its people engage in idolatrous practices like their Northern counterparts, kings do appear there who are righteous and walk in the footsteps of David,

11. It is specifically against the overindulgence in luxury goods while the poor go wanting that some of the classical prophets, like Amos and Isaiah, fulminate. See Isa 2:5–17; 3:16–26; Amos 6:4–8; 8:4–6; cf. Jer 22:13–17.

12. B. S. J. Isserlin, *The Israelites* (Minneapolis: Fortress, 2001), 181: "Certain of the ritual and ceremonial needs of the priesthood and monarchy could only be met by imports." For an extensive review of trade and economics in Israel, see Isserlin, *The Israelites*, 181–91.

13. This phrase is qualified only in one place by a reference to Uriah (1 Kgs 15:5).

notably Hezekiah (2 Kgs 18:1–20:21) and Josiah (2 Kgs 22:1–23:30). In a similar vein, God's sparing the nation is *for the sake of David* (e.g., 1 Kgs 15:4; 2 Kgs 19:34). Like the image of the land, the retrospective of King David in Kings is one of an idealized and perfect monarch, chosen by God, who did no wrong and for whose sake God preserves the people in their land for a time until the land is lost due to the weight of accumulated wrongs.

I have divided the text as follows:[14] Cycle I, "A New Day Dawns" (1 Kgs 1–11), reviews the end of David's rule and life in the midst of the struggle to determine the succession. It continues with King Solomon's violent suppression of possible challengers to his reign while his building programs and reputation of wisdom garner him the approval of his own people and admiration from abroad. Although the tone may be perceived as positive and approving, there are negative observations that lend an ironic cast to all the praise heaped on this king.[15] These notes are sprinkled throughout the material and culminate in the last chapter, with its severe denunciation of Solomon's idolatrous practices (11:1–13).

Cycle II, "The Beginning of the End" (1 Kgs 12–16), describes the division of the kingdom after Solomon's son Rehoboam alienates his father's subjects, providing an opening for the erstwhile rebel Jeroboam to take charge over the majority of the tribes. Rehoboam rules in Judah and Jeroboam in what from then on will be called Israel, the two at this period in constant confrontation (1 Kgs 12–14). The last half of the cycle (1 Kgs 15–16) records the rule of various kings in Israel and Judah and hostilities between the two kingdoms.

---

14. This division is loosely based on the outline of Jaap van Dorp in *De Bijbel Literair: Opbouw en Gedachtengang van de Bijbelse Geschriften en Hun Onderlinge Relaties*, ed. Jan Fokkelman and Wim Weren (Zoetermeer: Meinema; Kapellen: Pekelmans, 2005), 183–201.

15. For a thorough review of what he calls the "subversive" voice in 1 Kings 1–11, see Eric A. Seibert, *Subversive Scribes and the Solomonic Narrative: A Rereading of 1 Kings 1–11* (London; New York: T&T Clark, 2006). Others take a different view of the material and set chs. 1, 2 and 11 aside as a negative frame around what is otherwise depicted as a "golden age." See, for example, David Jobling, " 'Forced Labor': Solomon's Golden Age and the Question of Literary Interpretation," *Semeia* 54 (1991): 57–76.

In the North, the house of Jeroboam meets a violent end, and two dynasty changes result in the rule of the house of Omri in the first quarter of the ninth century.

Cycle III, "The Struggle for Life" (1 Kgs 17:1 – 2 Kgs 8:6), is dominated by the presence of the Israelite prophets Elijah and Elisha, who interact with the powerbrokers in the political and religious arena but also concern themselves with individuals and groups of people outside the courts and worship centers. The kings of Israel and Judah at times play a secondary role to these central characters. In terms of the monarchy, a good deal of attention goes to events related to the rule of Ahab and his wife Jezebel. The fall of Ahab's house and Jezebel's death are foretold but do not take place until the next cycle. The final three chapters of the cycle are devoted to wars with Aram and Elisha's role on the international stage. The cycle ends with a recollection of one of Elisha's greatest miracles and the return of one of his wealthy patrons to the story.

Cycle IV, "The Tumult of War" (2 Kgs 8:7–13:25), details turmoil in the reigns of Aram, Israel, and Judah. In Israel, Jehu's coup, in which he brings about the demise of the Omride house with the help of the prophet Elisha, is described elaborately (2 Kgs 9:1–10:36). From Judah comes the tale of the rule of Queen Athaliah, including her demise by a palace coup (2 Kgs 11), followed by the rule of the righteous King Joash, at the end of which renewed war with Aram breaks out (2 Kgs 12). The cycle begins and ends with Elisha on the stage (8:7–15 and 13:14–21); elsewhere, he appears briefly, indirectly involved with the anointing of Jehu (9:1–3).

Cycle V, "The Road to Collapse" (2 Kgs 14–17), presents the kingdoms at war with each other and the succession to the throne of the Northern Kingdom of Jeroboam II, by all accounts a successful ruler in the first half of the eighth century who receives short shrift in the biblical record. After his death, five kings follow one another in quick succession until Israel is overrun by Assyria, its capital Samaria is destroyed, and the population is taken into exile. Chapter 17 provides a long rationale for these events.

Cycle VI, "The Final Years" (2 Kgs 18–25), depicts the last century of Judah's existence as a semi-independent kingdom—in fact in vassalage to Assyria for much of the time. This is the period bookended by Kings Hezekiah and Josiah, faithful kings ruling a century apart, the latter in the final years of semi-independence while the mill of the Babylonian conqueror grinds on relentlessly (2 Kgs 18:1–23:30). Jerusalem is captured and destroyed in three subsequent stages between 597 and 586, and a great part of the Judean community is exiled to Babylon.

# Cycle I: A New Day Dawns (1 Kings 1–11)

*The two kings are an ideal pair, bringing unprecedented splendor to Israel.*[1]

Eleven chapters serve to describe Solomon's kingship, first with his appointment by his father's decree in the bridge chapters, 1 and 2, then in a review of his entire rule on different levels in the remaining chapters, with a great deal of attention given to the construction of the Temple in chapters 6 and 7. After Solomon takes the reins in his hands with determination and bloody suppression in chapter 2, God grants him wisdom, which results in his first act of judgment (3:16–27). Subsequently, the material deals with his administrative and building programs, especially involving the construction of palace and Temple (5:15–7:51 [5:1–7:51]), followed by sacrificial activity and a long prayer at the dedication of the sanctuary (ch. 8). The international relations of Israel with Egypt and Tyre through trade and advantageous marriages receive attention, including a visit from a foreign potentate, the queen of Sheba (chs. 9–10). Adonai *appears* to Solomon twice, once at the beginning and once at the height of his reign (3:5–14 and 9:2–9), the second time not only with promises but also with warnings. Twice he receives a direct word from the Deity (6:11–13; 11:11–13). Forced labor is mentioned on several occasions (4:6; 5:27–32[13–18]; 9:15–22). An extensive list of Solomon's wealth concludes the review of his rule (10:14–29), a list that runs counter to the requirements set forth about kingship in Deuteronomy 17:15–17

---

1. Terence E. Fretheim, *First and Second Kings*, Westminster Bible Companion (Louisville: Westminster John Knox, 1999), 19.

in all respects except one, idolatry, which is addressed in the assessment of Solomon's kingship in 11:1–13. In the end, Solomon is a king who arouses the anger of Adonai and as a consequence is beset by enemies without and within before he goes to his grave (11:14–43).

## Act I: Successful Succession (1 Kings 1–2)

*The sword lingers massively in this family.*[2]

Two long chapters take us into the court, where David is ailing and feeble without having regulated the succession. One of his remaining sons, Adonijah, the son of Haggit, takes the opportunity to declare himself king. This action arouses the resistance of the prophet Nathan, who forms an alliance with Bathsheba to promote Solomon for the position. Each party has important support, but Solomon wins the day, leaving Adonijah to survive for the time being. The second chapter reports David's instructions to his son, which include the charge to hold to account two individuals, Joab and Shimei, who have crossed David in some way or to his mind are guilty of past misdeeds for which they must pay the penalty. Solomon is established on the throne during David's lifetime, and after his father's death he complies with his requests, adding to the tally his brother Adonijah and, to some extent, the priest Abiatar.

### Act I, Scene I: Who Will Sit on the Throne? (1 Kings 1:1–31)

*David is old and cold.*[3]

Six units offer a great deal of activity within a short time. The scene begins with David, now an old man, as the subject of a number of negative verbs: "He did not get warm," "he did not know," and "he did

---

2. Walter Brueggemann, *1 & 2 Kings* (Macon, GA: Smyth & Helwys, 2000), 40.
3. Gina Hens-Piazza, *1–2 Kings*, AOTC (Nashville: Abingdon, 2006), 13.

not rebuke" (1, 4, 6). Over against this passivity on the king's part, a great amount of information is passed back and forth and there is a great deal of activity in the form of appearances before the king. The greatest amount of text is devoted to speech from one person to another: Nathan to Bathsheba (11–14), Bathsheba to David (17–21), and Nathan to David (24–27). At the end of the speeches, David makes his first pronouncement in verse 29. With the exception of six verses with Adonijah in charge, everything takes place within the confines of the court, beginning and ending in David's private quarters.

A central concern of both description and spoken word is obviously the matter of a successor to King David. First, there is Adonijah who "exalts himself"[4] and declares "I will be king" (5); later, both Nathan and Bathsheba refer to David having promised that Solomon "will sit on my throne" (13, 17). Nathan provokes the king by ascribing to him the declaration that Adonijah would be king "and he will sit on my throne" (24). Both Bathsheba and Nathan, in different ways, voice the question "Who will sit on the throne?" (20, 27). In the end, the phrase is turned into an affirmation of Solomon by David to Bathsheba when he swears that Solomon will succeed him as king "and will sit on my throne in my place" (30).

A second issue connected to the succession is King David's lack of knowledge. Each time a character speaks, he or she states that David "does not *know*" (11, 18)—turned into "you did not make *known*" by Nathan in his address to the king (27). David's abstaining from sexual intimacy with Abishag is expressed as lack of knowledge: "He did not *know* her." The Hebrew verb "to know" most often indicates more than intellectual knowledge, expressing intimate knowing, including sexual intercourse (1 Sam 1:19; cf. Gen 24:16; 38:26).[5] The concern is not so much with information the king possesses as with his lack of engagement with the matters of the greatest import for his people. The entire scene presents a detailed and clever account of the various eloquent persuasive techniques used to convince the

4. The *Hitpaʿel* of the Hebrew verb *nasaʾ* ("to carry") has this meaning. We might say "he got carried away."

5. The verb can also be used in this sense with a female subject (cf. Judg 11:39; 21:11–12).

king and to establish that Solomon's kingship is based on a royal appointment by King David himself.

The beginning of the first unit (1–4)—"King David was old, advanced in years"—does little to cast a positive light on the situation. Joshua, in his old age, faces a great deal of the land still to be conquered (Josh 13:1). At the opening of 1 Samuel, Eli is advanced in age and does not model strong leadership (1 Sam 2:22; 4:15). Even Samuel as an old man is unable to control his sons (1 Sam 8:1–3). The first unit paints the scene of an old man, perhaps in his bed, who is perpetually chilled, unable to get warm. His servants plan to find a young woman to warm him. Opinions differ on the extent of the beautiful Abishag's success. Verse 4 reiterates her beauty and declares her to become David's *attendant who served him*. The word "attendant" is based on a root meaning "to be useful." The verb "to serve" (*sharat*) is elsewhere applied to Joseph (Gen 39:4), to Joshua (Josh 1:1), and to Samuel (1 Sam 2:11; 3:1). Joshua is in *service* to Moses and Samuel to Adonai. Rather than diminishing Abishag's role, this description underlines the importance of her function. It is possible that her presence indeed achieves the goal for which the king's servants brought her to the king.[6] The purpose was physical warmth rather than sexual intercourse, the absence of which is spelled out at the end of verse 4 to make clear that there is no virile potency left in David. At the same time, the lack of virility on the part of the king is a serious matter because, in his context, there would be a natural connection between his natural powers and the "effectiveness of his rule."[7]

While the servants may have accomplished what they set out to do, the crisis of a king who is losing his powers is not averted,

6. So J. P. Fokkelman (*King David*, vol. 1 of *Narrative Art and Poetry in the Books of Samuel* [Assen: Van Gorcum, 1982], 345–48) who believes that the move of the servants is successful and that Abishag provides the needed warmth. She is to "lie" in the king's "lap," a phrase that occurred in the Nathan parable in regard to the lamb owned by the poor man (2 Sam 12:3). Others see Abishag only as "a signal of the king's impotence" (Richard Nelson, *First and Second Kings*, IBC [Atlanta: John Knox, 1987], 19). Also see Hens-Piazza, *1–2 Kings*, 13.

7. Nelson, *First and Second Kings*, 16.

and the question of who will be the next one to rule the kingdom is becoming acute. Into the gap created by this situation steps Adonijah, who has in mind to become king and has gone about creating a display of prominence in advance of his plan in the manner of Absalom (5–10). Like Absalom, he has a chariot and the personnel to go with it; like Absalom he gets no word of rebuke from his father; and like his brother, he is "very good-looking" (6). Moreover, he is next in line after Absalom. We get the picture. The note about the king's lack of reprimand in the face of his son's display of royal pomp and circumstance implies that these were preparations going on for some time and that David had information about it but refrained from interfering. In his machinations, Adonijah has managed to gain significant support: Joab and the priest Abiatar are on his side. Those not on his side are listed also: Zadok, the priest appointed by David (2 Sam 8:17; 20:25); Benayah, head of David's palace guard (2 Sam 8:18; 20:23; 23:22, 30); and the prophet Nathan and David's heroes (8). At first, this list omits the name of their candidate for the succession, but when repeated in modified form at the end of the unit, there is a strong hint that it is Solomon, the only one of Adonijah's brothers not invited to the feast to celebrate his kingship (10). In verse 9, Adonijah moves into action with sacrifices and a feast at Eyn Rogel, close to Jerusalem, to which he calls his brothers and a great number of guests—"all the people of Judah"—the only occasion in the scene for which the action moves outside Jerusalem.

Abruptly, the text draws us into an episode with Nathan speaking to Bathsheba, as if these two were habitually in one another's company (11–14). Bathsheba had only minimal presence in the earlier episode that featured her (2 Sam 11–12), and Nathan disappeared from the story after his interactions with the king in 2 Sam 12. Now both of them are on the stage in full force as if to make up for lost time.

1 KINGS 1:11–14

11 Then said Nathan to Bathsheba,
the mother of Solomon:

> Have you not heard about the kingship
> of Adonijah, the son of Haggit,
> while our lord David does not know?
> 12 Now, come, let me counsel you counsel,
> and you will save your life
> and the life of your son, Solomon.
>
> 13 Come and go to King David,
> and say to him: Did you, my lord King,
> not swear to your handmaid:
> Solomon your son will be king after me
> and he will sit on my throne?
> Then why does the kingship belong to Adonijah?
> 14 Behold, while you still speak there with the king,
> I will come in after you and confirm your words.

From the start, Nathan presents the issue of the succession explicitly in terms of family relations, especially between mothers and sons. The last line of the preceding unit mentions Solomon as the *brother* who was not invited, and in what follows Bathsheba is right away put on the scene as *the mother of Solomon*. Then Nathan refers to Adonijah as *the son of Haggit* and poses that his counsel will save the lives of Bathsheba and her *son, Solomon.*

In between the two mothers stands the unknowing father, David. That fact comes to the fore in both Nathan's counsel to Bathsheba and her words to the king, in which she calls Solomon "your son," emphasizing David's responsibility as a father. The speech has three elements, each of which will be repeated in the subsequent presentations before David, but with interesting variations: Adonijah has declared kingship, David does not know about this, and he swore an oath to Bathsheba that Solomon would succeed him.[8]

8. Verses 5–10 stop short of spelling out Adonijah's anointing and declaration, but possibly Nathan's words reflect that he had heard this had indeed taken place. There is no need to assume Nathan to be deceptive, as Richard Nelson does, for example (*First and Second Kings*, 19). He is certainly manipulating the situation in the direction he wants it to go. Also see Hens-Piazza,

Nathan hammers home the issue of succession in his counsel to Bathsheba with the four-times repeated mention of "king" coupled with "kingship" and "throne" (13–14).

Each time the king is spoken of and approached, it is with the utmost respect, as "my lord King" and "our/my lord" (11, 13, 17, 18, 20, 24, 27). "My lord King" is put in Bathsheba's mouth four times (13, 18, 20 [2×]) and is expanded in verse 31 to "my lord, King David." In the next unit (15–21), Bathsheba enters the private quarters of the king and makes prostration to David, waiting to speak until she is invited (16).[9] David's passive condition is emphasized by a renewed reference to his old age and Abishag's service (15). Instead of leading with the information about Adonijah, Bathsheba puts the issue of David's oath regarding Solomon up front, only then turning to Adonijah's kingship and David's ignorance. She adds detail about the activities of Adonijah, his feast, the guests, and the absence of an invitation for Solomon, now called "your servant" (19). She points out that all are waiting for an announcement by the king as to who will be king. Adonijah's de facto appointment of himself awaits only the word of the king, which, of course, will put her and her son ("I and my son Solomon") on the wrong side of the matter.[10] As Fokkelman points out, Bathsheba encloses her words within a frame of personal relationship references: "your handmaid," "Solomon, your son," "I and my son Solomon" (17, 21).[11]

Bathsheba is not yet finished when Nathan is announced and delivers his salvo (22–27). He too makes full prostration, "face to the ground" (23). Instead of beginning with the oath sworn about Solomon, he hypothesizes that David must have made a declara-

---

*1–2 Kings*, 15. Fokkelman (*King David*, 354n12) argues that the reference to the oath of David to Bathsheba creates ambiguity, which he considers to be a "literary asset" for which it is unnecessary to seek a solution.

9. The word *heder* ("chamber") indicates a private room (cf. Gen 43:30; Exod 7:28 [8:3]; Deut 32:25; Judg 3:24; 15:1; 16:9, 12; 2 Sam 4:7; 13:10).

10. The verb used is *hata'* ("missing the mark"), often translated in English with "sin." Fokkelman (*King David*, 357) suggests that the verb here has a "profane political meaning" approximating the "basic sense of the word – 'to fall short' " and translates that they will be "found at fault."

11. Fokkelman, *King David*, 357.

tion about the succession of Adonijah: "You yourself said Adonijah will be king after me" (24). He deduces this from the way Adonijah is carrying on with sacrifices and a feast at which "they said: Long live King Adonijah!" He then points to the omissions from the guest list: he ("your servant"), Zadok, Benayah, and Solomon were not invited. He ends with a convoluted sentence, the meaning of which is abundantly clear: It's perfectly possible of course that you, "my lord the king," are behind this event, just as I began by saying, but in that case "your servants" (enlarging the circle of people who were uninformed)—*all of us* were kept in the dark as to the succession.

David has heard enough and calls Bathsheba, who must have retreated on Nathan's entrance, back into the room. She now "stands before the king" while he swears to her a solemn oath.

1 KINGS 1:29–31

29 Then swore the king and said:
As Adonai lives, who has redeemed my life from all distress,
30 for as I swore to you by Adonai,
the God of Israel, that Solomon,
your son, will be king after me
and he will sit on my throne in my place,
yes, so I will do today!

31 Then knelt down Bathsheba face to the ground,
and she made prostration to the king,
and she said: May my lord, King David, live a long time.

David moves into his role of royal decision-maker with authority, swearing by God's holy name and referring to an earlier oath he swore. It is now decided that "Solomon, *your* son, [*he*] will be king after *me*." The last item is underlined by repetition, expressly stating that being king after David will mean "he will sit on the throne in *my* place." Bathsheba's full obeisance, "face to the ground," follows David's declaration as a sign of her gratitude and acknowledgment of the significance of the moment.

*Act I, Scene 2: Long Live King Solomon (1 Kings 1:32–53)*

*This day is a bottleneck in the history of David's dynasty. The right decision barely squeezes through and David is aware of its constriction.*[12]

Word is followed by action as David summons the people to make the kingship of Solomon a reality. It is worth noting that David does not intend to postpone the crowning of Solomon until after his own death and creates a co-regency by ceding the throne to Solomon.[13] With this decision, he not only gives the highest honor to their son, but he also honors Bathsheba.

The kingship of Solomon is achieved in three units (32–40), each of which repeats important details, underlining the importance of what is taking place by David's word. First, David summons Zadok, Nathan, and Benayah and instructs them in detail about the ceremony leading to Solomon taking his seat on the throne (32–37). As a priest, Zadok will be in charge of the anointing, together with Nathan, the one representing the court-appointed cultic personnel, the other God's spokesperson at the court.[14] Benayah, as the commander of the palace guard, is the stand-in for the military power. They receive seven precise commands: "to take," "make Solomon ride on a mule" (a symbolically royal ride), "bring . . . down," "anoint," "blow the shofar," "say," and "go up," completing the movement from going down to the Gihon spring to coming back to the city.[15] These commands are repeated by the same verbs in the past tense of com-

12. Fokkelman, *King David*, 364.

13. This goal was already implied in the words "after me" followed by "in my place" in v. 30, making clear that "the successor . . . will commence his rule during David's lifetime" (Fokkelman, *King David*, 368).

14. Fretheim (*First and Second Kings*, 24): "The rite is carried out with full priestly, prophetic and military participation." Palace and temple will be closely connected in the kingdom, together with prophets, who function as forecasters and advisors to the rulers (1 Kgs 22:5–28).

15. The spring was located on the city's east side, outside the walls, and was later, under King Hezekiah, to be connected by a channel to provide the city with a consistent supply of water, even under siege (2 Kgs 20:20; 2 Chr 32:30).

pleted action in the corresponding unit (38–40). Important features, such as the specifics of the military force accompanying the ride (the Creti and Pleti; cf. 2 Sam 8:18; 15:18; 20:7) and the precise manner of anointing are added in the second unit, together with references to a crowd participating in the proceedings, so that all the people "went up rejoicing" (40).[16] The phrase "long live King Solomon" occurs both times, the second time assigned to "all the people." David ends his commands with the declaration about Solomon that "he will sit on my throne and will be king in my place," the seventh repetition of this phrase in the chapter (the "after me" conspicuously absent), filled in with the words "Him I have commanded to be leader over Israel and Judah" in case there was any doubt where the decision about the succession originated (35). The confirmation of this action will appear in a report from one of Adonijah's supporters (46).

In between the royal commands and the follow-up, Benayah, the head of the royal guard, pronounces a blessing on the future kingship of Solomon, braiding together well-wishes for the future king ("may God make his throne greater," etc.) with repeated affirmations of David's kingship ("my lord the king" 3×, 36–37). In this way, he assures both David and Solomon of military support, a not insignificant matter in view of the brother-strife looming in the background of the scene.

A subsequent report brought to Adonijah by Jonathan, the son of Abiatar, who must have supported his father's choice of contender for the monarchy, verifies the specifics and fait accompli of Solomon's rule (41–48).[17] The sound of the shofar has been noticed by Adonijah and his guests, with Joab, the counterpart of Benayah as the agent of military power, wondering aloud why the town is in an uproar (41). When Adonijah receives Jonathan, he surmises that a good man must bring "good news" reminiscent of David ex-

16. Hens-Piazza (*1–2 Kings*, 22) notes the concluding phrase referring to the *quaking* of the earth foreshadows something "less joyous on the horizon." The Hebrew verb used in verse 40 elsewhere indicates a splitting or tearing (cf. Gen 7:11; Num 16:31).

17. Jonathan and Abiatar were on David's side during Absalom's rebellion (see 2 Sam 15:36; 17:17–21). Note that the location of Eyn Rogel is also part of the setting in the 2 Sam 17 episode.

pecting to hear good news from "a good man" after the battle at Mahanaim (2 Sam 18:27). Both question and remark cast an ironic shadow over the undertaking of Adonijah, who now receives the news of his brother's ascent to kingship. To the already twice-noted specifics, Jonathan adds the important fact that "Solomon has taken a seat on the throne of kingship." Jonathan attributes the detail of the blessing on Solomon's future earlier uttered by Benayah (37) to "the servants of the king"—his courtiers and bodyguard—adding that they "made prostration" to King David. To conclude, Jonathan expands the declaration about the one "who sits on the throne" with a divine blessing invoked by King David.

1 KINGS 1:48–49

48 Thus also said the king:
Blessed be Adonai,
the God of Israel, who has given today
one who sits on my throne
and my eyes to see it.

49 Then trembled and arose
all the guests of Adonijah.
And each man went on his way.

The final note puts to rest the aspirations of Adonijah for now and completes the repeated assertions about Solomon's kingship.

The chapter closes with Solomon's first activity as king: granting safety to his fearful brother (50–53). For the first time, Solomon speaks and acts, receiving from his brother the traditional gesture of prostration as a sign of recognition and respect. Adonijah is promised safety until he oversteps a boundary of unspecified nature (52). The clear program of the chapter, to argue the legitimate succession of Solomon to the throne of his father David, has been accomplished by the multiple references to this kingship originating decisively in his royal sire, finalized by the appropriate personnel, and acknowledged even by his rival. The undertone of the episodes is, however, one of contention, broken aspirations, and only a tentative peace in David's house.

*Act I, Scene 3: The Sword of Kingship (1 Kings 2)*

*If this is how it begins, how will it end?*[18]

David's deathbed instructions are the prelude to horrifying bloodshed at the onset of Solomon's kingship. As he nears death, David
instructs Solomon in a section that ends with his death and the
affirmation of Solomon's kingship (1–12). As the scene opens, David
admonishes Solomon to stick to the "Teaching of Moses" in words
that echo the teachings of Deuteronomy: "walk in God's ways, guard
his statutes, commandments, and just rules," etc. All of this is so
that God will maintain a descendant of David on Israel's throne.
Either the unconditional promise of God made to David in 2 Samuel
7:12–16 is here understood to contain a condition after all or the text
refers to the Northern Kingdom with the name Israel in verse 4. At
the least, David puts a condition on God's promises to his house.
We note that "the conditional and the unconditional stand in no
little tension in Kings."[19] In part, this tension is due to the multiple
voices in the text. In this chapter, we hear only from David what he
understands the promise to be.

The admonitions to this son bring to mind the words of God to
Joshua with their encouragement to "be strong" and "walk according
to the instruction given by Moses" (Josh 1:6–9). As in the encouragement to Joshua, specific orders follow the general admonitions.
In 1 Kings 2, these take the form of David's charge for Solomon to
eliminate old enemies. He names only two, but Solomon will find
four of them. David speaks first of Joab and the bloodguilt that is
on his head on account of his killing of Abner and Amasa (5). Never
mind that Joab is bound to him not only by his steadfast loyalty but

---

18. Lyle Eslinger, *Into the Hands of the Living God*, JSOTSup 84 (Sheffield:
Almond, 1984), 125.

19. Fretheim, *First and Second Kings*, 29. David Jobling (" 'Forced Labor':
Solomon's Golden Age and the Art of Literary Representation," *Semeia* 54
[Atlanta: Scholars Press, 1991], 69) argues that the unconditional subverts the
logic of the conditional at least in 1 Kings 3–10. One could, however, argue
the opposite case more easily. The conditional, after all, sets limits on the
unconditional.

by family ties. The second one is Shimei, who cursed David on his flight out of Jerusalem during the Absalom revolt (8). Never mind David's sworn oath on a subsequent occasion not to kill him (2 Sam 19:24[23]). The letter of his word will, after all, be kept if Solomon does the deed. Neither of these men is allowed to go to his grave in peace. With each command, David confirms Solomon's wisdom/ cleverness (6, 9).

The positive reference to Barzillai's offspring hardly makes a dent in this rancorous recital from David (7). That it may be less about Solomon and more about his own desire for revenge is disclosed in the way he commences the charges against Joab and Shimei, both of which put their transgressions against *David* in the center: "You yourself know what Joab did to *me*" (5) and "Shimei . . . cursed *me* with a terrible curse" (8). It's all about what lies between David and these two. Joab had sided with Adonijah, but that is not the charge David levels against him. Fokkelman believes that the source of the bitterness lies, for Joab's part, in the killing of Absalom and his harsh words to David in the aftermath.[20] Whatever the case may be, the reality is that Joab is a powerful force, especially in terms of the king's military support, and might be a dangerous man for Solomon to leave around. Yet Joab has come across as above all a realist; diplomacy and reason might have gone a long way to bring him around. Such tactics are not entertained, however, in dealing with Solomon's potential rivals and the threats to his kingship.

David's last words are "in blood to Sheol," and then he dies (10). It is an ignominious ending for the man we have followed from his youth through hardships and persecutions to a throne held in a shaky hand and through the ups and downs of his subsequent rule. Robert Alter writes, "David has had noble moments as well as affectingly human ones, but it is a remarkable token of the writer's gritty realism about men in the vindictive currents of violent politics that

---

20. Fokkelman (*King David*, 388) sees the dark side of David's personality revealed in this section, with its "vulgar settling of old accounts." He observes that "the true reason for his unfathomable bitterness and rancor is very personal yet remains concealed simply because David cannot give expression to it even now."

the very last words he assigns to David are *bedam Sheol*, 'in blood to Sheol.' "[21] His death notice is given in the way it will be for the rulers of Israel and Judah, referring to the ancestors and the location of the grave.[22] The narrators are not sentimental, and with this sober obituary lacking any reference to mourning, they may already be tolling the bell of doom that befalls such flawed human government. Solomon, in the meantime, sits firmly on his father's throne: "And Solomon sat on the throne of his father David,/ and his kingdom was firmly established" (12)—a declaration that will be repeated after the last of Solomon's victims, Shimei, has been killed (46).

The first one to fall victim to the death-wielding hand of the new king is not Joab, but Adonijah (13–25). He seeks an audience with Bathsheba and asks her to intercede for him with Solomon in order to be given Abishag as a wife. Once again, there is detailed conversation with Bathsheba at the center. She establishes first that Adonijah comes to her in peace and then listens to him declare that he understands the kingship to be Solomon's by God's will (even though it really already belonged to him!). Presumably, the statement intends to put Bathsheba at ease in regard to his intentions toward Solomon. He has come "in peace" (13) and fosters no plans of rebellion against his brother. In the next breath, he asks for the king to *give* him Abishag as a wife—she who, although not King David's consort, yet had shared his bed. Adonijah, already set up to recall Absalom when he first overreached in his display of royal grandeur, once again is depicted as stepping into a dangerous power zone too much like the one his brother occupied on the rooftop of the palace with his father's concubines. Bathsheba responds positively: "Very well. I myself will speak about you to the king" (18).

Solomon receives her with the utmost respect and already agrees to the request before she has made it, probably because the

---

21. Alter, *The David Story: A Translation with Commentary of 1 and 2 Samuel* (New York: Norton, 1999), 376n9.

22. The mention of "the city of David" (10) does not cohere with the reference to "his ancestors," who would have been buried in Bethlehem. Perhaps the notice means that an ancestral grave is established in Jerusalem for David and his descendants. All the kings of Judah that follow him will be buried there.

name of Adonijah is not a part of her opening gambit, which she couches as "a small request" (20). When Solomon hears what his brother has in mind, he sarcastically replies that she might as well have asked him to give the kingship to Adonijah, who is after all the elder, supported by David's general Joab and the priest Abiatar, and that this move will cost Adonijah his life. Benayah is the one to execute the king's orders, and Adonijah the son of Haggit becomes the first casualty of Solomon's reign (25).

Clearly, Solomon views Adonijah's desire as a power grab; his words sound sarcastic and angry. Bathsheba's mood and intention are more difficult to deduce. The narrative does not let the reader/listener glimpse her thoughts, and her tone cannot be inferred from her words. One word in her exchange with Adonijah may, however, hint at her frame of mind: when she agrees to speak *about* Adonijah to the king (18). Most translations settle on "for" or "on your behalf," but the word in Hebrew is *'al*, a preposition meaning "upon, over, above, or against." It is used with the personal pronoun and the verb "to speak" in two other places, where the meaning is negative.[23] At the very least, the phrase conveys ambiguity as to what she has in mind. Speaking *about* Adonijah can mean a lot of things, and the language leaves her intentions unclear.

From the course of the account, it becomes evident that Bathsheba is treated with great respect by those around her, as she occupies the position of queen mother, with which comes a good amount of authority. When Solomon welcomes her, he makes prostration to her and puts a throne down for her at his right hand (19). He accedes readily to what she is about to ask ahead of time. Bathsheba has shown herself to be a smart negotiator on her son's behalf in the previous episode, one capable of participation in political intrigue. It is difficult to conceive of her as in any way naïve, acting to support the extravagant claim of one who would remain an archrival to her son were he to remain alive. Most likely, she knows just how to phrase her words so as to get the maximum indignation out of her son. First, it is a "*small* request," to which he agrees right away. This she

---

23. 1 Kgs 22:23 and Jer 11:17 both have a negative meaning: "Adonai has spoken evil against you."

follows up with the reference to a gift of Abishag the Shunammite, perhaps raising Solomon's expectations that she desires her as an attendant for herself. Her last phrase, "to Adonijah, your brother, for a wife," holds the sting, even then delaying it until the final word.[24] It seems very unlikely that the narrative would have us understand she does not anticipate Solomon's outburst and his action.[25]

The next one to be deprived—if not of his life then of his livelihood—is Abiatar (26–27). The man who once, fleeing from the slaughter at Nob, brought David the Ephod, who stayed at David's side to be consulted when he fled from Saul, who together with Zadok brought the Ark into Jerusalem, who was appointed as priest by David, who together with his son Jonathan had risked his life on behalf of David during Absalom's rebellion—this man is exiled from Jerusalem. Solomon "drove him out from being priest before Adonai." It's all in fulfillment of a prophecy, of course (1 Sam 2:27–36; 3:11–14).

Joab, aware of Solomon's ruthless actions toward Adonijah and his supporters, takes the opportunity to flee to the sanctuary and like Adonijah before him holds on to the horns of the altar (28–34). Had not Adonijah first escaped with his life using this tactic? Benayah, ordered to kill Joab, is hesitant to violate the refuge of the sanctuary when Joab refuses to come out, but Solomon, offering a long justification for visiting bloodguilt on Joab, has him murdered there anyway.[26] It's all because he struck down "two men more

24. In Hebrew, the phrase contains only three words.

25. Alter (*The David Story*, 378n18), who shares this view of Bathsheba, remarks that she likely immediately agreed to Adonijah's request because "she quickly realizes what escapes him—that it will prove to be his death sentence, and thus a threat to her son's throne will be permanently eliminated." Others see Bathsheba as going to Solomon with good intentions on Adonijah's behalf (see Hens-Piazza, *1–2 Kings*, 32).

26. The Book of the Covenant orders protection at the sanctuary for someone who has killed inadvertently, but the one who has killed with intent shall be *taken from the altar* to be killed (Exod 21:12–14). It is of course difficult to know how many of the regulations in the Exodus texts were applied literally. It could be that a sanctuary was more generally conceived as a place where no killing should happen, as indeed the instruction in Exodus 21:14

righteous than he" (32): Abner, who had supported David's rival king, Ishboshet, and killed Joab's brother Asahel (2 Sam 2:8, 23), and Amasa, who had been in charge of Absalom's forces but was later appointed by David to lead the army (2 Sam 17:25; 19:14[13]). Joab was loyal to David throughout his life, and his support of Adonijah was a matter of backing the wrong horse for the succession rather than of betrayal. At least he gets a burial, unlike Adonijah and Shimei, albeit "in the wilderness" (34).[27]

Shimei's story is the most intricate, as Solomon sentences him to a kind of house arrest (36–38). Perhaps Solomon is tired of all the executions, and so he orders him to stay inside Jerusalem, to which Shimei agrees, probably glad to get away with his life. As a descendant of the tribe of Benjamin and a supporter of the Absalom rebellion, he may have been considered a special threat. When two of his servants flee to Gath and he goes there to retrieve them, it is over for Shimei (39–46). Once again, it is Benayah who executes the king's orders. So "the kingship was established in the hand of Solomon" is the concluding note, echoing the phrase following the report of David's death. In between these two statements, three men have been murdered, two of them kin to Solomon—his brother and his father's cousin—and a priest has been banished. There is little doubt that the narrative portrays a continuation of a house founded on rivalry, suspicion and bloodshed, something that hardly coheres with the admonition to follow the Teaching of Moses put in David's mouth as a preamble to the charges he gives his son regarding old enemies (3–4). Gina Hens-

---

stipulates, so that slaying even a guilty person at the altar was a violation of a moral code. For a detailed discussion of the finer legal points, see Jonathan Burnside, "Flight of the Fugitives: Rethinking the Relationship between Biblical Law (Exodus 21:12–14) and the Davidic Succession Narrative (1 Kings 1–2)," *JBL* 129 (2010): 418–31.

27. Alter (*The David Story*, 382n34) calls the "report of Joab's burial in the wilderness" a conclusion "on a haunting note." He also cites the medieval commentator Gersonides, who considered it fitting, for "it would not be meet for a man like him to be part of civil society because he had killed men by devious means and by deception." Of course, the same could be said of King David.

Piazza writes, "Whether read with an ancient sensibility or from a position of contemporary sentiment, the instructions of the dying king and subsequent murderous actions of his son can only leave us aghast and horrified."[28]

## Act II: The Fruits of Wisdom (1 Kings 3:1–5:14[29])

*And wisdom, where shall it be found? (Job 28:12)*

As Solomon settles into his kingship, he commences to forge alliances and engage in trade. The account of his dream and God's granting him wisdom, together with his exercise of wise judgment at the opening of his activities (3:5–27), balances the report on his royal household and the spreading reputation of his wisdom (5:9–14 [4:29–34]). References to Solomon's wisdom, already anticipated by King David in 2:6 and 9, are found in key places (3:28; 5:9-10, 14 [4:29–30, 34]). Wedged between the reports of chapters 3 and 5, chapter 4 contains an extensive list of administrative officials and their duties (4:1–19). The people of Solomon's reign come to the fore when they are said to be astonished by his wisdom (3:28; 5:14 [4:34]) or filled with peace and joy (4:20; 5:5 [4:25]). A more somber note is struck by the mention of "forced labor" (Hebrew *mas*), in this section occurring for the first time in 4:6.[30] It will not be the last.

28. Hens-Piazza, *1–2 Kings*, 33. Iain Provan ("Why Barzillai of Gilead [1 Kings 2:7]? Narrative Art and the Hermeneutics of Suspicion in 1 Kings 1–2," *TynBul* 46 [1995]: 103–116) argues that 1 Kgs 1–2 are constructed to arouse the suspicion of any reader by casting both David and Solomon in a negative light and thus undermining "the narrative which these two characters offer us."

29. I am following chapter divisions and verse numbering of the traditional Hebrew text. English versions present 5:1–14 as 4:21–34, noted in brackets in this section.

30. The Hebrew word *mas* is a so-called "collective" noun meaning both "forced labor, conscription or corvée" and the laborers conscripted for the tasks.

*Act II, Scene 1: A Word of Promise (1 Kings 3:1–15)*

*Shades of the bloodthirsty tyrant of chapter 2 have all but faded.*[31]

A seemingly innocuous introduction (1) sets the new king on the stage as an able negotiator, making smart alliances through marriage. At the same time, it introduces the notion of building plans that still lie ahead. There is as yet no fitting housing for the Egyptian princess. Solomon is said to *love Adonai* by "walking according to the rules of his father David" (3). Marrying foreign women will eventually be considered the cause for Solomon's worship of other gods, and making alliances with Egypt in itself is frowned upon in Deuteronomy in the prescriptions regarding kingship (Deut 17:16; 28:68). At the same time, sacrificing *on the heights* is mentioned twice, once in reference to the people and once to Solomon. The rationale is of course that there is as yet no temple; yet how had everyone managed to bring appropriate sacrifice until this point? The *heights* ring an ominous note, as offering sacrifice on them is considered a major cultic violation in Kings, becoming proverbial for the idolatry and betrayal of the God of Israel by all the kings of the North following Jeroboam (1 Kgs 12:31) and many of the kings of Judah.[32] To be sure, there is no outright condemnation intended here, but there is certainly a hint of foreboding regarding Solomon's kingship, which is all the more striking because it is juxtaposed with the observation about his *love* for Adonai. Hens-Piazza writes, "That Solomon's love for the Lord is encircled by references to high places may forecast just how fragile his love will be."[33]

Furthermore, there is already a hint of extravagance in the number of sacrifices brought by Solomon, even if we take the total of one thousand in verse 4 with a grain of salt. In addition, Solomon's worship takes place in Gibeon, encountered in Joshua as

---

31. Hens-Piazza, *1–2 Kings*, 35.

32. For example, 1 Kgs 14:23; 15:14; 22:44[43]; 2 Kgs 12:4[3]; 15:4, 35. The phrasing beginning with "only," as here in1 Kgs 3:3, is especially indicative of a less than wholehearted commitment to Adonai.

33. Hens-Piazza, *1–2 Kings*, 36.

a city with indigenous Canaanite inhabitants who tricked Joshua into a peace pact (Josh 9:3–27). In the opening chapters of 2 Samuel, it is a location of bloody murder (2 Sam 2:16), and at the close of Samuel, the inhabitants of Gibeon exact the slaughter of Saul's descendants (2 Sam 21:2–9). The name in Hebrew also includes a reference to a "high place." With Gibeon's history associated with deceit, bloodshed, and Canaanite habitation, few positive qualities emanate from this place.[34]

All the same, Solomon's first experience of a divine visitation occurs just here at Gibeon, a place where he has brought sacrifice (5–14). In the Historical Books, Solomon is the only person to whom God is said to *appear*—in Hebrew, literally "to be seen." Another appearance follows later in the cycle (9:2). The uniqueness of this experience is underlined in 11:9, where it becomes the basis of divine anger in the face of Solomon's idolatry. The medium through which Adonai appears is a dream, understood in the ancient world as a common means of divine-human communication.[35] As may be the case in parallel stories of this type, the Deity offers Solomon a wish. The king gets to his point in a roundabout way with elaborate references to God's kindness (*hesed*) toward David so that the phrase "you treated your servant David with great kindness" resolves into "you kept this great kindness . . . by giving him a son to sit on his throne today" (6). As his father did before him, Solomon refers to himself as "your servant" and in his own way declares his inadequacy for the task by referring to himself as a "small boy" who does

---

34. In Deut, the *geva'ot* are the places where Canaanite natives practice their worship, which are to be destroyed by Israel (Deut 12:2–3).

35. For parallel stories in the ancient Mediterranean world, especially comparing Solomon's dream to related myths in the Ugaritic literature, see Choon-Leong Seow, "The Syro-Palestinian Context of Solomon's Dream," *HTR* 77 (1984): 141–52. Seow draws especially on the KRT tablet for parallels. Keret, or Kirta, receives a visitation from the god El in a dream and is granted a wish; at the conclusion, the lines "Keret awoke and it was a dream,/ the servant of El and it was a vision" are especially close to the final note of Solomon's dream: "Then awoke Solomon and it was a dream" (3:15). See Cyrus Gordon, *Ugaritic Texts in Transliteration*, AnOr 38 (Rome: Pontifical Biblical Institute, 1965): 250–51, lines 154–55.

not know his way in or out (7; cf. 2 Sam 7:18–21). The Hebrew of verse 7 piles "ah" sound upon "ah" sound, evoking the bleating of the small lost child that he is.[36] Then, like his father before him, he moves to declare the greatness of God's people (8; cf. 2 Sam 7:23). Finally, he makes his request: to receive "a listening heart" in order to be a wise judge who discerns between good and evil. In return, God grants Solomon a "wise and understanding heart" (12), and because he has not asked for anything in the realm of the material, he will get that too: "riches and honor" (13). Only the last words raise a qualification.

1 KINGS 3:14

And if you walk in my ways,
to guard my statutes and my commandments
as walked David your father,
I will give you long life.

Long life is now conditionally guaranteed—reason enough for Solomon to send up more sacrifice, this time "before the Ark of the Covenant of Adonai" (15).

*Act II, Scene 2: The Sword of Wisdom (1 Kings 3:16–28)*

*This is a strange wisdom that governs by violence.*[37]

The story that follows to exemplify Solomon's wise judgment is so well-known today that even the biblically illiterate are familiar with it. Possibly, it was a story widely known in the biblical world as well—not necessarily connected with a particular monarch but attached to King Solomon because of his proverbial wisdom. The

---

36. 2 Kgs 3:7: *ve'attah ['adonai] 'elohay 'attah himlakhtta 'et 'avdekha tahat dawid 'avi ve'anokhi na'ar qaton lo' eda' tset vavo'.*

37. Walter Brueggemann, *1 & 2 Kings*, SHBC 8 (Macon, GA: Smyth & Helwys, 2000), 54.

name of Solomon is not found in the story. It concerns simply "the king," two women, and one baby. The two women, both of them whores, come and stand before the king.[38] The first woman to speak is the one who charges the second woman with stealing her baby after she had killed her own child by lying on him.

1 KINGS 3:19–21

19 Then died the son of this woman
   at night because she lay on him.
20 And she got up in the middle of the night
   and took my son from my side
   while your maidservant slept,
   and she laid him at her breast,
   and her dead son she laid at my breast.
21 I arose in the morning to nurse my son,
   and, behold, dead!
   I examined him in the morning,
   and behold, he was not my son I had borne.

Implied in her story is the expectation that the king will decide on her behalf that she is the mother of the surviving child. Before she can express her plea, the second woman cuts in with the accusation that the child of the first woman is the one who died and that hers is the one still alive. The two of them engage in a quarrel, and it becomes a classic case of "he said-she said," as pointed out by the king (23). His stunning command to bring his sword follows directly on his restatement of the case. He then proposes to cut the living child in two and divide it between the women. Upon hearing this, one of the women opts to let the other woman have the living child rather than see the baby die, but the other woman wants the king to follow through on his threat. The king judges the woman who

---

38. The Hebrew word for the women is *zonah*. For a discussion of the word as well as the profession, see my first volume in this series, *The End of the Beginning: Joshua and Judges* (Grand Rapids: Eerdmans, 2019), 61–62, 263.

chooses life for the child to be his mother and orders the newborn to be given to her (27).

Clearly, there are two women with one living child between them, and the king forces them to make a choice by threatening violence to the child. Because the narrator steps in with the information that the woman who speaks up in favor of saving the child is the real mother in verse 26, we know that she receives the living child. Woman One tells a story of birth-giving and dying and baby-theft; Woman Two accuses her of lying. Which of these two is the one who, according to the narrator, is the real mother (26)?[39] Stuart Lasine writes, "Readers are left with demonstrative pronouns without being able to determine at whom these verbal pointers are aimed."[40] The uncertainty of the riddle hovers over the story for the listener. The closing note states that "all Israel was in awe" because they saw that "the wisdom of God" was in the king (28). The effect of the story is to solidify Solomon's reputation for wisdom. And yet, as Brueggemann observes, "Solomon seems to have the sword excessively on his brain, the sword as a tool of control, coercion, and intimidation. . . . One may wonder what the king would have done with his threat of violence had the real mother not flinched."[41] A disturbing subtext runs through the narrative placed at this juncture of Solomon's reign.

39. Some translations, like the New American Standard Bible and the New Revised Standard Version, solve the issue by rendering verse 27, "Then the king answered and said: 'Give the first woman the living child' " (cf. NRSV). The Hebrew text, however, uses only preposition and pronoun: "to her."

40. Stuart Lasine, "The Riddle of Solomon's Judgment," *JSOT* 45 (1989): 67. Herbert Rand ("Pronunciation: A Key to Meaning [1 Kings 3:16–28]," *JBQ* 24 [1997]: 246–50) opts for the accused woman as the "real" mother. Ellen Van Wolde ("Who Guides Whom? Embeddedness and Perspective in Biblical Hebrew and in 1 Kings 3:16–28," *JBL* 114 [1995]: 638) decides that the reader will never know which of the women, complainant or accused, is the mother of the living child. In her detailed discussion of the episode, Van Wolde is especially interested in analyzing embedded speech in a narrative and its effect on the reader.

41. Brueggemann, *1 & 2 Kings*, 54. So also Hens-Piazza (*1–2 Kings*, 46): "Are threats to do horrific violence justifiable even if they end up producing acceptable results?"

On the face of it, one of the issues in the story is that the identification of the women's profession underscores their lack of status. They could only speak for themselves without the protection of a male, and the case before the king was therefore particularly difficult because their words could not be trusted.[42] While it thus emphasizes Solomon's "wisdom," the story also reverses expectations about whores by emphasizing one of the women's motherly compassion. Yet there may be more to the story. The opening of the episode introduces two women: "Then came in two women, whores, to the king and stood before him" (16). Not only is the king put in close proximity to "whores," spatially and grammatically, but the narrator draws attention to it with the deliberate phrasing, causing a suspicious reader to wonder what whores are doing at the court so close to the king. True, they have a case to present, but the introduction creates dissonance all the same.

More important, the word "whore" (*zonah*) is from a root that in the Bible is used most often as a metaphor to illustrate the practices of idolatry. In abandoning their God, Israel "whores" after "other gods." In the Torah, the Historical Books, and the Prophetic Literature, the verb is proverbial for Israel's disloyalty to Adonai.[43] It seems clear that the presence of the two women whores puts the king in a danger zone, for it is precisely his straying from the adherence to the worship of Adonai alone for which he will be castigated (11:9–11). The words with which the complainant opens contain multiple references to "house"—to the point of redundancy: "We were together;/ there was no one else with us in the house;/ only the two of us were in the house" (18). In addition, she mentions "giving birth" three times. Her speech draws attention to the *one house* where fertility is present. "House" is a well-represented word in the

42. I agree with Phyllis Bird ("Prostitution in the Social World and Religious Rhetoric of Ancient Israel," in *Prostitutes and Courtesans in the Ancient World*, ed. Christopher A. Faraone and Laura K. McClure [Madison: University of Wisconsin Press, 2006], 48) that we cannot "conclude anything from this account about the rights of prostitutes—or other citizens—to bring legal disputes to the king for adjudication."

43. See Exod 34:16; Lev 17:7; 20:5; Num 25:1; Deut 22:21; 31:16; Judg 2:17; 8:27, 33; Isa 1:21; Jer 2:20; 3:6, 9; 5:7; Hos 4:10–14.

Hebrew Bible, both in its literal sense and as a representation of family and people; we find it close to two thousand times in the text. The frequency of its use in 1 Kings 1–11 is striking, making up almost half of all the times it is mentioned in Kings. While the prostitutes are close to the king, they are also close together in one *house*, a word that can denote the entire people. Both king and people will participate in apostasy, and these terms can hardly be coincidental. At this point, a question is raised about the "moral state of the kingdom."[44]

Modern sensibilities may shrink from the violent instincts of King Solomon, but there may be hints at another issue implied by his command to cut the living child in two. The verb for "cut" in verse 25 is *gazar*, meaning "to cut off." We find it only a handful of times in the Bible, notably in Genesis 15, where it refers to the cut-up pieces of Abram's sacrifice.[45] The living child will become the sacrifice to one of the mothers' neglect of her responsibilities and ensuing transgression against her neighbor. When God condemns Solomon for his apostasy, the charge is accompanied by an announcement that God will "tear away" the kingdom, which after his death will be cut *in two*, with the larger part going to Solomon's enemy. As foretold by God and God's prophet, Israel as God's child will live on cut in two for a while before eventually succumbing, one part after the other, to the conquering zeal of surrounding empires, ending the dream of God's people living in their God-given land.

The mother of the living child in 1 Kings 3 is said to have her "compassion stirred"—another expression evocative of the fate of Israel. The prophet Hosea speaks of the people as God's child, called by God from Egypt (Hos 11:1), and of God's comfort as "stirred up" (Hos 11:8).[46] Jeremiah also refers to Ephraim as God's dear child and to the stirring of God's heart on its behalf, as well as God's "motherly

---

44. J. Daniel Hays, "Has the Narrator Come to Praise Solomon or to Bury Him? Narrative Subtlety in 1 Kings 1–11," *JSOT* 28 (2003): 164.

45. Outside of one neutral reference in 2 Kgs 6:4, where it refers to hewing down trees, the context of the verb *gazar* is dramatically negative. See 2 Chr 26:21; Isa 53:8; Lam 3:54; Hab 3:17.

46. This verb occurs only a few times and elsewhere is used of Joseph's *compassion* which is *stirred* when faced with Benjamin (Gen 43:30).

compassion" (Jer 31:20).[47] Both a somber future for God's people and God's enduring bond with Israel are strongly hinted at by vocabulary related to prostitution, a child to be divided in two, and motherly compassion—evoking at this point in the early days of Solomon's reign Israel's eventual apostasy, the division of the kingdom, and God's ongoing devotion to Israel.[48]

### Act II, Scene 3: The Burden of Kingship (1 Kings 4:1–5:14[49])

*It is Solomon that fulfills all the details of Samuel's prediction.*[50]

As if to offset the liveliness and intrigue of the previous episode, we encounter a long list of names in what follows, with descriptions of Solomon's practices in which he has no speaking or acting part (4:1–20). It will not be the last time that such material interrupts the narrative flow of the chapters devoted to Solomon, and tempted as

47. The word *rahamim* in 1 Kgs 3:26 is related to the word for womb, *rehem*, and used in reference to God's feelings for God's people (Deut 13:18[17]; 1 Kgs 8:50; Pss 25:6; 40:12[11]; 51:3[1]; Isa 54:7; 63:7; Jer 16:5). The adjective "compassionate" (*rahum*) is used in the praise accorded God in Exod 34:6 (see Neh 9:17; Jonah 4:2; Joel 2:13). For an extensive discussion of the noun, see Phyllis Trible, *God and the Rhetoric of Sexuality* (Philadelphia: Fortress, 1978), 31–58. Trible concludes that the root in its use in the Bible exhibits "semantic movement from the wombs of women to the compassion of God" (56).

48. I agree in this respect with Eric A. Seibert (*Subversive Scribes and the Solomonic Narrative: A Rereading of 1 Kings 1–11* [London; New York: T&T Clark, 2006]), who views the material on King Solomon as filled with negative notes. In this context Seibert considers 1 Kgs 1–2 in particular "ostensibly written as a piece of political propaganda but riddled with many subversive elements" (186). Unfortunately, Seibert omits a discussion of the episode of 3:16–28 in his illustrative material. Daniel Hays ("Has the Narrator Come," 164–65) raises the possibility of elements of the story pointing beyond the obvious reality to symbolic truths.

49. As noted above, I am following chapter divisions and verse numbering of the traditional Hebrew text. English versions present 5:1–14 as 4:21–34, noted in brackets.

50. Hays, "Has the Narrator Come," 165.

one may be to skip the difficult and tedious details, there are items of interest buried in the recital. Chapter 4 is framed by references to King Solomon and to the people. In verse 1, "Solomon was king over all Israel," and at the conclusion of the list, "Judah and Israel were numerous/ as the sand at the sea is numerous,/ eating, drinking, and rejoicing" (4:20). In this way, the frame of Solomon's rule and the people's expanded numbers and well-being surrounds the enumeration of the royal officials, cabinet ministers, and regional overseers.[51]

A list may function as glue that holds narrative together while it also preserves memories in a specific form. Although the text may be intended to testify in a positive way to the organized and extensive nature of Solomon's administration, it contains a number of negative notes—what Brueggemann calls "rumblings of troublesome things to come."[52] At the end of the list of court officials in 4:1–6, we find Adoniram as the overseer of "forced labor" (Hebrew *mas*).[53] This practice is mentioned also in connection with King David's officials (2 Sam 20:24), but in the Solomon narrative there are repeated references, including to the numbers of laborers (5:27–29[13–15]; 9:15,

---

51. As ch. 5 begins [= Eng. 4:21], the rule of Solomon expands its borders to the Euphrates and Egypt (5:1 [4:21]). It is thus within this vast realm that "Judah and Israel" dwell in safety. We may consider the reference to a vast empire to be stereotypical exaggeration characteristic of the narrative. The reference to the people as "Judah and Israel," as if they were a divided kingdom, heralds tension within this homage to Solomon's reign.

52. Brueggemann, *1 & 2 Kings*, 71.

53. Cf. 2 Sam 20:23–24. There is some overlap between the names of David's officials and those of Solomon, perhaps testimony to poorly preserved records. Adoram of 2 Samuel 20:24 is read the same as Adoniram in some medieval manuscripts of the Hebrew text and in Greek as well as Latin translations. On the face of it, Solomon's court officials include only men, but if we follow the testimony of Ezra 2:55 and Neh 7:57, there was a female ancestral scribe (*hassoferet* = the female scribe). See Wilda Gafney, *Daughters of Miriam: Women Prophets in Ancient Israel* (Minneapolis: Fortress, 2008), 127. With Gafney, I read the word *beney* in these texts as "descendants/disciples" rather than "sons." Gafney argues that "women cannot be automatically excluded from expressions such as "beney," "sons of," "descendants of" (128–29). Peruda of Ezra 2:55—a feminine passive participle from a root meaning to "spread, share"—may also be a female name, perhaps meaning "prolific."

21), and its mention here sets off alarm bells for the future of the realm (cf. 12:9–11). Also, the beginning of the list of regional overseers (4:7–19) states that each of these twelve regions provided for the royal household for one month of the year (4:7)—an enormous amount of food, as specified in 5:2–3 [4:22–23]. What takes place under Solomon is the practice of heavy taxation on the land to maintain the central administration. Worth noting also is that the regions listed are all in the north, coherent with the mention "all Israel" in verse 7 as excluding Judah. Judah is mentioned at the end of the list, but without a named official or other specifications (4:19). The concluding statement about the contentment of the people names them "Israel and Judah" as if they were already two kingdoms. Taken together, forced labor, taxation, and the burden placed on the north to provide for the king's table put a negative coloring on the details provided. What comes to mind are the warnings of Samuel on the eve of the monarchial period about a king who does little other than "take" (1 Sam 8:11–17).[54]

Each unit begins with a statement about Solomon's rule. "All Israel" of 4:1 becomes "all the kingdoms" in 5:1 [4:21], extending his domain from the "Euphrates to the land of the Philistines"—a vast territory that also contributes heavily to the royal court (5:1–3, 6–8 [4:21–23, 26–28]). In between, there is again emphasis on the *peace* that existed in Solomon's time and the resulting well-being of the people, again identified as "Judah and Israel" (5:5 [4:25]). While the text doubtless indulges in the usual exaggeration of size and numbers, it is hard not to hear the voice of irony in the statement about Judah and Israel.

1 KINGS 5:5 [4:25]

Then dwelt Judah and Israel in safety,
each man under his fig tree
from Dan to Beersheba,
all the days of Solomon.

---

54. "Thus the irony of the chapter. Solomon's organizational glory is the very thing that [Adonai] warned the nation about in 1 Samuel" (Hays, "Has the Narrator Come," 165).

Directly following this declaration is the reference to the vast number of horses kept by Solomon, an animal in this time and place kept only for the use of chariots, mostly in battle. A strong military guarantees but also offsets the "safety" of the people vis-à-vis other nations. Internally, the sense of safety and peace will be far to seek in the uproar eventually facing Solomon's successor (12:4). The number of horses kept by the king (forty thousand in the Hebrew text) can only add to the notes of dissonance present in the descriptions. For those familiar with the instruction of Deuteronomy, there is, in addition, the memory of the admonition that a king should refrain from maintaining a large stable (Deut 17:16).[55] Horses might lead the people back to Egypt, according to the Deuteronomic guideline, a country with which Solomon already has diplomatic relations. King Solomon does not sound as if he busies himself much with listening to the Teaching of Moses (Deut 17:16).[56] Taxation, forced labor, and a strong military—the Pax Salomonis is beginning to sound a bit like the Pax Romana![57]

The third unit in this accounting closes with praise for Solomon's "wisdom" (5:9–14 [4:29–34]). At the end, not only his own people but "all nations" and "all the kings of the earth" are acquainted with his wisdom (5:14 [4:34]). Two general statements, a comparison of Solomon's wisdom with sages of other nations and a reference to his literary output, are followed by specifics: wise individuals of the ancient world he surpassed and things of the natural world he understood. The "East" and "Egypt" (5:10 [4:30]) are generally recognized locations of knowledge in the ancient world. The individuals listed as illustrations (5:11 [4:31]) are no longer known; Ethan the Ezrahite is cited also in the superscripts of Psalms 88 and 89. The natural world of which Solomon "spoke" (5:13 [4:33]) includes what grows and moves on the land (trees, herbs, and beasts) and in the

55. In 5:6 [4:26], read "horses" for the NRSV "horsemen."

56. Deut 17:16–20 warns against keeping many horses because it might tempt a king to "return the people to Egypt . . . of which God said that they should never return on this road" (16), as well as against keeping a large harem and the accumulation of wealth (17).

57. Brueggemann (*1 & 2 Kings*, 70) suggests that the tax collection system of the Solomonic era was "not unlike the one known in the Roman period."

sky and water (birds, creeping things, and fish; cf. Gen 1:20–25). Biblical tradition maintained the connection of wisdom with Solomon by attaching his name to the collection of sayings in the book of Proverbs (Prov 1:1; 10:1; 25:1), and the Song of Songs (identified in its superscript as the Song of Solomon; Song 1:1; 3:9, 11; 8:11, 12).[58]

## Act III: Royal Building Projects (1 Kings 5:15–8:66[59])

*In these verses the temple is the clear access point to heavenly forgiveness.*[60]

Everything in these chapters takes place in connection with the construction of the Temple. First, Solomon engages in an international trade agreement in order to plan the building. The preparations are told in some detail in chapter 5, while the building begins and is finished in chapters 6 and 7. In the report of the details, the focus is on the Temple, the account of which surrounds the shorter and more general account of the construction of the palace (7:1–12), although the palace took almost twice as long to build. The dimensions of the Temple and its furnishings, including their fashioning, are elaborately described. Chapter 8 reports on a solemn assembly during Sukkot, with appropriate rituals performed by Temple personnel and the king, including a long dedicatory prayer (8:23–53).

### Act III, Scene 1: Terms of Trade (1 Kings 5:15–32[61])

*Solomon is consistently portrayed in the First Kings as employing an exclusionary strategy of power.*[62]

58. In addition, two psalms are dedicated to Solomon: 72 and 127.

59. As noted above, I am following the chapter divisions of the traditional Hebrew text. Thus, 1 Kgs 5:15 will appear as 1 Kgs 5:1 in most English translations.

60. Brueggemann, *1 & 2 Kings*, 119.

61. For verse numbering, see footnotes above.

62. Stephen C. Russell, *The King and the Land: A Geography of Royal Power in the Biblical World* (Oxford: Oxford University Press, 2017), 3. Russell

The first unit (15–26[1–12]) reports on negotiations between Hiram, the king of Tyre, and Solomon. The initiative is taken by Hiram, who "sends" servants to Solomon (cf. 2 Sam 5:11). This "sending" without a stated purpose likely is for the purpose of bringing good wishes to the successor of David from a foreign ruler who is said to "have loved David always"—the last individual in the Historical Books to be so described. In Hiram's case, it is likely a testimony to his loyalty to David and his house rather than an indication of deep emotion.[63] Good wishes from a ruler to a new king reflect a customary practice of the time and the region.[64] Solomon uses the occasion to enter into negotiations for material and a labor force to execute his plan "to build a house for the name of Adonai" (17[3]).

Solomon refers back to his father, whose inability to construct a temple he ascribes to his preoccupation with war.[65] This reference

---

argues that power strategies used by political actors fall "along a continuum that lies between two poles. An exclusionary strategy tends toward the centralization of power, while a corporate strategy tends toward its distribution." Furthermore, he maintains that the "prominence" of those who employ exclusionary strategies "depends on their ability to become central to a network of extragroup exchange partnerships." See also Norman C. Habel (*The Land Is Mine* [Minneapolis: Fortress, 1995], 17) who argues that basic to the "royal land ideology are the concepts of the land as a source of wealth" and "the divine right of the monarch to appropriate that wealth."

63. The word "to love" in Hebrew (*'ahav*) often has this connotation, although it may also connote emotional and romantic attachment. In 2 Sam 5:11, Hiram of Tyre provides David with the personnel and materials to build his palace in Jerusalem. The two Hirams can hardly be the same person; the name may be a general indication for the rulers of Tyre, who exhibited habitual loyalty to the royal house to their south.

64. Victor (Avigdor) Hurowitz (*I Have Built You an Exalted House: Temple Building in the Bible in Light of Mesopotamian and Northwest Semitic Writings*, JSOTSup 115 [Sheffield: Sheffield Academic, 1992], 174–75) cites examples from the Amarna letters that testify to the practice.

65. In 1 Chr, which ascribes the temple construction and its completion to a Davidic initiative he passes on directly to Solomon himself, the denial by God's decree is also associated with his activities on the battlefront: "For you are a warrior and have shed blood" (28:3). It is also David who warns his son to stay loyal to Adonai, who will abandon him if he becomes disloyal (28:9–10). David provides the plan for the construction of the temple, which

opens up in two directions: First, it enables him to emphasize the fact that he, Solomon, is not occupied in this way, perhaps allaying any fears on the part of the king of Tyre that he might step on someone's toes in assisting Solomon. Second, he brings to mind that it is God who had announced to David that his son, put on the throne by God, will undertake the task, thus underlining that both the succession and the Temple construction are a God-ordained undertaking. We recall that the initiative in 2 Samuel 7 to build a temple came from David. Solomon uses that occasion and its negative outcome to turn the matter into a divine mandate in accordance with customs of the time and the region.[66]

Not until the end of the discourse does Solomon raise the issue of the trade he proposes, which consists of "cedars from Lebanon" for the cutting of which he will send his workers to labor alongside the servants of Hiram, with wages paid by Solomon according to the rate set by Hiram (20[6]). Hiram, following custom, professes to be overjoyed and renegotiates the terms of the deal so that in the end Solomon puts out quite a bit more than just the wages for the workers, providing lavish food provisions for the Tyrian royal house rather than paying wages to the workers (25[11]). Hiram will have his own servants cut the timber and transport it by sea to a port of Solomon's choosing. It is not clear how well Solomon fares by this deal, but the exchange concludes with a pact: Besides the chopping of trees the *cutting* of a covenant takes place (26[12]).[67]

More negotiations may have gone back and forth, for in the last section of chapter 5, Solomon sends workers to Lebanon—forced

---

is financed through a volunteer labor force (28:21) and "freewill offerings" (29:6–9), clearly patterned on the Exodus account and the making of the tabernacle. The differences between the Kgs and Chr texts are multiple, including the omission of forced labor in connection with building the temple. The palace of Solomon receives only a cursory reference in 2 Chr 8:1.

66. For comparative examples, see Hurowitz, *I Have Built You an Exalted House,* 131–67.

67. I agree with Hurowitz that we should understand the Solomon-Hiram exchange as epistolary. See the many comparisons with letters from elsewhere in the region with parallel terminology, marshaled in *I Have Built You an Exalted House,* 171–223.

labor consisting of thirty thousand workers, ten thousand per month according to the text (27–28[13–14]). It may be that a compromise was reached with Hiram. In addition, there are stone cutters and carriers to transport the stones from the quarries in Israel. Even taking into account the habitual exaggeration of numbers, the use of forced labor and the extremely arduous task of stone cutting and carrying for the benefit of constructing the sanctuary lends an aura of oppressive practices the likes of which Israel has not experienced until this point. The account brings to mind the harsh labor exacted of the Israelites in Egypt (Exod 1:11–14). In that context, the Israelites as a people were subjected to the *mas* (Exod 1:11), a situation from which they were liberated by the hand of Adonai through Moses. After the Babylonian destruction, the poet bewails the fact that Jerusalem has been put to *forced labor* (Lam 1:1). We may think also of the construction of the Tabernacle in the wilderness, when the divine command to create a sanctuary included the *gift* of what each person's *heart* moved it to contribute (Exod 25:2), later called a *voluntary donation* or *free-will offering* (Exod 35:29). What people gave then out of their enthusiasm for the project has become enforced toil for a construction devised by rulers. In verses 27–31[13–17], Solomon is the subject of multiple verbs related to the *mas:* "Solomon raised up forced labor," "he sent them," "he possessed," "he commanded." After these actions, the workers are said to "hew" timber and stone. The verb *hew* used for cutting the timber and stone is rare (unlike v. 20[6]) and occurs in a positive sense only in Exodus 34:1, 4 and Deuteronomy 10:1, 3 regarding the cutting of the tablets with the Ten Words. Its noun, *pesel*—literally *hewn image*—occurs more than thirty times, exclusively in a negative context as a word for idol.[68]

### Act III, Scene 2: The King and His Temple (1 Kings 6–7)

*Disquiet hangs over the narrative.*[69]

---

68. For example, Exod 20:4; Lev 26:1; Deut 4:16; 27:15; 2 Kgs 21:7; Isa 40:19; 42:17; 44:9, 10, 15, 17; Hab 2:18.

69. Hens-Piazza, *1–2 Kings*, 73.

The connection with the exodus raised subliminally in the last episode rises to the surface with the beginning of the actual building, which is dated with reference to the "going out of the children of Israel from Egypt" (6:1).[70] The link with the exodus from Egypt highlights continuity but also difference. The collectors and editors of the material in the Historical Books ascribe the desire for a central sanctuary to King David. According to the account in 1 Kings, the project is clearly a priority for Solomon, emphasized by the central location of the material concerning the Temple and the amount of text devoted to it. What motivated Israel's kings to construct a central sanctuary? In Exodus, the sanctuary is made on the basis of *divine instruction*, and it is *portable*, going where the people are (Exodus 25–40). Also the purpose of the structure in Exodus is so that God may "dwell" in the midst of the people, using a root of the Hebrew verb *shakhan*, which indicates settling for a period of time, a sojourn with the possibility of moving and without the connotation of dwelling in a fixed and clearly demarcated place. A sanctuary made of cedar and stone is by its nature stationary. Solomon, in his rationale to Hiram, does not cite the reason provided in 2 Samuel 7:6–7 for Adonai's refusal of a temple but rather refers to David's preoccupation with war. In fact, David's notion about the Temple comes about after God has given him "rest . . . all around from his enemies" (2 Sam 7:1). At the core of God's denying David the opportunity to build a temple is the notion that God has no need of a house, but it is David who does.

2 SAMUEL 7:6–7

6   For I have not stayed[71] in a house
    from the day I brought the Israelites up from Egypt until today.
    I have been going about in tent and tabernacle.

---

70. The number 480 years is most likely not to be taken literally but is a symbol of "the orderliness of God's plan for Israel" (Everett Fox, *The Early Prophets: Joshua, Judges, Samuel, and Kings* [New York: Schocken, 2014], 593) and may also intend to establish "continuity and relationship between past sacral events and the present undertaking" (Hens-Piazza, *1–2 Kings*, 63).

71. The Hebrew verb *yashav* means "to stay," "to live," "to sit."

7  In all my going about with all the Israelites,
   did I speak to one of the tribes,
   whom I commanded to shepherd my people Israel,
   saying: Why have you not built me a house of cedar?

It could hardly be more strongly stated that Adonai is not a god whose nature it is to *sit* or *stay in* a house but one who *walks about* with the people in *tent and tabernacle* (Hebrew *mishkan*) and has no need for a permanent residence; rather, people and monarchs have need for a place and for houses. The statement that David's successor will build a house for God sounds like a concession in this context (2 Sam 7:13).[72] In addition, the housing of a divine image, one of the reasons to provide a sanctuary elsewhere in the ancient world, was not an issue for a religion that prohibits the making of such images.

One response to the question of the monarchial need for a temple—and by no means a trivial one—is that Israel's neighbors had large temples. This may have become quite important once Israel was set on the map as a kingdom. What kind of people did not have a central sanctuary to give glory to their deity, their protector who vouchsafed the well-being of the people and its leaders? Israel, a latecomer on the scene of powerful civilizations before and during Solomon's time, could hardly claim to be a player in its social and political context without a structure to show to the world a concrete exhibit of its religious commitments. Once, the people had clamored to have a "king" to rule them like "all the other peoples" (1 Sam 8:5, 20). It would not be so far-fetched to assume that the people also wished for a sanctuary in the manner of "all the other peoples" to properly worship and show pride in their God. According to the biblical record, however, the desire for the Temple does not arise with the people but with the monarch. In the period we assign to King

72. In pondering the question of God's presence, Samuel Terrien (*The Elusive Presence: Toward a New Biblical Theology* [San Francisco: Harper & Row, 1978], 201) wrote that there exists "a grievous tension between two cultic views of the divine presence" in the Bible, one related to understanding and articulating the presence of God through *space* and the other through *time*.

Solomon, the second half of the tenth century BCE, the city of Tyre was far more important and affluent than Jerusalem, and trade with it was probably more beneficial for Israel than vice versa. Erecting a building for the national deity might cohere with a wish of the court to not appear too shabby in comparison to such a significant trading partner. According to the description furnished in chapters 6 and 7, the Temple in Jerusalem resembled sacred structures of the region in its design and ornamentation. Some scholars suggest that the Solomonic Temple constituted a rebuilding of an already existing structure of Jebusite origin.[73] Whatever the case may be, the tradition records a richly furnished and decorated House of Adonai with Solomon in charge, referring to "the house that King Solomon built" (6:2). Throughout, Solomon is in charge of the work of *building*, with the phrase "he built" repeated eleven times in chapter 6. Three times, the text adds that "he finished it" (6:9, 14, 38), according to verse 38 in "seven years," with strong echoes of God, who "finished" the creation in seven days (Gen 2:2).

While the king may have had complex motivations for the project, it is clear that the Temple not only creates a new bond between the God of Israel and a place, but it firmly anchors the position of the king within this bond as the one who mediates between God and people. As Rainer Albertz points out, what happens is an attempt to make "the king a comprehensive guarantor of salvation for Israel" so that all the crucial parts of the bond between the community and God "run through the king."[74] In this light, it is difficult not to

73. So Rainer Albertz, *A History of Israelite Religion in the Old Testament Period*, trans. John Bowden, vol. 1, OTL (Louisville: Westminster John Knox, 1994), 130; trans. of *Religionsgeschichte Israels in alttestamenlicher Zeit* (Göttingen: Vandenhoeck & Ruprecht, 1992): "A former Jebusite temple which Solomon had renovated and splendidly adorned for the cult of" the God of Israel. Albertz considers it "intrinsically questionable" that the Ark, once in Jerusalem, was kept in a tent for more than forty years and suggests that pre-Davidic Jerusalem had a sanctuary on the supposed "threshing floor of Arauna." It is true that 2 Sam 12:20 refers to David going "into the house of Adonai" after the death of his child.

74. Albertz, *The History of Israelite Religion*, 121; see Habel, *The Land Is Mine*, 32.

see the construction of the Temple as another attempt by the monarchy to accrue power to the throne. To be sure, this step did not take place without resistance from sectors of the community. We hear counter-voices as early as the first stages of the appointment of a king in 1 Samuel 8 and continue to discern them not only in breakaway movements such as the rebellions of Absalom and Sheba (2 Sam 15–19; 20) but also in other texts that function as a critique of the power and royal entitlement of the monarchy in Israel. In some ways, the entire narrative of David and his court in 2 Samuel 9–20 provides a counter-voice by its depiction of a king who is vulnerable, open to chastisement by the prophetic voice, unable to restrain his offspring, and maintaining only a fragile hold on his rule. In 1 Kings 5–7, there is the proviso added that Solomon desired to build "a house for the *name* of Adonai my God" (5:19[5]), a declaration reiterated multiple times in chapter 8 (vv. 16, 17, 18, 19, 20, 29, 33, 35, 41, 42, 44, 48). Also, and remarkably, the description of building is going at full speed in 6:1–10 when the narrator interrupts with a divine admonition.

### 1 KINGS 6:11–13

11 Then happened the word of Adonai to Solomon, saying:
12 [About] this house you are building:
   If you walk in my ordinances
   and my justice you will do,
   and if you keep my commandments,
   walking in them,
   then I will maintain my word with you
   that I spoke to David, your father.
13 I will sojourn in the midst of the Israelites
   and not abandon my people Israel.

The opening words—"this house you are building," rather than "my house" or "building for me"—do not exactly sound enthusiastic, and subsequently the remarks do not pertain to the sanctuary at all but to the way of life God demands of the king. This extraordinary moment reflects on the consequences of the king's heightened stature with God and people. The well-being of the people and God's bond with them will henceforth be connected to the way the king stays the course in terms of God's ordinances. God's concern for the people and his continued divine presence with them is here front and center.[75] The big "if" already once uttered at the time of the granting of Solomon's wish (3:14) is augmented at the moment when the king seeks to guarantee God's permanent presence with the people, which according to these words will not be provided by *building* but by *living* according to God's instruction (Hebrew *torah*).

The description of the construction proceeds from the outside in, and although compared to most temples of the period it may not have been all that grand at ninety feet long and thirty feet wide with three rooms in a row, the holiest place in the back, it was splendid enough in its small city and well-appointed with furnishings and decorations (6:14–38; continued in 7:13–50).[76] Especially impressive are the Cherubim, a type of four-winged sphinx—composite creatures common to the region and used to guard royal and sacred enclosures.[77] Hens-Piazza writes, "From the description of the imposing outer framework reported at the onset, to the individual bronze and gold implements within the building, described at the conclusion, the account bespeaks a king who left nothing to chance."[78]

75. The concern of these verses clearly reflects that of the Deuteronomistic theologians, and at some point, they were inserted into the record of construction, where the final editors maintained them.

76. Temples in both Egypt and Mesopotamia of the period were certainly large even by contemporary standards. Robert Alter (*Ancient Israel: The Former Prophets: Joshua, Judges, Samuel, and Kings* [New York: Norton, 2013], 631n2), who estimates the Jerusalem temple of Solomon to have been 30–36 m long (100–120 ft), observes that the Chartres cathedral is three times as long. B. S. J. Isserlin (*The Israelites* [Minneapolis: Fortress, 2001], 249–52), who judges the length to have been 50 m (165 ft), notes that the structure was more impressive for its "architecture and fittings" than its size. The modesty of its size may reflect accurate tradition. Isserlin has a helpful description of Solomon's temple, about which we still know so little archaeologically.

77. Fox, *The Early Prophets*, 597.

78. Hens-Piazza, *1–2 Kings*, 71.

As Hens-Piazza also points out, questions still hang over the narrative. One issue not directly addressed in the description but underlying the listing of the costly materials is the question of financing. On our faculty at Louisville Presbyterian Seminary, we had a colleague who was in the habit of raising the issue of financial support at inconvenient moments. He might raise his head during a theological discussion at one of our annual faculty retreats, which included overnight lodging and meals, and ask who was paying for "all of this." It was and is a good question. Who was paying for all the splendor of Solomon's Temple? For sure, he brings the treasures looted by David from neighboring peoples inside (7:51), but those are only a small part of what the entire undertaking must have cost in the seven years it took. This is not to speak of his own palace, which takes almost twice as long to construct, is larger in size than the Temple, and about the furnishings of which very little is said (7:1–12). It leaves the impression that the less said about them the better, for they may have outshone the sanctuary. The *taking* of the king announced by Samuel in 1 Samuel 8 has begun in earnest. Eventually, of course the costly furnishings will be stripped, and the building destroyed—*taken* by one conqueror or another.[79]

There are three records of sanctuary construction reported in the Hebrew Bible: one during the wilderness wanderings under the care of Moses (Exod 25:1–31:11; 35:1–40:38), the most detailed; another at the time of the monarchy under Solomon in 1 Kings 6–7; and the third and last following the Babylonian exile under the guidance of Ezra (Ezra 3:8–6:15).[80] The first structure, which represented the presence of a God who moves about with the people, also paints

79. Hurowitz (*I Have Built You an Exalted House*, 224–59) provides a thorough review not only of the parallels to trade negotiations and building materials in preparation for the building project but also of similar descriptions of the details of size and furnishings in official administrative documents of the region and period.

80. The report in 2 Chr 3–4 provides a parallel to the text in 1 Kgs 6–7. I do not include the description of the postexilic temple in Ezekiel, which is presented as a vision rather than an event. It closely resembles the 1 Kgs 6–7 text, albeit in greater detail. For an overview of biblical building stories, see Hurowitz, *I Have Built You an Exalted House*, 106–128.

the most evocative word picture of lavish beauty, and the work includes many contributors.[81] Compared to it, the description of the Solomonic structure is sparse, omitting any prescriptions for Temple service and personnel, concentrating more on the role of the king than that of the people who would serve the sanctuary.[82] The Ezra account offers almost no detail, with a focus mostly on opposition and negotiations for continuing the work under difficult circumstances, but it registers many workers who were active in the rebuilding of the Temple (Ezra 3:8–9). Each account notes the "finishing" of the work: "Moses finished the work" (Exod 40:33); "Solomon built the house and finished it" (1 Kgs 6:14; cf. 6:9, 38; 7:51); "they finished their building" (Ezra 6:14, with the "elders" as the subject).[83]

### Act III, Scene 3: A Royal Prayer (1 Kings 8)

*The ability to pray is the acid test of faith.*[84]

As the work is completed, the Ark is brought up and put into the innermost chamber with dedicatory sacrifices, in which the king takes a leading role. The Ark is deposited "in its place" in the innermost room of the sanctuary, the holy of holies, "under the wings of the Cherubim" (6). It is carefully defined as "the Ark of the Covenant of Adonai" (1, 6), and the text stipulates that the Ark contained nothing except the tab-

---

81. See Johanna W. H. van Wijk-Bos, *Making Wise the Simple: The Torah in Christian Faith and Practice* (Grand Rapids: Eerdmans, 2005), 204–207, for a brief discussion of the possible historical provenance of the wilderness tent.

82. Hurowitz (*I Have Built You an Exalted House*, 224–59) has argued that the detail of size and furnishings in 1 Kgs 6–7, though seemingly unique in terms of literature on temple construction in the ancient world surrounding Israel, resembles similar descriptions in administrative documents of the region and period.

83. Notes on the completion of the work are common to many Mesopotamian building stories. Since such a note also occurs at the close of the first creation story, Hurowitz (*I Have Built You an Exalted House*, 242) speculates that the creation narrative in Genesis 1:1–2:4a belongs to the genre of building story.

84. Nelson, *First and Second Kings*, 59.

lets that testify to the covenant of Adonai with Israel (9).[85] In an echo of the conclusion of the Tabernacle account, a cloud fills the house upon the placement of the Ark, representing the "glory of Adonai" (10–11; cf. Exod 40:34–35). We have encountered the Ark in all the Historical Books: It travels with the army in the first chapters of Joshua (Josh 1–7) or is stationed at a location for a solemn religious occasion (Josh 8:33); in Judges, it appears out of nowhere in Bethel (Judg 20:27); in Samuel it pops up at Shiloh (1 Sam 3:3) and subsequently with the Israelite army at Aphek and among the Philistines (1 Sam 4–6); it appears with Saul during a skirmish with the Philistines (1 Sam 14:18) and is eventually transported by David to Jerusalem (2 Sam 6). It is carried out of the city during David's flight in the face of Absalom's rebellion, but on David's orders it is taken back (2 Sam 15:24–25). We find it in Jerusalem again in 1 Kings 3:15. Different traditions clung to the Ark, yet even when it is defined emphatically as "only" a testimony to the covenant between God and Israel, it still represents the presence of Adonai. Unlike the gods of the neighboring peoples, there were no images of the Deity to be placed in the Temple, but like those other images, the Ark is placed in the Temple to symbolize divine presence.

Solomon begins speaking in verse 12 and goes on through verse 61. His speaking is framed by two narrative sections (1–11, 62–66), with the discourse in turn in a frame of two blessings (15–21, 56–61). Descriptive phrases connect the whole.

1 KINGS 8:14, 22, 54–55

14 Then the king turned his face
and blessed the whole assembly of Israel,
and the whole assembly of Israel stood.

. . .

22 And Solomon stood before the altar of Adonai
in the presence of the whole assembly of Israel
and spread out his palms to heaven.

. . .

85. This reiteration was most likely added to avoid the notion that the Ark functioned in the Temple as the footstool of God.

54 Now when Solomon finished praying to Adonai
all his prayer and his supplication,
he arose from before the altar of Adonai,
from kneeling on knees with his hands outspread to heaven,
55 and stood and blessed the whole assembly of Israel
with a loud voice saying. . .

The phrase "the whole assembly of Israel" highlights the presence of the people at this event; they are the recipients of the second blessing and the subject of the greatest part of Solomon's prayer. The entire section is a grand symphony on the theme of the importance of the "house" (16×) Solomon "built" (12×) as a place of prayer and on the majesty of God who is in "heaven" (15×), who is implored to "listen" (14×) to the cries and supplications of the king and God's people. Solomon's preface highlights the contradiction embedded in the theme.

1 KINGS 8:12–13

12 Then Solomon said:
Adonai thought to dwell in deep darkness,
13 I have surely built for you an exalted house,
a firm abode for your dwelling for the ages!

Are the two statements contradictory or complementary? Did God have it in mind to be hidden and remote, but Solomon firmly pinned the Deity down into one place, even if it is in the innermost sanctuary and not visible?[86] Or is the phrasing intended to reconcile the irreconcilable: The unfathomable God is also the one who dwells in a house, a firm place to live in?[87] To undercut the notion that God

86. Alter (*Ancient Israel*, 643n13): "The Lord meant to abide in thick fog./ I indeed have built You a lofty house,/ a firm place for Your dwelling forever." In a note, Alter makes clear that he understands Solomon to be announcing a new era.

87. The verb for "dwelling" in verse 13 is the Hebrew *yashav* ("to sit" or "to stay"). See p. 47 above. In Exod 15:17, where the "abode for your dwelling" can also be found, it is the Holy God who established it; here the emphasis

is permanently located in a building, the emphasis in the context and the prayer is repeatedly on a "house for the name of Adonai" (5:17[3], 19[5]; 8:14–53 16×). Likewise, Solomon exclaims in the opening section of his prayer:

1 KINGS 8:27

For will indeed God dwell on the earth?
Behold, the heavens and heaven of heavens cannot contain you;
how much less this house that I have built?

Evidently, the text intends to hold on to both the notion that the God of Israel cannot be tied down to one place and the notion that there is a special place established in Jerusalem to which people can turn in prayer because God's "eyes may be open to this house day and night" (29). As Alter puts it, it is "a kind of terrestrial communications center for speaking with God."[88] It is certainly interesting that sacrifice is not mentioned in the prayer, although both the opening and closing narrative units make mention of a great abundance of sacrifices (5, 63–64).

The initial blessing (15–21) is addressed to God, who has verified through his *word* the choice of David as ruler and of his son as the one to build a sanctuary for God's *name*, and it opens onto the person of Solomon: "I arose. . . . I sat on the throne. . . . I built the house. . . . I put . . . the Ark" (20–21). Likewise, the initial part of the prayer (23–30) has its focus on David as God's servant and Solomon as his successor. Three times, Solomon uses "your servant" to refer to David (23–26) and four times to himself (28–30) as the one to whose prayer and supplication he pleads with God to *listen*. From this focus, the prayer moves to the pleading of the people, a move anticipated at the end of the introductory section, which also notes God's dwelling place as *heaven* (30).

is on Solomon's building. Eslinger (*Into the Hands of the Living God*, 158) understands vv. 12–13 to reflect Solomon's purpose "to confine the divinity to a temple to Solomon's and Israel's advantage."

88. Alter, *Ancient Israel*, 646n30.

Seven hypothetical situations are listed—occasions when the people might have reason to pray and ask forgiveness (31–50). They move from individual disputes (31–32) through defeat in battle (33–34) to drought (35–36), a variety of disasters such as famine, plague or failed harvest (37–40)—including also the "foreigner" who might have occasion to pray to the God of Israel (41–43)—to success in battle (44–45) and finally the possibility of exile (46–53). The last section, anticipating exile, is the most elaborate and notably does not request return or deliverance but "compassion" from their captors (50). The last intercession also includes a motivation for God, in that God brought them out of Egypt and set them apart as his "inheritance," so that the entire prayer ends in an extended reference to the exodus.

1 Kings 8:51–53

51 For your people and your inheritance are they
    whom you brought out of Egypt
    from the midst of the furnace of iron.[89]
52 May your eyes be open
    to the supplication of your servant
    and to the supplication of your people Israel
    to listen to them in all they cry out to you.[90]
53 For you separated them for yourself as an inheritance
    from all the peoples of the earth,
    as you spoke by the hand of Moses, your servant,
    when you brought out our ancestors from Egypt, Holy God.

The concluding blessing (56–61) begins with praise to God for the fulfillment of God's promise to Moses in giving "rest" to the people. In Deuteronomic language, it wishes for a heart that in-

89. Egypt is referred to as the "iron furnace" from which God delivered the people in Deut 4:20.
90. Cf. 1 Kgs 8:30, in the opening section. This expression, "may your eyes be open," is unique in the Hebrew Bible. The idea here is that God is involved with a sense of both seeing and hearing.

clines to God in order to "walk" in God's ways, "to guard" God's instructions, statutes, and rules (58). In verses 57–58, the verbs and pronouns are in the first-person plural: "May God be with us," "not forsake us," "incline our hearts." Finally, Solomon asks for justice for himself and the people in order that "all the peoples of the earth may know that Adonai is God, there is none other" (60).[91] The narrative conclusion (62–66) sets everything in light of the festival of Succoth, at which the dedication of the Temple is said to have taken place (2, 65). A fantastical number of sacrifices and great celebrations end the festivities so that the people can go away happy and in good spirits (66).

The prayer is a composite dating back to different times and experiences in the history of Israel but has been woven into a grand whole, bridging the tensions between adherence to a God who is incomparably great and who dwells in "heaven" and the idea that there is a special place, the Temple in Jerusalem, where God can be reached more than in any other place. The emphasis on sin, pleading and forgiveness is noteworthy and fits well into the postexilic context, when a sense of responsibility for the loss of the land on account of disloyalty toward God pervaded the community. At the time of the Festival of Succoth in Judah during the restoration, the prayer of Ezra reflects on God's goodness and the people's rebellious and disobedient behavior both in the wilderness period and afterward, summarized in the words "you have dealt faithfully and we have acted wickedly" (Neh 9:33).

### Act IV: The Fruits of Riches (1 Kings 9–11)

*A critique of national pride, high standards of living, and cultural ingenuity.*[92]

---

91. The statement that there is no other god besides Adonai is at home in the prophetic poetry of Second Isaiah, texts dated to postexilic times (Isa 45:5, 6, 14, 18, 21, 22; 46:9).

92. Nelson, *First and Second Kings*, 67.

Three chapters reporting various visitations, trading adventures, divine judgment, the rise of adversaries against Solomon, and a prophetic announcement draw the curtain on the reign of King Solomon and at the same time on the enterprise of one people under one monarch. Throughout the first two chapters, there is an emphasis on the gathering and display of riches. First, God provides Solomon with guarded approval of the Temple in a second dream that contains a stern warning and announcement of future disaster in case of the king's apostasy (9:1–9). Trade with Tyre, more building projects, and the accumulation of possessions and gold follow the divine visitation (9:10–28). When the queen of Sheba visits and is overwhelmed by what she sees and hears, more possessions are yet added to the rich display, especially of gold, but also chariots and horsemen (10:1–29). The final chapter details Solomon's apostasy and God's judgment (11:1–13). After this, adversaries begin to plague Solomon, among them Jeroboam, who receives an announcement from a prophet that the kingdom will be divided in two after Solomon's death, with the greater part assigned to Jeroboam.

With Solomon's lengthy prayer we have heard him speak in this material for the last time. His subsequent absence is ironic in view of his reported utterances of thousands of sayings and speaking of so many growing things and animals (5:12–13 [4:32–33]). Although he is an active participant in the events, he participates only by description, is not said to react verbally to either praise or chastisement, and undergoes little character development. His eventual apostasy does not come as much of a shock in view of all the warning signs the text has shown before, especially in regard to his attachment to riches rather than to walking in God's ways. The prescription in Deuteronomy not only lists negatives in its stipulations, avoiding too many of this and too much of that, but requires that the king of the future will spend time every day reading God's *torah*—his Teaching—"lest his heart lifts itself above his brothers/ and lest he turn aside from the commandment to right or left;/ in order that he may prolong the time on his throne,/ he and his descendants in the midst of Israel" (Deut 17:20).

*Act IV, Scene 1: A Word of Caution (1 Kings 9:1–9)*

*Solomon isn't the only one who can cite the Davidic covenant.*[93]

The opening statement sounds a positive note with its repeated emphasis on Solomon's finishing all his building projects, the fifth such reference in the chain of stories (6:9, 14, 38; 7:1). One might thus expect the second divine visitation he receives to be one of approval, and indeed it starts in the right direction by God expressing approval of the prayer and divine "sanctification" of the Temple, affirming the sanctification completed by Solomon (8:64). The careful wording is that God consents to "put my name there for the ages," and in response to Solomon's plea "my eyes and my heart will be there always" (3).[94] No mention is made of God's *dwelling* there. The emphatic indication of the Temple as "this house that you built" can be seen as a mere repetition of the identical references from Solomon's mouth in his prayer, although it occurred earlier in a context of divine warning (6:11–12; see pp. 50–51 above). Then, in the middle of his building activities on the Temple, Solomon had received a word from God that presented him for the second time with an "if," the first having occurred during his dream (3:14). In chapter 9, too, God adds an "if" to the directives. The speaker turns the attention forcefully to Solomon with the reiterated "you": "And you, you will walk before me" (4). The ordinances, commandments, and justice are mentioned as on the two previous occasions, and in all three the concern is with *walking* in the ways God ordained.[95] All three recall God's promise to "David your father." The outcome of Solomon's loyalty is defined as a "long life" in 3:14 and as a promise of presence

93. Eslinger, *Into the Hands of the Living God*, 145.

94. The "heart" used in the sense of the core of a person and especially the will and understanding (but also including the emotions) can be found in reference to God in the Bible about fifteen out of the roughly eight hundred occurrences. Eight of these are in a context where God directly refers to "my heart," as here (1 Sam 2:35; 2 Kgs 10:30; Isa 63:4; Jer 3:15; 7:31; 19:5; 32:41; Hos 11:8). In Kgs, the wisdom God grants to Solomon is a matter of his heart (1 Kgs 3:9, 12; 5:9 [4:29]; 10:24).

95. "If you walk in my ways" (3:14); "if you walk in my ordinances" (6:12).

with Israel in 6:12–13. On this occasion, Solomon gets a promise of continued possession of the throne through his descendants: "There shall not fail you a successor on the throne of Israel" (5).[96] That is not where the warning ends, however.

In a sharp continuing rebuke, the consequences of royal disloyalty for the people, the land, and the Temple are spelled out.

### 1 KINGS 9:6–7

6  If you will turn, yes turn away,
     you all and your descendants from following me
     and not guard my commandments,
     my ordinances that I have set before you [all],
     and walk after and serve other gods
     and bow down to them,
7  I will cut off Israel from the face of the land
     that I gave to them,
     and the house I consecrated to my name
     I will cast away from me,
     and Israel will become a proverb
     and a taunt among all the nations.

The address expands in verse 6 to the second person plural. Whereas everything before was spoken to Solomon alone, the words are now directed to the people: *you all.*[97] Nothing could spell more clearly that the fate of the king and the fate of the people are connected. The monarch's missteps will bleed into the transgressions of the people; thus also the punishment. Israel will become a proverb and a taunt, mocked by the nations, who will wonder, "Why has Adonai done this/ to this land, to this house?"[98] To this rhetorical question the

96. Literally, the phrasing is that "there will not be *cut off* for you a man on the throne of Israel." Subsequently God threatens to "*cut off* Israel from the face of the land" (9:7).

97. Hebrew verbs are inflected to make a distinction between the second person singular and plural that cannot easily be reflected in English translations. In this discourse, the second person verb forms are plural as of verse 6.

98. The word for "taunt" (*sheninah,* from a verb "to sharpen") occurs

response (from outsiders!) will be that it happened because "they abandoned Adonai" (9). The last word of God's speech is "evil." "This house you have built" will become a sanctuary God casts away, a ruin, so that it is a source of derision, of schadenfreude for outsiders, who are all in the know about the cause of the disaster.[99] Solomon has no reply to this announcement of a potentially calamitous future.

### Act IV, Scene 2: Embarrassment of Riches
### (1 Kings 9:10–28; 10:11–29)

*The expansionist ambitions of powerful rulers are often realized in the shadow of policies that diminish the value of human beings.*[100]

The section opens with Hiram and closes with him. He is the donor of much gold (9:11, 14) and at the end participates in a seafaring adventure with Solomon from which both gain gold (9:28). Since "Ophir" itself can mean "gold" (a noun that occurs eleven times in this last section), chapter 9 ends with the sight and the sound of this glittering commodity. First, Hiram is the recipient of Solomon's gift of twenty cities, with which he is not satisfied, so that a storm threatens to brew between the trade partners; but it seems to blow over (9:12–14). This brief mention of Hiram is interrupted by another catalog of *forced labor*, the building of more cities, and the gathering of goods, including a return to the mention of "chariots" (9:15–19). Forced labor is this time limited to surviving peoples in the land, who make an unexpected appearance (9:20–22). The text

---

only three other times in the Hebrew text, each time accompanied by *mashal* ("proverb," "by-word"): Deut 28:37; 2 Chr 7:20; Jer 24:9. A person or community's suffering can be exacerbated by taunting or mocking (see Ps 44:14[13]).

99. Reading "ruin" with the Vulgate and Syriac rather than the Hebrew "most high," which does not fit the text but may be a euphemism. See Fox, *The Early Prophets*, 616. In his prayer, Solomon has not specifically mentioned the possibility of apostasy, although one might consider it subsumed under the category of "sin" in 8:33, 35, 46, 50.

100. Hens-Piazza, *1 & 2 Kings*, 94.

states emphatically that Solomon did *not* put the Israelites to forced labor, a reassurance that carries little weight in view of what came before and what will happen after.

The scene ends with a notation of Solomon's sacrificial offerings three times a year, most likely on the occasion of the major festivals. Like the qualification regarding forced labor, the note serves as a reassurance of appropriate conduct, this time in terms of his faithful worship observance. More building ensues, however, in the shape of a fleet, sent to Ophir at the south end of the Red Sea—the "land of gold" (9:26–28). Solomon is fast becoming part of the "one percent" in his environment, and the accumulation of vast wealth, although not directly counter to the warning issued by God at the beginning, creates dissonance with the admonition to "do" all God's "commandments and justice" (9:4). Solomon's "justice" sounds more and more like the justice of the king Samuel warned about (1 Sam 8:11–17). He is not yet said to "serve other gods," but the repeated mention of "silver and gold" reminds one of the prophetic warnings that mention these metals in connection with idols almost exclusively (Isa 30:22; 31:7; 40:19; Jer 10:4, 9; Hos 8:4). Sayings in Proverbs warn of the *fall* to come for those who "trust in riches" (Prov 11:28) and against toiling "to gain wealth" (Prov 23:4). That's not to mention the admonitions regarding chariots and wealth specific to kings in Deuteronomy 17:16–17. The attention paid in the text to the time and energy spent by Solomon on these very things should give the reader/listener pause for thought if not cause for downright suspicion that perhaps this is not what God had in mind for the king and his people. Eslinger writes, "In the person of Solomon the gifts that God has granted are a deadly pitfall, leading to wrack and ruin."[101]

The account of the acquisition of gold is continued in the second half of chapter 10. At his court, it is truly all gold that glitters. The text even records that "there was no silver;/ it was not valued in the days of Solomon as anything," although in the next breath the collecting of "gold and silver" is reported beside "ivory, apes, and peacocks," a startling collection of items that have little value except for show, found only here in the Hebrew Bible (10:21–22; cf. 2 Chr

---

101. Eslinger, *Into the Hands of the Living God*, 153.

9:21). The abundance of goods is partly due to the fleet the king operates jointly with Hiram. Naturally, the whole world is astonished, and comes to "hear his wisdom," which in this context can hardly be read without a sense of irony (10:24–25). Surely, if people came to visit, the visual splendor of the court would distract them from hearing anything at all!

### Act IV, Scene 3: The Riddle of Sheba (1 Kings 10:1–10)

*This text, like so many others, sits on an interpretive knife edge.*[102]

Such is the bedazzlement of the queen of Sheba, who comes to visit on hearing reports about her neighbor. Her purpose is to test Solomon with *riddles*, a beginning that sets up the expectation of an example, another way for Solomon to prove his wisdom. The first unit ends with the assurance that Solomon answered all her *questions*, which could refer to the solving of riddles, but all hopes of an example are dashed, as we never find out what she asked or what he answered (1–3). Solomon is once again spoken *about* in the episode rather than appearing as an active participant; as the queen of Sheba does, we behold him in all his glory. The queen of a country most scholars put in the Arabian Peninsula arrives with splendor of her own, a retinue in tow, and "perfumes, much gold, and precious stones" (2). The text reports on what she sees.

1 KINGS 10:4–5

4 And the queen of Sheba saw
all the wisdom of Solomon
and the house he had built;
5 also the food on his table,
the seating of his servants
and standing of his attendants,

---

102. Danna Nolan Fewell and David M. Gunn, *Gender, Power, and Promise: The Subject of the Bible's First Story* (Nashville: Abingdon, 1993), 177.

and their clothing,
his cupbearers, and the sacrifices
that he sent up in the house of Adonai;
it took her breath away.

The "wisdom of Solomon" consists in all she *beholds*: the palace, food, and so on, which robs her of *ruah*—spirit or breath.[103] So what exactly does she *see*? Wisdom, the first thing mentioned, is spelled out as concrete articles: buildings, food, the seating and standing of servants and other attendants, their clothes, and the sacrifices. This enumeration leaves aside everyone outside the court. What she sees is the wisdom used by Solomon to construct a house, the number of his servers, how well they are provided for, and all the offerings going up. All of it begs the question of where all this lavishness is coming from. The text has already let it be known how food came to the king's table (4:7), and no doubt, once the Temple was built, its personnel and the sacrifices that "went up" exacted more provisions from the land. What the queen of Sheba does *not* see is the toll all this "good stuff" (7) takes on the people who furnish it for the court, the Temple, and all the personnel. Well may she declare the king's servants—those who are in the presence of such abundance—"happy," but it is an extremely limited view of what makes for a "happy" land and population (8). Three times she mentions "wisdom" in her report to the king (6–8), first as hearsay in her own land, then as she has *seen* it with her own eyes, and finally as overheard by all in attendance at the court. In the meantime, not one word has passed Solomon's lips. Her eulogy ends with the avowal that the God of Israel must be devoted to Solomon's people to have established him as king "to do justice and righteousness" (9). Eslinger calls the queen's observations a "piece of dramatic irony" and "justice and righteousness conspicuous only by their absence."[104]

103. Cf. Josh 2:11; 5:1, where *ruah* is used of the "spirit" leaving the inhabitants of Canaan in the face of the invading Israelites.

104. Eslinger, *Into the Hands of the Living God*, 151. Eslinger notes that the queen is not "aware" of the irony. The point is not whether her speech is deliberately ironic but the effect the narrator intends to create with the speech.

The incongruity of these words in the context of the queen's visit can hardly have escaped the narrator who set them on the page. In fact, following the gift of wisdom in chapter 3, "all that the narrator has described . . . is Solomon's incessant efforts at material gain for himself and his monarchy."[105]

As summarily as the story of the queen is told in 1 Kings 10, so elaborate has her life been in the life of religious interpretation and imagination. Whether viewed as a demon with hairy legs or as producing the line of King Nebuchadnezzar together with Solomon, as suffering from a variety of impairments or as the founder of the Ethiopian conversion to the God of Israel, she has taken up a large space in the religious imagination.[106] In the Hebrew Bible, her story is not only short in terms of the extent of text but also in regard to characterization, which leads to the conclusion that the writers and compilers had other goals in mind than setting a complex character on the page. Chapter 9 ended with a report of Solomon's fleet and wide-ranging trade adventures, which may also have served to spread rumors about him. The queen's abrupt entrance in 10:1 is based on just such reports. The Hebrew of the first verse is filled with sibilants echoing the sound of whispered rumors: *umalkat sheva shoma'at 'et shema' shelomo leshem 'adonai*—"and the queen of Sheba heard the report[107] of Solomon for the name of Adonai."[108] The upshot of this phrase may be that trade has brought in its wake reports about both the king and the God of Israel. The story functions also to illustrate the homage of the foreign potentates who are said to have brought Solomon gifts (5:1 [4:21]).

---

105. Eslinger, *Into the Hands of the Living God*, 151.

106. For an overview of the many ways in which the queen of Sheba lived on in religious literature and imagery, see Alice Ogden Bellis, "The Queen of Sheba: A Gender-Sensitive Reading," *JRT* 51 (1994–1995): 17–28.

107. The noun "report" is *shema'* in Hebrew: that which is "heard."

108. The words "for the name of Adonai" do not fit well in the text and are left out in a number of translations. It is possible that some letters or a word dropped out. A contemporary German translation adds the words "and of the house he built for the name of Adonai." Greek versions read for both nouns the word "name," producing "heard the name of Solomon and the name of Adonai."

On its own, it is not significant that the potentate is a queen rather than a king, but in view of what follows, both femaleness and foreignness strike a potentially negative note. According to the next and last chapter of the cycle, King Solomon was seduced into the worship of "other gods" by the many "foreign women" he loved (11:1–8). The queen's foreign identity needs no emphasis, as it is clear enough; she is also described as wealthy and powerful. She comes with a "great train" of animals and goods (2), literally in Hebrew with a "mighty army." As the curtain opens, everything is over the top: She arrives with a *"very* mighty army" and *"very* much gold" and speaks of *"all* that is in her heart." In return, Solomon tells her *"all* her words; not a word was hidden from the king" (3).

The riddle of the story is not in the test with which she faces Solomon, of which we hear nothing, but in the meaning of her praise for the ostentatious display of wealth. Rather than hearing a match of wits, we see a mighty, rich queen overwhelmed by what she beholds. Truly, here are riches beyond the imagination if they could reduce even such a one to silence! "What remains to be done but for her to tell the man what he wants to hear—that he is incredibly brilliant and amazingly wealthy, and that the wine goblets really leave hers completely in the shade."[109] While we see with the queen's eyes the lavishness of the court, we hear nothing from Solomon and indeed have to take her word for it that his wisdom surpasses everything she had heard (7). Her declaration invoking the name of Israel's God with a blessing may be seen as a literary stereotype in which foreign powers have heard of the power of Adonai, but it is not therefore meaningless.[110] Like Rahab, the queen of Sheba is a foreign woman who highlights the power and grandeur of Israel, in this context in the person of its king, as well as the stature of its God. Is she thus the "foreign" woman upholding the name of the God of Israel in contrast to the women in the next chapter? Or is she speaking with great irony because to gather heaps of gold does

109. Fewell and Gunn, *Gender, Power, and Promise,* 176.
110. We can think of Rahab, who makes a statement about Adonai's *giving* of the land to the Israelites (Josh 2:9); the expression to take "the breath away" occurs also in that context (Josh 2:11; cf. 5:1)

nothing to promote the cause of justice and righteousness and in fact may do the reverse?[111]

### Act IV, Scene 4: A Word of Judgment (1 Kings 11:1–13)

*The final assessment that unfolds in these verses . . . is less about [Solomon] breaking one law of Deuteronomy than it is about his repeated choices that now culminate in comprehensive waywardness.*[112]

What comes about in chapter 11 should not be a surprise after all the warning signs leading up to it. Eight verses describe the condition of Solomon in light of his excesses in marriages. The phrase "and King Solomon loved women, many foreign women," encapsulates what is to follow. Not only in riches but in his harem, he practices extravagance, and it is only the last step in a series of choices that, if not outright evil, is not conducive to a life in accordance with God's instruction. "At the end of his reign, the indictment of apostasy narrates as well as climaxes a lifelong series of decisions to pursue other powers, to become caught up in other preoccupations, and to succumb to other attractions."[113] Three times God warned Solomon, and yet here we find him constructing "a high place" for gods introduced into his household (7). More ominously, it is said of him that he himself followed other gods (5).[114] The word "heart" occurs five times in the first four verses: The traditional warning is that other peoples would endanger the "heart" of Israel, and in Solomon's case the foreign

111. It is not at all clear that the story intends to highlight Solomon's, and by extension Israel's, superiority, as proposed by Susanne Gilmayr-Bucher in "She Came to Test Him with Hard Questions: Foreign Women and Their View on Israel," *BibInt* 15 (2007): 135–50. Gilmayr-Bucher sees both Sheba and Rahab as a mirror of Israel's supremacy.

112. Hens-Piazza, *1–2 Kings*, 108.

113. Hens-Piazza, *1–2 Kings*, 117.

114. The text qualifies Solomon's idolatry by assigning it to his "old age," but this note does little to undo the many negative notes in the text that precede this qualification. Oppressive practices and unwise use of resources, people, and land are strongly connected to idolatry in the prophetic literature of the Bible.

women "turned his heart" (3, 4). The heart is where the inclinations and will are located. When the Holy God contemplates the evil of humanity at the beginning of creation, it concerns the "imaginations of their heart" (Gen 6:5). Solomon's heart is not "wholly with Adonai his God" (4). Where in Deuteronomy the danger lurks among the native inhabitants of Canaan (Deut 7:1–4), here the threat comes from foreign imports, the daughter of Pharaoh in the lead (1). The blame falls on the company Solomon keeps, the "foreign women," a concern that arose especially after the Babylonian exile in the small community of the restoration period of fifth-century Judah. We note that the consequences of Solomon's apostasy fall squarely on his shoulders and not on those of the women, however.[115]

God is angry, especially in view of the privileges experienced by Solomon: two divine visitations and clear directives. So, the results of this behavior are spelled out directly by God (9–13). We note that Solomon does not receive word via a prophet but that Adonai addresses him personally and announces that the kingdom will be "torn away" from Solomon and given to his "servant" (11). For the first time, Solomon is charged with not "guarding my covenant," indicating the totality of the "ordinances and commandments" mentioned earlier (3:14; 6:12; 9:6).

115. This aspect differs from the "foreign women" of Ezra and Nehemiah (Ezra 9:1–10:44; Neh 13:23–28), who were banished from the community together with their children" (Ezra 10:18–44). The postexilic community labored under anxiety about its identity and fear of divine punishment in view of the exile. The biblical text witnesses to tension between the (mostly Deuteronomic) view of the danger presented by outsiders and the love expected for the outsider, especially the stranger. (Thirty-six laws in the Torah concern the existence of the stranger in the midst of Israel, all of them positive.) The Historical Books present a number of women who contribute to the community in remarkable ways, among them Rahab and Yael. Ruth, a Moabite, the great-grandmother of David and thus related also to Solomon, provides an example of what it means to live according to the family devotion required in the Torah. The anxiety about identity formation through fear of the outsider is certainly not alien to the social and political context of the United States, as well as many other parts of the Western world, today. See Johanna W. H. van Wijk-Bos, *Ezra, Nehemiah, and Esther*, Westminster Bible Companion (Louisville: Westminster John Knox, 1998), 42–48.

1 KINGS 11:11–13

11 And Adonai said to Solomon:
   Because it is this way with you
   and you have not guarded my covenant
   and my statutes with which I charged you,
   I will tear, yes tear, the kingdom from you
   and give it to your servant.
12 Only in your lifetime I will not act
   for the sake of David, your father.
   But from the grasp of your son I will tear it.
13 Only I will not tear away the entire kingdom;
   one tribe I will give to your son,
   for the sake of David my servant
   and for the sake of Jerusalem, which I chose.

The expression *tearing the kingdom* is reminiscent of the announcement by Samuel to Saul (1 Sam 15:28; 28:17), which also included *giving it* to someone else—"to your neighbor" in 1 Samuel, but in Solomon's case to his "servant." The verb "to tear" occurs four times in these few lines to emphasize the importance of this violent action. Unlike in King Saul's case, the verdict is immediately qualified by two limitations: the kingship will not be taken from Solomon himself but from his son, and the Davidic kingship will continue, albeit over only one tribe. An attachment has formed between the Deity and the house of David, as well as the city of Jerusalem, which is left intact, at least for the time being.

### Act IV, Scene 5: Adversaries (1 Kings 11:14–43)

*The prophet is a mouthpiece for the theological verdict given earlier in the chapter.*[116]

The sequel to this dire beginning continues in a downward spiral, with threats to the peace of Solomon and the land. First, two "adver-

---

116. Brueggemann, *1 & 2 Kings*, 147.

saries" or "accusers" are aroused by God: an Edomite and a Syrian, Hadad and Rezon (11:14–25).[117] Both go back to the days of David, and their characters involve background stories. The first, Hadad, is an Edomite who had fled to Egypt on account of military action against Edom by Joab (14–22). The second, Rezon, who likewise endured defeat under King David (2 Sam 8:3–10), ends up in Damascus (23–25). Both characters take us back to David's campaigns in 2 Samuel 8 and his aggressive, ruthless behavior toward neighboring peoples. The story of Hadad is difficult to piece together on account of problems in the text and its uncertain ending. He may have been significant because he combines in his person features of Joseph and Moses. Midianites sold young Joseph to an official of Egypt, where he eventually found great favor with Pharaoh, as did Hadad. Moses is raised in the household of Pharaoh, as is Hadad, and Midian is the destination for Moses on his flight out of Egypt (Exod 2:15). Hadad's plea to Pharaoh "send me" (2× in vv. 21–22) recalls Moses' plea to Pharaoh (cf. Exod 9:1).

Rezon's story, amounting to little more than a short note, shows parallels to that of David. He is not royalty but a leader of a band of fighters who is eventually elevated to be king in Damascus. God's guidance and choice are important factors in the lives of these characters, underlining the divine intent that directs the breakup of the kingdom and its aftermath. An interesting postscript to the Hadad and Rezon accounts makes clear that they created difficulties for Solomon during his entire reign.

1 Kings 11:25

And he was an adversary of Israel
all the days of Solomon,
together with the evil that Hadad did,
and he loathed Israel
and became king in Aram.

---

117. The word in Hebrew is *satan*, meaning "accuser" or "tester," not the usual word for enemy. Alter (*Ancient Israel*, 663n14) suggests the word "troublemaker" or a "stumbling block."

The verb "to loathe," found fewer than ten times in the Hebrew Bible and only here in Kings, elicits a strong reminder of Israel under oppression in Egypt, when the Egyptians "loathed them" (Exod 1:12).[118] The verb indicates disgust as well as fear. Solomon himself claimed that Adonai gave him "rest" (5:18[4]), and there are no accounts of military campaigns in the review of his reign. The text, however, lists soldiers and a great number of chariots, apparatus mostly used in warfare (5:6 [4:26]; 9:22; 10:26). The Solomonic period may not have been as peaceful as it appears on the surface of the Kings narrative.

The accounts of Hadad and Rezon prepare for the appearance of Jeroboam, who arrives with all his antecedents—father, mother, region, and town (26)—and gets most of the attention in the rest of the chapter (26–40). The introduction states that he "raised his hand against the king" and then continues to tell of the events that led to his rebellion. The king apparently puts a great deal of trust in him and has charged him with serious responsibilities, assigning him to oversee "all the burden of the house of Joseph,"[119] which could be a reason for Jeroboam to rebel, or at least add fuel to the fire of his indignation with Solomon's regime, as he is an Ephraimite. Whatever the case may be, as Jeroboam is leaving Jerusalem, he has an encounter with a prophet that changes his life (28–39).

All the attention of the text in verses 29–39 is focused on the prophetic oracle rather than on the mindset, actions, or reactions

---

118. "Loathe" is one possible translation for a verb that indicates both disgust and fear. In the Dutch language, the word *kotsen*, meaning "to vomit," is a possible Hebraism that is also used both literally and metaphorically. Both words could be onomatopoetic.

119. The word for "labor" in v. 28 is *sevel* rather than *mas*, from a verb that means "to carry a burden." Thus, Jerome T. Walsh (*1 Kings*, Berit Olam [Collegeville, MN: Liturgical Press, 1996], 143) interprets the activity in 1 Kgs 11:28 as that of "hauling." It appears to have this meaning in 1 Kgs 5:29[15] and Neh 4:4[10], where the action is also clarified as carrying (Neh 4:11[17]). It seems likely that although the activity described in 1 Kgs 11:28 may be carrying a burden or hauling, it is a part of forced labor. It is used in Gen 49:15 of the burden on a donkey (metaphorically for Issachar); in Isa 9:3[4] and 14:25, the word is parallel to "yoke."

of the recipient, who never gets to speak.[120] Ahiyah is from Shiloh, according to Brueggemann "a seat for older, radical Mosaic notions of social organization."[121] More likely, Shiloh at this moment functions as a seat of judgment, linking this prophecy to the judgment given there against the house of Eli, also by a prophet, as well as the direct divine announcement to Samuel (1 Sam 2:27–36; 3:11–14). First, Ahiyah repeats God's message about tearing the kingdom with a symbolic action. Tearing a robe as a symbol of separation evokes the image of the torn robe in 1 Samuel 15, declared by Samuel to be a symbol of God's tearing of the kingdom away from Saul. Here, the ten pieces of the robe symbolize the ten tribes that will be under the rule of Jeroboam, constituting a specification of God's words to Solomon. Such a symbolic action undertaken by a prophet is a powerful event, anticipating the future as an accomplished fact. Jerome Walsh writes, "Together the prophet's oracle and the symbolic action have power, they unleash what they announce."[122]

There are two main issues that Ahiyah takes up in his oracle: the ceding of the ten tribes to a king who does not descend from David and the sparing of one tribe for David and his house.[123] These two are intricately woven together, going back and forth from the one

---

120. Nelson (*First and Second Kings*, 72) judges the oracle to be "verbose and overfull." Most likely, the compilers were intent on highlighting both the importance of Jeroboam's appointment by divine choice, while at the same time holding on to the importance of David's house and God's protection of Jerusalem.

121. Brueggemann, *1 & 2 Kings*, 145.

122. Walsh, *1 Kings*, 144.

123. We assume the one tribe to be Judah, although this begs the question of a remaining unassigned tribe. The Greek text has "two tribes." It is possible that the omission in the Hebrew text is a sign of a seam where two traditions are combined, as Ernst Würthwein (*Das Erste Buch der Könige Kapitel 1–16*, ATD 11 [Göttingen: Vandenhoeck & Ruprecht, 1977], 139–49) would have it. Würthwein traces one strand to the Northern Kingdom, the one that legitimizes Jeroboam's kingship as a divine appointment, and the second, the one that emphasizes the importance of David's rule over Judah and God's choice of Jerusalem, to the South. His argument leans on the theory of two Deuteronomic traditions, one hailing from the Northern Kingdom and one completed under Josiah.

topic to the other, although they may originate in different strands of the tradition. The prophet begins with an indictment of Solomon and a brief mention of the sparing of one tribe for the sake of David and Jerusalem (32). He then launches into a strong condemnation of idolatrous practices, all of which are assigned to the people rather than to Solomon alone, once again emphasizing the consequences of the monarch's actions for the community.[124] Verse 34 returns to the appointment of a successor for Solomon as a descendant of David, here called "my servant." Returning to the gift of ten tribes to Jeroboam, the next statement emphasizes the importance of Jerusalem because God chose it for God's *name* (35–36).[125] Finally, Jeroboam, as the one appointed by God to be king "over Israel," is warned that the gift includes a condition.

### 1 KINGS 11:38–39

38 And if you heed all that I command you
   and walk in my ways and do what is right in my eyes
   by guarding my statutes and my commandments
   as did David my servant,
   then I will be with you, and I will build for you
   a trustworthy house as I have built for David,
   and I will give you Israel.
39 And I will afflict the seed of David
   because of this, but not forever.

124. One would expect the third person singular, referring to Solomon, as both RSV and NRSV translate, but the Hebrew text has plural verbs throughout verse 33. The Greek text has a singular, but the Vulgate maintains the plural.

125. In addition, the text mentions that the one tribe will provide "a lamp for David my servant always" (v. 36) The lamp as a symbol of life and light referring to David occurs again in 1 Kgs 15:4 and 2 Kgs 8:19. The word used here is related to the noun *ner* used in 2 Sam 21:17 for David himself. It occurs in reference to God or God's commandment in poetry (2 Sam 22:29; Ps 119:105; cf. Ps 18:29[28]; 132:17: "I will cause to grow a horn for David/ I will arrange a light for my anointed."

The requirements for a lasting house are clear, and the constant references to David are striking. David is held up as an example of one who kept God's commandments, but the reminder of a *lasting house as I have built for David* also sounds a note of warning. By now it is evident what is going to happen to that house!

Either Jeroboam undertook some type of rebellious action that has dropped out of the story or Solomon got wind of Ahiyah's oracle, because at the resumption of the narrative Solomon seeks to kill Jeroboam, who flees to Egypt (40).[126] The narratives close with the death notice of Solomon, like his father's in the style that will be used for subsequent rulers: The rest of his deeds are recorded elsewhere, he ruled for so many years in his capital, he lay down with his ancestors and was buried in the city of David, and his son became king in his stead (41–43).

## Solomon

*The wisdom for which he becomes world famous is not the ability to listen but the ability to speak.*[127]

Since half of the first book of Kings is spent on Solomon's ascension to the throne and his rule, we may assume that the compilers of what became Kings considered the person and the period to be of enormous significance for the community's self-understanding in view of its past.[128] Clearly a great deal of attention is paid to his suc-

---

126. Walsh (*1 Kings*, 148) suggests that the Jeroboam account serves as "a sort of hinge connecting the story of Solomon in chapters 1–11 to that of Jeroboam in chapters 11–14." Walsh also points to the parallels between the Solomon-Ahiyah-Jeroboam story and the Saul-Samuel-David accounts.

127. Walsh, *1 Kings*, 155.

128. The forty-year kingship assigned to Solomon (11:42) is most likely a symbolic number, as was that of his father, David (2 Sam 5:4). For a balanced discussion of Solomon as a historical person and of the period, see J. Maxwell Miller and John H. Hayes, *A History of Ancient Israel and Judah*, 2nd ed. (Louisville: Westminster John Knox, 2006), 186–220. Miller and Hayes judge the reign of Solomon to have ended "approximately in 925 BCE" (194).

cession, taking up almost a quarter of the entire narrative. Beyond the elaborate machinations by Nathan and Bathsheba, there is the oath David takes in God's name that Solomon will be "king after me and will sit on the throne in my place" (1:30), appointing him even before his death. In addition, Solomon is *anointed* as king by a priest at his father's command, in the presence of a prophet, while the people acclaim his kingship and rejoice in it—an event mentioned again as something people have *heard* about both around the court and outside Israel, underlining its significance (1:33–40, 45; 5:15[1]).[129] Solomon was not the logical successor to the throne; Adonijah was clearly an older brother and there may have been others (see 2 Sam 3:4; 5:13). Were there questions about the legitimacy of Solomon's succession, making it necessary to ground it firmly in his father's appointment and in sacred anointing?

On the other hand, while David's imprimatur is crucial, the portrait of the aging king is hardly flattering. He is old and impotent, manipulated by his family and a court prophet, and filled with ill-will toward those who have crossed him in the past so that his last words to his son are "you will cause his grey hair to descend in blood to Sheol" (2:9). A different picture emerges of this David than of the one we met in the Samuel narratives, stripped as he is of charisma and magnanimity. It is difficult to reconcile this depiction of David with the various portrayals of 1 and 2 Samuel, even the most negative ones, and it seems that another hand is at work here.

The image of Solomon in the first chapters is of someone who will do most anything to hold on to his grasp of the throne, and in that sense he may be considered "wise" as his father judged him to be (2:6, 9). Wisdom (*hokhmah*—mentioned more than twenty times in these chapters in reference to Solomon), together with its linked concept "insight," is a complicated notion in the ancient world and the Hebrew Bible, related to knowledge about living in such a way as to avoid hazards and temptations. True wisdom helps one to get along, to elude major pitfalls or follies, and to be successful. It

---

129. Outside of Solomon, the anointing of kings in Israel and Judah is mentioned only in the cases of Jehu (2 Kgs 9:6), Joash (2 Kgs 11:12), and Josiah's son Jehoahaz (2 Kgs 23:30).

comes about through close observation of what transpires in human relationships, conversation, and so on, but also in nature, so that it can be said of Solomon that:

1 KINGS 5:13 [4:33]

He spoke of trees,
from the cedar of Lebanon
to the hyssop that comes out of the wall;
and he spoke about domestic beasts
and birds and creeping things
and about fish.

His elimination of enemies and possible contenders for the throne could thus be considered "wise," as it forestalled further bloodshed and violence in the future. The order to cut the baby of the prostitutes in two and give each woman half of a child is "wise" in the sense that it works to stir the compassion of the mother. On the other hand, it is an extreme solution and could have produced horrific results.

Solomon is the only king who experiences divine appearances directly, to whom the word of God comes without an intermediary—a factor that highlights the extraordinary status of this king. He receives large gifts from God, one for which he asks and two more given freely without his requesting them. Such gifts, however, still need to be managed well by the person who receives them. The gift of wisdom needs handling with great care, in a manner that benefits not only the king himself but also the people of his rule, as he discerns when he asks for a "listening heart" in order to judge God's people.

Solomon refers to the people as "vast" or "weighty" with the Hebrew adjective *kaved* from the root *kavad*, whose primary meaning is "to be heavy" (3:9). The adjective can refer to numbers, as may be in the case of 1 Kings 3:9, because of Solomon's preceding reference to the people in terms of a multitude (3:8). It can also mean "difficult" or "obdurate," as with Pharaoh's heart in Exodus 7:14. Used with people, it can mean "strong." It is translated "heavy" when related to a burden or yoke (12:4, 10, 11, 14). When Moses is displeased with the people during the wilderness wanderings, he complains to God that he cannot "carry all this people, for it is too *heavy* for me" (Num 11:14). So, which of these meanings is intended here? Are the people vast (although he already mentioned that)? Are they weighty in the sense of honored or heavy in the sense of a burden? Are they mighty and strong or obdurate and difficult? All of the above? When faced with the prostitutes, Solomon is certainly presented with the obdurate and finds his way quickly out of the predicament they pose. Yet Solomon's hand reaches all too quickly for the sword—in spite of his name, which includes the Hebrew word "peace," "wholeness"[130]—and the same hand imposes forced labor on the people, which is not a wise or just thing to do. Also, the hand that reaches for the sword stretches to gain great wealth and in so doing not only imposes forced labor on his people but burdens them with the maintenance of a lavish household. We found many hints in the narrative that Solomon's way of managing his wisdom and wealth led him in the wrong direction.[131]

Another event of the highest importance for the compilers was the construction of the Temple, to which they devoted almost a third of the narrative in 1 Kings 1–11. The preparations and trade in materials for the Temple are carefully detailed, as is the building

130. For different interpretations of the Hebrew name *shelomo*, see *HALOT* 4:1541.

131. Taking the negative details into account in chapters 3–10 demonstrates their cohesiveness with chs. 1–2 and 11, keeping us from viewing the framing chapters as pasted on by a Deuteronomistic hand to an overall positive account of a "golden age" of the past. For interesting but unpersuasive arguments of this latter view, see Jobling, "Forced Labor," 68–69, 72–73. To Jobling's view, "the unconditional traditions . . . have their own power to subvert the conditional." One can, however, as easily argue that it is the other way around—that the conditional undermines the unconditional. In addition, and in agreement with Daniel Hays ("Has the Narrator Come to Praise Solomon?" 151), the entire Solomon narrative fits into the text of 1–2 Kings and the rest of the Historical Books, which track a "downward spiral." Hays identifies the standard to be Deuteronomistic, a standard that certainly applies to 1–2 Kings.

itself. Amid these descriptions, we read about Solomon's palace, which took twice as long to finish and involved similar rich materials and accoutrements (7:1–12). In an earlier day, the prophet Samuel warned about a king who would be mostly skilled in *taking* (1 Sam 8:11–18), and much later another prophet will sarcastically question the "justice" of a king who is "passionate about cedar" rather than about providing justice for the poor and the needy (Jer 22:13–17). From the narrator's perspective, God is angry about the idolatry of Solomon, judging him by his cultic practices, just as all the kings after him will be judged. The people of God, this "weighty-difficult-honored" people, are suffering under a king who lacks the wisdom to devote his attention to them, God's people—surely a dedication demanded of someone who is said to *love* Adonai. The Temple, and without doubt the palace too, is built on the backs of those forced into service by the king, who is held directly responsible for putting this "burden" on the people (5:27–32[13–18]; 9:15–25). Did the king become a *heavy burden* for the people instead of the other way around? The gift of wealth, granted because he did not ask for it, may require even more care than that of wisdom and the application of a wise and listening heart. Did the hand that gathered riches know when to stop? While wealth in itself is not judged negatively in the Hebrew Bible, the instruction for a king is that "silver and gold he shall not multiply for himself to excess," a prohibition found side by side with the rule forbidding a large harem (Deut 17:17). Solomon crashes through both of these injunctions to an extreme.[132]

Finally, King Solomon is described as *loving*. He is said to have *loved* Adonai (3:3) and many women (11:1). Love in the Bible can mean dedication, devotion, and passion between individuals. It is used in Kings only of Solomon (besides the reference to Hiram's love for David in 5:15[1]), which makes it an observation of particular interest. The love Solomon had for his wives is emphasized by repeating the root in the noun derived from it: "And King Solomon loved women / many foreign ones / along with the daughter of Pharaoh/ . . . ./ To them Solomon clung in love" (1 Kings 11:1–2). We may safely

---

132. In addition, he of course violates the prohibition of acquiring many horses (see p. 42 above).

conclude that Solomon was a passionate man. He was passionate in his devotion to God but passionate about other matters besides: his throne, trade, building projects, gathering possessions, chariots, silver and gold. And he was passionate about women. In the end, his many passions divided his heart so that he burdened the land and his people through his devotion to buildings and piles of goods and he burdened Adonai through his devotion to other gods. God could not overlook this last disloyalty, and the people were not willing to put up with the first.

# Cycle II: The Beginning of the End (1 Kings 12–16)

*Two kingdoms existed alongside each other for approximately two centuries.*[1]

Five chapters take us the better part of a century forward, from Solomon's death through the first half of the 800s to the second king in the Omride house of the Northern Kingdom. Chapter 12 presents a detailed picture of the country's division into two kingdoms, with lively verbal exchanges and attention to underlying social and economic tensions created during Solomon's reign, already evident in the account of his rule (chs. 3–11). Rehoboam, Solomon's son, takes the throne in Judah while Jeroboam becomes king over the ten northern tribes, identified as "Israel," establishing his own capital and worship centers. From then on, the focus stays on Israel and its kings. Only one section is devoted to Judah (14:21–15:24), in which Rehoboam and his son Abiyam are both found wanting in their devotion to Adonai (14:22–24; 15:3).

In Israel, it becomes clear very soon that Jeroboam is not abiding by the standard set for faithful followers of Adonai. Rather than presenting a more or less complete record of a king's rule, the text lingers over specific episodes during each king's reign, sometimes of a puzzling nature—particularly in the case of Jeroboam. On a few occasions, hostilities with neighboring peoples and resulting negotiations take up space in the text. On the whole, this record does not offer a picture of social, economic and political events during a specific monarch's time but highlights the ways in which rulers

---

1. Miller and Hayes, *A History of Ancient Israel and Judah*, 221.

conducted their lives in loyalty to Adonai. Because of the failures of the kings of Israel in this area, the history of the kingdom moves in a constant downward spiral, with frequent coups and assassinations of monarchs and entire royal houses taking place in response to God's command. Between the death of Rehoboam and that of King Asa of Judah, who according to the record reigned for forty-one years, one descendant of Jeroboam, Nadav, has followed him on the throne, and three dynasty changes take place—from Ba'asha to Zimri to Omri—when Ahab, Omri's son, begins his rule (16:29).[2] Every time a royal house is overthrown in Israel, it is according to God's command and announced by a prophet (14:6–17; cf. 15:29; 16:1–4, 9–12).

The presence of prophets is felt throughout the text, beginning in chapter 13. Sometimes an individual is identified only as "a man of God" or a "prophet," but on other occasions someone is mentioned by name, like Ahiyah, familiar from the Solomon narratives, in chapter 14. Their function in the stories is complex: They are critics of the monarchs but also miracle workers, foretellers, and creators of general disturbance. Old legends may lie at the foundation of a number of them, now woven into the accounts of the kingdoms. Their frequent appearance in Kings testifies to the increased importance of the prophetic voice as the kingdoms continue and the existence of the people in their land becomes more threatened.

The close attention paid to individual kings prevents much insight into the lives of ordinary people. Only in chapter 12 do we hear their collective voice speaking in relation to the burdens laid on them by King Solomon. The engagement in trade that became evident as of the late tenth century under Solomon must have created a merchant class of some significance, exacerbating divisions between rich and poor. For most people, a self-sustaining agricul-

---

2. Precise dating is not always possible, but the dates covered from chs. 15–16 are approximately as follows according to J. Maxwell Miller and John H. Hayes, *A History of Ancient Israel and Judah*, 2nd ed. (Louisville: Westminster John Knox, 2006), 222. In Judah: Abiyam, son of Rehoboam (909–907); Asa (906–878); Jehoshaphat (877–853). In Israel: Nadav, son of Jeroboam (905–904, assassinated); Ba'asha, in the first dynastic change (903–882); Ela (881–880, assassinated); Zimri, in the second dynastic change (880 for seven days, suicide); Omri, in the third dynastic change (879–869); Ahab (868–854).

tural lifestyle would have been the norm. Taxation, conscription into the armies, and the obligation to sustain an elaborate administrative and cultic apparatus would have borne down on them severely. Four times, we read that there was war between the two kingdoms (14:30; 15:6, 7, 16), a context that would have created chaos and unrest in the land even if these "wars" consisted mostly of skirmishes. War, at any time in human history, is always harmful to a land as well as to its people. Apart from physical danger to living beings, crops get burned and farmlands overrun and devastated: "Your land a desolation, your towns burned with fire, your soil before your eyes by aliens devoured, a desolation overthrown by aliens" (Isa 1:7). This lament by the prophet Isaiah is not relevant to his time alone.

After the kingdoms divide, there is a prolonged time of turmoil and uncertainty, of hostilities from outside (Egypt and Damascus) and inside (struggles between Judah and Israel). Markedly, the presence of God is recorded as most active in the North, especially through prophetic presence and the judging voice of the narrator. The collectors may have wanted to emphasize how nothing could stop the kingdom's decline and eventual fall—not even God's availability to them with counsel and reproach. Moreover, the presence of God's warning and admonishing voice serves to underline that although the kingdoms are two, God's people are still one people under God's care for good or ill.[3] All the kings except one in these chapters, Asa of Judah, are denounced for their idolatry. Jeroboam, who builds two worship centers to compete with Jerusalem, comes in for special censure, and his disloyalty is the proverbial standard by which his successors are measured; they "walk in the way of Jeroboam (the son of Nevat) and in his sins that he caused Israel to sin" (15:1; 16:3, 26, 31; 21:22; 22:53[52]; 2 Kgs 3:3; 10:29; 13:2, 11; 14:24; 15:9, 18, 24, 28; 17:22). His name is often listed together with his patronymic, "the son of Nevat," perhaps to distinguish him from the Jeroboam who ruled in the eighth century (788–747), the period of the prophets Amos and Hosea.

---

3. "[Adonai]'s people is one, but by God's will it lives under the rule of two kings" (Jerome T. Walsh, *1 Kings*, Berit Olam [Collegeville, MN: Liturgical Press, 1996], 208).

### Act I: Two Kings in the Land (1 Kings 12:1–14:20)

*What was Solomon's relationship with the northern tribes?*[4]

The first scene (12:1–24) presents the attempt of Rehoboam to become king over all the tribes, which ends with his rejection by the majority and the crowning of Jeroboam (12:20). As with the succession of Solomon, a great deal of text is devoted to speech—by the people, by two groups of counselors, and by Rehoboam—so that the action slows down and we view everything from a close-up perspective. Once Rehoboam is ensconced as king over Judah, he attempts to wage war, presumably to regain his kingship over all Israel, but is stopped in his tracks by a prophet (21–24).

The rest of the focus of act 1 goes to the newly minted kingdom of Israel and especially to its king, Jeroboam. He comes back into the picture early in the first scene, and once he is on the throne of the ten tribes now called "Israel," in scene 2 (25–33), he begins with making fortifications in certain towns before turning his attention to matters of worship. He ends up constructing two sanctuaries, one in Bethel and one in Dan—the first as far south as possible without crossing the boundary to Judah and the other as far north as possible, the town formerly called Laish that was brutally conquered by the Danites (12:28–33; cf. Judg 18).

Worship practices instituted by Jeroboam are clearly against regulations prescribed in Deuteronomy, and at the beginning of scene 3 (13:1–34) a "man of God" from Judah appears to condemn the sanctuary in Bethel, announcing doom over the altar and Jeroboam's house. The man of God works a miracle by healing the hand of Jeroboam, who had tried to have him arrested, but refuses to go to the king's house for a meal and a reward (13:4–10).Subsequently, the attention shifts to the interaction between the man of God and an old prophet in Bethel, in a story probably drawing on an existing legend made to fit into the ongoing events and the larger context of the book of Kings (13:11–32; see 2 Kgs 23:17–18). The engagement of the two and the ensuing death of the man of God from

---

4. Walsh, *1 Kings*, 160.

Judah is told in great detail and exhibits characteristics of a fable with the presence of animals as God's instruments.

In spite of what has happened to him, King Jeroboam does not repent of his wrongdoings, and the scene ends with a repeated condemnation and the announcement of the future fall of his house (13:33–34). In the last scene of this act (14:1–20), the doom of his house, not yet announced to Jeroboam himself, is voiced by the same prophet Ahiyah who earlier promised Jeroboam his kingship (11:29–39). It is framed by the story of Jeroboam's ill child and its mother, who is sent to the prophet to inquire about the child's future.

### Act I, Scene 1: Who Will Sit on the Throne? (1 Kings 12:1–24)

*Clearly all was not happiness and bliss under Solomon's rule.*[5]

A first unit (1–4) has Rehoboam in Shechem waiting for "all Israel" *to make him king.* At the end, there will be someone who *is* made king, but it will not be Rehoboam (20). Shechem is a location of historical significance in the texts from Joshua through Kings. It is near Mount Ebal and Gerizim, where once an important ceremony took place to affirm the covenant bond between God and people (Josh 8:30–35). It is where Joshua pledged the people to set aside other gods and commit themselves to serve only Adonai (Josh 24:1–28). It is a town with a tradition of solemn assemblies, but it is not an immediately obvious one to choose as a place for crowning a king unless complaints from the northern tribes had reached the court in Jerusalem and Rehoboam went north to assure himself of the support of tribes other than Judah.[6] In connection with king-making, we encountered the town when Abimelek was *made king* there by the "masters of Shechem" in the period of the Judges (Judg 9:6), an event that did not turn out well. Saul, David, and Solomon were *anointed* by prophet or priest, but neither is represented on this oc-

---

5. Miller and Hayes, *A History of Ancient Israel and Judah*, 219.
6. Walsh (*1 Kings*, 160) judges that Rehoboam was "obliged to travel north to Shechem to obtain the allegiance of 'all Israel.' "

casion. The division of the kingdom has already been announced to us in the previous episode, and the ground is only prepared further by the opening lines and by what follows.

Immediately, Jeroboam is reintroduced, having been called back from Egypt. He is present to address Rehoboam together with "all the assembly of Israel" (3). Jeroboam's appearance destabilizes the proceedings, and he is central to the challenge presented to Solomon's would-be successor to the throne—the demand for concessions in terms of the burdens King Solomon had laid on them.[7] The words they use refer to their service and yoke as *hard* and *heavy*:

1 KINGS 12:4

Your father made hard our service,
and you now, you make light
the service of your father, the hard one,
and his heavy yoke that he put upon us,
and we will serve you.

It's between *you*, *your* father, and *us*. He made our life impossible, and now it's up to *you* to lighten the load of service. Under that condition, we will *serve* you. Rehoboam's reply asks for time, presumably so he can consult the right people.

In the next unit, he does just that, taking counsel with two groups: the elders who were his father's attendants and another group of his own attendants (6–11). We already know that he rejects the counsel of the first group by the time he goes to the second one. His father's men advocate for the soft approach while his own counselors go for the hard one. Absent once again is anyone who could speak to him on God's behalf, whether priest or prophet. The first group is indicated with the word "elders" and the second with "boys" (*yeladim*)—an unusual term in this context, which one would be inclined to translate with "youngsters." The phrases that

---

7. Grammatically, Jeroboam sits in the center of the actions surrounding him: they sent, they called, they came, and they spoke.

accompany the two categories may be the most important for a correct understanding of who these people are. The elders are the ones who "were standing before Solomon" (12:6) while the "youngsters" are the ones "who were standing before" Rehoboam (12:8). Nili Fox has argued that the term *yeladim* indicates a group of offspring of court personnel brought up with the children of the royal house to rise later to the position of court officials.[8] Rehoboam is already 41 years old when he ascends the throne, so the emphasis here may not be so much on age—the sagacity of the "elders" of Solomon versus the impetuosity of the "youngsters" of Rehoboam—as on allegiance. In verse 10, the second group is still called *yeladim* and defined as those "who had grown up with him." Thus, they are hardly children.[9]

The group "standing before Rehoboam," indicating a type of attendance, is not a part of the old regime; they owe their allegiance to their prince, and he allies himself with them.[10] They speak their mind bluntly. In fact, they speak very bluntly and advise him to approach the people with threats rather than the "good words" Solomon's elders had counseled.[11] Different theories about effective government are embodied by the two groups: a willingness to accommodate and compromise versus an assertion of authority exerted by force. It is easy to consider the latter advice poor, especially for those who know what lies ahead, but threats and fearmongering often work to the advantage of leaders, then as now. Notably, each time the people and their concerns are mentioned by Rehoboam, as well as by the different groups of advisors, they are referred to

8. Nili Fox, "Royal Officials and Court Families: A New Look at the ילדים (*yĕlādîm*) in 1 Kings 12," *BA* 59 (1996): 225–32.

9. *Yeladim* occurs for the last time in verse 14. Nili Fox ("Royal Officials and Court Families," 226) points out that the word with the connotation it has here only occurs in this passage and its equivalent in 2 Chr 10:8, 10, 14.

10. There are subtle hints of this in the use of the verb in first person plural in verse 9: "What do you advise we respond [lit. return word] to this people?"

11. Literally, they advise that Rehoboam claim his "little finger" to be larger than his father's "thighs." It is quite clear that the reference here is to genitals.

as "this people." While this can be a more or less neutral term, it carries at least a hint of negativity, used, for example, during the incident of the golden calf in the wilderness when God calls them "this people" (Exod 32:9). Moses identifies them in the same way when he questions his brother Aaron (Exod 32:21; cf. 32:31; 33:12; Num 11:12). It is used almost exclusively with a negative slant by the prophets Isaiah and Jeremiah.

Mistrust on both sides and a decision to side with the hard-liners cause Rehoboam to face the crowd that returns to him on the third day with the announcement that he will make things harder. If they thought it was burdensome under his father, they have not seen anything yet! (12–14). Had his father made their service *hard*? He will give them *hard* words. Had Solomon *disciplined* them with whips? He will *discipline* them with scourges—the lash with multiple thongs and sharp objects to cause multiple injuries. The narrator assures the reader/listener that a turn of events is about to come from Adonai as announced by the prophet Ahiyah. In other words, it is part of the divine plan!

As the people decide to part ways, they use the phrases heard earlier from the rebel Sheba: "What share have we in David?/ No inheritance with the son of Jesse!/ To your tents, O Israel!/ Now see to your house, O David!" (16; cf. 2 Sam 20:1). The rupture that has threatened as of the first period of the entry into the land and many times along the way has become reality. The people stone to death the overseer Adoram sent by Rehoboam—whether as negotiator or enforcer is not clear—and Rehoboam flees back to Jerusalem. This is the same Adoram we met as Adoniram, Solomon's overseer of forced labor in 4:6 and 5:28(14) (see p. 40 above). When the northern tribes, who have gone their own way, hear of Jeroboam's return, presumably from Shechem (?), they make him king "over all Israel" (20).

As once before, in the days of King David (2 Sam 2:8–4:8), there are two kings in the land: Rehoboam and Jeroboam—in Hebrew *rehav'am* and *yarov'am*. Both the names end in the Hebrew word "people" (*am*). The verb *rahav* ("to be broad, wide, large") is significant in the story of Rahab.[12] The name of Rehoboam/Re-

---

12. Josh 2:1–24; see Johanna W. H. van Wijk-Bos, *The End of the Begin-*

hav'am could be a play on the words "the people are large/extensive," congruent with observations in chapters 1–11. In the Solomon narratives, different entities were identified as a great multitude, among them the people, who were said to be "as numerous as the sand at the sea is numerous (4:20; cf. 5:21[7]). Rehav'am, initially intended to be a name related to a multitude of people, in the end turns out to be an ironic name for a ruler whose kingdom extends "to the tribe of Judah alone" (20).

The opening syllables of the name Jeroboam/Yarov'am may hint at the word "strife" or "dispute" among other possibilities. Since the people separated from David's royal house in a dispute, this name is particularly appropriate for Yarov'am. A similar play on "dispute" as part of a name may be found in Judges when Gideon's father renamed him Jerubbaal (*yerubba'al*), referencing a fight or dispute with Baal in a narrative concerning crucial issues of idolatry.[13] A name such as Yarov'am may well have brought Gideon/Yerubba'al's name to mind. The way it harkens back to the struggle with apostasy in Israel's past bodes ill for this king's future as measured by the standards of 1–2 Kings. Another connection with the Gideon story is the town of Penuel, destroyed by an angry Gideon (Judg 8:8, 17) and rebuilt by Jeroboam (25; see below).

Rehoboam wants to go on the warpath immediately and begins to gather troops (we hear nothing more about his being "made king") in order to force Israel to accept him as king (21–24). A word from God through the prophet Shemayah stops the proceedings and thwarts the king's plan. It is worth noting that soldiers are mustered not only from Judah but also from Benjamin, which may have straddled the two kingdoms (21). The mention of the Israelites as "your brothers" (24) is rare and striking in this context—an attempt to emphasize the unity of the people even when divided into two realms. The verb "return" is key to the unit and will play a central role in the episodes that follow. Rehoboam intends to "return the kingship" to himself (21); the command from God to halt the prepa-

---

ning: *Joshua and Judges*, A People and a Land 1 (Grand Rapids: Eerdmans, 2019), 61.

13. Judg 6:32; see van Wijk-Bos, *The End of the Beginning*, 232.

rations includes the directive to "each return to his house" (24); it is repeated for a third time when, in response, the people "turned to go" (24). Every time the text uses a form of the verb *shuv*, a term not only meaning to literally go back from one place to another but in many texts theologically laden with the sense of a return to God's ways of life and worship.

### *Act I, Scene 2: Devisings of the Heart (1 Kings 12:25–33)*[14]

*One gains the impression of a king who, like Solomon, gets right down to the important business of religious obligation.*[15]

War preparations for the moment put to rest, Rehoboam and Judah are left behind as the text turns its attention to Jeroboam, whose voice has not been heard and about whom as yet very little is known. His first action is to "build"—most likely fortify—Shechem and then to do the same with Penuel, the town across the Jordan destroyed by Gideon in another age and once again connecting Jeroboam with those episodes. This impression is strengthened by the fact that Penuel gets rare mention in the Bible and does not appear again in the Jeroboam period.[16] His fortifications both west and east of the Jordan could be in reaction to Rehoboam's preparations. We do not know, for the interest of the text goes immediately to other matters. Jeroboam speaks for the first time in verse 26:

14. I divide the text this way because I hope it facilitates understanding the focus on Jeroboam and what happens in the immediate aftermath of his instituting new worship centers in Israel. The division reflects no judgment on what the writers and editors of the material may have considered a "unit." See the discussion in D. W. Van Winkle, "1 Kings xii 25–xiii 34: Jeroboam's Cultic Innovations and the Man of God from Judah," *VT* 46 (1996): 102.

15. Gina Hens-Piazza, *1–2 Kings*, AOTC (Nashville: Abingdon, 2006), 128.

16. About Penuel very little is known outside the reference in the Jacob cycle (Gen 32:31–32[30–31]) and the passage in Judges 8:8–17.

1 KINGS 12:26–27

26 Then said Jeroboam to himself[17]:
   Now the kingship will return
   to the house of David.

27 When this people goes up to make sacrifices
   in the house of Adonai in Jerusalem,
   the heart of this people will return to their lord,
   to Rehoboam the king of Judah.
   They will slay me and return
   to Rehoboam the king of Judah.

A major character's private thoughts give insight about motivations and subsequent actions (cf. 1 Sam 18:17, 21; 27:1). When father Judah sends his daughter-in-law Tamar back to her family home after his second son has died through having coitus interruptus with her, the narrator informs us of his thoughts, which open up a world of suspicion about his posture toward Tamar and his future plans for his third son (Gen 38:11).[18] Gaining access to an individual's thinking privileges the reader with information that people in the story do not have. The narrator assigns to Jeroboam fear of being assassinated. Strangely for someone who received a prophecy that promised him the kingdom and subsequently was elected by the

---

17. Literally "Jeroboam said in his heart," meaning that he spoke or "thought" to himself. The verb is "he said" (*'amar*) but in this context can be translated "he thought." The expression occurs elsewhere with the "hearts" of Abram (Gen 17:17), Esau (Gen 27:41), and David (1 Sam 27:1). See also Haman in Esth 6:6. In the Psalms, fools say "in their heart/to themselves" that there is no God (Pss 14:1; 53:2[1]) and evildoers say the same (Ps 10:6, 11, 13). God speaks in soliloquy in Gen 1:26; 6:5–7; and 11:6, where the text provides "said" without an indirect object. The same is true for Saul, who contemplates killing David in 1 Sam 18:17, 21—clearly without voicing the words aloud.

18. Gen 38:11 furnishes another example of a soliloquy lacking the word "heart," simply stating "Judah said." These must be his own thoughts, for overtly he promises Tamar his third son, but inside himself he does not plan to give her another chance, "for he *said* that this one might die also like his brothers."

people, sealing the promise he got earlier, he becomes immediately mistrustful. The storyteller portrays a character who is unsure of himself and his position and essentially mistrustful of God. The lines of his rumination abound with the word "return." His thoughts swirl around in his anxiety about the people's "return" to Rehoboam, expressed three times surrounding the slaying of him, Jeroboam. It will all come about when everyone goes to Jerusalem to make sacrifice. There is logic in this paranoid thinking. The "house of David" and the "house of Adonai" are strongly connected and may reinforce a longing for reuniting what is now divided. He needs to keep the people geographically separated.

Thus, the construction of two worship centers follows, overtly based on Jeroboam's suggestion that it is too much for the people to go up to Jerusalem (28–33). The text states that he "took counsel" but not with whom or what, which gives the impression that once again he is relying on his own insights. In language that emphasizes flagrant violation of worship codes articulated in Deuteronomy 12, 16, and 18, he comes up with "images, new festivals and non-Levite priests" to initiate the new order of Israel's worship.[19] Jeroboam is busy *making* all sorts of things: "golden calves" (28), "a house on high places," "priests" (31), and "a feast" (32–33), inventing a new liturgical calendar. Without doubt, the narrative paints all of this in the most negative colors, signaled immediately by Jeroboam's words about the bull calves—"These are your gods, Israel, who brought you up out from the land of Egypt!" (28)—clearly referencing the idolatrous activities of the Israelites under Aaron's leadership and their aftermath during the wilderness wanderings (Exod 32:4). The text underlines the way Jeroboam himself participates in worship to the fullest extent, listing three times when he "went up on the altar" (32–33). Even if a prophet had not appeared almost immediately to denounce the state of affairs, the informed reader then and now would understand what the narrative intends

19. Stuart Lasine, "Reading Jeroboam's Intentions: Intertextuality, Rhetoric, and History in 1 Kings 12," in *Reading Between Texts: Intertextuality and the Hebrew Bible*, ed. Danna Nolan Fewell (Louisville: Westminster John Knox, 1992), 140.

to convey: This is not how a God-appointed leader walks in God's ways, does what is right in God's eyes, and guards God's statutes and commandments (11:38).

### Act I, Scene 3: The Way of Return (1 Kings 13)

*Certainly, this powerful story deserves to be better known than it is.*[20]

Although this scene contains two distinct episodes, we read them together as centered on the theme of Jeroboam's unwillingness to *return* from his frightened, misguided way in spite of a prophetic announcement and a miracle. It is illustrated by the story of the two prophets set inside the theme. The frame around the prophets' story is the future doom of the altar announced to Jeroboam (1–3) and the doom of Jeroboam's house because of his refusal to "return from his evil way" (33). A prophetic announcement always holds open the possibility of repentance, of *return.* In the face of Jeroboam's obduracy, the prophesied doom includes not only the sanctuary but his entire house. At every point, the reaction of Jeroboam to prophetic presence is important and comes up wanting. The expression "by the word of Adonai," rare elsewhere in the Hebrew Bible, occurs in this section seven times, predominating in the opening units and appearing again at the end (1, 2, 5, 9, 32). The man of God comes with a word and a "portent," one that Jeroboam in the end ignores.[21] Equally, the healing of his hand and the adventures of the

---

20. Nelson, *1&2 Kings*, 90.

21. The word used for "portent" in vv. 3 and 5 we find only here in the Historical Books. It is more common in Deuteronomy together with the word "sign" for the wondrous events by which God led the people out of Egypt (Deut 4:34; 6:22; 7:19; 26:8; also see Exod 4–11) and to indicate false or true prophetic presence (Deut 13:2-3). Thomas B. Dozeman ("The Way of the Man of God from Judah: True and False Prophecy in the Pre-Deuteronomic Legend of 1 Kings 13," *CBQ* 44 [1982]: 379–93) understands the theme of the chapter to be true and false prophecy, a subject which is undoubtedly present. More important, however, seems to be the response to the word of Adonai. Dozeman's approach is historical-critical, separating sources and redactional

two prophets are portents that could guide him to *shuv*—to turn from his chosen path—but they fail to do so.

In the opening unit (1–3), Jeroboam is going about his business, officiating at the altar told of in the previous episode in repetitive detail, so that the opening words "Look, a man of God!" startle us to attention. He has come from Judah on God's command, and ignoring the king's presence, he makes a prophetic announcement (identified by the phrase "thus says Adonai") to the altar. The prophecy concerns a prince from the Davidic house who will sacrifice the "priests of the high places" (i.e., illegitimate priests who engage in illegitimate worship practices), and they will be burned upon the altar (13:2; cf. 2 Kgs 23:19–20). A portent of things to come is that the altar will be "rent" and the ashes on it will be "poured out." The word for rending is the same verb used in chapter 11 for the tearing of the kingdom from the house of David (11:11, 12, 13; see p. 70 above). Ashes are ordinarily not poured out, and the verb is found usually in connection with blood; metaphorically, it occurs in the Prophetic Literature for God's anger with Israel's shortcomings. When the king attempts to have the doomsayer arrested, his hand stiffens so that it stays outstretched over the altar, which indeed splits, causing the ashes to scatter.[22] The king begs for a miracle, and his hand is healed. When the hand becomes stiff, the text literally states that the king could not "return" it to himself; he prays that the hand "may return to me," and when he is healed "the hand of the king returned to him."[23]

---

levels, while my focus is on the text in its final form and the possible intention of the compilers for the inclusion of this material in the Jeroboam cycle. Van Winkle ("1 Kings xii 25–xiii 34," 106–7), whose approach is to the text in its final form, sees obedience and disobedience to God's commandments as the heart of 1 Kgs 12:25–13:34.

22. Literally, the king's hand is "dried up," something that in the Bible happens to land or water, grass or plants. Of body parts it can be the palate (Ps 22:16[15]), the skin (Lam 4:8), or bones that dry up (Ezek 37:2, 4, 11). One other passage mentions a "dried-up arm" in a prophecy against the "worthless shepherd" (Zech 11:17).

23. The repetition of the root is obscured in most translations, which read something like "could not draw it back" in v. 4 and "restored" in v. 6 (so

Jeroboam has received a sign and a healing, and his reaction is to invite the man of God for refreshment and a reward, but his offer is met with a refusal.

1 KINGS 13:8–10

8  Then said the man of God to the king:
   If you will give me half of your house,
   I will not come with you;
   I will not eat food,
   and I will not drink water
   in this place.
9  For thus I was commanded by the word of Adonai:
   You will not eat food,
   and you will not drink water,
   and you will not return
   by the way that you came.
10 And he went by another way
   And did not return by the way
   by which he came to Bethel.

A word from Adonai has instructed the man of God regarding his *return*, and it does not involve staying in "this place" for nourishment or going back the same way he came. "Eating and drinking" can be a source of contentment, as their absence is a sign of deprivation. But it may also indicate an occasion filled with ambiguity, ending in horrifying violence, as told, for example, in Judges 19 (4, 6, 21). "This place" is an expression that can bode ill from the mouths of the prophets as they announce impending destruction (2 Kgs 22:17; Jer 7:3, 6, 7; 22:3).[24] The man of God

---

NRSV). Everett Fox (*The Early Prophets: Joshua, Judges, Samuel, and Kings* [New York: Schocken, 2014], 639–40) maintains the key word by translating "he was not able to return it to himself" in v. 4 and "returned-in-health" both times in v. 6.

24. Jacob refers to Bethel (!) as "this place" after his dream when he declares it "fearful, for it is nothing but a house of God" (Gen 28:17).

from Judah gives no other reason than that God commanded him to this effect, including not *returning* by the way he came. The way he came is not the way to go back. His faithfulness consists in *not returning*.

He of course fails to live up to the charge in the strange and detailed story that follows (11–32). Another prophet is around, one not from Judah but from Bethel, who goes looking for the man of God from Judah. When on his invitation he receives the same message of not eating and drinking and not returning (16–17), he lies that he, as a fellow prophet, had a message directly from God that it's okay to come and do exactly as he had been told *not* to do. The repeated statement to the Bethel prophet that he is *not to return* and *not to eat food or drink water in this place* changes to "he returned with him and ate food in his house and drank water" (19).

Once at table, the lying prophet becomes a true prophet and foretells doom over the disobedient man of God (20–22). In a certain way, the man of God from Judah has become the mirror image of Jeroboam in being swayed by a false argument; he, after all, had no word from God himself about the matter, only that of a Bethel prophet! His *return* has taken him in the wrong direction, and in the next installment he is killed on the road by a lion. From man of God he has become a "corpse," "flung" on the road with donkey and lion "standing beside it." Corpse (Hebrew *nevelah*) is a word very close to the word for "folly" or "wicked error" (*navelah*; cf. Josh 7:15; Judg 19:23; 2 Sam 13:12). The lion and donkey standing watch, "as if in death the man of God acquires an honor guard to watch over his remains,"[25] act against their nature of predator and prey. They are still standing there when the other prophet has received word and comes looking. In fact, the text reports the odd behavior of lion and donkey three times (24, 25, 28). Here are two of whom one at least should have been eating but who are, unlike the man of God from Judah, not partaking![26] The animals acting against their nature become the image of faithfulness to God's instructions.

25. Walsh, *1 Kings*, 186.
26. Walsh, *1 Kings*, 187.

The prophet of Bethel, false prophet become true prophet, now becomes a true host to the body of his guest, whom he takes home (literally "causes to *return*"), buries, and bewails, calling him "my brother." He then gives his sons, who have together with the donkey been a constant presence in the story, instructions to inter him in the same grave as the man of God and reaffirms the prophecy of the man of God from Judah, expanding it to include the destruction of "the houses and heights and cities of Samaria."[27] The tail-end of this story will not arrive until the waning days of the Kingdom of Judah, when King Josiah, already brought to mind with the man of God's announcement over the altar (2), will destroy all that the prophet of Bethel has mentioned and honor the tomb in which the prophets from Judah and Bethel are buried (2 Kgs 23:17–20).

That day is still far off, but in the face of all that has happened—the torn altar, the stiffened hand, the healing, and the events involving the two prophets—Jeroboam persists in his wayward conduct.

1 KINGS 13:33–34

33 After this event,
Jeroboam did not return from his evil way;
he returned and appointed from the ranks of the people
priests for the high places.
Anyone who wanted it he gave a mandate[28]
and he became a priest on the heights.
34 This matter became a sin of the house of Jeroboam
so it would be blotted out and destroyed
from the face of the ground.

27. The reference to Samaria is of course out of place even within the boundaries of the text, for it will not become Israel's capital until later, under Omri (1 Kgs 16:24). The editors of Kgs here have a larger purpose and aim to bring to mind the bridge between this section and King Josiah, already mentioned at the beginning of the story.

28. Literally "he filled his hand." I take this translation from Everett Fox, *The Early Prophets*, 644.

## The Man of God from Judah
## and the Old Prophet of Bethel

*One of the more puzzling prophetic legends in the OT.*[29]

The story about the man of God and the old prophet of Bethel makes a certain sense in its context. There is, first of all, a link through the emphasis on responding and not responding to the "word of Adonai" through the various uses of the verb "return." Second, a direct connection is made in the text with references to King Josiah (1 Kgs 13:2, 32).Yet, some questions remain. The introduction "there was a certain. . ." (13:11; see Judg 13:2; 1 Sam 1:1; cf. its variant "there was a man" in Judg 17:1; 1 Sam 9:1) draws the reader's attention to what follows.[30] Also, the episode is told in unusual detail, taking up the larger part of chapter 13 and setting before us with vivid specificity two characters central to the action—which stands out all the more in view of the fact that neither one of them receives a name. One effect of their namelessness is that their places of origin are drawn into the foreground—one from Judah, the other from Israel. The struggle between the two kingdoms may be personified in the story's positioning them initially in opposition: one is a true prophet, the other lies. Yet, their roles switch, with the prophet from Bethel becoming a mouthpiece for Adonai and the one from Judah disloyal to his charge from God. In the end, however, the two are reconciled in a common grave. In some ways, the two prophets personify the two kingdoms: under different rule, but one people under God's guidance.

Why did the prophet from Bethel go looking for the man of God from Judah, and what were "the words" the prophet from Judah "spoke to the king," reported by the sons to their father (13:11)? If they heard everything, the condemnation of the altar may have aroused anger in the Bethel prophet so that he set out to deliberately deceive his Southern colleague. Or he could have just been curious

---

29. Dozeman, "The Way of the Man of God from Judah," 379.

30. In Hebrew, the phrase can be *vayhi eesh ehad* (so Judg 13:2; 1 Sam 1:1) or *vayhi eesh* (Judg 17:1; 1 Sam 9:1).

and wanted to show hospitality. He finds the "man of God sitting under the oak" (13:14), a tree with cultic significance.[31] Is this a hint that the prophet from Judah is about to "turn" from the instructions he had received? Why is he *sitting*? Is his stopping on his journey home another subtle hint at a failure to follow God's command? He was presumably on foot and thus tired, hungry, and thirsty. In short, a human being, protesting that he really can't accept any hospitality, is quickly persuaded by the lying prophet from Bethel.

In verse 18, the narrator interjects with the comment "lying to him," which everyone assumes to refer to the old Bethel prophet. Yet his first assertion, "I also am a prophet like you," is not a lie; he has been introduced as a prophet and will speak a word from Adonai in the future. The Hebrew phrase about lying is extremely terse and follows directly on the line about the messenger from Adonai. Literally translated the text runs, "And a messenger spoke to me by the word of Adonai:/ Return him with you to your house,/ and he will eat food and drink water,/ lying to him" (13:18). Who then is doing the lying? It may sound shocking to ascribe a lie to a messenger from Adonai, but in a later episode, a lying spirit sent from God influences prophets (1 Kgs 22:21–23), and it is not unthinkable that such a thing may be happening in this case. God's presence pervades the story. It is there at the table when the old prophet speaks a true word to the man of God from Judah, and it is there in the events that follow. A lion kills the man of God and then acts against his nature by not tearing the donkey apart. Even his victim, the man of God, and the prophet who finds him are not torn by the lion, although the Bethel prophet assumes this is what happened to his guest (13:26). The God of Israel is compared to a lion in the Prophetic Books (Isa 31:4; Jer 49:19; Lam 3:10; Hos 11:10; Amos 3:8). Certainly, there is something of an uncanny presence in the unnatural behavior of both lion and donkey. More than one theme may be present in the chapter, with a sub-theme centered on true and false prophecy, a subject that will be

---

31. The *elah*, an oak or terebinth, is not just any tree; it is closely related to the *elon*, which in the prophets is connected with idolatry (cf. Ezek 6:13; Hos 4:13). In earlier literature, it is not necessarily a sign of disloyalty to the God of Israel, but it is always a tree of significance (cf. Josh 24:26; Judg 6:11, 19).

taken up in chapter 22.[32] It is at least ambiguous as to who is doing the deceiving in verse 18.

Finally, in the presence of prophets, we are necessarily also in the company of average people in terms of routines and customs rather than in the exclusive company of royalty. There are the saddling of donkeys, sitting at table, eating and drinking; sons help their father, gossip goes back and forth. We get drawn into the story because it works on the level of human interest. Both prophets in 1 Kings 13 are human beings, open to being deceived and deceiving, to anger and kindness. In their presence we meet once again the complex characters we encountered in the earlier narratives. We will find complexity of character for the most part in the circle of the prophets of Israel and Judah in contrast to the relatively flat and formulaic depictions of monarchs.

### Act I, Scene 4: The Verdict (1 Kings 14:1–20)

*She is a shuttlecock sent back and forth between stiff-necked king . . . and hostile prophet.*[33]

The doom of Jeroboam's house has been announced but the king himself has yet to be told. The prophetic speech against him and his house is set in the frame of a short narrative about Jeroboam's family (1–3, 17–18). He and his wife have a sick boy by name of Abiyah, and Jeroboam sends his wife to a prophet for information about the outcome of the illness.[34] He chooses Ahiyah of Shiloh, the one who earlier foretold him his impending kingship.[35] The choice

32. See Dozeman, "The Way of the Man of God from Judah," 392.

33. Walsh, *1 Kings*, 200.

34. The son is called a "lad" or "boy" throughout the story and may have been a teenager or young man.

35. The names of both Abiyah and Ahiyah, respectively meaning something like "my father Adonai" and "my brother Adonai," are so-called theophoric names, with the "yah" syllable at the end indicating Adonai. Other names will have the two syllables "yahu" at the end, such as Yeshayahu (Isaiah) or Jirmyahu (Jeremiah).

is interesting since we know there were other prophets available. He trusts this particular prophet to tell the truth; but all the same, he does not want him to know where the inquiry originates, so he tells his wife to go in disguise. Perhaps he feared that she would get an earful—not so much about the boy, but that Ahiyah would use the occasion to speak ill about him, which is of course exactly what happens. We observe that he does not send her to ask for healing for the child's sickness, which would have been a natural favor to ask for. Rather, the goal is to find out "what will happen to the boy" (3).[36] At the conclusion of the frame, the boy dies as soon as his mother enters the house on her return (17). A sick boy in a doomed household is surely another sign of the decline of Jeroboam's fortunes.

Jeroboam's wife does not get a name, she does not get to speak, she is the subject of the same three verbs twice ("she arose, she went, and she came"), and in the Hebrew text only thirteen words are devoted to her. Here there is no detailing of her travel, no saddling of donkeys, no sitting down and eating after what must have been an anxiety-filled and arduous journey, no text devoted to her response to either Jeroboam or the prophet. We watch her leave the house in silence, enter Ahiyah's house in silence, and come home to find her son dead in silence. A cloud of grief hangs over her story, as she has no agency but makes her trek in disguise and comes back to a doomed house. It is to her that Ahiyah delivers his long and devastating speech. All in the king's orbit, family and nation, will be drawn into the vortex of disaster on account of his apostasy. The king sends her "so they will not know you as the wife of Jeroboam," but unfortunately she is his wife, and a disguise will not save her from this fate.

The main scene takes place in Shiloh, Ahiyah's residence, perhaps still or once again a center for prophetic activity. Two units (4–7) continue the narrative style before the speech section. As soon

---

36. Walsh (*1 Kings*, 194) assumes that the request to the prophet is for healing: "Jeroboam hopes that he will now speak another word of power, both announcing and effecting Abiyah's recovery." This is a possibility of course, but it is striking that any references to healing are omitted and that Jeroboam's wife does not make such a request when faced with the prophet.

as the queen gets to Ahiyah's house, perspective shifts to the prophet with an observation that reveals the futility of her pretense, for the prophet is now old and cannot see (4–5). Like old Eli (1 Sam 4:15), his "eyes are set" and "he could not see her," making it all the more ironic that he knows precisely who she is. Ahiyah has already had a warning from Adonai that Jeroboam's wife is on the way and that she is in disguise—literally that she is "pretending to be another"—and what he should say to her. So as soon as he hears her coming, he calls out to her, asks why she is pretending "to be another," and, not waiting for a response or inquiring what she wants, he begins his oracle, emphasizing her silence in the story. She never gets to ask her question about her son, for he launches into the verdict with the classical prophetic introduction: "Go, say to. . ., thus says Adonai, the God of Israel."

It's a long speech, consisting of three parts. The first (7–11) concerns Jeroboam and his house directly; the second and shortest (12–13) is about the issue for which she came, her son; and the last part (14–16) concerns the future of Israel. As a lead-up to the pronouncement over Jeroboam, the prophet rehearses God's past gifts to him, the *giving* of princely status and the kingdom and the *tearing away* of the kingship from David's house. Jeroboam's failures are all the more glaring in view of such benevolence. The charge is making idols and abandoning God: "Me you flung behind you" (9). God has been discarded as the corpse of the man of God from Judah was "flung" on the road (13:24, 25, 28). Because of this, God will destroy the house of Jeroboam, cutting off all males ("wall-pissers") and sweeping away the house "as dung is swept away" (10).[37] He ends this part of the pronouncement with "Adonai has spoken," sealing its trustworthiness.

As if becoming aware that the woman in front of him may still be waiting for word about her son, he makes clear that there is no

---

37. I agree with Alter (*Ancient Israel*, 681) that the expression "wall-pisser," used also by David in 1 Sam 25:22 in connection with the house of Nabal, is a coarse epithet but probably "formulaic in pronouncing resolutions of total destruction." The verb *ba'ar* in verse 10 can either mean "to burn up" (so NRSV) or "to sweep away" (New American Standard Bible).

good news in this quarter either. That this may have been her main concern is signaled in verse 12 by the emphatic "you."

### 1 Kings 14:12–13

12 Now as for you, you arise and go to your house.
   When your feet enter the city, the boy will die.
13 All Israel will bewail him and bury him,
   for only this one of Jeroboam will enter a grave,
   for in him was found something good
   toward Adonai, the God of Israel,
   in the house of Jeroboam.

Not to be buried, not to "lie down with one's ancestors," was viewed as a terrible fate in ancient Israel, a reason why the last words against Jeroboam's house hit especially hard, for it allows for no burial place for any of his descendants (11). We think of the bodies of Saul and his sons (1 Sam 31:8–13) and the executed sons of Saul (2 Sam 21:10–14). At least this mother will not have to keep watch over the desecrated bones of her child. Within the speech context, it is also the logical place to turn to the destiny of the sick boy, who will die but will also be the one to receive a funeral ("bewailing") and interment, for "in him was found something good to Adonai." The "something good in him" stands out for its vagueness, but anything "good" in this setting of offenses is worth mentioning. It may have been a small comfort to the mother. Who knows?

Ahiyah is not done and goes on to announce the future: Another king will "cut off" the house of Jeroboam (14). The phrase "on this day, even now" is hyperbole for the imminent arrival of the destruction. Then the entire kingdom is indicted: Adonai will "strike" Israel, "shake" it like a reed, "uproot" it (15)—broad hints of the eventual fall of Israel to Assyria. "It was first simply 'sin' (12:30), then 'the sin of the house of Jeroboam' (13:34), and finally 'the sin which he sinned and which he caused Israel to sin' (16)."[38] Everything and everyone is affected by the spreading pool of the king's sinful behavior.

38. Walsh, *1 Kings*, 198.

Ahiyah has had his say; the mother of the sick boy goes home, and as she is entering the house, her son dies (17). The prophet had announced the hour of his death to be as soon as she would "enter the city" (12), and here the text has his death taking place at the moment of her entering the house. Perhaps she ran home in her anxiety and grief and almost got there to see him still alive, but not quite. The only sign of the narrator's awareness of this mother's pain is buried in a phrase in most English translations put in the past tense, where the Hebrew can be read as a participle[39]: "She comes across the doorstep of the house and the boy dead!" He is buried and properly mourned.

Mourning does not take place in the case of Jeroboam, who dies in the final note of the scene (19–20) according to formulaic obituaries for the kings of Israel: a reference to royal annals we no longer possess where everything he did is written down, the duration of his reign, and his successor, who will not come back into the text until 15:25. The reference to other records that would perhaps reflect more particulars of what took place during his administration, here summarized with "the rest of the affairs, his battles and his rule," highlights that much has been left out, but the compilers have transmitted what they thought the most important—almost all of which is related to his apostasy.

## Act II: Reign after Reign (1 Kings 14:21–16:34)

*The feel of a dry chronicle rather than a story with dramatic movement.*[40]

Two and a half chapters cover approximately 70 years in the history of the kingdoms, beginning with Rehoboam in Judah and ending

---

39. As Walsh (*1 Kings*, 199) observes correctly, the phrasing would be more accurately reflected by the English historical present: "She comes to the threshold of the house, and the child dies." Hebrew participles do not reflect tense. Her coming into the house is a third feminine participle; the verb with the boy as subject can either be "he died" or "dead."

40. Walsh, *1 Kings*, 206.

with the onset of Ahab's rule in Israel. From now on, the listing of different kings will follow the pattern of synchronizing the rule of each king with that of the king of the other kingdom. Each monarchy receives a formulaic introduction and conclusion, although the turmoil in the Northern Kingdom will result in abbreviated notices for Nadav, Ela and Zimri. The introductions for the kings of Judah include their age and the duration of their reign as well as the names of their mothers, perhaps indicating a higher status for this position in Judah, or else that the records of the mothers' names were lost in the North during the chaotic dynasty changes. For Israel's kings, ages are not provided, but often there are notes on the location of their reigns, and all the kings in each kingdom receive a theological judgment. The concluding notes for both Judah's and Israel's monarchs refer to records of all the things they did, their burial with perhaps another note of interest added, and the name of the successor to the throne. Because of the constant dynastic changes in Israel through assassinations, Nadav, Ela, and Zimri receive notices of death but not of burial. Time goes by fast, with few details added, apart from references to hostile engagements with neighbors. In general, kings do not get a voice, so we gain little sense of their individuality.

With the end of the tenth and the beginning of the ninth century, we are entering an era when some corroboration is extant to support material in the Hebrew Bible. Although Sheshonq's late-tenth-century inscription does not mention the kingdoms of Judah and Israel or the names of the kings in spite of a successful military campaign in Canaan, the report about his robbing the Temple and palace in Jerusalem is not impossible. We met this Pharaoh, with the biblical name Shishak, as one who provided refuge for Jeroboam during his flight from Solomon (11:40), and he will appear on a hostile campaign in Judah in the time of Rehoboam. For the period beginning with Omri, there is extrabiblical testimony from Moabite and Aramean inscriptions and fragments, while Assyrian records report hostile engagement with Israel in the ninth century.[41]

41. For a review of extrabiblical records during this period, see Miller and Hayes, *A History of Ancient Israel and Judah*, 244–52.

*Act II, Scene 1: Three Kings in Judah (1 Kings 14:21–15:24)*

*A well-seeded spirit of enmity and hostility is the legacy of both Jeroboam and Rehoboam.*[42]

Eleven verses cover the reign of Rehoboam in chapter 14, seven of them devoted to the stereotypical introduction and conclusion. Only four verses mention a significant event during his rule. The assessment following the notation of his age and duration of his reign in 14:22 is noteworthy because it refers to the sins of Judah rather than of the king: "Judah did evil in the eyes of Adonai/ . . . more than all their ancestors did/ in their sins that they sinned." A list of specific practices—building "heights and sacred poles and Asheras," sacred prostitution, and other "abominations"—portrays a people fallen into complete apostasy. The specifically Deuteronomic word "abominations" does not occur in the Historical Books outside of Kings. After the list of depraved behaviors, the invasion of Shishak (14:25–28) is a logical follow-up, befitting a perspective that holds people and kings accountable for the international disasters that befall them. The record has Shishak robbing the Temple of its treasures and the golden shields of Solomon. Alas, the fancy decorations did not last long. Rehoboam replaces them with bronze ones, another metal of great worth, and has them kept under guard. Whether the note is of historical value or not, the robbing of the Temple's treasures reported here is a harbinger of far greater destruction to come in the future.[43]

That's it for Rehoboam; we are encouraged to read about "all that he did" in the "scrolls of the days of the kings of Judah," and he goes to his ancestral grave (14:29–31). A detail not usually a part of the formula is added about continuous war between Rehoboam and

---

42. Hens-Piazza, *1–2 Kings*, 146.

43. For possible connections between 1 Kgs 15:25–28 and the invasion of Canaan by Pharaoh Sheshonq I (the biblical Shishak) in the late tenth century, see Miller and Hayes, *A History of Ancient Israel and Judah*, 198, 261–62, 278–79. It could be that Sheshonq's name became attached to the destruction and looting of other periods in Judah's history.

Jeroboam, which, even if it only refers to skirmishes that took place with regularity, all the same testifies to continued strife between the kingdoms. The repeated note on the name of his mother, Na'amah the Ammonite, causes one to suspect a negative judgment from the collectors, who implicitly may have blamed her for the idolatry taking place at that time. Rehoboam is succeeded by his son Abiyam.

Abiyam, whose mother is listed as one Ma'acah, the daughter of Abishalom, reigns for only three years and receives a negative evaluation: "He walked in all the sins of his father" (15:1–3). Because of the negative reports on both him and his father, an explanatory note emphasizes the continuation of the line of David in Judah. The clarification in 15:4–6 refers to the "lamp in Jerusalem" (cf. 11:36; 2 Kgs 8:19) for the sake of "David" who did what was right in God's eyes "except in the affair of Uriah the Hittite"—the only time this allusion to Uriah accompanies the mention of David in texts that hold him up as standard for measuring the kings of Judah. "The point is not that David was a flawed paradigm but that he was a paradigm nonetheless."[44] Abiyam's short rule closes with his death and burial and the name of his successor (15:7–8). War as a recurring aspect of the relationship between the kingdoms appears regular as clockwork in these chapters, especially during Abiyam's reign (14:30; 15:6, 7, 16, 32).

More text is devoted to the reign of Asa, Abiyam's son, than to either Rehoboam or Abiyam, with greater detail regarding the hostilities between Israel and Judah (15:9–24). He is evaluated positively in terms of his loyalty to Adonai, with the qualification that "the heights did not disappear" (15:11–14). Unlike in the case of Abiyam (15:3) Asa's heart was "wholly" with Adonai. Ma'acah, the daughter of Abishalom, the mother of Abiyam (15:2), is also called the "mother of Asa," causing speculation that Asa was in reality Abiyam's brother. Her name occurs for a third time in this section when Asa removes her from her position as *gevirah* in his efforts to clean up idolatrous worship practices (15:13). The Hebrew word, "queen" or "queen mother" in the translations, is a feminine form of *gevir* ("master") from a root meaning "to be superior, to be lord over." In Genesis 16,

---

44. Walsh, *1 Kings*, 211.

the only place where we find *gevirah* in the Torah, it is usually rendered as "mistress" for Sarai (Gen 16:4, 8, 9). It may have indicated an official position at the court about which information is lost, or it may simply refer to specific royal women who became especially powerful.[45] The threefold mention of Maʿacah surely points to her importance, also signaled by Asa's removing her from her station. The first Maʿacah in the histories is one of David's wives, identified as the granddaughter of the king of Geshur, a region in the far north across the Jordan that the Israelites reportedly were unable to occupy under Joshua (Josh 13:13).[46] She was the mother of Absalom (2 Sam 3:3). The mother of Abiyam is called "the daughter of Abishalom" (15:2), perhaps a son or grandson of Absalom, who may have married into the royal family of Geshur, where he stayed for three years after the murder of Amnon (2 Sam 13:37–38). The name Maʿacah would thus be carried beyond one generation.[47] It seems most likely that the Maʿacah of 1 Kings 15:10 and 13 was the grandmother of Asa (Hebrew has no specific word for this relationship), so that Asa was her "son" in the sense of being her descendant.[48] She manages to gather a good deal of power and influence—too much in the eyes of the king, who removes her from the position and destroys the image of the *asherah* she had made.[49]

45. The title occurs in only fifteen verses, three of them in Gen 16, four in Kgs (1 Kgs 11:19; 15:13; 2 Kgs 5:3; 10:13), and one in Chr in the context of the Asa story (2 Chr 15:16). In a psalm and a proverb (Ps 123:2; Prov 30:23), it is used generally of a female of high rank, and in Isa 47:5, 7 it is a metaphor for Babylon. In Jer, the reference is to a royal person of high rank (Jer 13:18; 29:2).

46. Maʿacah is also a region to the north of Geshur. For its significance, see Ktziah Spanier, "The Queen Mother in the Judean Royal Court: Maacah—A Case Study," in *A Feminist Companion to Samuel and Kings*, ed. Athalya Brenner (Sheffield: Sheffield Academic, 1994), 189.

47. The biblical references to Absalom's offspring are conflicting, one of them referring to sons and a daughter, Tamar (2 Sam 14:27), and one to a lack of any children (2 Sam 18:18). For the suggestion that Absalom married a member of the Geshurite royal family, see Spanier, "The Queen Mother," 190.

48. Thus Martin Buber (Martin Buber and Franz Rosenzweig, *Bücher der Geschichte* [Cologne: Jakob Hegner, 1965], 389), who translates the word *gevirah* here with "grandmother" (German *Grossmutter*).

49. The fact that she was "removed" argues for there being some sort of

The "asherah" was a "stylized tree-image, pole or actual tree" standing next to an altar, representing perhaps the natural world "and its powers of regeneration."[50] It was probably quite ubiquitous as an object of worship in the period of the monarchy but taboo according to the rules determining the worship of Adonai alone in Deuteronomy and the strict theological perspective that governs the text of Kings, which views idolatry as *the* cause of the downfall of both kingdoms. Asherah was also a Canaanite goddess, the consort of El, the head of the pantheon according to the texts from Ras-Shamra Ugarit. It is not easy to tell in the Hebrew text which is intended, the tree image or the goddess.[51] In Ma'acah's case, we are not helped by the use of the word *mifletset*, "abominable image," to describe the object she made, but since it could be burned, it was most likely made of wood.[52] The notation that Asa brings the "sacred

official position connected to the role, even if the details of it are not maintained in the biblical record. This is contra Zafrira Ben-Barak's ("The Status and Right of the *Gebira*," in *A Feminist Companion to Samuel and Kings*, ed. Athalya Brenner [Sheffield: Sheffield Academic, 1994], 185) position that "as a rule the *gevirah* or queen mother had no official political status in the kingdom." The mother of a king in most cases must have reached an older age than most women, which in itself would have accorded her special reverence and privileges in the ancient Near Eastern culture.

50. Tikva Frymer-Kensky, *In the Wake of the Goddesses: Women, Culture and the Biblical Transformation of Pagan Myth* (New York: Macmillan, 1992), 155. According to Frymer-Kensky, the asherah as sacred tree image was part of "Israel's own native tradition of worship until the 8th century." Debates about the precise identification of Asherah or the asherah have occupied scholars for more than a hundred years and took on new energy with the discovery at Kuntillet Ajrud and Khirbet el-Qom in the seventies of inscriptions that contain the Tetragrammaton combined with the word "asherah." The inscriptions caused ongoing speculation that there was a time Adonai was understood to have a consort.

51. Frymer-Kensky, *In the Wake of the Goddesses*, 156.

52. Walsh, *1 Kings*, 211: "The NRSV's 'abominable image' is a guess; we have no idea what the Hebrew term means." The Latin translation of this word as *priapus* leads one to think of a sacred pole, some sort of phallic image as part of a cultus in which Ma'acah filled a leading role. *Priapus* is usually capitalized in the printed Vulgate editions, but in Latin the word also means "phallus," besides being the name of a fertility god. The entire line in

things" into the Temple (15) is a virtual verbatim repetition of the same action reported of Solomon (7:51).

A good king then, Asa, but not one who could by himself stop the aggressive moves of his counterpart in the North, Baʻasha, who begins to fortify Ramah—only a few miles north of Jerusalem—coming far too close for comfort (15:16–17). The gold that still remains in the treasuries is sent to the king of Aram in Damascus with a plea for help (15:18–20). Verse 19 records the only words from a king in Judah in these chapters as Asa appeals to a covenant between himself and King Ben-hadad, one that is transgenerational and should negate the more recent one with Baʻasha of Israel. Ben-hadad responds positively and makes a smart move in going on a rampage in the North, both east and west of the Jordan (15:20), alarming Baʻasha enough to make him withdraw from his action in the South so that Asa can begin some fortifications of his own (15:21-22). Fortifying cities was apparently one of the strong points of Asa's long 40-year reign since it's a detail mentioned in his death notice, in addition to a disease that affected his "feet" in his old age (15:23–24).[53] His son Jehoshaphat succeeds him, and we are close to the halfway point in the ninth century. It sounds as if little of the "gold" amassed by Solomon is left in Jerusalem.

---

verse 13 in Jerome's translation reads "ne esset princeps in sacris Priapi." Some have argued that the "asherim" were phallic pillars, "symbols of human and agricultural fertility" (Fritz Muntean, "Asherah: Goddess of the Israelites," *Pomegranate* 5 (1998): 43. The rendering of "[Adonai] and his asherah" from the aforementioned inscriptions from Kuntillet Ajrud and Khirbet el-Qom could thus be "Adonai and his sacred pole." For a recent discussion and new archaeological evidence, see Garth Gilmour, "An Iron Age II Pictorial Inscription from Jerusalem," *PEQ* 141 (2009): 87–103.

53. What disease affected Asa is unclear. If it relates literally to his feet it could be a reference to gout. The parallel passage in 2 Chr 16:7–12 includes a sharp prophetic rebuke to Asa by the prophet Hanani for having sought the help of Aram, as well as a narrative condemnation for his consultation with healers about his disease instead of consulting God. The word "feet" can be a euphemism for genitals in the Bible, which leaves the possibility that Asa was affected in his virility in old age, a bad omen for the kingdom. See Walter Brueggemann, *1 & 2 Kings*, SHBC 8 (Macon, GA: Smyth & Helwys, 2000), 192.

### Act II, Scene 2: Plots and Counterplots (1 Kings 15:25–16:34)

*The sorry tale of royal failure.*[54]

The period that in Judah covers the reigns of Jeroboam, Abiyam, and Asa provides a chronicle of seven kings in Israel: Jeroboam's son Nadav, Ba'asha and his son Ela, Zimri, Tivni, and Omri and Ahab.[55] Ba'asha, Zimri, Tivni, and Omri all represent dynastic changes and get to the throne by assassinating its occupant. Zimri is on the throne only seven days and commits suicide; Tivni and Omri are kings at the same time in competition with one another for four or five years. None of the kings who die violent deaths—Nadav, Ela, Zimri, and Tivni—receive a burial notice. All of them "did what was wrong in the eyes of Adonai" (15:26, 34; 16:19, 25, 30), which in Ela's case is simply referred to as "the sins they sinned and caused Israel to sin" (16:13). Of Tivni's activities or death there is no mention at all. Omri is the only king in this section whose reign does not include either an announced or actual violent death. Of him it is stated that "he did more wrong than any before him" (16:25). Although he was a significant ruler of this period, he gets scant mention in the text, which, including his death notice, consists of five verses in chapter 16. A hallmark of the kings is that they vex/provoke Adonai with their idols, also called "futilities"—a charge already leveled at Jeroboam in 14:9, 15. Of some interest is the information that a Philistine town, called Gibbeton, undergoes a siege in the period of both Nadav and Ela, both of whom are assassinated during this campaign (15:27; 16:10, 15–19). Apparently, the Philistines are still very much a part of the landscape!

Every time a king ascends the throne, the year of King Asa's reign is mentioned, so that Nadav becomes king in the second year of Asa (15:25) and Ba'asha in his third (15:33); Ela is king in Asa's

---

54. Brueggemann, *1 & 2 Kings*, 204.

55. According to the biblical record, Ahab became king in Asa's thirty-eighth year. The actual dates may be somewhat different, with Ahab coming to the throne at the time of Asa's son Jehoshaphat. See Miller and Hayes, *A History of Ancient Israel and Judah*, 222 chart 13.

twenty-sixth year (16:8), Zimri takes over in his twenty-seventh but is king for only seven days before his suicide (16:10); Omri becomes king in Asa's thirty-first year (16:23) and Ahab in his thirty-eighth (16:29; see p. 111 above). The record is unrelentingly negative, while in actuality a new period began with King Omri and his successors. An extensive building phase took place, including the cities of Megiddo, Hazor, and Jezreel besides Samaria. Omri and Ahab of this dynasty were the most powerful kings, whose building programs and foreign alliances are also mentioned, albeit sketchily, in the biblical account (16:24; 16:31). The strong rule of Ahab can be inferred in the next cycle from the Elijah stories. In addition, there is archaeological evidence about the influence and successful rule of these kings and their increasing significance in an international arena.[56] At the same time, we date the beginning of the Neo-Assyrian Empire to this era, and both Omri and Ahab are contemporaries of King Ashurnasipal II (883–859). We note also that Omri and his descendants are the first to establish a house that lasts for more than two generations. Among Omri's building projects is Samaria, from that time on the capital of Israel.

The sad recital ends with Ahab, who is as bad as the kings before him with the added element that he takes a wife named Jezebel, a Sidonian princess, and becomes a worshiper of Baal (16:30–33). Besides erecting an altar for Baal, he also makes an ashera (16:32–33) and "vexed" Adonai "more than all the kings of Israel before him." A horrifying final note includes references to the sacrifice of children as foundations for the town of Jericho and its gates by one "Hiel of Bethel" (16:34).[57]

---

56. For information on extrabiblical evidence, such as the Mesha Stone and Assyrian inscriptions, see Miller and Hayes, *A History of Ancient Israel and Judah*, 291–99.

57. Brueggemann, *1 & 2 Kings*, 204: "It is possible, though not certain, that the verse alludes to the practice of 'foundation sacrifice' wherein a child was killed and entombed into the foundation of a new building as an act of piety to assure the well-being of the structure." In English, the King James Version expresses this by translating "he laid the foundation thereof in Abiram his firstborn, and set up the gates thereof in his youngest son Segub."

# Cycle III: The Struggle for Life
## (1 Kings 17:1 – 2 Kings 8:6)

*The tale of Elijah is scattered with symbols for life.*[1]

Fourteen chapters are dominated by the presence of two prophets, Elijah and Elisha, as they upset the status quo in the Northern Kingdom for both rulers and common people, for good and ill. Their stories probably originated independently in prophetic circles to be eventually enfolded in the material about the monarchy in Israel and Judah in the last three-quarters of the ninth century BCE. Both prophets are at home in the arena of politics as they interact with the ruler of the day, but they can also be about other business, associating with ordinary people. Both function as the mouthpiece for the God of Israel to the reigning house—Elijah for the most part to Omri's son Ahab. Elisha interacts with monarchs inside and outside of Israel. The focus is on the kings in the North, with only short references to the monarchy in Jerusalem. King Jehoshaphat of Judah, whose long reign stretches over most of the period, comes into view as he engages together with Ahab in the war against Aram in 1 Kings 22 and receives a brief notice at the end of that chapter. Prophecy was a common feature of the landscape in the entire ancient Near East and was not unique to Israel. Courts and sanctuaries had prophets in their employ as advisors and forecasters; we get a glimpse of this profession in 1 Kings 22. Elijah and Elisha are not attached to an institution, and with them we experience rather the life of a prophet as wandering teacher and miracle worker.

1. Neil Glover, "Elijah versus the Narrative of Elijah: The Contest between the Prophet and the Word," *JSOT* 30 (2006): 451.

They are not the only prophets on the scene, but their presence dominates and enlivens narratives that otherwise come across as chronicles of gloom and doom with their consistent negative outlook on kingship and the kingdoms. Their words are generally not received positively by the ruling house, especially by Ahab, who is on the scene for most of the period in which Elijah is active. It is he who calls Elijah a "bringer-of-disaster to Israel" (1 Kgs 18:17). Although there are only two scenes in which Elijah and Elisha appear together, we may assume that Elisha was Elijah's disciple as of the time he was called to his task from behind the plow upon Elijah's return from the wilderness (1 Kgs 19:19–21; cf. 2 Kgs 2). They are not particularly "nice" people; they may be bloodthirsty in their zeal for Adonai, fearful in the face of a vengeful queen, or on the verge of giving up the entire effort; they may want to tell the truth, but the first words out of their mouths may be a lie; they may ask for too much or try to give too much. As much as the legends about them partake of the miraculous and fantastic, the two characters come to life on the page with their own peculiarities and sometimes less than admirable traits.

Women come into focus in this material by the side of prophet and king in various roles—sometimes villain, sometimes patron and host, and sometimes recipient of God's care and concern for the poor represented in the person of the prophet. Ordinary people going about their business of providing food and keeping a household intact against the odds appear side by side with a queen who goes too far in indulging her husband and consequently acts without scruple or regard for the life of an ordinary person. These chapters sit in the center of 1 and 2 Kings, and they take us on a journey that moves from kitchen to palace, from the intricate web of international politics to domestic affairs, from Mt. Carmel to Mt. Horeb within a relatively short period. At the point where Elisha foretells the kingship of Hazael of Aram at the end of the cycle, barely thirty years have passed from King Ahab to Jehoram.[2] It is an era of war, especially with Aram, waxing and waning through the decades. There is for the most part peace and cooperation between Judah

2. Jehoshaphat is king in Judah for almost this entire time span.

and Israel in contrast to the period immediately following the death of Solomon.

Idolatry in the form of worship of Baal or Asherah is always the hallmark of disloyalty to the God of Israel in Kings, and no less so in the Elijah-Elisha stories. By the time the material that constitutes the Former Prophets was collected and put into its present form, Baalism was a thing of the past and no longer an acute danger in the life of the community, but worshiping other gods than Adonai was still an imminent threat. Idolatry for Israel is symbolic of the abandonment of the life-giving presence of Adonai. An idol is a dead thing: "A pursuit of ashes, it does not deliver life" (Isa 44:20). Much of the material under review in this cycle can be summarized under the subject of a struggle for life, a topic represented by the ubiquitous presence of words for life and its opposite, death—which, although frequent enough in other places, here crowd the narratives to an unusual degree. This theme is coherent with an emphasis on provisions, be they food, water, shelter, or land, in a world of scarcity. Life teeters always on the brink of being extinguished. It is extinguished and is resurrected, but there are no guarantees that it will continue—that a woman and her child will survive food shortage, that a landowner will remain in possession of property and life under the greedy eye of a king, that the people will continue to live in the land. Possibilities of life are presented to leaders and people, but the choice is theirs to make.[3]

Historically, hostile engagements with Aram/Syria belong more likely to the era of Jehu following the Omri-Ahab period than to the time of Ahab, going by evidence from Assyrian inscriptions that testify to a successful coalition of Syria-Palestinian forces against the encroaching power of Assyria during Ahab's reign.[4] The Kingdom of

---

3. The phrase "as Adonai lives" or "by the life of Adonai" is only two words in Hebrew, juxtaposing Adonai and life. It emphasizes the connection of Adonai with life. The phrase is not unusual in the Historical Books but occurs mainly in Samuel and Kings, and in Kings it is almost entirely reserved for the Elijah-Elisha cycle.

4. J. Maxwell Miller and John H. Hayes, *A History of Ancient Israel and Judah*, 2nd ed. (Louisville: Westminster John Knox, 2006), 287–326. One monolith inscription "indicates that Shalmaneser was either defeated or

Judah may have been more or less subservient to Israel in Omri and Ahab's time. We consider the stories regarding the hostile relationship with Aram paradigmatic for a gradually deteriorating situation, no matter which king was in charge, emblematic of the theme of the cycle with its emphasis on the struggle for survival in an international as well as national arena. At the end of the cycle, Elisha is still active, but a new period begins with the ascendancy of Jehu.

## Act I: Look! Elijah! (1 Kings 17–19)

*The Elijah stories are unruly pieces of literature.*[5]

Three chapters revolve around Elijah's activities. He appears announcing absence of rain, which means absence of life in his rain-dependent country, and moves from a dry riverbed east of the Jordan to dried-up food supplies in a household in Sidon. He challenges rival prophets to a duel of deities and comes out victorious only to flee in fear for his life to the south. On that journey, he finds himself finally at Mount Horeb, that is to say Sinai, for an encounter with God, who sends him back with new tasks to fulfill and a disciple to appoint.

### Act I, Scene 1: Elijah and Ahab, Part 1 (1 Kings 17:1–7)

*An abrupt and decisive interruption in the royal narrative.*[6]

The ending of the previous chapter with its description of the evils committed by King Ahab and the horrifying image of possible child sacrifice, if not perpetrated by the king then taking place under his

---

brought to a standstill even though he claimed a great victory" at the time of King Ahab. This inscription, dating to 853 BCE, lists Israel among the coalition members as well as Aram-Damascus (308).

5. Glover, "Elijah versus the Narrative of Elijah," 449.

6. Walter Brueggemann, *1 & 2 Kings*, SHBC 8 (Macon, GA: Smyth & Helwys, 2000), 207.

supervision, in no way prepares for the abrupt opening putting Elijah directly in the king's neighborhood (1). His name means "my God is Adonai"; his origin is Tishbe, a location now forgotten or perhaps never exactly known, except that it is in Gilead, in Israelite territory across the Jordan; and he comes on the stage speaking: "Then said Elijah the Tishbite to Ahab" (1). He is not called a prophet, and he defines himself as one who *stands* "before the presence of Adonai"— that is to say as God's servant—before taking an oath "by the life of Adonai" on the prediction of a total absence of rainfall unless he announces otherwise. Famines were all too common in the uncertain climate of ancient Israel and often ascribed to divine interference. The announcement of something as overwhelming and disastrous as the one uttered by Elijah runs the risk of raising the king's ire, especially since he makes it sound as if he rather than God has the power to end the drought. There is a gap between verses 1 and 2, leading one to surmise that the king had a strong reaction—strong enough to make it necessary for Elijah to go under cover. In the next breath, God commands him to *hide* across the Jordan and promises to provide for him (2–4). We find Elijah next at the Kerit creek, literally meaning the "cut-off creek," fed by ravens with bread and meat, while water from the creek quenches his thirst (5–7). As could be foreseen, the creek bed dries up, and without water Elijah cannot survive.[7] If the first hitch in the story is the lack of any reaction on Ahab's part, which bodes ill for Elijah, lack of water is the second.

### Act I, Scene 2: Elijah and a Widow in Sidon (1 Kings 17:8–24)

*"Now I know that you are a man of God." (1 Kgs 17:24)*

Elijah receives a new command from Adonai, this time to go to Zarephat in Sidon, a rather long trek for a man who is suffering

---

7. The name of the creek or wadi, Kerit, a side stream from the Jordan, in Hebrew means something like "cut-creek," not a name that holds a great deal of hope for sustaining Elijah during a long period of time under the circumstances of a drought.

from dehydration and, moreover, a place not in Israel (8–9). But the story does not spend time on the details of travel. We assume that the famine stretched as far north as Sidon, and this may be so, but widows in the ancient world were extremely vulnerable to poverty without adult males in the household, even when resources were abundant. Life was not really viable for them, especially not with a small child as the Sidonian woman appears to have. Widows, together with their children (the "orphans" of the Bible), and "the stranger" belong to the most protected categories of people in the Torah because the assumption is that their lives are fragile and frequently lived on the verge of disaster.[8] Unless they are extremely well-off or protected by other family members, a famine would bring their existence closer to the edge of death. The widow's presence in the story spells absence of viable life. In view of this reality, it is interesting that God intends to "command a woman, a *widow*, to provide" for Elijah (9). The source of provision sounds no more promising than food from ravens and water from a soon-to-be dried-up creek.

Elijah obediently sets out for a foreign country, and we find him facing a woman gathering sticks in the town of Zarephat.

1 KINGS 17:10–11

10 He arose and went to Zarephat
and entered the city gate,
and, Look!, a woman, a widow,
gathering wood.
He called to her and said:
Get me please a little water
in a cup so I may drink.
11 She went to get it
and he called to her and said:
Get me please a bit of bread in your hand.

---

8. The story of Ruth and Naomi offers an extended example of the situation of widows, and many laws in the Torah testify to the ongoing concern for their well-being. See Exod 22:21[22], 23[24]; Deut 10:18; 14:29; 24:17, 19–21; 26:12–13; 27:19; cf. Pss 68:6[5]; 146:9; Isa 1:17, 23; Jer 7:6.

It is not clear how he knows this is a widow or that this is the woman God had in mind; perhaps her status was identifiable by her dress. The text skips over such details, speeding Elijah through his journey until he is faced with the woman and asks her politely for a *little* of this and a *little* of that. She is already on her way to get him water when he halts her in her tracks to add his request for food. He must have been dusty from his travels, clearly not thriving, famished and thirsty, and she is obliged to offer hospitality to this stranger, a social obligation shared throughout the ancient world. Just here, the third snag happens, for the widow balks (12). She may have some water, but there is not enough food to share. In fact, she has decided to use the little she has left for herself and her son so they may "eat and die."

Because of the earlier announcement that the widow would act under divine command, her reply presents the first surprise in the episode. The woman's words are strong. As Elijah did earlier, she swears on Adonai's life that she has nothing "baked," using the phrase "by the life of Adonai your God." Elijah, however, insists that she make him "a little cake" and bring it to him (13).[9] He then adds a foretelling in the name of Adonai: "The jar of meal will not be finished/ and the jug of oil will not diminish/ until the day Adonai gives rain on the ground" (14). The words introducing this message, "thus says Adonai the God of Israel," are a stereo-typical prophetic announcement formula, placing Elijah clearly in prophetic company. All's well that ends well, and the widow's household together with their guest eat for days. It all happens "ac-

---

9. The Hebrew word for cake (*ugah*, from a verbal root meaning "to bake") does not occur often. It is found in relation to scarcity in Exodus for the preparation of flatbread at the first Pesach as well as for the manna in the wilderness (Exod 12:39; Num 11:8). In addition, it is part of the meal Sarah is to prepare for the guests visiting Abram in Gen 18:6. All three occasions are set in the context of the miraculous. Another Exodus reminder may be found in the verb for the widow's *gathering* sticks (17:10), which is used for the people under oppression in Egypt gathering straw (Exod 5:7, 12). Jerome T. Walsh (*1 Kings*, Berit Olam [Collegeville, MN: Liturgical Press, 1996], 230) draws attention to the connection between the words used by the woman, "a baked thing" (Hebrew *ma'og*), and those of the prophet, who asks for a "baked bread" or "cake" (*'ugah*).

cording to the word of Adonai," the third time this phrase occurs in the scene (15–16; cf. vv. 2, 8).

Then the fourth, and most ominous, obstacle arises: The widow's child falls ill and dies or is near death (17).[10] First, this event occasions sharp words from the distraught mother, who blames Elijah for the disaster (18). Her charge is interesting for a number of reasons. First, she calls him "man of God," an alternative identification for a prophet, and second, she refers to an offense or guilt.

### 1 Kings 17:18

She said to Elijah:
What is there for me and you, man of God?[11]
You came to call to mind my guilt[12]
and to cause the death of my son!

She clearly believes that Elijah is to blame and caused her son to die and that he did this on account of a wrong she committed. It is possible, as many interpreters suggest, that her "guilt" refers to a common human lack of perfection, a kind of "general sinfulness," but she may have something more specific in mind.[13] Earlier, when Elijah asked her

10. The expression in v. 17, "there was no breath left in him," does not make it entirely clear whether he has expired. Richard Nelson, *First and Second Kings*, IBC (Atlanta: John Knox, 1987), 111: "Sickness or old age brought one down to the realm of death even while one was technically alive."

11. The phrase "what is there for you and me?" occurs also in Judg 11:12 from Jefta to the elders of Gilead and will later be directed by Elisha to the king of Israel (2 Kgs 3:13) and by Pharaoh Neco to Josiah (2 Chr 35:21). We should perhaps understand it to mean something like "what do you want from me?"

12. The Hebrew word *awon* means the offense, the guilt, and the punishment. Cain announces to God that his *awon* is too great for him to bear (Gen 4:13). She may mean here that Elijah is the one bringing her the punishment for whatever she did wrong.

13. Nelson (*First and Second Kings*, 111) is of this opinion, as is Walsh (*1 Kings*, 231), who says, "The sin of which she speaks is nothing specific"; cf. Terence E. Fretheim, *First and Second Kings*, Westminster Bible Companion (Louisville: Westminster John Knox, 1999), 98. In historical narrative, however, ʿ*awon* usually refers to a specific transgression.

for a bit of bread, she initially refused. We never heard whether this woman was indeed the one who had received a command from God. The text ascribes to her some familiarity with Israel's God, going by the oath she takes on "the life of Adonai your God" at the very moment of her refusal (12; see p. 119 above). If she did receive direction from Adonai, then her refusal to provide further for Elijah was certainly an offense, not only against the general rule of hospitality to the stranger but against a divine command. This issue may have been gnawing at her for a while, as she experienced abundance of food through the presence of Elijah, and it finds a voice in her present anguish.

Elijah has no verbal reply but engages in swift action. He takes the boy from his host's lap and to the room where he lodges. He puts the child on his bed and addresses God in a manner similar to how the widow spoke to him, accusing by question: "Even on the widow, with whom I lodge as a stranger, have you brought evil by causing her son to die?" (19–20). The word "even," or "also," acknowledges that it is God who is bringing the evil of drought upon the land and thereby also on Elijah, now piling it on by causing death to the child of the woman who housed him, though he is a "stranger."[14] Thus, he accuses God of potentially violating God's own rules against harming stranger, orphan and widow. If anything, Elijah's words to Adonai are more accusing than those of the widow. Then he lies down on the boy and prays that the "life" may return to the boy's body (21). Earlier, the *life-breath* (Hebrew *neshamah*) had left him. Elijah prays for the return of his *life* (Hebrew *nefesh*). God grants the request so Elijah can return the child alive to his mother.

1 KINGS 17:22–24

22 And Adonai heard the voice of Elijah,
and the life of the boy
returned to his body, and he lived.

14. The text uses the verb *gur*, from which the noun "stranger," *ger*, is derived, a category of people even more protected in the Torah than widows and orphans. Protective laws for strangers are more prevalent than any other kind of ethical prescription in the first five books of the Bible.

23 Elijah took the boy
and brought him down from the upper room
to the house, to his mother, and said to her:
See, your son is alive.
24 The woman said to Elijah:
Now I know that you are a man of God
and that the word of Adonai in your mouth is true.

This last unit wraps up the predominant theme of the episode, which is crucial for this cycle of stories: the life and death struggle. Elijah has come out of nowhere announcing drought, which spells death, in the name of Adonai. He fears for his own life, not for the last time, and is sent by God to unlikely places to find life: first to a drying up creek where birds come to feed him, then to a foreign country where a starving widow is to provide resources. Life carries on against the odds, but all goes south once again, and life is threatened by the impending death of a child—in fact, the guarantor of the widow's future well-being. The miracle of resurrecting the dying or dead child results in the verification of Elijah's prophetic appointment from the mouth of the widow. At the end of the day, Elijah the Tishbite has become the "man of God" who speaks a "true word of Adonai." The presence of God is found where no life appears to flourish, next to a drying riverbed, with a woman who is at the end of her resources, and with a child at the end of his short life. It is the woman—and a foreign woman at that, in a country where Baal is god—who proclaims Elijah a true prophet of Adonai! Of course, the various obstacles and their resolutions have not brought an end to the life-threatening drought announced by Elijah at the beginning.

### Act I, Scene 3: Elijah and Ahab, Part 2 (1 Kings 18:1–20)

*We may well reread the Bible with attention to "minor" figures who live at the edge of the narrative in dangerous, faithful ways.*[15]

---

15. Brueggemann, *1 & 2 Kings*, 221.

There are at least two stories in this chapter: one about the return of rain to the country, the other a contest of gods and prophets on Mount Carmel. The first story (1–20, 41–46) is interrupted by the second (21–40), and we read them as three scenes. The first scene begins with the message to Elijah that after three years of drought, Adonai will cause the rain to return once Elijah appears before Ahab (1). It looks as if Elijah is on his way ("Elijah went") (2) when there is a shift in perspective, with Ahab taking center stage, together with Obadiah, the overseer of the palace (3–4). The narrator provides essential facts in such a way that we view everyone on the move: Elijah toward Ahab, while Ahab and his majordomo go out to search for water. Twice the phrase "appear before Ahab" (lit. "be seen by Ahab") occurs in the introductory lines. Next, we hear that the famine was *severe* in Samaria—no surprise after more than two years without rain—emphasizing the seriousness of the situation.

Most of us will remember the contest between God and Baal on Mount Carmel but have probably forgotten Obadiah, the *servant of Adonai* who is in Ahab's employ.[16] Obadiah is defined as a God-fearing man. "He feared Adonai greatly," and in the face of Jezebel's elimination of God's prophets, he has hidden one hundred of them, providing them with bread and water (4). Like Elijah's God-sent ravens, he has managed to keep these faithful alive—under the circumstances an act of rebellion both difficult and extremely dangerous. In other words, this character is not just himself an obedient servant of God, but he understands what it means to live a life that serves *torah*, God's instruction for the well-being of members of the community who are unable to take care of themselves. He puts his life on the line in this service.

In the next unit (5–6), Ahab and Obadiah go looking for water on Ahab's urging to see if they can find a blade of grass near springs and streams in order to keep some livestock alive, specifically horses and mules. The reasoning sounds odd, but perhaps there is still

---

16. Obadiah's name literally means "servant of Adonai," and as with all biblical names ending in "ah" in English, the last syllable represents a form of the sacred name of God in Hebrew. Like Elijah's name, Eli*yahu*, Obadiah's name is Ovad*yahu*.

enough food in the palace for human beings and they can ill afford to slaughter the beasts needed to carry the necessary provisions. Tellingly, Ahab is concerned about *cutting down* animals, while Jezebel is *cutting down* the prophets of God (5; cf. v. 4).

Ahab and Obadiah divide the task, and each goes his separate way. Obadiah comes upon Elijah, presumably on his way to appear before Ahab. Elijah commands Obadiah to announce his presence to the king. The wording is terse and to the point.

1 Kings 18:7–8

7  Now Obadiah was on the road
   and, Look!, Elijah coming to meet him.
   He recognized him and fell on his face and said:
   Is this you, my lord Elijah?
8  He said to him: It is I.
   Go, say to your lord:
   Look, Elijah!

The twice-used word "look" (*hinneh*) draws attention to the unexpected nature of this encounter, both for Obadiah and for Ahab, who will receive the announcement of Elijah's impending appearance. The term "lord" (*'adon*) is used to special effect, first when Obadiah calls Elijah "my lord" and second when Elijah refers to Ahab as "your lord." A number of lords seem to be competing for the loyalty of a man whose name means "servant of Adonai/the Lord." In addition, Elijah's name means something like "my God is Adonai" so that the message about his arrival also sounds like a declaration of allegiance.

Obadiah presents elaborate reasons for his refusal to go along with Elijah's command (9–14). He marshals three arguments. First, he is sure that Ahab, who has been looking for Elijah everywhere, will kill him if he comes with the news "look, Elijah!" The fact that Ahab has been searching high and low for Elijah is new information and explains why the prophet went into hiding in the previous chapter. Second, Elijah has proven to be elusive; what if he disappears and then Ahab doesn't find him—another reason for doing away with Obadiah, a servant who could not deliver. Finally, and perhaps most important, by risking his own life, Obadiah risks the lives of the hundred prophets he has hidden as a faithful servant of Adonai, giving them food and drink in the face of the queen's active persecution. He ends by stating for the third time that Ahab will kill him.[17] The speech winds itself around his repeated, reproachful "Now you are saying: Go say to your lord: Look! Elijah" (11, 14), literally repeating Elijah's command. The speech reveals information so far not known—Ahab's active search for Elijah—and repeats the reports of Jezebel's extermination of prophets loyal to Adonai and the hidden prophets of Adonai, who are continuing in the service of the God of Israel together with Obadiah and who knows how many others.[18]

The theme of life and death continues in this episode. Life is represented by adequate supplies of *food and water*, the prophets in the cave, and the search for springs of *water* in the land that may cause something to grow and *keep alive* the animals, preventing them from being *cut down*. The prophets of Baal *eat* at Jezebel's table, while death is the fate of the faithful to Adonai who are *cut down* by Jezebel. Water is the source of life and growth in the uncertain climate of ancient Israel and is thus the sign of fertility and productivity, but it is also a powerful symbol for the power of both life and death.[19] Obadiah claims three times that Ahab will *kill* him.

There is a second theme present: *searching* and *finding*. Obadiah refers to Ahab's *searching* high and low for Elijah without *finding*

---

17. The first time, he uses a form of the verb *mut*, "to die": lit., "Ahab will cause me to die!" (18:9). The second and third time, he uses the more graphic verb *harag*, "to slay."

18. Walsh (*1 Kings*, 243, 260) considers the presentation of Obadiah ambiguous because he refers to both Elijah and Ahab as "my lord." Rather, it seems that the entire exchange introduces some ambiguity into the character of Elijah, who appears now and later unaware of the existence of others, including other prophets, who have stayed loyal to the God of Israel.

19. Poets may lament that threatening waters are about to overcome them (Ps 69:2[1], 3[2], 15[14], 16[15]; Jonah 2:6[5]) or long for the presence of God as the deer longs for "streams of water" (Ps 42:2[1]). Most powerfully, water represents God's life-giving presence in Isa 55:1: "Come to the water, all you who are thirsty."

him. Ahab and his overseer go throughout the land in search of water, which of course they do not find, but both *find* Elijah.

1 KINGS 18:17–18

17 When Ahab saw Elijah, Ahab said to him:
Is this you, bringer-of-disaster on Israel?[20]
18 He said: I have not brought disaster on Israel,
but you and the house of your father have
by you (all) abandoning the commandments of Adonai
and you walking after the baals.[21]

Both Obadiah and Ahab meet the prophet with the question "Is this you?" but while the first addresses him as "my lord Elijah," the king calls him a "bringer-of-disaster on Israel." To give Ahab his due, when Elijah met him for the first time, he had announced there would be no rain until he gave the word, making it sound as if both the drought and the return of rain were up to him (17:1), so the charge is not entirely unreasonable. The accusation employs the participle of a verb used in connection with adversity brought on Israel by Achan (Josh 6:18; 7:25) and again on the occasion when Jefta blamed his daughter for the calamity he had himself caused by his thoughtless oath (Judg 11:35). Jonathan used it when his father had disadvantaged the troops with the order of an ill-timed fast (1 Sam 14:29). The word "troubler," adopted by most translations, is not quite as strong as what is intended here. Elijah, in Ahab's view, is not just an agitator but someone who has actively caused a calamity for the land. Elijah throws it back at Ahab, of course, pointing to the people's abandonment of Adonai and Ahab's running after idols.[22] It is at this point that the

20. I take the translation "bringer-of-disaster" from Everett Fox, *The Early Prophets: Joshua, Judges, Samuel, and Kings* (New York: Schocken, 2014), 670.

21. The verb form "abandoning" is in the plural, while the "walking after the baals" is in the second person singular, appearing to apply specifically to Ahab.

22. The word here is the plural *be'alim* ("baals"), used also in Judg (Judg 2:11; 3:7; 8:33; 10:6). The Hebrew word *ba'al* is complicated; it can be a noun

drought is connected specifically with Ahab's idolatry, emphasized at the end of chapter 16. It is clear to Elijah where the fault belongs, and he orders the king to call together "all Israel" as well as the prophets of the gods he worships, all of whom are provided for by Jezebel. One of the remarkable features of this story is Elijah ordering the king to do his bidding and the king following through (19–20). Unlike Obadiah, Elijah has no lord but Adonai.

### Act I, Scene 4: Elijah and the Prophets of Baal (1 Kings 18:21–40)

*There are times when you have to choose.*[23]

During the events on Mount Carmel, Ahab is absent from the story, with action and dialogue taking place between Elijah, the people, and the prophets of Baal. Before the drama begins, Elijah challenges the people to make a choice, for they cannot follow both Adonai and Baal (21). Then he launches into a speech in which he proposes the course of action to follow (22–24). First, he claims that he is "the only prophet left for Adonai" facing a multitude of Baal prophets, true on this occasion, but untrue in the larger context since it flies in the face of the revelation about the prophets hidden in a cave (4, 13). At least, the statement raises the question why Elijah did not call on his own community to be present at the impending showdown. It may be important to show that one man in the service of Adonai can outperform hundreds of those who serve the wrong powers. But it may also not be the best thing for Elijah to be so solitary in this struggle. In suggesting the process, he makes sure to leave the choice of the sacrificial animal up to the prophets of Baal. Once the sacrifice is prepared and ready to be burned, without lighting a fire, each party will call on its deity, and the one who "answers with fire" will be confirmed as "the God" (24). The people agree to this.

---

meaning owner, master, or husband (!) as well as the fertility god of Canaan, and in the plural, it becomes a catch-all word for idols.

23. John Goldingay, *1 and 2 Kings for Everyone* (Louisville: Westminster John Knox, 2011), 84.

Then the theater begins. The Baalists go first, hopping around the altar and calling at length on their deity ("Baal, answer us!"[24]), but not a sound is heard in reply (25–26). Instead of going about his own preparation, Elijah becomes a heckler in the audience, mocking their prayer, suggesting that this powerful god is chatting, has gone on vacation, or is asleep, and the Baalists, who seem to go along with everything Elijah advises, call louder.[25] Next, the Baal prophets begin self-mutilation—a ritualistic practice not unusual in the ancient world—while they rant like prophets.[26] The show goes on until late afternoon, all of it in vain, when Elijah finally goes into action.

Elijah calls on the people to approach and builds an altar. The action of constructing an altar of twelve stones according to the number of the tribes evokes the image of Moses at Mount Sinai (30–33; cf. Exod 24:4).[27] More unusual action begins with the digging of a trench around the altar.[28] Elijah commands the people to pour water in the trench and on the wood for sacrifice so that everything is soaked and less likely to be affected by fire. In contrast to the minimal preparations for sacrifice by the Baal prophets, Elijah's arrangements are extremely elaborate and detailed, involving the construction of the altar, the preparation of the sacrifice, the digging of the trench, and the pouring of the water. The prophet of God apparently had no difficulty finding an abundance of water at a time when Ahab and his servant had gone out to look for "a blade of

24. The verb used for their *hopping* is the same as the one Elijah employed when talking of the necessity for the people to choose instead of "*hopping* on two branches" (18:21).

25. The translation of a few of the preoccupations of Baal is difficult, and some suggest a scatological reference. I have opted for Alter's (*Ancient Israel: The Former Prophets: Joshua, Judges, Samuel, and Kings* [New York: Norton, 2013], 702) "chatting" for one of these verbs, which in other places has that meaning. Very attractive is Walsh's (*1 Kings*, 249) "Cry louder! After all, he's a god; he's busy, in a tizzy, he's off on the road!"

26. Cf. Saul in 1 Sam 10:6, 10, 11; 18:10; 19:23–24.

27. This also recalls the ancestor Jacob at his altar building and renaming (Gen 35:1–10).

28. The word for "trench" is rare in the Bible, occurring in Kgs only here and for the water conduit constructed under Hezekiah in 2 Kgs 20:20.

grass" on dry ground (5). Groundwork and ritual on the part of the protagonists are in this way depicted as starkly dissimilar. It is also worth noting that the people are involved with Elijah's activities, first called on to "come near" (30), drawn into Adonai's sacred zone, and subsequently engaged in pouring the water, coming closer to making their choice. Elijah's prayer constitutes his only ritual.

1 KINGS 18:36–37

36 At the time of the grain-gift offering,[29]
Elijah, the prophet, came near and said:
Adonai, God of Abraham, Isaac, and Israel,[30]
today may it be known that you are God in Israel
and that I am your servant
and at your word I have done all these things.
37 Answer me, Adonai, answer me
so this people may know that you are Adonai
and have reversed their hearts.[31]

For the first time, the narrator refers to Elijah as "the prophet," a telling characterization at this crucial moment. Elijah names God as the God of the ancestors, using "Israel" instead of "Jacob" and thus emphasizing the link between the people of Israel and Adonai.

The recognition that has to come from God's fire is of both Adonai as Israel's God and of Elijah as Adonai's servant: "May it be known/ . . ./ so this people may know." When the fire "falls down" in response and devours everything, including the stones of the impromptu altar, the people confess Adonai with one accord. Their

29. I.e., the evening sacrifice.
30. This identification of God is unusual; the phrase is ordinarily "God of Abraham, Isaac, and Jacob." In v. 31, the people are called "the children of Jacob" rather than "of Israel."
31. I take the translation "reversed" from Fox, *The Early Prophets*, 672. Literally, the text reads that they "have turned their hearts backwards." Some understand this to mean that God had allowed the Israelites to backslide, but it seems more natural to understand it as a reversal back to Adonai. Some ambiguity remains. See Alter, *Ancient Israel*, 704n37.

acknowledgment of Elijah as Adonai's servant goes unmentioned (38–39). After this, Elijah commands the people to grab the prophets of Baal, not one of whom is to escape the wrath of Adonai's prophet. They are slaughtered as animals are killed for sacrifice at the Kishon stream, where once the armies of Deborah and Barak had defeated Sisera (Judg 4:7, 13; 5:21), although it is unlikely to be the raging wadi of Deborah's poem at this time of drought. We note that the killing of the Baal prophets is not commanded by Adonai.

The parties heard from in this episode are Elijah and the people, while the prophets of Baal are described as engaging in prophetic ranting but only get to say "Baal, answer us!"—two words in Hebrew (26). There is throughout an emphasis on who does and who does not answer. First, the people do not *answer* Elijah when he challenges them to make a choice between Baal and Adonai (21). When Elijah proposes that the proof of who is God will be in the one who *answers* with fire, the people *answered* with approval (24). Both the Baalists and Elijah pray for an *answer* (26, 37). To the plea of the Baal prophets "there was no voice and no *answerer,*" a phrase repeated with the added "no response" (26, 29). The petition "answer me, Adonai" voiced by Elijah is at home in Israel's psalms of lament as a crucial element—a personal cry arising from deep distress (Pss 13:4[3]; 69:14[13]; 86:1; 102:3[2]; 143:1).

We may assume that the fire *falling down* constitutes God's answer, but this is nowhere articulated, nor is God a party to any of the proceedings. In contrast to the experiences in chapter 17 and the beginning of chapter 18, where God issues directives and commands and is recorded as *hearing the voice* of Elijah when he prays on behalf of the child (17:22), there is a curious absence of such divine involvement on Mount Carmel.[32] The sign of God's presence is a devouring fire that eats all in its path, including the stones that form the altar, and licks up the water, giving the impression of a wild animal. Hens-Piazza writes, "Since shrines and altars elevated their builders, as well as the builder's deity, the destruction of the altar may be a subtle reproach of the prophet who constructed

---

32. Glover, "Elijah versus the Narrative of Elijah," 456: "Nothing happens . . . to confirm that Elijah has acted according to the word of [Adonai]."

it."[33] Perhaps this is so. In any case, Elijah on this occasion may be putting himself rather in the center and is possibly going too far with the slaughter of the prophets of Baal.

A logical follow-up to the first scene of the chapter, the encounters of Elijah with Obadiah and Ahab, would be a struggle on the mountain about which god was the better rain-giver, but this is not the case. The contest between gods and prophets and the resulting conversion of the people take place in response to the falling down not of rain but of fire, a peculiar element to call forth in the midst of a drought. One of Baal's titles as a deity in charge of fertility was Lord of Rain and Dew; he is a god who would not ordinarily be asked to send fire. Fire, apart from being a destructive natural phenomenon, traditionally represents the awesome presence of the God of Israel, who appeared to Moses in a burning shrub, at Mount Sinai in fire and smoke, and to the people in the wilderness as a column of fire (Exod 3:2; 13:21; 19:18; Num 9:15–16).

As this episode was probably part of the original cycle of prophetic legends, a question arises as to why the compilers inserted it just at the point where it delays the promised arrival of rain. In terms of narrative style, it keeps alive the tension created by the announcement of the chapter's first lines, with their anticipation of rain coming down as soon as Elijah shows himself to Ahab. The meeting of the two came about in a circuitous way and in the end took place on Ahab's rather than Elijah's initiative. Yet rain has been announced and is going to appear, and when it does, would it not be the simplest thing for the people who are "hopping on two branches" to ascribe its return to the god who is Lord of Rain and Dew rather than to Adonai? In terms of content, then, the Mount Carmel episode might function to insert a resounding defeat of Baal while at the same time playing with the irony of asking a god of rain for fire, and it accomplishes the people's confession of their true allegiance *before* the promised event of rainfall. After this, there will be no doubt as to who has caused the return of the rain! Once it has been made clear who is in charge of the fate of Israel and the land, who is

---

33. Gina Hens-Piazza, *1–2 Kings*, AOTC (Nashville: Abingdon, 2006), 180.

the true life-giver, the threat of death that still hangs over the land because of continuing drought can be resolved.

### Act I, Scene 5: Elijah and Ahab, Part 3 (1 Kings 18:41–46)

*Throughout this section Elijah will always be one step ahead of things.*[34]

#### 1 KINGS 18:41–42

41 Elijah said to Ahab:
   Go up, eat and drink,
   for [there is] a roar of rushing rain.
42 Ahab went up to eat and to drink,
   and Elijah went up to the top of Carmel,
   crouched down to the earth,[35]
   and put his face between his knees.

The scene fits well with the opening episode of the chapter, which ended in a meeting between Elijah and Ahab, whose presence is not mentioned during the drama on Mount Carmel. In the opening verse, Elijah addresses Ahab as if they have not been apart and commands him to ascend and "eat and drink" on account of the sound of rain. The next verse repeats the verbs as completed action with the result that *eating and drinking* surround the "roar of rushing rain," all of it a sign that life is returning to the land. Elijah also goes up and sits in a crouched position, face down. Evidently, it is not he but a servant who will witness the sign of rain on the horizon and announce it to Ahab. From this description and the use of a go-between, it does not appear that Ahab and Elijah are in the same

---

34. Walsh, *1 Kings*, 257.

35. The verb I have translated "crouched" is extremely rare and will occur in only one other place (2 Kgs 4:34-35). Elijah's action is sometimes explained as a position of prayer (so Hens-Piazza, *1–2 Kings*, 181; Nelson, *First and Second Kings*, 119); prayer in the Bible can involve bowing down, but usually not with one's face also downward. Face and hands would be lifted up.

place on the mountain. Elijah's crouched-down position may have been for the sake of concentration or because he is restraining his impatience.[36] The style of the short scene centers on the action of *going up*, the root occurring seven times in four verses and implied another seven times by Elijah's instruction to his lad in verse 43. This doubling of the mythological significant number seven without doubt serves to emphasize the mysterious and sacred nature of the event of rain-giving, understood to derive from divine interference. The *descending* movement on Elijah's and Ahab's parts (Elijah *crouching down*, v. 42; Ahab commanded to *go down*, v. 44) are corresponding downward movements symbolizing the return to the earth, which once again will be the site of fertility and abundance. In a grand finale, Ahab rides ahead of the wind and heavy rain with Elijah running ahead of the chariot as far as Jezreel under the power of Adonai (45–46), ending the chapter on a triumphant note.

### Act I, Scene 6: Elijah and Adonai (1 Kings 19)

*Uniqueness is a lonely place where death is sometimes craved.*[37]

The first unit (1–2) links the events to come with what has taken place on Mount Carmel. "Ahab told Jezebel all that Elijah had done," including the slaughter of the prophets, and Jezebel responds by sending a threatening message to Elijah. The queen's reaction sets in motion Elijah's flight, initially to Beersheba in Judah, where he leaves his servant behind, and then further into the wilderness.

1 KINGS 19:4

He himself went into the wilderness,
one day's journey,
and came and sat under a juniper bush

---

36. Fox (*The Early Prophets*, 673) interprets it as concentration.
37. Glover, "Elijah versus the Narrative of Elijah," 459.

and asked for his life to die
and said: Enough already, Adonai.
Take my life, for I am no better than my ancestors.

The response he receives to his death wish is a messenger, in verse 7 identified as a messenger of Adonai, who brings food and water and urges him to get up and eat. It is worth noting that the messenger "touches" him. Although the verb for "touch" (*naga'*) can imply simple contact, it is often used with a connotation of aggression, and the noun derived from it means "affliction." A messenger of Adonai's *touching* may result in a blemish or disfigurement. Being "poked" might come closer to what Elijah experiences and is indicative of the fact that Elijah needs to be stirred back to energy and life.[38] This happens two times, the second time for the specific purpose of going on another journey. Strengthened by the food, he goes on his way "forty days and forty nights" until he reaches Horeb—that is to say, Sinai. The first supply of food consists of items identical to those in the story of the woman of Zarephat: a baked cake and a jug of water, the words for both of which are rare.[39] Elijah is once again at the mercy of someone else to provide for him, and he partakes of the same miraculously augmented nourishment the widow had at hand. Again, the miracle of food in the midst of scarcity represents the power of life on the verge of life being extinguished.

It may seem strange for the mighty Elijah, who singlehandedly maneuvered the prophets of Baal into a corner and did away with them afterward, who presided over the dramatic sacrifice of a burnt offering without having fire at hand, who ordered Ahab to be the first witness to life-restoring rain, who ran in front of a chariot—it may seem strange that this man runs away upon a threat issued by

38. We can think of Jacob being "touched" by the Being at the Jabbok, which he certainly interpreted as a divine appearance (Gen 32:26[25], 33[32]), or the food touched by God's messenger in Judg 6:21.

39. The term for "jug" or "flask" is found only in these two chapters in Kings and in 1 Sam 26:11, 12, 16. The flask in 1 Sam 26 is the one taken by David from a sleeping Saul (see p. 119 above). For the occurrences of the word for "cake," see above.

a woman. Once again, we must ask the reason why the compilers inserted the episode precisely here.

According to the traditional Hebrew text, Elijah "saw" and took off to Beersheba "on account of his life." Ancient versions of verse 3 read that he "was afraid"; either he was in fear or he saw which way the wind was blowing and went as far as he could to the south.[40] His request for God to let him die is unusual in the Bible, but it puts him in the company of the prophets Jeremiah (Jer 20:14–18) and Jonah (Jonah 4:3, 8), and even Moses (Num 11:15), with Jonah offering the closest parallel as a prophet in circumstances he considers unbearable asking for "his life to die."[41] The desire to die may not be so much a suicidal wish as the articulation of a general giving up, a sinking of the spirit to a point at which it loses the will to go on.[42] The comment that he is no better than his ancestors is unique and could mean he does not think of himself as any more valuable or capable or suitable for his task than they were. In any case, the statement testifies to a lack of confidence. Walsh suggests that the phrase constitutes a sort of challenge to Adonai. "If Elijah has failed, it is because Adonai expects too much of him."[43] It sounds like Moses at his first encounter with God in the wilderness, when he protests his assignment because he is not well-spoken and has not improved in God's presence (Exod 4:10). Like Moses, Elijah will acquire an assistant.

40. The difference constitutes no changes in the Hebrew consonants, only in the vowel pointing, and both readings are possible. Many modern translations, including the NRSV, have "he was afraid." We may let the ambiguity stand and keep both options alive: *seeing* the state of affairs, he became *afraid*. In either case he acts on fear.

41. Moses sounds the most radical with his statement: "If you act like this to me, then slay, yes, slay me, please" (Num 11:15). His motivation is that he considers himself unable to put up with the demands of the people in the wilderness.

42. So Micha Roi, "1 Kings 19: A 'Departure on a Journey' Story," *JSOT* 37 (2012): 32. According to Roi, Elijah's prayer is "an expression of resignation to the fact that he is likely to perish. His flight into the wilderness is intended to *save* his life, not to lose it."

43. Walsh, *1 Kings*, 268.

The second visitation and supply of food is for the specific purpose of the journey, which in the words of the messenger is "too much for you" (7). What is intended with "the journey"? The road back or another journey Elijah must undertake? And, if the latter, is Horeb the intended destination (8)? Horeb, another name for Sinai, is where he ends up—a place of enormous significance in Israel's religious traditions. Everything, including the forty days and forty nights it takes Elijah to get there, is invested with sacred connotation (8). That he enters a cave is testimony to the fact that he is still in hiding and at the same time brings to mind the prophets hidden by Obadiah in a cave (18:4, 13). In this place, Adonai addresses him with the question, "What are you doing here, Elijah?" The phrase in Hebrew is very short: literally, "what for you here, Elijah?" This may be a neutral or a challenging question, depending on tone or context.[44] Here no clue is provided about Adonai's state of mind. Why are you here? What is your business here? What do you want here? All of these are possibilities.[45] Some interpreters understand the emphasis to be on the word "here," which implies that Horeb is perhaps the last place God expected to find the prophet and suggests a reproach.[46]

In most cases where the phrase occurs, either with or without the qualifying "here," it elicits an explanatory response, as it does from Elijah. But Elijah's is a very indirect answer.

### 1 KINGS 19:10

He said: I have been exceeding zealous
for Adonai, the God of Hosts,
for they have abandoned your covenant,

44. For examples of the phrase in the Historical Books, see, Josh 15:18=Judg 1:14; Judg 18:23, 24; 2 Sam 14:5.

45. Martin Buber and Franz Rosenzweig, *Bücher der Geschichte* (Cologne: Jakob Hegner, 1965), 406: "Was willst du hier?" ("What do you want here?"); Fox, *The Early Prophets*, 676: "What [brings] you here?"

46. So Walsh, who understands the emphasis to mean that Adonai expects Elijah to be somewhere else and that the food for "the journey" was meant to help him make his way back to his task as a prophet.

the Israelites;
your altars they have demolished,
and your prophets they have slain with the sword,
and I am left, I alone,
and they sought my life to take it.

The answer reveals as much as it conceals. He reviews his career of dedication to God in the face of the disloyal actions of God's people, who have demolished God's altars and killed God's prophets, and he ends by underlining the solitary nature of his existence in the face of attempts on his life. The "I . . . I alone" echoes the words of Moses, who pled with God that *he alone* could not *carry* the people before he asked God to kill him (Num 11:14–15). Elijah's speech ignores the fact that there are other prophets still faithful to Adonai, even if they are in hiding, and that there has been a magnificent conversion on the mountain. Even if the Israelites have gone backsliding in the intervening period, surely there are some left who have maintained their loyalty. Also, the reply does not answer the question, no matter how we understand it or interpret its tone. An added phrase, "so I came here to hide," would have worked, or "I was looking for you" or "Help me, please, because I am afraid." None of these cross his lips, but as if they had, God's reply comes in the form of an appearance (11–12).

First, Elijah is commanded to "go out" and "stand on the mountain before Adonai" (11). Then Adonai comes by with a great storm that tears at the mountains, then with a quake and a fire. But God is *in* none of them; they merely herald God's presence. They are followed by a "a sound of soft stillness" (12).[47] In agreement with Richard Nelson, I understand all the phenomena, including the "sound of silence," to be heralding God's presence, but the last one no more than the former.[48] Storm, quake and fire are traditionally understood

47. The final expression evokes numerous different translations. The "still small voice" of the KJV is still popular. Alter (*Ancient Israel*, 708) opts for "a minute stillness," while Buber (*Bücher der Geschichte*, 406) has "eine Stimme verschwebendes Schweigens"—something like "a voice of drifting silence."

48. Nelson, *First and Second Kings*, 124.

in the Bible as accompanying God's presence, not *containing* God.[49] The climax of the silence is not traditional but is what is left in the wake of the upheaval that preceded it. Elijah heard (the verb has no object in Hebrew, so we may assume he heard all of it), although nothing draws him out until he "hears" the silence as a sign for him to come out of the cave.[50] He, like Moses at the bush that burns and is not consumed (Exod 3:6), covers his face before he goes out and stands at the cave opening, where Adonai once again asks him what he wants "here" (13). Elijah replies with an answer identical to the one he gave earlier (14). Nelson's suggestion that the noisy accompaniments of God's presence are failed attempts to bring Elijah out of his cave and that once he has emerged he is in the same place he was before, still as stuck as ever, is certainly attractive.[51] Perhaps the stillness signaled to him that God was gone, making it safe to emerge, and the voice asking him the same question he heard before comes as a surprise.

The next unit reports the longest speech from Adonai to Elijah in these chapters, one that constitutes something of a divine commission for the tasks that lie ahead (15–18). The charges—to anoint an Aramean king, a new king for Israel, and Elijah's own successor—are framed by a general instruction and a promise. First, the instruction: Elijah is to *return* on his way, to go back to his task, which contains specific directives. Finally, the promise: Elijah is not alone; God will preserve Israelites who have not abandoned the worship of Adonai. The first charge certainly sounds odd. Since when do Israelite prophets anoint foreign kings? The announcement of all the blood that will be shed by the anointing of both the Aramean and the Israelite king is appalling. Even the hopeful note that Elisha the son of Shafat will carry on the work for Elijah includes a message about killing. The downward spiral of the kingdom will continue,

---

49. So, correctly, Walsh, *1 Kings*, 276: "They point to the divine presence but do not *contain* the divine presence."

50. Walsh's (*1 Kings*, 276) explanation for the silence is that in the mystery of its phrasing it represents the "divine not only beyond all natural phenomena but also beyond all human ability to comprehend it."

51. Nelson, *First and Second Kings*, 125.

and a remnant of seven thousand is not much after all. Yet it is perhaps enough to go on with some hope.

The final unit begins with Elijah leaving and finding Elisha, whom he does not anoint but in some sense appoints by throwing his mantle on him as he is plowing his land (19–21). Elisha appears enthusiastic, although Elijah tries to discourage him, and the tale ends with the phrase "he arose and followed Elijah and attended him" (21).[52] Even though we are not to hear from or about Elisha again until 2 Kings 2, we may assume that from here on he stays with Elijah, so that the solitary, depressed prophet who ran away from his oppressor and his assignments can once more go about what God called him to do.[53] He is no longer the only one left serving God in splendid isolation.

### Act II: Ahab's Wars (1 Kings 20–22)

*At the end of the book there is no sense of conclusion.*[54]

In this section, Ahab is at the center of the action. Prophets appear in every chapter speaking to Ahab in the name of Adonai. Their presence continues the references to other prophets begun in the previous episodes of the cycle (18:4, 13) and underlines the assurance given to Elijah that there are those left in Israel who are faithful to Adonai (19:18). With the exception of chapter 21, the only chapter in which Elijah appears, the events concern war with Aram, the powerful country to the northeast of Israel, with

---

52. The verb "to attend" points to an important function and is used in the Torah and the Former Prophets for Joseph, Moses, and Samuel, as well as Abishag (Gen 39:4; Josh 1:1; 1 Sam 2:11, 18; 3:1; 1 Kgs 1:4). See p. 17 above.

53. Unlike some interpreters, I do not view the episode at Horeb as one in which God decommissions Elijah. The tasks he does not fulfill will be carried out by his disciple, and the intent of the list could be to get Elijah back to his vocation rather than a literal expectation that it will all be accomplished by him. Elijah's discouragement to Elisha may have been a standard formula to avoid attracting thoughtless or impulsive followers.

54. Walsh, *1 Kings*, 368.

portrayals of vivid incidents in episodes leading up to war, in the heat of the fight, and in the aftermath. According to historians, the events described belong to a later historical period than the second quarter of the ninth century, but the compilers ascribe them to the reigns of Ahab in Israel and Jehoshaphat of Judah.[55] The picture of Ahab in the first engagement with Aram is complex. There is evidence of an able and successful ruler, which eventually tilts in a negative direction through prophetic judgment in the second part of the story. In the story of Naboth's vineyard, the king and his queen come in for blunt condemnation by Elijah, but Ahab shows himself repentant before Adonai. The final chapter of the book portrays prophets functioning as advisors to the kings of Israel and Judah, who are together involved in a war of aggression against Aram. The act closes with notes on king Jehoshaphat of Judah and Ahab's successor in Israel.

### Act II, Scene 1: Ahab Victorious (1 Kings 20:1–34)

*The plot moves through a triple rise and fall of narrative tension.*[56]

The first scene describes two battles framed by two sets of negotiations. The battles are a part of a war between Israel and Aram, and the negotiations take place between King Ben-hadad of Aram and King Ahab of Israel. At the end of the first exchange between the two individuals, they are on the verge of battle after rising tension between them (1–12); at the end of the second, there is a peace treaty after Israel has come out victorious (31–34). The prophetic condemnation that follows (35–43) gives the interaction of Ahab with Ben-hadad a negative twist. If King Ahab had gone home before verse 35, he would not have been "dejected and sullen," as he is said to be in verse 43.

---

55. For a reconstruction of historical events citing biblical records from both Kgs and Chr and comparing them with archaeological evidence, see Miller and Hayes, *The History of Ancient Israel and Judah*, 286–326.

56. Nelson, *First and Second Kings*, 131.

Twelve verses in three units set the stage for the battles with Aram in a lively lead-up with a back and forth between Ben-hadad and Ahab, who will mostly appear in the scene as "the king of Israel."[57] The first unit (1–4) introduces a siege of Samaria by Aram, laying down a false trail before veering off in another direction as the negotiations go on. Ben-hadad, who has the upper hand, lays claim to all that is Ahab's—the most valuable property, including members of the king's household. To this, the king politely agrees: "Yours I am and all that is mine" (4). In the second unit (5–6), negotiations take place through messengers, who on returning to the king in Israel report that Ben-hadad, once he has received the goods from the king of Israel, will send his servants to take possession of everything else that is still in the court and its precincts. The king of Israel will *give*, the Aramean king will *take*.

In a third unit (7–12), Ahab consults with the "elders of the land," something not reported in 1 Kings since the unsuccessful meeting called by Rehoboam (1 Kgs 12:6). They, with "all the people," advise him not to go along, so a polite message of refusal goes to Ben-hadad. Ahab will agree to everything he promised earlier but is not open to the second proposal. Aram's king flies into a rage and sends back a threat to reduce Samaria to rubble. Ahab sends back a smart proverb in return, to the effect that it might be wise not to count one's chickens before they have hatched, omitting any of the earlier polite references to "my lord the king." Verse 12 gives a brief glimpse of Ben-hadad, with the intriguing detail that "he was drinking" with his allies "in the tents" before he gives the order to his army to go into attack position.

The word for "tents" usually means something like a hut or booth, a temporary shelter, best known for its association with the Feast of Succoth/Booths held in commemoration of the exodus (Lev 23:34, 42, 43). The word is used a few times unconnected to this

---

57. The predominance of references by title only is one sign pointing to the origin of the story in a different period. Walsh (*1 Kings*, 293) suggests that each episode with Ahab at the center is a complete story without the prophetic condemnation, reflecting "the original independence of the Ahab stories and their subsequent expansion in prophetic circles."

festival; it can be found in 2 Sam 11:11, for example, when Uriah refused to go home to sleep with his wife while the army was staying in "tents."[58] There is also a town called Succoth about 20 miles east of Samaria on the other side of the Jordan. A word with three possible allusions, at least one of them evoking the liberation of Israel from Egypt, injects a note of hope for Israel into the preparations. The fact that the king of Aram is drinking gives the Aramean prospects a negative coloring.

In regard to the structure of the story, the point of the protracted exchanges with a hostile force, probably determined to wage war from the outset, could be to delay action long enough for Israel to make its own preparations. In addition, they paint Ahab in a different light than the mostly negative portrait offered at earlier stages of the narrative. He is canny in his bargaining, takes the leaders of the land into his counsel, and in his recounting of Ben-hadad's outrageous demands, he mentions his wives and children before the property.[59] As Burke Long observes, "Through contrastive dialogue and sparse connective prose . . . the 'historian' suggested character, and sought the reader's sympathies for Ahab."[60]

Two battles ensue. First, there is an engagement in the area around Samaria that begins with a prophetic foretelling and ends in a "severe blow" dealt to Aram—but not a decisive defeat (13–21). The text draws us into the incident in verse 13 with the word "Look!" (*hinneh*) so that we hear the prophet addressing Ahab directly in Adonai's name and promising him victory over this "great throng." The stated purpose of this triumph will be so that Ahab will acknowledge Adonai.[61] Here again a window of possibility opens for

---

58. See Johanna W. H. van Wijk-Bos, *The Road to Kingship: 1–2 Samuel*, A People and a Land 2 (Grand Rapids: Eerdmans, 2020), 278.

59. Walsh (*1 Kings*, 297): "Ben-hadad places wealth before people. When Ahab recounts those demands to the elders, he cites his family before his silver and gold."

60. Burke O. Long, "Historical Narrative and the Fictionalizing Imagination," *VT* 35 (1985): 410.

61. "You will know that I am Adonai" (20:13). The same purpose was stated by Elijah on Mount Carmel (18:36–37) and is deeply embedded in the tradition of the exodus, where God's acts of miracles and liberation are done

a king who was earlier judged to have done "more evil in the eyes of Adonai than anyone before him" (16:30). God will be on his side in the upcoming struggle. The prophet is not identified by name and may have been a member of a prophetic circle advising Ahab—one who is faithful to Adonai.

Ahab receives instructions as to how to engage in combat, although we cannot be sure what is meant by "the lads of the leaders of the districts" (14). They could be a special commando unit or the opposite—those not as heavily armed as the usual soldiers to trick the enemy. Ahab himself is to lead them as kings did of old. It looks as if they form a kind of vanguard, with the mustered army, also conducted by Ahab, following behind (15–16). In the meantime, Ben-hadad has had too much to drink, and on the report that "men have gone out of Samaria," he can only utter garbled instructions to take them prisoner whether they come in peace or not (16–18).[62] Battle is joined and won by Israel (21), but in the manner of men in their cups sometimes miraculously surviving potentially deadly events, Ben-hadad gets away (20). The "great blow" dealt by Israel to Aram will not be enough to keep him away forever.

Following the victory, first the prophet arrives again to warn Ahab that it isn't over yet: "Be strong; know and see what you shall do" (22). Then the scene shifts to the Aramean king, whose "servants" advise him about the kind of gods or god the Israelites have on their side and how this insight might be related to the armies' choice of battleground (23–25).

1 KINGS 20:23

The servants of the king of Aram said to him:
Gods of the hills their gods;
therefore, they are stronger than we.

---

to elicit the same confession from outsiders as well as from Israel (Exod 6:7; 16:12; 29:46; 31:13).

62. "If for peace they have gone out,/ take them alive;/ and if for war they have gone out,/ take them alive" (20:18). It looks as if he meant "kill them" for the second order.

If, however, we fight them in the plain,
then surely we will be stronger than they.

Understandably, God's representative in Israel will take great offense at this statement about Adonai and proclaim it the reason for the upcoming defeat of Aram (28). The idea is of course not so strange from an Aramean point of view. The fame of Sinai and Carmel may have spread, and Israelites are known for worshiping on "the heights," besides occupying a very hilly country. It is a common idea in the ancient world that the gods fight on the side of their people, and Israelites thought the same thing. Then too, rationally speaking, with chariots it might be a better idea to fight on even ground than in hills. They encamp near the Jordan at a place called Aphek, with the Israelites looking like two flocks of goats compared to the host of Arameans (26–27).[63]

Once again, a prophet, here called "a man of God," appears and predicts victory for Israel—or actually for Adonai—on account of the insulting claim that the only location under Israel's God's control is the hill country. The goal is again to acknowledge Adonai, although this time the recognition encompasses the people: "And you will all know that I am Adonai" (28, cf. v. 13). As is typical, only a few words are spared for the actual fight. We hear only that the "Israelites struck Aram" in incredible numbers. Here, too, the people, rather than just the king, are involved. Ben-hadad once again gets away in the rout toward Aphek. In the aftermath, the Aramean king's servants plead for mercy and receive it from a king who swears brotherhood to the king's servants and to Ben-hadad himself, and it all ends in a peace treaty (31–34).

Ahab received prophetic messages at each crucial turn, before the first and the second battle, but in this last encounter he is acting entirely on his own. Yet one might be inclined to admire a king who behaves with grace in victory. The Arameans count on *hesed*,

---

63. The location is unlikely to be the same as the one of the notorious battle with the Philistines on the coastal plain in 1 Sam 4. Yet the similarity in name may conjure up some tension in the story, as it would bring to mind a resounding defeat for Israel.

the same quality that Rahab counted on (Josh 2:12), and they get it from Ahab. There is, on the other hand, little motivation for such kindness toward a king who once threatened to pillage Ahab's entire house. It seems a bit peculiar and brings to mind Saul, who spared the Amalekite king when he had received instructions not to do so (1 Sam 15:9). "Brotherhood" is well and good, but there may be times when it serves king and country better to keep some distance from the despots of the world.

### Act II, Scene 2: Ahab Judged Wanting (1 Kings 20:35–43)

*The clash of prophet and king in this chapter is a model for the inescapable tension between faith and politics.*[64]

1 KINGS 20:35–36

35 A certain man from the disciples of the prophets
said to his companion on the word of Adonai:
Strike me down please.
And the man refused to strike him down.
36 He said to him:
Because you did not listen to the word of Adonai,
Look!, you will be going from me
and a lion will strike you down.
He went from his side,
and the lion found him and struck him down.

Prophets were followed by "disciples," and here one of them engages in seemingly bizarre behavior. Politely asking his companion to *strike him down*, the poor companion is himself *struck down* by a lion upon refusing. It's a disorienting beginning to a brief, disorienting story. The prophet, for so he will be identified later, apparently does not reveal he has had a command from Adonai, so the companion has no clue as to why he would wound his friend. There could hardly be a

64. Brueggemann, *1 & 2 Kings*, 254.

greater repetition of the word *strike*, which occurs four times in two sentences. Of course, another man comes along who does the job, for so it goes in a tale of this sort, with another piling up of the same verb. Once the prophet who started it all is wounded, he stands on the road with his eyes covered as a disguise, waiting for the king to come by. In this way the prophet himself becomes the message (37–38).[65]

The prophet has a story to tell the king about pledging to guard a man—presumably a prisoner—in the midst of the battle and letting him get away (39–40). The king is being set up, as David was set up by Nathan's parable (2 Sam 12:1–12), and like David he utters his judgment that either a huge sum of money is due or the life of the prophet is forfeit: "Thus your judgment;/ you yourself determined it" (40). At this point, the prophet removes his bandage and utters his judgment as a prophet. Indeed, the king's life will be forfeit because the man he let escape was under the *herem.* Not only will Ahab's life be demanded but also that of his people. The story ends with the king going home "dejected and vexed" (43).

The story echoes other narratives. First, of course, the lion killing a disobedient prophet brings to mind the tale in 1 Kings 13. In Kings, the phrase "by the word of Adonai" occurs only in that chapter and here. The story opens with "a certain man" in the same way as 13:11. At the time of the incident involving the prophet, the lion, and the donkey, the king was Jeroboam. Is part of the purpose thus to bring to mind the king who got the entire downslide started? Or does the story evoke the king who also saved another king in disobedience to the total destruction commanded by God through a prophet—Saul in 1 Samuel 15? The *herem* coming out of nowhere in this case is certainly unsettling. It is not mentioned as a practice in Kings except as a reference to the past (1 Kgs 9:21). This prophet appears to go to extremes to bring home a message that King Ahab will be punished in spite of his ignorance about the rules of the game. And behind the prophet is God.

Ahab was apparently a successful leader in a military campaign against Assyria, according to historical records.[66] As part of a

65. Walsh, *1 Kings*, 311.
66. His name occurs in the so-called Monolith Inscription as a member

Syro-Palestinian coalition, he was able to stop Assyrian aggression midway through the ninth century. This victory may be what is remembered here in the war with Aram, which in reality took place later. Is the verdict story a prophetic warning that victory against no-matter-which aggressive force is not going to halt the march of mighty empires? Aram and Israel will both be swallowed by the greedy maw of the Assyrian empire; there is no treaty-making that will avert the fate that will befall the Northern Kingdom—king, people, and land. Or is the victory story and Ahab's deed of loyalty and kindness a sign of hope even amid anticipation of the avalanche of destruction to come?

*Act II, Scene 3: Ahab, Jezebel, and Naboth (1 Kings 21:1–16)*

*Here we have a classic economic issue: the enlargement of estates where there is no empty land.*[67]

The story begins and ends with a vineyard. At the opening, it is in the possession of one Naboth of Jezreel, a town in the fertile valley west of the Jordan, about forty miles north of Samaria (1). At the end, Naboth is a dead man whose vineyard is taken as a *possession* by Ahab (16). How we get to this final point is told in four stages: Ahab wants the property, close to a royal residence, and makes an offer, which Naboth refuses and Ahab goes home visibly unsettled (1–4); Jezebel comforts him and promises she will take care of getting Ahab the vineyard (5–7); Jezebel writes letters in Ahab's name to leaders in Jezreel to set Naboth up for a fall (8–10); the community

---

of a coalition that halted the advance of the Assyrian king Shalmaneser III at Qarqar in Northern Syria. See Miller and Hayes, *A History of Ancient Israel and Judah*, 292–94; Rainer Albertz, *A History of Israelite Religion in the Old Testament Period*, trans. John Bowden, vol. 1, OTL (Louisville: Westminster John Knox, 1994), 149; trans. of *Religionsgeschichte Israels in alttestamenlicher Zeit* (Göttingen: Vandenhoeck & Ruprecht, 1992). Albertz describes the successes of Ahab's foreign policy as "impressive."

67. Tikva Frymer-Kensky, *Reading the Women of the Bible* (New York: Schocken, 2002), 210.

bosses do exactly as she instructs them, and Naboth is killed in a manner that leaves Ahab free to take possession of the vineyard (11–16). Ahab plays an active role regarding the vineyard only in the first and the last stage, and in the final part only because Jezebel urges him to act. Jezebel is at center stage throughout most of the scene. The episode stands out in Kings because it describes a royal transgression committed in the socioeconomic realm rather than in the setting of ritual and worship.

Naboth has a vineyard; Ahab wants it. Ahab offers a fair price for it, or another property in exchange—a king could apparently not just *take* what he wanted—but Naboth refuses because he does not want to part with his ancestral land: "God forbid that I should give my ancestral inheritance to you" (3). What he owns is literally the "inheritance of his fathers."[68] Naboth has a special attachment to the vineyard on account of the fact that it is ancestral, "connecting households, ancestors and land."[69] Within this network of ideas, bonds with the ancestors were not cut off by death and were maintained in part by the land belonging to a family. It is telling that Ahab does not report Naboth's term to Jezebel but refers to the property as the "vineyard" (6). Yet this is precisely what "vexes" Ahab—that Naboth said, "I will not give you my ancestral inheritance!" (4).

Enter Jezebel, who notices her husband's glum demeanor and speaks to him like a spouse: "Why is your spirit low, and why do you not eat?" (5)—an echo of Elkanah's words to Hannah (1 Sam 1:8). Ahab explains his offer to Naboth and the refusal as follows: "I said to him: Give me, please, your vineyard, . . . and he said: I will not

68. For the word "inheritance" (*nahalah*), see above. Norman C. Habel (*The Land Is Mine* [Minneapolis: Fortress, 1995], 33–35) considers the translation "inheritance" to be misleading in most passages. He judges the word *nahalah* to be "a rightful share or allotment, an approved entitlement to land, property or people" (35). There is in Naboth's case little doubt that the land is inherited because of the defining term "ancestral."

69. Stephen C. Russell, "Ideologies of Attachment in the Story of Naboth's Vineyard," *BTB* 441 (2014): 30. Russell argues that the core story is not Deuteronomistic and is not tied to the concept of Adonai's land allotment to the tribes. Habel (*The Land Is Mine*, 31) agrees that the basic issue in 1 Kgs 21 is one of conflicting ideologies: peasant versus royal ideology concerning land.

give you my vineyard" (6). Speculation that his change of terms is deliberate on account of Jezebel's lack of acquaintance with Israel's customs and laws founders in the next unit, where her acquaintance with such regulations is obvious. Jezebel tells her husband to man up and do his job while she takes care of things. She will see to it that he gets his vineyard (7).

She writes letters to the leadership of Jezreel—"the elders and dignitaries"—in the king's name, attaching his seal, and instructs them to call a communal fast at which two scoundrels (*beney belia'al*) are to accuse Naboth of a crime deserving the death penalty: cursing God and king. Her instructions are very precise.

1 KINGS 21:9–10

9 She wrote in the letters as follows:
Call a fast and seat Naboth
at the head of the people.
10 And seat two scoundrels opposite him,
who will testify against him as follows:
You have cursed god and king.[70]
Then take him outside and stone him so he dies.

She uses six verbs to spell out the details, down to the seating and the taking Naboth outside to be executed, as well as the method of the murder. There are proscriptions in the Torah against speaking ill of God and leaders (Exod 22:28; Lev 24:16), and a regulation in Deuteronomy states the sufficiency of two witnesses to execute a person (Deut 17:6).[71] There is no legislation that specifically stipulates a punishment for speaking ill of the king. Jezebel's letters (how many exactly did she write?), however, specify exactly what they must do to take care of the matter and show a clever manipulation of what must have been a traditional moral code.

70. The Hebrew verb "to bless" here means its opposite and is apparently used as a euphemism for "curse," as in Job 2:9.
71. In none of these texts do scribes exhibit the scruple of using a euphemism for cursing God as in 1 Kgs 21:10.

The notables, in any case, follow her instructions to the letter, and Naboth becomes a victim of the queen's machinations. As of verse 13, the "scoundrels" are in charge of the action: They "testified," "led him," "stoned him," "sent a message"—they may well have been, as Walsh suggests, in Jezebel's employ.[72] Jezebel can now go to Ahab and tell him that Naboth is dead, so he can have his vineyard (15–16).

The repeated mention of Jezebel's letters, four times in four verses (8–11), is striking. She did not send a messenger but "wrote letters" (8, 9, 11) and "sent the letters" (8). Here, then, is a literate queen in communication with the upper ten of Jezreel to execute an innocent man in order to cheer up a king who can hardly need more property. She manages everything from a distance, as David once managed Uriah's death through orders to a subordinate (2 Sam 11:15–17), and it is as sordid a story, depicting manipulative power at its worst. The leadership of Naboth's city is implicated also. Was there no one to stand up on Naboth's behalf? And what about Ahab? Did he manipulate matters in this direction all along, knowing that Jezebel would go into action as long as he goaded her? Was his seal just lying around for her to use? Are there two ways of "reading" the main characters: a weak king and an all-powerful queen or a clever king who "keeps his own hands clean of direct involvement in the crime of judicial murder"?[73] Neither one of them comes out well in either case. The king may be feeling better, but Naboth, the Jezreelite, is dead—his death, impending or completed, mentioned five times and emphatically stated by Jezebel when she encourages Ahab to arise and take possession: "Naboth is no longer alive, for he is dead" (15).

The planned murder of the owner of a vineyard, a royal couple committing crimes against the land and its citizens, death hovering over the participants—the story of Naboth and his vineyard, inserted in between chapters on the war with Aram in which Ahab will

---

72. Walsh, *1 Kings*, 324. So also Anne-Marie Kitz, "Naboth's Vineyard after Mari and Amarna," *JBL* 134 (2015): 542: "They are hirelings, personally answerable to their employers."

73. Jerome T. Walsh, *Ahab: The Construction of a King* (Collegeville, MN: Liturgical Press, 2006), 53.

eventually meet his own death, sheds a somber light on the future of the land. Perhaps we should consider neither Naboth nor Ahab nor Jezebel the main character but rather the vulnerable vineyard that lies there for the taking. "I will sing to my beloved/ a song of my beloved to his vineyard:/ A vineyard had my beloved/ on a very fertile hill./ . . ./ What more could I have done for my vineyard that I did not do?/ . . ./ The vineyard of Adonai of Hosts is the house of Israel,/ the people of Judah the planting of his delight;/ he waited for justice, and, Look!, injustice,/ for equity and, Look!, iniquity" (Isa 5:1, 4, 7).[74] So run the words of the poet writing a hundred or more years after Naboth and his property fell victim to aggression and greed just as the entire "house of Israel" will fall victim to its ferocious neighbor.

### Act II, Scene 4: The Verdict (1 Kings 21:17–29)

*Has Elijah identified so wholeheartedly with the judgment that again he has taken initiative to embellish on behalf of Yнwн?*[75]

God's judgment as voiced by Elijah is not long in coming. The scenes are linked by the instruction of verse 18, which sends Elijah to Ahab at the "vineyard of Naboth, where he went to take possession." The unit begins with the classic prophetic introduction "the word of Adonai happened."[76] Earlier Jezebel told her husband to "arise, take possession" (Hebrew *qum resh*, v. 15), now God's servant is commanded to "arise, go down" (*qum red*, v. 18). Ahab is labeled as "the

---

74. I borrow the felicitous rendering of the Hebrew wordplay in the last line from the Jewish Publication Society translation: *The Jewish Study Bible*, ed. Adele Berlin and Marc Zvi Brettler, 2nd ed. (Oxford: Oxford University Press, 2014), 776.

75. John Olley, "Yнwн and His Zealous Prophet: The Presentation of Elijah in 1 and 2 Kings," *JSOT* 80 (1999): 43. Olley argues that Elijah rarely conforms to the words Adonai gives him to speak. See also Neil Glover ("Elijah Versus the Narrative of Elijah," 456), who judges that in chapter 21, "Elijah decides that this oracle requires editing and embellishment."

76. The traditional translation "came" smooths the radical nature of what takes place when the word of God interrupts the flow of events.

king of Israel who is in Samaria" even though in the next breath he is clearly in Jezreel, the place of Naboth's vineyard. The Samaria identification serves the purpose of linking Ahab to the capital city, where he built a temple and altar for Baal (16:32). God's word commences with a sarcastic question: "Have you killed and also taken possession?"[77] It continues with a prediction of dogs licking up Ahab's blood in the same place where they licked the blood of his innocent victim (19). We note there is no word from Adonai about Jezebel.

Ahab, perhaps in the middle of enjoying a walk-through of his new property, greets Elijah with a new epithet. Earlier he had called him a bringer-of-disaster (18:17); this time he chooses a more personal label.

### 1 KINGS 21:20–21

20 Ahab said to Elijah:
  Have you found me, my enemy?
  And he said: I have found that you sold yourself
  to do evil in the eyes of Adonai.
21 Look, I will bring upon you evil;
  I will sweep away your posterity
  and will cut off from Ahab every wall-pisser,
  whether bound or free, in Israel.

This a great deal more than what God instructed Elijah to say, and he is not yet done, as he elaborates that the house of Ahab will become like the house of Jeroboam, referring to the "provocation"—that of Ahab himself and that in which he caused Israel to engage (22; cf. 14:9, 15; 15:30; 16:2, 7, 13, 26, 33). Also, Jezebel comes in for indictment; she is to be eaten by dogs. Both Ahab and Jezebel will become carrion (19, 23–24). Here, the narrator interrupts the spate of Elijah's

---

77. The Hebrew expression is difficult to render in English in its sound alliteration of *s*, *ts*, and the harsh *het* in between: *haratsahta wegam yarashta?* Walsh (*1 Kings*, 329) suggests, "Did you kill to get your will?" In a subsequent writing (*Ahab: The Construction of a King*, 55), he offers "Have you murdered then plundered?"

words by noting how evil Ahab truly was, pointing to his idolatry, seduced as he was by Jezebel (25–26). Swerving away from the social injustice committed by Ahab and Jezebel, the narrative picks up the familiar thread of condemnation of idolatry. Yet this turn to matters of worship serves as a reminder that ethical mandates and cultic ones in Israel were not conceived of as belonging to separate spheres. Idolatry and conducting one's life with "bloody hands" were considered to be all of a piece (cf. Isa 1:15).

Then the unexpected happens: Ahab repents. He shows the depth of his penitence by dressing in sack and ashes and walking around softly, or despondent or depressed (27). Elijah most likely does not expect this, for God points out to him the thoroughness of Ahab's self-abasement and promises a delay of the disaster for his house (28–29). The text does not record Elijah's passing on the word of God's mercy to Ahab, leaving an unresolved question at the end of the episode, which may be an appropriate way to end the story of Naboth's vineyard. Ahab has become an unexpectedly contrite villain and once again shown a different side of himself, leaving an understanding of this king's character and his standing with God an open question. When people repent in the Bible, God often responds by showing mercy, albeit a qualified mercy in Ahab's case. The flat depiction of character that in many portions of the text marks Israel's kings is absent in the case of Ahab. He shows a more complex human face, and so we become more interested in his fate.[78]

### Act II, Scene 5: Nothing but the Truth (1 Kings 22:1–28)

*You want the best people on your staff, and you especially want on your staff really able people who disagree with you.*[79]

The last chapter of 1 Kings involves three stories, or two stories and the snippets of another. The first, our scene, takes place at the en-

---

78. For a thorough analysis of the different voices in relation to Ahab, see Walsh, *Ahab*, 61–64.

79. John Goldingay, *1 and 2 Kings for Everyone*, 101.

trance of the gate to Samaria on a threshing floor where the kings of Israel and Judah, Ahab and Jehoshaphat, are seated in full regalia.[80] Before them, 400 prophets are prophesying. This takes place in the third year of peaceful co-existence with Aram, in which Israel and Judah have formed an alliance, making it possible to plan a joint expedition to take back a city from the Arameans (3–10). Time flows quickly in the introduction to the main action outside the city gate (1–5), with the king of Judah coming down from Jerusalem to Samaria and deliberations taking place about a war to retake Ramoth Gilead from the Arameans.

### 1 KINGS 22:3–4

3  The king of Israel said to his servants:
Did you know that ours is Ramoth Gilead?
And we stay silent without taking it
from the hand of the king of Aram?

4  He said to Jehoshaphat:
Will you go with me to war with Ramoth Gilead?
And Jehoshaphat said to the king of Israel:
Like me like you,
like my people your people,
like my horses your horses.[81]

According to the biblical text, Ramoth Gilead, in the north of the Transjordan, had been a city in one of King Solomon's districts (1 Kgs 4:13), a Levitical city under Joshua (Josh 21:38) and a city of refuge in Deuteronomy (Deut 4:43). At some point, then, it was considered to be a part of ancient Israel's territory, but at this point

---

80. Threshing floors were located outside city gates and afforded a large gathering space following the harvest when not in use. The time may have been the spring of the year, "when kings go out to battle" (2 Sam 11:1), before the first harvest.

81. This is a literal translation of the Hebrew, meaning something like "I am your man!" Cf. NJPS: "I will do as you do; my troops shall be your troops, my horses shall be your horses."

it belongs to Aram's domain.[82] The unit presents a short version of two deliberations: one of Ahab with his advisors and one with his royal visitor. King Jehoshaphat, who may have been in somewhat of a subservient position to Israel at this time, commits himself readily to Ahab's proposal. He has, however, a request of his own to "inquire first of Adonai" (5), a unique request from a monarch in 1 Kings.

Ahab follows up readily by gathering a large crowd of prophets, of whom he asks directly: "Shall I go up to war with Ramoth Gilead?" (6). Where in earlier times divine guidance might be sought through a priest with the ephod (see 1 Sam 23:6–11; 30:7), here groups of prophets are pictured as attached to the court in the function of advisors to the administration. Four hundred prophets may seem over the top for this kind of deliberation, but it is a standard figure for a large number, which in this case also recalls the numbers of Baal and Asherah prophets cited in 18:19 and 22, casting some doubt on this crowd's religious allegiance. They predict good fortune for the king in the name of Adonai.[83] The unanimous prediction does not satisfy Jehoshaphat, who may have mistrusted the allegiance and trustworthiness of these prophets anyway, and he asks if there is no one else available to provide a second opinion on the issue (7–8). Ahab allows there is someone, but not one he is overly fond of on account of his never telling him anything "good." At Jehoshaphat's demurring,

82. As noted above, the war with Aram was probably conducted at a later time than Ahab, who was instead involved in a coalition to oppose Assyrian progress. See p. 140 above.

83. Some scholars argue that the allegiance of the prophets is called into question further by the consonants used in the Hebrew text, which are not the usual ones for the name of Adonai. See Walsh, *1 Kings*, 347; *Ahab*, 68–69. The traditional text, however, points the Hebrew word 'adon with the vowels belonging to the sacred name, and the same spelling occurs in other places in the Hebrew Bible where the reference is clearly to the God of Israel (cf. Gen 18:27, 31; Exod 4:10, 13; 5:22; 15:17; 34:9; etc.). It is not of great import, for the prophets of Ahab may have invoked the name of either Baal or Adonai as it suited them. The issue Elijah addressed on Mt. Carmel was the importance of making a choice between the two (1 Kgs 18:21).

Ahab has the prophet, Micaiah ben Yimlah, called through the agency of a eunuch.[84]

The time-flow, gradually slowing down in response to Jehoshaphat's request, comes to a halt in verse 10, which brings into view the two kings seated in their regalia at the Samaria gate with the prophets in action before them. The next verses present a split-screen vision, one half showing the threshing floor with kings and prophets and another the messenger on his way to the gate with Micaiah (11–14). At the threshing floor, Ahab's prophet Zedekiah enacts the defeat of Aram with two horns made of iron while the other prophets join him in foretelling victory. Meanwhile the messenger instructs Micaiah to join the rest of the prophets in predicting good fortune for the king, eliciting a strong protest from Micaiah, who invokes an oath while pledging that he will say what Adonai tells him to say (14).

1 KING 22:15–16

15  He came to the king,
    and the king said to him:
    Micaiah, shall we go up to battle with Ramoth Gilead
    or shall we refrain?
    He said to him: Go up and triumph;
    Adonai will give it into the hand of the king.
16  The king said to him:
    How often must I adjure you
    not to speak to me anything
    but the truth in the name of Adonai?

The narrator provides no motivation for Micaiah's word-for-word repetition of the predictions uttered by Ahab's other prophets. One

---

84. Eunuchs served as court officials in the ancient world; their presence is especially notable in Esther, reflecting customs at the Persian court. This is the first time we meet this type of royal servant in Kings and may be a subtle hint at the adaptations of Israel's royal households to the customs of the larger world.

possibility is that on being faced with the large crowd in front of the two kings, he loses his courage and starts to repeat the words he heard on his way down from the messenger or overheard from the prophets. It is entirely within the realm of possibility that Micaiah was afraid, for in speaking truth he runs enormous risks to his own well-being. Also possible is that he speaks in a sarcastic tone, mimicking the prophetic crowd on purpose, perhaps to goad Ahab. The story then takes an ironic turn when the king actually insists on Micaiah telling the truth "in the name of Adonai."[85] It is noteworthy that Micaiah does not introduce his first prophecy with the words "thus says Adonai." Since tone in this case is difficult to discern, fear and sarcasm are both options, but the second becomes more likely if we consider what Micaiah is hoping to achieve. In the commentary on Samuel I reviewed the notion that prophecy in the Bible is more than a straightforward prediction of events and is always aimed at the hearer's repentance.[86] On this occasion too, we assume that all of Micaiah's efforts are aimed at turning Ahab from his stated purpose of making war on Aram.

The king's demand for the real truth elicits from Micaiah a description of his vision of "all Israel scattered like sheep without a shepherd." Only then does he insert the word of Adonai, proclaiming in regard to the people "these have no master"—in other words, they are without their king (17). King Ahab's reaction to this is merely an "I told you so" to his colleague. What escapes him is that Micaiah's words concern Israel's as well as his own fate. "It is a vision about *Israel*, the people for whom he has responsibility; they are scattered and leaderless. YHWH's concern is for them and their safe return home."[87] Because his words do not evoke the desired response, Micaiah pushes further to try to

---

85. This is the view of R. W. L. Moberly ("Does God Lie to His Prophets? The Story of Micaiah ben Imlah as a Test Case," *HTR* 96 [2003]: 7), who argues that the king is being mocked by Micaiah and then is forced to take the moral high ground by demanding the truth.

86. See van Wijk-Bos, *The Road to Kingship*, 46–47.

87. Moberly, "Does God Lie to His Prophets?" 7–8. Moberly argues that the prophet's words are in "essence a challenge to the king to remember his responsibility as a shepherd before it is too late" (8).

make Ahab see the error of undertaking a war with Aram. It may seem fruitless to us, for the king is already committed publicly, supported by his crowd of prophetic advisors, but like the woman of Tekoa in front of David, the prophet keeps approaching his subject, each time from a different angle. Now he begins with the announcement "hear the word of Adonai" and tells the story of God and the host of heaven and a lying spirit who goes out to "fool" the prophets so "Ahab will go up and fall in Ramoth Gilead" (18–23). Such a tale of Adonai sending a lying spirit is intended to goad Ahab further into recognizing that the plan is ill-conceived. Micaiah ends his inventive anecdote with the words "Adonai has spoken evil regarding you" (23). This type of prophetic warning is aimed specifically at evoking repentance, as it did successfully through the announced "evil" God planned to bring on Ahab through the message of Elijah (21:21). "The second vision has the same purpose as the first vision. If the message is that the king will die, it is given so the king may not die."[88]

The first reaction to the oracle comes not from Ahab but from the prophet Zedekiah:

1 KINGS 22:24–25

24 Then Zedekiah Ben Kena'anah came near
   and struck Micaiah on the cheek and said:
   How did the spirit of Adonai pass from me to speak to you?
25 Micaiah said: Look, you will see it
   on the day that you go from room to room to hide.

Zedekiah, whose name means "Adonai is Righteous," with a patronymic indicating his origin as a Canaanite, not only takes the liberty of dealing Micaiah a physical blow but accuses him of possessing the lying spirit which he assigned to Zedekiah and his cohort. Micaiah retorts that the truth will eventually come out when Zedekiah himself will look for a place to hide. In other words, Zedekiah's fate is no safer than Ahab's. Ahab's reaction is

88. Moberly, "Does God Lie to His Prophets?" 9.

to imprison Micaiah and put him on short rations until the king's safe return (26–27). Micaiah, who must have feared the danger to himself, replies that Ahab's safe return will indeed prove that Adonai has not spoken through him (28). The final phrase—"He said: Hear this all peoples!"—a duplicate of the prophet Micah's first words (Mic 1:2) and commonly viewed as a scribal error, can also be understood to be spoken by Ahab to the crowd in the vein of "you all heard what he said!" Ahab may here take on a mocking tone in mimicking prophetic speech.[89]

The entire scene has provided an interruption between the first verse and its continuation in verse 29, when the kings of Israel and Judah go to war. The effect of the large amount of dialogue is that we are very close to what has transpired at the Samaria gate, as the narrator *shows* what is happening rather than merely describing it. "Why, if this section does not advance the plot, does the narrator make it so prominent and present?"[90] On the surface there is the obvious issue of true and false prophecy. False prophecy is not so much connected to an outcome as to telling people what they want to hear. Jeremiah will announce that the prophets who promise "peace and security" in the name of Adonai are "false prophets." Those who proclaim there will be no hunger or violence in the land will themselves perish through hunger and violence (Jer 14:13–16). In addition, prophecy is an appeal, even if it means assigning to God a lying spirit, for king and people to return to their calling of being a community under the guidance of *torah* even in the face of war and destruction. The scene thus plays a role in the larger history of the kingdoms, in which the prophets will issue their constant challenges and calls for repentance.

---

89. Keith Bodner ("The Locutions of 1 Kings 22:28: A New Proposal," *JBL* 122 [2003]: 539) suggests that the words are spoken by Ahab in a "brazen mimicry of prophetic speech, rhetorically intended toward Micaiah as he is being led toward his place of confinement." This mockery of the prophet, then, has the purpose of conveying the message both to the troops and to the army of Judah that Ahab has every "intention of returning."

90. Walsh, *1 Kings*, 353.

*Act II, Scene 6: A Ruse Confounded (1 Kings 22:29–40)*

*Everything pivots on King Ahab, who is to die.*[91]

As they go to war, Ahab counsels Jehoshaphat to be recognizable as his royal self while he, Ahab, goes in disguise (29–30). Clearly, Micaiah's prophecy has sown at least a seed of doubt in Ahab's mind. The natural tendency of the enemy will be to search out the royal leader—especially Ahab himself, the more powerful of the two kings. By annihilating the leader in battle, one undermines the fighting spirit of the troops. His disguise will serve to make him less of a target. Disguise has functioned in important ways in what came before. In Ahab's story, it functioned to bring home to him an unwise decision he had made—one that may at this moment come back to haunt him. At that time, a prophet came to him "in disguise" (20:38) to force Ahab to recognize his mistake. Now, Ahab himself puts on a disguise in reaction to a prophecy that came to him disguised as a lie. There is also a gloomy echo of Saul who went "in disguise" to hear a word of his doom from the Shaman at Endor (1 Sam 28:8–25).[92] He is correct in anticipating the enemy's plan to target him (31). But what initially seems to work is deflected by the king of Judah, who is recognized as not being the king of Israel so that the officers turn away from him, presumably still looking for Ahab (32–33).

We should probably understand the next section to have taken place simultaneously with the attack on Jehoshaphat, for a random shot has hit Ahab at a vulnerable place, causing a wound from which he dies in the evening (34–35). He instructs his charioteer to take him from the fight but is kept upright in his chariot until he is dead. Then the cry goes out through the camp for the troops to go back home (36). For the second time, the text notes the king's

---

91. Brueggemann, *1 & 2 Kings*, 275.

92. Different verbs in the histories refer to the action of appearing as another, going in disguise. The 1 Sam 28 text employs the identical form of the same verb used here for Ahab (see 2 Chr 18:29; 35:22), which also recalls the action of the blindfolded prophet in 1 Kings 20:38.

death, followed by his return to Samaria and his burial. He had obviously bled out in the chariot, because the blood mingles with the water for washing the chariot so that dogs come and lick the blood, and prostitutes wash themselves there—animals and humans of low status desecrating the remains of Ahab (38). In counterpoint, there is the reference to "all he did" and the buildings he undertook, written in another record (39). Then he is reported to "lie down with his ancestors" while his son Ahaziah succeeds him (40). The final notices reflect the complicated view of the compilers on the character of Ahab.

Few kings in the history of the kingdoms receive as complex a narrative as Ahab. On the one hand, he is more evil than any other king (21:25); on the other hand, he follows the advice of his advisor prophet Elijah. Hounded by prophetic presence (not only Elijah but other prophets appear to upbraid him and call him to account), he can respond to their message and go into full repentance. He buys into the optimistic announcement of the lying prophets but elicits truth from one who never tells him anything "good." He is a brave fighter who goes into battle with his people, resembling Saul and David. He is greedy for more property than he needs, wanting someone's ancestral property for his vegetable garden, wanting another city for his realm. He is blind as the blindfolded prophet but also generous to a fallen enemy and perspicacious in his view of Elijah, who rarely comes to him for a friendly chat. The final view of this king and his reign may not be positive, but the stories show more than anything that there is always an opening for things to go otherwise, for kings as well as for ordinary people.

### Act II, Scene 7: Jehoshaphat and Ahaziah (1 Kings 22:41–54[41–53] [93])

*A strange and abrupt end to this book of Kings.* [94]

---

93. I am following the verse numbering of the traditional Hebrew text. English versions present 22:45–54 as 22:44–53, noted in brackets.

94. Hens-Piazza, *1–2 Kings*, 221.

The end of 1 Kings returns to the dry recital of reigns in Israel and Judah with snippets of information and stereotypical expressions of approval and disapproval. Jehoshaphat of Judah, the son of Asa, turns out to be a "good" king, modeling his behavior after his father and "doing what was right in the eyes of Adonai"—only not quite measuring up because he left "the heights" where people sacrificed intact (41–47[46]). The notice in verse 45[44], "Jehoshaphat made peace with the king of Israel," links back to the preceding episode and the coalition between North and South (1–40). The reference to the rest of his affairs and his heroic deeds recorded elsewhere is inserted before his death report, with the addition of a note on his removing inappropriate cultic personnel from Judah's worship (47[46]; cf. 14:24; 15:12).[95]

Three verses give an abbreviated account of incidents during Jehoshaphat's reign that the compilers considered important (48–50 [47–49]). Edom is weak at the time, which makes it possible for Jehoshaphat to undertake a maritime adventure involving the port of Ezion-Geber that would otherwise be under Edom's control. The goal is to acquire gold from Ophir, a place renowned for this precious metal, but the ships founder close to the port (cf. 1 Kgs 9:28; 10:11). An offer by Ahaziah of Israel before this mishap to make it a cooperative adventure is rejected by Jehoshaphat (50[49]); Judah may have become less dependent, or else the king is not willing to ally himself with his neighbor after the unfortunate war with Aram. Also, he may be wary of associating with a known worshiper of Baal (see 54[53]). The death notice of Jehoshaphat is standard (51[50]). It would have been nice to know how he got away from the battlefield at Ramoth Gilead, but that information was either preserved in other sources or never recorded.

King Ahaziah, who succeeded Ahab in verse 40, receives an entirely negative judgment, walking "in the way of his father, and in the way of his mother, and in the way of Jeroboam, the son of

---

95. Here, as in 14:24 and 15:12, the term is one that in the past was understood to refer to a type of male cultic prostitute. Walsh, *1 Kings*, 209: "All we can say for sure is that the *qadesh* and the *qedesha* were cultic personnel who did not belong to the worship practices" of Adonai.

Nevat" (52–54[51–53]). The mention of the mother of one of Israel's kings is unique and, together with the negative judgment of this king, gives rise to the inference that Ahaziah's mother was Jezebel. We assume that Ahab had other wives, but besides Jezebel none are named individually or as a group; they are only alluded to in 20:3, 5 and 7. The short section presents the standard introduction but not his death notice, and the conclusion of 1 Kings is not an ending, since Ahaziah's story continues in the first chapter of 2 Kings. This strange and ragged conclusion of 1 Kings is due to the eventual division in two of what was originally one book, making one wish for a more orderly transition from the first part to the second. It may in itself be illustrative of the strange and ragged progress and eventual chaotic ending of the kingdoms of Israel and Judah under the monarchies.[96]

### Act III: From Elijah to Elisha (2 Kings 1–2)

*"Is there no god in Israel?" (2 Kgs 1:3)*

Negative judgment has already been announced for Ahaziah, the king of Israel, in the last chapter of 1 Kings, but there is still a story to tell, beginning with an example of how far he went in his idolatrous inclinations. The main story serves to bring Elijah back into the picture to issue his last verdict against a monarch. The second chapter tells of Elijah's ascension and the continuation of his task by Elisha, who performs his first miracles. A new era has begun with the activities of Elisha, who will be present in every subsequent episode through 2 Kings 8. Some of this material exhibits a characteristic style of its own, especially evident in the account of Elijah's ascension. Brief miracle stories will alternate with more extensive tales of Elisha in his environment dealing with either kings or the people of the land.

---

96. The division of Kings into two books goes back to the Greek translation of the Hebrew text, the Septuagint. In Jewish Hebrew tradition, there was only one book until 1516.

*Act III, Scene 1: Between the Lord of the Flies*
*and the Lord of Hair (2 Kings 1)*

*An elemental figure who in his very appearance brings out the struggle*
*between the powerless and those who rule.*[97]

The opening line about the rebellion of Moab appears to lay down a false trail, for that event and its consequences will not be told until chapter 3, but it also makes a connection to the situation of the king of Israel, who is injured from a fall and thus in no shape to pursue this matter.[98] After the note on the king's illness, the account goes immediately to the information that Ahaziah sent to "inquire" about his recovery from a god in Philistine territory named Baal Zevuv, which is literally "lord of flies" but most likely a Hebrew deliberate pejorative misnaming of Baal Zevul, "exalted lord" or "Baal the exalted."[99] The verb "to inquire" can be used as a technical term for seeking Adonai's advice, concerning illness as well as other matters (1 Kgs 14:1–18), and the name Baal Zevuv next to this verb sends a shockwave through the opening of the story. This will not be about human enemies but will concern the threatening presence of a deity that has derailed the allegiance of Israel's monarchs to Adonai from the start (1–2).

The *messengers* sent by the king are juxtaposed with the *messenger* of Adonai commanding Elijah[100]:

97. Robert L. Cohn, *2 Kings*, Berit Olam (Collegeville, MN: Liturgical Press, 2000), 12.

98. Historians assume the domination of Moab by Israel during the period of Omri and Ahab, preceding Ahaziah. See Miller and Hayes, *A History of Ancient Israel and Judah*, 295–307.

99. The name Baal Zevul occurs in the Ugaritic texts for Baal. It is also possible that Jezebel's name, which in Hebrew is *Izevel*, puns in a similar manner on Baal's name: "Where is the exalted?" See Fox, *The Early Prophets*, 663, 701. The name Beelzebub, the common English rendering of Baal Zevuv, survived in Christian tradition as a name for the devil (see Matt 10:25; 12:24). The famous novel by William Golding, *Lord of the Flies*, took its title from this Hebrew epithet for Baal.

100. For the translation of the word *mal'akh* as "messenger" rather than "angel," see van Wijk-Bos, *The End of the Beginning*, 199n13.

2 KINGS 1:3–4

3  A messenger of Adonai spoke to Elijah, the Tishbite:
   Arise, go to meet the messengers of the king in Samaria.
   Say to them: Is there no God in Israel
   that you are going to inquire of Baal Zevuv, the god of Ekron?
4  Therefore, thus says Adonai:
   From the couch on which you went up
   you will not come down,
   for you will surely die.
   And Elijah went.

The message of doom is preceded by a sarcastic rhetorical question, setting the "God in Israel" in direct opposition to the "god of Ekron." The fall from a window will not be the cause of the king's death but rather his perfidy in seeking counsel from a foreign god, as the word "therefore" makes clear.

Between verses 4 and 5, there is a gap where the encounter of Elijah with the messengers of Ahaziah should be told, with the result that we move quickly from the prophet's side back to the court, where the king's messengers report to him exactly what Elijah has told them (5–6). The inquiry of the king, "If I will revive," has now been met twice with the message "you will surely die." Because the Hebrew phrase repeats the root "die"—literally, "You will die, yes die"—in both verses 4 and 6, the verb "to live" is countered four times by the verb "die." The king wants to know what sort of man it was who gave them this message, and they describe him as a man with a lot of hair (most likely on his garment) girded with a leather belt (7–8).

Descriptions of appearance are rare enough in the biblical text that they give pause to the reader/listener. Samuel was identifiable by his cloak, David's daughter Tamar by her tunic, and here the description apparently marks the person clearly as Elijah. The insertion just at this point serves another purpose than finding the man who presented the king with his bleak outlook, for he is now faced with two "baals"—one a "master of flies" and the other a "master of hair," the literal translation of the term used for Elijah by the king's messengers.[101] According to the narrator, one, the "lord of the flies," represents every wrong turn taken by Israel's kings in the footsteps of Jeroboam the son of Nevat, and the other, the "lord of hair," personifies the uncompromising presence of the God of Israel, to whom alone the people and their leaders owe their allegiance.

Ahaziah has received the response to his inquiry, but rather than repenting of his waywardness, he commands a search for Elijah, who is found sitting on a mountaintop. Once again, the story leaves a gap concerning the king's motivations, the method of locating Elijah, and where they find him exactly to move immediately to the encounter of the king's representatives with God's agent (9–15). That a commando of fifty soldiers goes out to get hold of the prophet makes clear that if need be, he may be apprehended forcefully. The commander orders Elijah to descend: "He said to him: Man of God, the king says, come down!" (9).[102] Elijah apparently inspires enough awe that no one attempts to *go up* to overpower him. We note that it's the king who "will not come down" from his couch who commands Elijah to "come down" from his mountain. Rather than Elijah, however, fire "comes down" from the sky and devours the commander and his soldiers. Instead of the "man of God" (*ish elohim*), what comes down is "fire from the sky" (*esh min hashamayim*, v. 10). This scene repeats itself almost exactly once more (11–12), and success is not achieved until the third effort, when the commander approaches Elijah with appropriate humility and courtesy, pleading for not only his *life* but the *life* of the soldiers, "your servants" (13–14). God's messenger then instructs Elijah to "go down" and "not be afraid"—a sign that Elijah has indeed been afraid for his life (15).

Elijah's movement of "going down" to the king is followed directly by the phrase "he said to him" of the final unit (16–17). This

101. The god of Ekron is Baal Zevuv, and Elijah is called a *ba'al se'ar.* *Ba'al* is also a Hebrew noun meaning "owner," besides indicating the name of a Canaanite deity. The clothing described, including the leather girding Elijah, must have been unusual enough to make him identifiable by it.

102. The text actually has Elijah sitting on top of *the* mountain, perhaps because the reader is familiar with this location as one of Elijah's habitual stopping places, but the exact location is no longer clear.

time the "therefore" is preceded by the cause: "Because you sent
. . . to inquire of . . . the god of Ekron . . . therefore you will die, yes
die"—an announcement immediately followed by "and he died" (17).
In between the spelling out of the cause and the result, the phrase "is
there no god in Israel?" occurs one more time, an indignant inter-
jection amplified by "to inquire about his word?" Ahaziah receives
no death notice, and the narrative closes with a reference to his
successor Jehoram, perhaps his brother.[103]

The story has clear folkloristic motifs, filled with repetitions
and miraculous events like fire coming down from the sky. At the
same time, it closes Elijah's career as spokesperson for Adonai, especially to the kings of Israel, in a significant way. The central theme of
the episode of unfortunate Ahaziah is the struggle between life and
death. The king wants to know if he will *live* and is told three times
that he will die with a sixfold repetition of the verb. This theme is
also at the heart of the fate of the kingdoms: Will they live or die?
Will they, in their desire to live, appeal to the right source of life for
their well-being and continued existence? At the same time, on the
level of the context of the Elijah legends, the theme also anticipates
his upcoming departure from this life while the motif of *going up*
and *not coming down* looks forward to the manner of his leaving in
the next chapter.

### Act III, Scene 2: Taken Away (2 Kings 2:1–14)

*Visionary space, and indeed Elijah and Elisha it seems, belong to a nu-
minal realm set apart from the ordinary.*[104]

---

103. The succession becomes confusing at this point. Jehoram is also
called Joram, and either there were two kings—one in Israel and one in Judah—by the same name or there was a period of about ten years when one
king ruled both kingdoms. We will not become entangled in the difficulties of
the synchronic listing of kings. For an overview of the possibilities, see Miller
and Hayes, *A History of Ancient Israel and Judah*, 320–23. In this volume, the
longer form is used for the king of Israel and the shorter form for the king
of Judah.

104. Burke O. Long, *2 Kings*, FOTL 10 (Grand Rapids: Eerdmans, 1991), 27.

2 KINGS 2:1–2

1  When Adonai was about to bring up[105]
   Elijah in a storm to heaven,
   Elijah and Elisha came from Gilgal.
2  Elijah said to Elisha:
   Stay here please,
   for Adonai has sent me to Bethel.
   And Elisha said:
   By the life of Adonai
   and by my own life,
   I will not abandon you!
   And they went down to Bethel.

We note the continuation of the motif of upward and downward movement as it frames this first unit in the first and last sentences. It will find resolution in the report that "Elijah went up" in verse 11. Initially, the movement is back and forth, taking Elijah and Elisha on what appears a strange circuitous journey, from Gilgal, a little west of the Jordan, to Bethel, about ten miles to the west of Gilgal, and back to Jericho, only a few miles from where they started (1–6). The point of the stopping places is not to create an impression of an orderly progression or a likely distance covered, which even at only 20–25 miles in hilly country would be a formidable trek to make on foot in one day.[106] The locations are significant for their traditional associations: Gilgal with the first solemn celebration and commemoration of the crossing of the Jordan under Joshua (Josh 4:19–24),[107] Bethel with its numerous occasions of divine revelation and altar building (Gen 12:8; 28:19; 35:7; Judg 20:26;

---

105. The verb form is from the root "to go up," one of the leading motifs in ch. 1.

106. Ernst Würthwein (*Die Bücher der Könige: 1 Kön. 17 – 2 Kön. 25*, ATD 12 [Göttingen: Vandenhoeck & Ruprecht, 1984], 274) uses a proposed distance of sixty miles to argue that vv. 2–6 are secondary to the core of the story.

107. The prophet Samuel and King Saul are also associated with Gilgal (1 Sam 7:16; 10:8; 11:14; etc.). I believe the reference to Joshua to be the primary association the narrator wishes to evoke in this text.

1 Kgs 12:29), Jericho as the first city conquered by the Israelites after they crossed the Jordan and entered the land (Josh 2:1; 4:13; 6:25; cf. 1 Kgs 16:34), and finally the river Jordan, the place of the miraculous crossing itself (Josh 3–4). The two go from one place that resonates with numinous importance in Israel's remembrance to the next. Because the narrator begins the episode by disclosing that Adonai will "take Elijah up in a storm to heaven" the progression from town to town creates a moment of suspense, as each important location could be *the* place where it is going to happen. Indeed, nothing here is "ordinary."

The description of this extraordinary journey by Elijah and Elisha, who turns up as if he has never been absent from his "master's" side, is one of short lines in poetic repetition and contrast: "they came from . . . they went to"; "Adonai has sent me . . . stay here, please"; "by the life of Adonai and my own life, I will not abandon you." Each phrase is repeated three times until they come to a standstill at the Jordan in verse 7. Elisha's insistent pledge to stay with Elijah turns the general "they" of "they went" into "they went, the two of them" (6), then to "the two of them stood at the Jordan" (7), and finally to "the two of them crossed on dry land" (8). The crossing with Elijah dividing the waters of the river by striking it with his mantle serves to recall the miraculous crossing by the Israelites of both the Sea of Reeds and the Jordan in reverse direction (Exod 14:15–25; Josh 3:14–17). Elijah is here not the lonely figure at Mount Horeb, and Elisha not simply the one who "attended to him." Already, Elisha is coming closer to receiving the prophetic office. Twice, a group of prophet disciples comes to foretell the impending "taking away" of Elijah to Elisha, who twice responds, "Also I myself have known it" and commands them to be silent (3, 5). Elijah makes three attempts to stop Elisha from going with him, but Elisha refuses to allow his master to go on in isolation.[108] How Elisha knows of Elijah's ascension ahead of time is not disclosed; he may actually know something or he may be intent on getting rid of the pesky questioners. The disciples of the prophets evidently know of it, and in the case of

---

108. There is a close resemblance to the vow of Ruth not to "abandon" Naomi (Ruth 1:16).

everyone, including Elisha, the foreknowledge may simply underline the powerful predictive abilities of these characters.

The moment of the climactic event, at this point revealed three times (1, 3, 5), is very near once they have crossed the Jordan. Now Elijah is the one to speak of being "taken" (8–10). He asks what he can do for Elisha, who boldly requests a double share (literally "two shares") of Elijah's spirit (9). A questioning and giving mode is not characteristic of Elijah, and while gift-asking and giving is a standard motif of folkloristic tales, it may point to a change in Elijah—certainly in his relationship with Elisha. He determines that the gift Elisha asks for is a difficult one (lit. a "hard" thing) and not one he judges to be in his control to give. The sign of it being granted will be if Elisha will "see" Elijah's "being taken." Verse 11 interrupts their speaking together so that the moment still comes as a surprise. A chariot of fire and horses of fire divide them.

### 2 Kings 2:11–12

11  As they were going on speaking,
    Look!, a chariot of fire and horses of fire,
    and they divided the two of them.
    Then Elijah went up
    in a windstorm of heaven.
12  And Elisha saw
    And he was crying out:
    My father, my father,
    chariots of Israel and its horsemen!
    And he saw him no more.
    Then he took hold of his clothes
    and tore them in two pieces.

A storm is frequently associated with divine power in the Bible; God speaks to Job in a storm (Job 38:1; 40:6); Isaiah speaks of a destructive storm originating with "Adonai of Hosts" (Isa 29:6); Jeremiah announces a punishing tempest descending on the prophets who promise peace in Israel (Jer 23:19), and in Ezekiel the storm heralds the vision of a divine appearance (Ezek 1:4). Elijah's spectacular leave-taking and its vision evoke Elisha's ecstatic cry. Only after he stops *seeing* does he tear his clothes in "two pieces" in mourning—a traditional gesture, but also a specification that reiterates the "two shares" of Elijah's spirit. In addition, what was heretofore "the two of them" has become divided: One has been taken and one left behind.[109] Elijah's cry is framed by his seeing: "He saw . . . and he saw him no more." The qualification necessary for him to receive a double share of Elijah's spirit has indeed taken place, so he lifts up Elijah's mantle and stands with it at the edge of the Jordan (13). As Elijah did, he strikes the water, and he asks: "Where is Adonai the God of Elijah, even He?" (14). While this phrase is read by some as a challenge, we can also hear in it the cry of desperation frequently voiced in the Psalms.[110] The continuation of this phrase repeats the striking of the water, which divides hither and yon, and Elisha "crossed over," leading to the conclusion that Elisha's attempt to divide the water succeeds only after he calls on the "Adonai the God of Elijah."

Beside the upward and downward movement, the motifs of "parting" and its opposite, "attachment," are central to the story. Elijah attempts to *part* from Elisha by telling him to *stay* before he is taken up, but Elisha will not hear of it, expressing his attachment through his vow not to *abandon* (2, 4, 6). Disciples of the prophets

109. Long, *2 Kings*, 27: "Here *lishnayim qera'im*, 'into two pieces,' alludes to the *shenehem*, 'the two of them together,' of vv. 6 and 11 and suggests the depth of change by the trajectory from Gilgal to Transjordan."

110. The words "even he" (*af hu*) are taken into the next phrase by many translations; for example, "And he too struck the water" (Alter, *Ancient Israel*, 737), but in the Hebrew sentence, the following verb is preceded by a copula, which makes this an unlikely reading. Fox (*The Early Prophets*, 707) follows the reading of the Septuagint, "indeed." Wesley J. Bergen (*Elisha and the End of Prophetism*, JSOTSup 286 [Sheffield: Sheffield Academic, 1999], 64) reads as the text stands: "Where is [Adonai], the God of Elijah, even he?" and argues that the text intends to distance Elisha from Adonai, in line with his argument that the text presents an overall negative portrait of Elisha. Bergen's argument that "A narrative that portrays [Adonai] acceding to the demands of an impatient prophet does little credit to either prophet or god" appears entirely modern and alien to the biblical context. Questions posed to God about divine absence and pleas for a renewal of God's favor may be found throughout the Psalms (see Ps 89:50[49]; Isa 63:11, 15; Jer 2:6).

appear to warn Elisha that "Adonai is taking" his "master" away from him, and Elisha professes to be aware of this final parting that lies ahead (3, 5). Eventually, the refusal by Elisha to *abandon* resolves itself into a unified pair of prophets going together, "the two of them" (6, 7, 8), which in the end resolves into a division between the two (11), a separation that also expresses itself in the *two pieces* of Elisha's clothes and in the divided waters of the Jordan. The double share of Elijah's spirit, which rests on Elisha, symbolizes the connection between the two, persisting in spite of the final parting.

### Act III, Scene 3: Elisha among the Prophets (2 Kings 2:15–25)

*One has seen his power—for weal and woe, whether or not the matter is congenial to modern tastes.*[111]

Prophets have appeared throughout the text of Kings, once before in the guise of one of the *disciples of the prophets* (1 Kgs 20:35). Such groups are apparently especially attached to Elisha, and they step onto the stage in verse 3 without a special introduction, speaking to Elisha rather than Elijah.[112] There will be other references to this band in the Elisha stories. Prophets may have worked more or less on their own, like Elijah, or as members of a type of guild. We witnessed the group of prophets advising King Ahab in 1 Kings 22 and heard about another group hidden by Obadiah in 1 Kings 18:4. The picture that emerges is of prophets functioning as a unit under the guidance of one teacher, exemplified by Elisha. Fifty of these have been standing on the west side of the Jordan (7) awaiting Elisha's return, upon which they proclaim that the spirit of Elijah rests on Elisha (2:15). They bow down to him—a sign that he is held in reverence—and refer to themselves as "your servants." These

---

111. Long, *2 Kings*, 35.

112. The translation of *beney hannevi'im* should be "disciples of the prophets" rather than "sons of the prophets." Here as elsewhere we cannot automatically exclude women from membership in the prophetic circles. See p. 179 below.

prophets-in-the-making know that the spirit of Adonai has taken Elijah, and they propose to go in search of the body, wondering if the spirit has thrown him down somewhere. Elisha opposes this but eventually gives in. Their search is in vain, emphasizing that they are not prophets equal to the stature of Elijah and Elisha and that Elijah was truly taken away from Elisha and the earthly realm (16–18).

Two events of a miraculous nature round off the account of Elisha and his first activities as successor to Elijah; first, he clears up a spring of water that has gone bad in Jericho (19–22). Second, on his way to Bethel, little boys mock him and are torn to pieces by two bears after Elisha curses them. The first, a healing miracle, will be the more characteristic of Elisha's interventions. It takes place in Jericho, the rebuilding of which was cursed by Joshua (Josh 6:26; cf. 1 Kgs 16:34), and the cleansing of the spring not only rehabilitates the productivity of land and people but absolves the effect of the curse.

### 2 KINGS 2:19–22

19 Then said the men of the city to Elisha:
The location of the city is good,
as my lord sees,
and the water is bad;
the land miscarries.
20 He said: Get me a new bowl
and put salt in it.
And they got it for him.
21 He went to the spring of water
and there threw the salt
and said: Thus says Adonai:
I have healed these waters.
No longer shall there be from there
death and miscarriage.
22 And the waters were healed until today
according to the word of Elisha that he spoke.

So far, prophets have surrounded Elisha, counseling him and proclaiming his gift. Their search for Elijah arose from a desire that if there was a body to find, it should receive burial. Presumably, they are still with Elisha since the text notes that they "returned to him" (18). In the episode about the healing of Jericho's spring water, the initiative is taken by "the men of the city," enlarging the circle in which Elisha moves and acts. Elisha involves the people in the action by asking them to get the receptacle for the salt—a new bowl.[113] This is a simple request, but it asks the citizens not only to contribute to the endeavor but also to trust the prophet's ability.[114] Not a dead body *thrown* on the land, but salt *thrown* in the water brings healing. In contrast to Elijah, who involved the people around him only on Mount Carmel, Elisha's activities will involve both individuals and the community in acts of restoring life. His declaration, "Thus says Adonai," is the first time he makes this prophetic statement and ascribes to God the result of human activity. Instead of *death* for both land and people, God has brought life. The comment of the narrator in the final note serves to underline the lasting effect of the cleansed waters as well as the authority of Elisha.

The second example of Elisha's access to divine power offers a grim counterpoint to the first (23–25). On his way to Bethel, little boys come out of the city to jeer at Elisha, mocking his bald head.[115] Lack of hair may have been a sign of weakness or shame in the ancient world, a cause for insecurity and lack of self-confidence.[116] It may have struck especially hard at Elisha because of the contrast to Elijah, who is at least once referred to as a "master of hair" (1:8).

---

113. Involving a *new* item may be what is called for in a sacred action. We think of the Philistines as well as King David placing the Ark of the Covenant on a *new* cart (1 Sam 6:7; 2 Sam 6:3) or the prophet Ahiyah tearing his *new* cloak (1 Kgs 11:29).

114. Cleansing the water brings to mind the action of Moses at Mara (Exod 15:22–25), but Elisha's miracle is unique in that Elisha engages the community in participatory action.

115. The verb for their taunting is serious, not simply "making fun." It is used in connection with defamation and shame.

116. Note the shaming of men by shaving off half of their hair by the king of Ammon in 2 Sam 10:4 and a hint at the shaming of victims by shaving their heads in Jer 2:16. Hair as a sign of power is associated with Samson, Absalom, and Elijah.

In light of this, we may excuse Elisha's cursing the boys. He curses them, however, in the name of Adonai, which in his case unleashes divine power even he may not have counted on. Bears come out of the forest and tear the boys apart. The horrifying result exemplifies what Cohn identifies as the "raw and amoral power at Elisha's disposal."[117] Bethel is a city known both in sacred ancient tradition and as the place where Jeroboam commenced his idolatry, and the boys may function as a symbol of the transgression that clings to it. Elisha in any case seeks no shelter there and goes on first to Mount Carmel before ending up in Samaria, the seat of power in the kingdom.

### Act IV: A Prophet in Israel (2 Kings 3–5)

*The narrative will continue to move between these two worlds.*[118]

Three chapters all contain reports of Elisha's activities. They move from the plight of armies preparing for battle when a shortage of water arises, to the distress of a single woman householder who faces the threat of losing her sons, to a wealthy patron who receives a gift through Elisha she may not have wanted, to food issues facing the community, and finally to the healing of a Syrian court official. The last episode results in complications in Elisha's immediate environment. Elisha is present in each scene, although not in identical ways. Change occurs through the life-giving interventions of Adonai, whether the context is the center of power or the more modest setting of home and family. Shortage of means to sustain life is an issue at every turn and alleviating the shortage the key issue.

#### Act IV, Scene 1: Water without Rain (2 Kings 3)

*Has the prophet been wrong?*[119]

---

117. Cohn, *2 Kings*, 17.
118. Bergen, *Elisha and the End of Prophetism*, 4.
119. Hens-Piazza, *1–2 Kings*, 246.

The rebellion of Moab, already announced at the opening of the first chapter, takes shape in a narrative that combines battle story and prophetic activity somewhat in the manner of 1 Kings 22, but with its own twists and turns.[120] First (1–3), Jehoram of Israel receives the evaluation that was missing when he was introduced in 1:17. He gets a negative judgment, partially alleviated by the comment that he is not as evil as "his father and mother" (Ahab and Jezebel) and that he removed a stele dedicated to Baal (2). Yet, this "faint praise" is not enough to redeem him, and ultimately he does not depart from the sins of Jeroboam.[121]

The narrator describes the huge tribute paid by Moab until this time and the subsequent rebellion after the death of Ahab, which motivates Jehoram of Israel to invite Jehoshaphat of Judah to take on Moab together (4–8). Identical phrases to the ones used by the kings in 1 Kings 22 follow, which causes one to suspect that they are two versions of one story. Together with the king of Edom, they choose to come up from the south, which has the advantage of being the least obvious route and the disadvantage of taking them through desert land (8–9), causing a water shortage for the army and the animals. The same motif we found in 1 Kings 22 surfaces with the king of Judah requesting counsel from a prophet of Adonai (3:11), with the result that the three kings go to consult Elisha. Elisha is introduced by a servant of the king and mentioned in close connection with Elijah to enhance the trust the warriors should put in him.

A lively dialogue presents Elisha in a sarcastic exchange with the king of Israel, counseling him to ask the Baalist prophets of his parents for advice and only agreeing to be of service because Jehoshaphat is among the company (13–15). Kings bring out the sharp and caustic side of both Elijah and Elisha. He orders them to get a

120. Some scholars suggest that 1 Kings 22 and 2 Kings 3 are two versions of the same story. So Cohn, *2 Kings*, 18.

121. The wording of the condemnation of Jehoram is not entirely stereotypical. The phrase "to cling to" transgressions is elsewhere in Kings used only of Solomon (1 Kgs 11:2), and the phrase "he did not depart from it" has not been as common in citing the transgressions of the kings of Israel before this moment, although it will be standard as of this point and become especially frequent beginning with 2 Kings 13:2.

string player,[122] and when the musician plays, "the hand of Adonai was upon" Elisha, and he prophecies that water will fill the wadi without a natural phenomenon—"You will not see wind, and you will not see rain" (17). The armies and the animals will be able to drink, and they will go ahead and annihilate Moab. The miracle that ensues is the land filling with water.

2 Kings 3:20–22

20 In the morning, when the offering was going up,
   Look!, water was coming from the Edom road,
   and the land was full of water.
21 And all of Moab had heard
   that the kings had gone up to fight them.
   And they summoned together all
   fit for military service and above
   and took a stand at the border.
22 When they woke up early in the morning
   and the sun rose on the water,
   the Moabites saw the water on the other side
   red as blood.

The Moabites are looking east, and the rising sun colors the water, causing them to believe there are pools of blood from a battle among the advancing armies of Israelites and Edomites. This motivates them to begin the attack, which ends in a devastating victory for the Israelites (23–25). The closing paragraph, however, reports the withdrawal of Israel from a further fight, caused by great "wrath" in the wake of the king of Moab sacrificing of his firstborn son. Verses 26–27 leave puzzlement in their wake. Does the king of Moab succeed in breaking through to the king of Edom on a second attempt? Whose great wrath comes upon Israel (27)? The word used here is often associated with Adonai, but if God's wrath came upon Israel, why not state this? Is this a contest between

---

122. The same noun is used to describe David in 1 Sam 16:16–18. The lyre or harp was considered to be a powerful instrument to conjure spirits.

gods, and because they are in non-Israelite territory, does the god of Moab win? Or is it precisely because Adonai does not stoop to a contest involving the sacrifice of children that wrath ensues? Does the wrath refer to Israelite loathing in the face of child sacrifice?[123] Should the kings have withdrawn the troops after the destruction they wrought, making extreme measures like child sacrifice unnecessary? There is no answer to any of these questions from either prophet or narrator.

### Act IV, Scene 2: Elisha and a Woman Disciple (2 Kings 4:1–7)

*The prophet serves as God's instrument of life.*[124]

Chapter 4 moves away from the battlefield into the realm of everyday life and its problems. The stories share an absence of specific time references and political events; the individuals and groups at their center represent those with specific needs, often related to food but also to disease and death. In the first scene, Elisha faces a woman.

2 KINGS 4:1

And a certain woman
from the women of the disciples of the prophets
cried out to Elisha:
Your servant, my husband, is dead.
You yourself know well that your servant
was one who feared Adonai.
Now the creditor has come
to take my two boys for himself as servants.

---

123. This appears to be the opinion of Marvin Sweeney (*I & II Kings: A Commentary*, OTL [Louisville: Westminster John Knox, 2007], 279, 284) who writes, " 'The Israelites' disgust at Mesha's sacrifice of his son prompts them to break off the battle.'"

124. Hens-Piazza, *1–2 Kings*, 248.

This story begins with "a certain woman" and continues to define her as one of the women of the prophetic circles, either one gathered directly around Elisha or one of the amorphous groups found in many locations, including in his neighborhood as depicted in chapter 2. Hebrew, unlike English, has only one word meaning both "woman" and "wife." Translations and commentaries almost uniformly identify her as a wife of one of the members of the prophetic circle.[125] By repeating the word "women," the narrator clearly attempts to stress the presence of *women* among the disciples.[126] Women prophets are known from the Hebrew Bible by name (Exod 15:20; 2 Kgs 22:14; 2 Chr 34:22; Isa 8:3; Neh 6:14), and we cannot exclude the possibility that the woman who addresses Elisha is herself a member of the prophetic circle, which is the more natural reading of the Hebrew text.[127] As a member of such a circle, she has a claim on Elisha's attention.

125. So NRSV, TNK, and many modern translations. Fox (*The Early Prophets*, 714; cf. Long, *2 Kings*, 49) adheres more closely to the Hebrew text: "a woman from the wives of the sons of the prophets." Würthwein (*Die Bücher der Könige*, 288) translates, "eine Frau, eines des Prophetenjünger," which is as ambiguous as the Hebrew because German, like Hebrew, does not differentiate between "woman" and "wife." He clearly understands her to be the wife of a disciple in his discussion. Sweeney (*I & II Kings*, 287–88) translates "and one woman from the sons of the prophets," and in his discussion of the unit assumes she is the widow of a prophet who had income that she lost with his death, making no distinction between prophets and their disciples. Nelson (*First and Second Kings*, 171) identifies her simply as "the widow" and offers no close analysis of the story. He clearly understands her to be a wife of one of the disciples. Fretheim (*First and Second Kings*, 146) identifies her as "the needy widow of a prophet."

126. For the reading "disciples of the prophets" rather than "sons of the prophets," see p. 172 above.

127. See Johanna W. H. van Wijk-Bos, *Reformed and Feminist: A Challenge to the Church* (Louisville: Westminster John Knox, 1991), 79. Wilda Gafney (*Daughters of Miriam: Women Prophets in Ancient Israel* [Minneapolis: Fortress, 2008], 39) argues the same point: "She could be a woman from the women of the prophetic guild, in other words a disciple herself, since the masculine plural *beney-hannevi'im* can include but would also mask the presence of female disciples."

She is indeed a widow, and about her deceased husband all we hear is that he "feared of Adonai," a phrase—also applied to Obadiah the court official under Ahab (1 Kgs 18:3, 12)—which identifies someone loyal to the God of Israel. The woman facing Elisha lays claim to the same loyalty through her husband, likely also one of the prophetic circle since she refers to him as "your servant," the same term employed by the prophetic circles vis-à-vis Elisha in 2:16.[128] She and her family are evidently not people of means, because the death of her husband has left her with two sons and debts, a situation that allows a creditor to demand her offspring to become his indentured servants until such time as he considers the debt paid, or after six years according to Torah prescription.[129] This practice would deprive her of needed sustenance through contributions to the family by her sons. The woman, widow, mother—soon to be unable to sustain herself—"cried out," a verb used for crying in distress. The Torah states that the widow and fatherless person deserve the special attention of the community and that when these *cry out* to Adonai, God will pay special attention to their cries (Exod 22:22[23]). She does not ask for specific help; she only cries out the tide of woe about to overcome her.

2 KINGS 4:2–4

2   Then said to her Elisha:
    What shall I do for you?
    Tell me: What do you have in the house?
    She said: Your maid has nothing in the house

128. Lacking is a reference to herself as "one who fears Adonai," but the observation about her husband is juxtaposed to the notation about the creditor—perhaps in counterpoint to it, as incurring debts might cast a poor light on her dead husband.

129. Indentured servitude existed in ancient Israel as well as in the rest of the ancient Near East (Exod 21:1–11; Deut 15:12–18) and is not the same as the chattel slavery that existed, for example, in the United States. "Slaves" is thus a misleading translation of what is at stake here. We have little information about how closely ancient Israelites adhered to the law of the seventh-year manumission.

but a flask of oil.
3 He said: Go, ask for yourself containers
 from outside, from your neighbors;
 empty containers, not too few.
4 Then go in, close the door
 behind you and your sons,
 and pour in all these containers.
 What is full put away.

Elisha's first intervention constitutes his asking what he can do for her, meaning that he assumes the position of waiting for the woman to tell him a way forward out of her predicament rather than presuming to know what she needs. Then he asks her to consider her resources. Her despairing reply is that she has "nothing in the house"—nothing, that is, except a small jar of oil. A juglet of oil was enough for the widow of Zarephat, and for this widow also it will be the beginning of her liberation from servitude to debt and anxiety. The advice she receives from Elisha must have sounded exceedingly odd. Requesting empty containers from her neighbors assumes she has something to put in them and flies in the face of her destitute reality. This action demands a great deal of trust on the part of the woman, and it also means that her entire community is involved in facilitating supplies so that the extent of the miracle will depend on both her courage and the generosity of her community. Unlike the very public miracle of the desert filling with water in the previous episode, the increase of the oil will not take place in public. The miracle happens behind closed doors, and the life-giving oil flows in the circle of her small family, the place where she experienced her deprivation most sharply.

### 2 KINGS 4:5–7

5 She went from him
 and closed the door behind her and her sons.
 They brought; she poured.
6 When the containers were full,
 she said to her son:
 Bring me another container,

and he said to her:
There is no other container.
And the oil stopped.

7 She came and told the man of God,
and he said: Go, sell the oil, pay your debts,
and you and your sons will live on the rest.

The story skips the step of the widow gathering the empty containers, taking us immediately into the household to witness the *bringing* and *pouring*. The woman becomes the subject of active verbs:
she *went, closed, poured*, and *said "Bring me"* showing her movement
from panicked inactivity to full participation in what is taking place,
together with her sons—the ones who were on the verge of disappearing into semi-permanent servitude. In the end, she goes to tell
Elisha, who gives her counsel that sends her off into a potentially
independent life. The universe that seemed to close in on the woman
disciple of the prophets has opened up to new possibilities.

Such a short story, told with the greatest economy of words,
paints a vivid picture of circumstances possibly besetting a great
number of common people in Elisha's day. By listening to her cry,
responding to her need, and drawing on her resources both concrete
(a flask of oil) and insubstantial (courage, trust, and faith), he helps
this disciple to become actively engaged in gaining a foothold for
herself in an uncertain social and economic context. Elisha steps
aside, and the woman moves into the center of the action, anticipating her more promising future. In its own way, this account injects
into the downward trajectory of the history of the kingdoms a note
of confidence that, for Israel also, the universe is not closed, and
new possibilities may open up beyond a horizon of loss and despair.

*Act IV, Scene 3: The Great Woman of Shunem (2 Kings 4:8–37)*

*Will the woman bring Elisha back to his calling as "man of God"?*[130]

130. Jopie Siebert-Hommes, "The Widow of Zarephath and the Great

Another story of interactions between Elisha and a woman follows, in which Elisha is initially the one in need who is cared for by a woman of substance, contrasting with the first encounter. I divide the text into five units, beginning with the verses that function to set up the story (8–17). The woman of Shunem goes unnamed, like the widowed disciple, but receives her own epithet.

### 2 KINGS 4:8

One day Elisha passed through Shunem,
and there was an important woman,
and she pressed him to eat food.
So, whenever he passed that way,
he turned aside there to eat food.

The adjective qualifying the Shunammite, literally translated, means "great," indicating a woman of substance, with standing in her community. In the opening section, the main characters are introduced: Elisha, the Shunammite, and eventually Gehazi, the servant of Elisha. The woman's husband is not on the scene as an actor but is mentioned in the discourse. Shunem is a bit north of the Kidron river on the west side of the Jordan, and the phrase "whenever he passed that way" points to Elisha being a wandering prophet without a permanent location to call home who depends on the goodwill and patronage of local people to cater to his needs. The Shunammite is clearly taken with Elisha, as she "pressed him"—literally "took hold of him"—to profit from her hospitality. She suggests that they

Woman of Shunem: A Comparative Analysis of Two Stories," in *Samuel and Kings*, ed. Athalya Brenner, A Feminist Companion to the Bible, Second Series (Sheffield: Sheffield Academic, 2000), 106. Siebert-Hommes continues an analysis begun by Fokkelien van Dijk-Hemmes, "The Great Shunammite Woman and the Man of God: A Two-Part Interpretation of 2 Kings 4:8–37," in *The Double Voice of Her Desire: Texts by Fokkelien van Dijk-Hemmes*, ed. J. Bekkenkamp and F. Dröes (Leiden: Deo, 2004). This article by van Dijk-Hemmes is a translation of her 1989 essay "De grote vrouw uit Sunem en de man Gods: Een tweedelige interpretatie van 2 Koningen 4:8–37," *Mara, Tijdschrift voor feminisme en theologie* 2 (1989): 45–53.

prepare a room for this "holy man of God," furnished with all the necessities, for him to stay in when he passes by their place.

It is in and around this room that the different characters have a conversation, instigated by the desire of Elisha to reward his patron with a suitable return for her efforts (11–17). First, he approaches her through Gehazi, asking if she would like him to put in a good word for her with the king or the commander of the army. To this generous offer, the Shunammite replies with only three words in Hebrew: "In the midst of my people I live" (13). In effect, she says, "No, thanks, I do fine on my own. My people will provide if I have need."[131] The great woman of Shunem knows who she is, is respected in her community, and does not need intercession on her behalf. Rather than wishing for the powerful men around her to do anything for her, *she* likes to do things for *them;* witness her actions for the benefit of Elisha.

Elisha is not satisfied and urges his servant to keep wondering what they "can do for her" (14). Here is a woman who has not declared any need, but he is convinced that she must need something. This reflection causes Gehazi to point out that the woman has "no son" and "her husband is old" (14), implying that the likelihood of her *ever* having a son is very small. Next, the woman is standing at the door opening to the chamber, and Elisha speaks to her directly.

2 KINGS 4:15–17

15 He said: Call her,
and he called her.
And she stood at the door opening.
16 And he said: At this season, next year,
you will embrace a son.
And she said: No, my lord, man of God,
Do not lie to your maid.
17 Then the woman conceived and bore a son,
in the same season the next year,
as had spoken to her Elisha.

131. Mary E. Shields, "Subverting a Man of God, Elevating a Woman: Role and Power Reversals in 2 Kings 4," *JSOT* 58 (1923): 56–69.

Elisha announces the birth of a son with a phrase reminiscent of God speaking to Sarah in Genesis 18:10, 14. Sarah too is at the "opening" of her dwelling and reacts with disbelief in the face of her advanced age (Gen 18:12).[132] The response from the woman with two negatives ("No . . . do not") surrounding a term of address is rare, and we find it elsewhere only in the context of illicit sexual intimacy (Judg 19:23; 2 Sam 13:12).[133] The happy ending in verse 17 suggests a completed story, although the narrator does not comment on further reactions from the Shunammite. While some interpreters understand her to be a "barren woman" about to become a "fully realized mother," we note that the narrative does not present a woman who has needs—a contrasting picture to that of Hannah in 1 Samuel 1 or the widow in 2 Kings 4:1–7.[134] It is clear that the narrative assigns the desire for the woman to have a son to Elisha.

In the second unit (18–24), Elisha is absent, and the focus is on the family, with the action of the son and the father on the one hand and the woman and her husband on the other. The text leaps over pregnancy, birth and early childhood to present the boy old enough to be out in the field by himself, perhaps six or seven years old. Once there, he falls ill and cries, "My head, my head," to his father—the only words he utters in the entire passage (19). The father does not behave with any parental concern and orders a servant to take him to his mother. He subsequently dies in his mother's arms, and she takes him to Elisha's room, puts him on the bed, and leaves him behind a closed door (21). The woman calls for a servant and a donkey to go to the "man of God," an action questioned by her husband, who neglects to ask after the welfare of their son (23). The woman also does not speak of their

132. For other parallels between the annunciation and birth of Isaac story and 2 Kings 4:8–37, see Gershon Hepner, "Three's a Crowd at Shunem: Elisha's Misconduct with the Shunamite Reflects a Polemic against Prophetism," *ZAW* (2010): 387–400.

133. Shields, "Subverting a Man of God," 118.

134. Sweeney (*I & II Kings*, 289) refers to "the barren woman" while Long (*2 Kings*, 56) comments that Elisha "hints at the Shunammite's future transformation into a fully realized mother." Hens-Piazza (*1–2 Kings*, 252) speaks of the "shame of childlessness in a patriarchal society."

child but merely assures her husband that she will be back and that all is well.[135] Then she is on her way to find Elisha, who is on Mount Carmel. The action slows down for verbal exchanges in the third unit (25–28).

Unlike the Shunammite's husband, Elisha's first words through Gehazi, whom he sends to meet her, concern everyone's welfare: "Are you well? Is your husband well? And is the boy well?" (26). Reflective of the haste with which everything is taking place, the text does not report the woman's meeting with Gehazi, abbreviating the account to make it sound as if she responds directly to Elisha while she is still some distance away. Gehazi, on Elisha's behalf, asks her three times if everyone is "well," and she answers "well."

2 KINGS 4:27–28

27 When she reached the man of God on the mountain,
   she grasped his feet.
   Then Gehazi came near to push her away,
   and the man of God said:
   Let her be, for her heart is bitter,
   and Adonai is hiding it from me
   and is not telling me.
28 She said: Did I ask for a son from my lord?
   Did I not say: Do not put me at ease?

The verb in verse 27, where she takes hold of Elisha's feet, is the same as the one used in verse 8 for her "pressing" food on Elisha. Gehazi tries to prevent her, but his master tells him to let her be, for he perceives the bitterness of her heart, or soul (Hebrew *nefesh*). Bitterness of the spirit or soul occurs in the text when people are faced with loss through death (Ruth 1:13, 20; 1 Sam 30:6). Yet that is all the "man of God" perceives, for he states that God is hiding the truth from him in a double statement: *hiding* and *not telling*. The Shunammite responds with a double rhetorical question that in its

---

135. In 4:23, she says, "Shalom"—in modern English parlance, "It's okay." She will repeat this answer to Gehazi.

harshness makes clear to Elisha what has happened: Did I ask? Did I not say? I told you so! (28).

Elisha tries to solve the situation by sending Gehazi with his staff to put on the face of the boy, presumably in an effort to resuscitate him (29–31). The great woman of Shunem refuses to leave Elisha and, in an echo of Elisha's earlier pledge to Elijah, swears she will not leave him: "By the life of Adonai and your own life, I will not leave you" (30; cf. 2:2, 4, 6). In her failing to rush back home with Gehazi, she shows herself to have little trust in his effectiveness—an intuition that proves correct, as Gehazi fails to raise the boy. It is not until Elisha himself goes into the house and finds the boy lying on his bed that he, behind closed doors, prays to Adonai and performs the act of raising the boy to life (32–35). The action is depicted in detail as a kind of mouth to mouth resuscitation.

2 KINGS 4:36–37

36 He called Gehazi and said:
   Call this Shunammite. And he called her.
   And she came to him,
   and he said: Take your son.
37 She came and fell at his feet
   and bowed to the ground
   then took her son and went out.

In the end, this is not a story of a miraculous birth but of the miracle of resurrection from death. It is also a story that raises questions.

The first two units (8–23) begin with a type reversal for which we may not be prepared. The woman of Shunem is not in a victimized position or in any kind of need, a fact reiterated four times in the opening unit: by her being called a "great" (i.e., important) woman, by her providing for Elisha, by her confident statement in response to his first question, and by her protest to the second offer. It is, after all, possible that even in a patriarchal society there are women who do not long for offspring. The Shunammite is the most active of the four characters in the episode. She is presented by the narrator as "taking hold of Elisha" to give him food, she has "knowledge" about his identity (a "holy man of God," vv. 8–9), and she takes the initiative to make a guest room and furnish it comfortably. She consults her husband in this endeavor but clearly does not wait for his consent (10). She is deferential to Elisha, calling him "my lord," but speaks her mind, expressing self-confidence and mistrust. When her son dies, she keeps her own counsel, not broadcasting his death to the household, and sets out to find Elisha. In the matter of her journey to Mount Carmel, she informs her husband but again clearly goes her own way (22–24). She is a member of a family of means, able to construct a guest room and host the man of God and his servant. They have servants and donkeys, signs of the well-to-do. The text gives no hint that she experiences lack of any kind until the death of her son, when she sets out to find the man of God, the source of her present trouble, on whom she counts to provide a solution. In the third and fourth units (25–30) she lies to Gehazi and does not reveal her secret until she is on the mountain *taking hold* of his "feet," a well-known euphemism for genitalia in the Bible, and reproaching him for granting her something she did not ask for only to take it away (28). Finally, she echoes Elisha's words to his departed master, putting her trust in him rather than his servant. She disappears from the action when Elisha revives her son and at the end surfaces once more to leave the story together with her son.

Fokkelien van Dijk-Hemmes suggests that the Shunammite speaks more "from a desire for the man of God than for a child" and that "the woman desires Elisha."[136] Gershon Hepner has pointed to many words that, in his opinion, denote sexual intimacy and concludes that the Shunammite importuned Elisha, taking "the initiative in the relationship."[137]

---

136. Van Dijk-Hemmes, *The Double Voice*, 152.

137. Hepner, "Three's a Crowd," 392. See also Bergen's (*Elisha and the End of Prophetism*, 104) overall negative interpretation of Elisha: "In the end I am left with a picture of a prophet whose claim to power/status arises from his ability to perform unnecessary miracles." Thalia Gur-Klein (http://www.lectio .unibe.ch/03_2/gur.htm) puts forward that "sexual hospitality existed in the ancient Near East, including ancient Israel," and that certain stories in the Hebrew Bible provide possible examples of narratives with residual traces of this practice, including the story of Elisha and the woman of Shunem in 2 Kings 4.

Elisha in this episode is a "man of God" who is "pressed" by a woman to "eat food" in Shunem and who "turned aside there." The name of the location Shunem occurs only here and in the first chapters of 1 Kings as the origin of Abishag, who attended David (1 Kgs 1:3)—a beautiful young woman who was brought to the king's bed. It is thus a place that brings to mind activity of specific intimacy. The emphasis on eating food (twice in v. 8) draws attention to Elisha's physical needs and perhaps alludes to more than basic nourishment.[138] The verb for "turn aside" (*sur*) is found three times in the opening verses (8, 10, 11). While this can be a neutral action, it can also denote a significant or dangerous turn of events and is used as a technical term in Deuteronomy for the people's turning to the worship of other gods (Deut 7:4; 9:12, 16; 11:16, 28; 17:11, 20; 28:14; 31:29).[139] The term Elisha uses for the birth announcement is that the woman will "embrace" a son (16), a verb that can certainly occur in connection with affectionate family embraces but also with sexual intimacy (Prov 5:20; Song 2:6; 8:3). The text skips any reference to the act of impregnation; no man here "knew" the Shunammite (cf. 1 Sam 1:19), leaving one to speculate about the identity of the father. Elisha refers to the great woman of Shunem as "this Shunammite" to Gehazi when they are in her house (12, 36), and "that Shunammite" when he spies her from afar on Mount Carmel (25); if this is not an outright disrespectful reference, it is still a term that puts verbal distance between himself and the woman.[140] A shift takes place in his attitude when she approaches him on Mount Carmel. He does not dissuade her from taking hold of his "feet," he discerns her bitter grief, and he confesses that Adonai is hiding the truth from him. He sends Gehazi to do the work he should be doing himself, and once the Shunammite has made her vow not to leave him, *he* follows *her*

---

138. Hepner ("Three's a Crowd," 392) maintains that "eating bread" is an expression "that can denote sexual intercourse." The verb I have translated with "press," from the root *hazaq* (lit. "to seize, take hold") is also used in connection with sexual intimacy (2 Sam 13:14; Prov 7:13).

139. Cf. Judg 18:3; 19:15. See van Wijk-Bos, *The End of the Beginning*, 293–94.

140. Adding the demonstrative pronoun to someone's name can indeed be derogatory, as in David's references to Goliath (1 Sam 17:26, 32, 33, 36, 37).

instead of the other way around. In the end, he prays and achieves results, but the character of Elisha has become unstable in the narrative. He is consistently called "the man of God." First, he has his needs of food and shelter met—of a bed to lie on—and one wonders if other needs are met also. Gehazi observes that the woman has no son, but there is another person in the story without a son: the prophet himself.

The servant Gehazi is present throughout the story and consistently acts as the person who mediates between Elisha and the woman both in the initial unit and subsequently at Mount Carmel (11–16, 25–26). In both instances, Elisha calls on Gehazi to speak to the woman, and in both it is not clear to whom she is speaking because the text is unclear about her location and skips directly to her speech, blurring the distance between the woman and Elisha. Gehazi speaks directly only twice, both times to Elisha, and both times his words refer to the woman's lack of a son: "She has no son, and her husband is old" (14) and "the lad has not awakened" (31). He tries to push the woman aside on Mount Carmel when she comes close to Elisha (perhaps too close for his liking), and he fails in raising the child. There is nothing here to condemn him, and he stays a rather flat character, but the woman clearly does not trust him, and there may be an allusion to some negative qualities in his character embedded in Elisha's admonishment not to speak with anyone when he sends him to try to revive the boy (29).

The husband of the Shunammite remains a vague presence, as does the child, who mainly serves the purpose of being brought back to life. Both speak only once: the child when he is in the field and cries, "My head, my head"—words that could point to a question about his origin.[141] The father asks why his wife is going to Elisha when there is no holy day to observe (23), and she answers with a lie. The father does not behave like a father to the boy when he falls ill, and the mother does not treat her husband as the father when she keeps her son's death a secret.

141. Van Dijk-Hemmes, *The Double Voice*, 153: "The boy wants to know who his head, his father is. He wants to know where he belongs and where he comes from."

If Elisha is indeed the biological father of the child, as the text insinuates—either by the Shunammite's initiative or his own—does the narrator intend to portray Elisha as an example of an immoral adulterer? Is this narrative indeed a part of a "polemic against prophetism"?[142] I believe that Yairah Amit comes closer to the truth by identifying the story as one of "development."[143] The prophet, no matter how powerful, shows himself here to be not as connected with God as he should be and falters in his task as Adonai's servant. He behaves with arrogance toward the Shunammite woman; his freeing the woman from her childless state is an "answer to the prophet's needs rather than hers."[144] Amit believes that such a story was needed in order to maintain the boundary between God and the prophet, who is an emissary.[145] In light of the power to which the prophets Elijah and Elisha have access, identification of the "man of God" with the Deity is a danger to be averted. The story of Elisha and the great woman of Shunem shows an all too human prophet and guards against aggrandizing his person. In the meantime, the legend has set on the stage not only a prophet in all his humanity but also a woman who, even while she goes unnamed, comes to vibrant life in the story in all her pride, self-confidence, and vulnerability.

### Act IV, Scene 4: Food Matters (2 Kings 4:38–44)

*Despite [Israel's] apostate kings and people . . . God's power is yet available through Elijah's successor.*[146]

The two short stories that close the chapter both concern food in times of scarcity. In both, Elisha is found in the company of a circle of people—prophets' disciples, perhaps his own acolytes, and oth-

---

142. Hepner, "Three's a Crowd in Shunem," 387, 399.

143. Yairah Amit, "A Prophet Tested: Elisha, the Great Woman of Shunem, and the Story's Double Message," *BibInt* 11 (2003): 279–94.

144. Amit, "A Prophet Tested," 288.

145. Amit, "A Prophet Tested," 291.

146. Long, 2 *Kings*, 65.

ers. It is quite remarkable how much objects pertaining to everyday life come into view in all the scenes of chapter 4. Their appearance highlights how infrequent they are in biblical narrative, and they serve to draw readers and listeners directly into the accounts. Utensils, a flask, pots and pans, foodstuff, oil and bread, gourds, corn, a room with its furnishings, a bed, a table, a seat, and a lamp are all key parts of the stories. They take us far from court and Temple into the households of Israel.

In verses 38–41 of this chapter, the "disciples of the prophets sitting in his presence" function as the household of Elisha. Almost as an aside, the text reports "a famine in the land," evoking the picture of a crowd of hungry people. In light of this statement, Elisha's order for his lad to put a "large pot" on the fire to cook a dish for the circle around him sounds almost as illogical as the widow's asking her neighbors for empty containers in the first scene. With what is the servant to fill the pot? Is he supposed to conjure vegetables out of nothing? One of the company goes out to the field, comes back with produce from the field, and cooks it without knowing its properties. The stew either tastes terrible or makes the people feel terrible so that they cry "death in the pot, man of God!" (40). Elisha clears up the matter by throwing meal into the pot, and all is well: "There was no longer anything bad in the pot" (41). A self-sufficient prophet solves a food problem by perhaps natural means, although we may not understand exactly how "meal" would help matters. For the time being, the wolf of hunger is kept at bay.

In the second story (42–44), there is food, but not enough for the large crowd around the "man of God." The word "give" occurs five times, along with the fourfold "eat" and the double mention of "leftover" to draw the ironic picture of surfeit where there should have been scarcity. Elisha is mentioned in the first unit, while the second speaks only of "the man of God," who makes a prophetic announcement: "Thus says Adonai" (43). The word from God is to "eat and have leftovers," creating the impression that the multiplication of food comes directly from Adonai with no action needed from the prophet. The chapter is thus framed by two feeding miracles in which the role of the prophet is minor: the multiplication of the oil behind closed doors (1–7) and the multiplication of bread and corn on God's command. Each story exhibits miraculous intervention to make life possible in the midst of scarcity and death.

### Act IV, Scene 5: The Great Man of Aram (2 Kings 5)

*It is surely ironic that such an insignificant little girl could deliver words of such profound importance.*[147]

The drama of Naaman, an Aramean general with a skin disease, plays out in three parts. In the first (1–12), Naaman is introduced while still in his home country. He travels to Israel and refuses the treatment recommended by Elisha. In the second (13–18), Naaman is healed and swears fealty to Adonai before Elisha, who refuses to take a gift in payment and sends him on his way. In the third (19–27), Gehazi resurfaces to request a gift from Naaman through subterfuge, an act for which he is severely punished. A tale that opened with a Syrian who has an affliction of the skin ends with Elisha's servant suffering the same disease.[148] Naaman has a role throughout, taking center stage in the first part, sharing the action in the second with Elisha, and gradually disappearing in the third, in which Gehazi first takes a central role before eventually sharing the stage with Elisha.

The Hebrew word *lifney* ("in the presence of/before") serves as a keyword to put individuals in relation to one another. As the story begins, Naaman is "a great man *before* his lord" while a "little girl from the land of Israel serves *before* the wife of Naaman" (1–2). This young captive wishes, "Oh, that my master were *before* the prophet who is in Samaria" (3). As the story progresses, the word for "before him" (*lepanaw*) starts to play a crucial role, with Naaman, now healed, *standing before* Elisha who *stands before* Adonai; meanwhile, Gehazi has his loot carried *before him* and in the end stands *near his lord*, ending up with a skin affliction and completing the

147. Jean Kyoung Kim, "Reading and Retelling Naaman's Story (2 Kings 5)," *JSOT* 30 (2005): 53.

148. Both Cohn (*2 Kings*, 35–42) and Long (*2 Kings*, 66–79) provide excellent analyses of this chapter.

oppositional picture with Naaman, who was *before his lord* with his skin disease when the narrative opened. The story is full of motion: Naaman travels to Israel to the house of Elisha, dips into the waters of the Jordan, returns to Elisha, and goes on his way home. Gehazi runs after Naaman, takes the silver from his lads, secures it in his house, and stands before his master. The only stationary person appears to be Elisha.

Naaman receives a surplus of accolades in verse 1.

### 2 KINGS 5:1–3

1  Now Naaman was commander of the army
of the king of Aram,
a great man before his lord,
and he stood in high regard
because by him Adonai gave victory to Aram.
And the man was a strong warrior
with a skin disease.

2  Arameans had gone out in war bands
and taken captive from the land of Israel
a young girl who served before the wife of Naaman.
3  She said to her mistress:
Oh, that my master were before the prophet
who is in Samaria.
Then he would cure him of his skin disease.

A counterpart to the "great woman of Shunem," Naaman is a "great man." He is held in "high regard" because he has won an important battle, and he is a "strong warrior." After all this praise, the sting comes in the last word of the verse: he has a "skin disease" (*metsora*). We do a disservice to the lines by introducing qualifying conjunctions, revealing too soon what the sentence leaves till the end.[149]

---

149. The NRSV's "the man, though a mighty warrior, was a leper" is typical in this regard. There is an important buildup in Hebrew that should be left intact.

In the first two units, the word "skin disease" is emphasized by its position at the close of the sentence. The disease was certainly not leprosy, or Hansen's disease, which did not exist in the Mediterranean world of the period, would not have been curable, and would have made it impossible for a person to fulfill important functions such as Naaman's.[150] Noteworthy is the statement about Adonai granting "victory to Aram," claiming intervention from the God of Israel on behalf of the affairs of foreign peoples.[151]

Opposite Naaman the great is a young girl who fell into the hands of Aramean bands raiding her country (2). This girl is not great in any sense; literally, she is called "a little girl." She is captive, and she serves her mistress, the wife of Naaman. From this unlikely source come words that hold a promise for healing: "if only." If only he were in the presence of, *before*, the prophet in her home country in the capital Samaria, he would be cured of his illness (3). We have so far not witnessed Elisha healing sick people, and Naaman's story will present a unique example. The female in the story is of no account, a "little" girl, not a "great woman," and yet she becomes the channel through which the waters of healing begin to flow.

150. Although allowing for this reality, most translations and commentaries persist in using the word "leprosy," creating a mistaken impression and omitting attention to the nature of Naaman's affliction. As *The Hebrew and Aramaic Lexicon of the Old Testament* argues, the Hebrew *tsara'at* and the verb derived from it, *tsara'*, point to vitiligo and related diseases (*HALOT*, 3:1056–57, s.v. *tsara'at*). Vitiligo causes loss of pigmentation, which explains the expression "white as snow" used to describe the effect on Gehazi in 2 Kgs 5:27. Alter (*Ancient Israel*, 751n3), who observes the difference between the disease mentioned in the Bible and leprosy, opts for "skin-blanch," which is accurately descriptive. Fox (*The Early Prophets*, 721, 722, 725) leaves the word untranslated as Tzaraat. A disadvantage of the translation "skin-disease" is that *tsara'at* was not confined to skin and could be found in clothes, furnishings and the walls of a house (Lev 13:47–58; 14:34–53). For insight on the nature of the biblical *tsara'at* and leprosy, see John F. A. Sawyer, "A Note on the Etymology of Tsara'at," *VT* 26 (1976): 241–45; Samson O. Olanisebe, "Laws of Tzara'at in Leviticus 13–14 and Medical Leprosy Compared," *JBQ* 42 (2014): 121–27. Adhering to the word "leprosy" may have the unfortunate byproduct of maintaining the cultural prejudices that accompany this disease.

151. Presumably, the victory referred to is the one recorded in 1 Kings 22.

Word reaches the king of Aram, who decides this is a matter to be taken care of between kings. He sends Naaman off with a load of gifts and a letter to the king of Israel, asking him to cure the man of his skin disease. This does not work, of course, and causes a dramatic and humorous scene with the Israelite monarch tearing his clothes, uttering sarcastic questions, and wondering if this kind of challenge is in reality a threat from the Arameans (6–7). Relations between Aram and Israel are clearly somewhat fraught at this time, and "none of the power people 'get it.'"[152] When Elisha gets wind of Naaman's visit and the king's reaction, he asks for Naaman to come to him: "And he will know that there is a prophet in Israel" (8).

Everything comes to a halt as Naaman arrives with his entire entourage and stands "*before* the door of the house of Elisha," who does not bother to greet his important guest but sends a messenger out to give him instructions on what to do in order for his flesh to become "clean." Washing himself seven times in the Jordan sounds ridiculous to Naaman, who had an entirely different idea of what the prophet would do to accomplish his healing (10–12). Like the king before him, he engages in sarcastic rhetorical questions as he wonders how all the waters of Israel stack up against the rivers of his own country. Naaman's words are presented as an interior dialogue so that one gets a direct insight into his mood and also into what he thought would have happened during a healing: the waving of a hand "on the spot" and calling on "the name of Adonai his God." He apparently has a clear idea about what constitutes an appropriate ritual for his healing. To underline his mood, the text ends this unit by stating that he "turned around and went away in anger" (12).

It could have ended here had not Naaman's servants intervened, pointing out that it was after all a rather simple thing he was asked to do, he who could and *would* have taken on something so much greater! The servants, like the little Israelite girl, are of course far below Naaman in standing and power, but to his credit he heeds their words.

---

152. Brueggemann, *1 & 2 Kings*, 338.

2 KINGS 5:14

He went down and dipped into the Jordan seven times
according to the word of the man of God,
and his flesh was restored as the flesh of a young boy,
and he was clean.

Naaman gets his ritual, for the terminology in this sentence makes
clear that this is exactly what is taking place. Elisha's messenger
told Naaman to *wash* seven times in the Jordan, a verb repeated
in Naaman's soliloquy as well as by the servants (10, 12, 13). At the
point of Naaman's immersion, the verb changes to "dip" (*taval*), a
word applied to ritual cleansing in half of its occurrences (eight out
of sixteen) and specifically related to skin disease in Leviticus 14:6,
16, and 51. "To be clean" (*tahar*) is also the word for *cleansing* in a
ritual context and is especially dominant in Priestly material in the
Torah (Lev 13:6, 13, 17, 23). The flesh of Naaman is "restored"—literally "it returned"—to that of a "young/little boy." A *little girl* had
set in motion the journey of Naaman that turns his flesh into that
of a *little boy.* The waters of the Jordan have turned Naaman into a
cleansed Israelite prepared to appear before Adonai.[153]

How the experience affects Naaman is made clear by his "return" to the man of God *before* whom he now stands and confesses
his faith in the God of Israel (15–19).[154] When Elisha refuses a gift,
Naaman asks for soil to take back to his country so he will be able
to bring proper sacrifice, and he prays for forgiveness in case he has
to join his king in prostration before Aram's deity.[155] Elisha sends

153. Purity and impurity regulations set boundaries on what and who is in
a state of holiness, as the body was viewed as the vehicle for the approach to
God. See Johanna W. H. van Wijk-Bos, *Making Wise the Simple: The Torah in
Christian Faith and Practice* (Grand Rapids: Eerdmans, 2005), 213–23. I thank
my former student Manasses Fonteles for a conversation in which the ritual
expectations of Naaman became clear.

154. The confession of Naaman is all the more remarkable since there has
been no mention of prayer or Elisha calling on God's name in the account.

155. The Aramean deity is called Rimmon, i.e. "pomegranate," belittling
the name of the god Ramman.

him away in peace. Naaman's being healed of a skin disease has forced from him the acknowledgment that there is "no God in all the world except in Israel," and the story of a cure has become a conversion story. In addition, he promises to worship no other god than Adonai. His request regarding soil does not bind God to one location but recognizes the "continuing import of links to the particular community that is inextricably associated with the confession and guards its integrity."[156]

Once again, it could have ended here. The story has a sad ending, however, when Gehazi, who most likely overheard his master refusing "by the life of Adonai" the gift offered by Naaman, invokes the same oath to do the opposite (20–24). He runs after the Syrian commander and tricks him into donating a part of the treasure he carries: two talents of silver and two gala garments,[157] carrying them to his house and hiding the matter from Elisha.

## 2 Kings 5:25–27

25 Then he came in and stood near his lord,[158]
and Elisha said to him:
From where, Gehazi?
He said: Your servant went neither here nor there.
26 He said to him:

---

156. Fretheim, *First and Second Kings*, 155.

157. The Hebrew word rendered "gala garments" or "party clothes" is found only eleven times in the Hebrew Bible, six of them in the Samson story and here (Judg 14:12, 13, 19; 2 Kgs 5:5, 22, 23). The fancy garment is found elsewhere only in the Joseph narrative (Gen 45:22). Elsewhere it means "change" (1 Kgs 5:28[14]; Job 10:17; 14:14; Ps 55:20[19]). The link with the Joseph and Samson tales suggests the connection of party clothes with trickery. Also, they likely represent affluence outside the reach of common people. The treasure illicitly taken by Achan during the destruction of Jericho also included a piece of clothing, "a fine robe from Sinar" (Josh 7:21, 24).

158. The preposition in this phrase is not *lifney* ("before") but *'el* ("next to, by" or even "opposite, against"). Gehazi no longer stands *before* Adonai or *before* his master.

> Did not my heart go
> when a man turned away from his chariot to meet you?
> Is it a time to take silver
> and to take clothes,
> olives and vineyards,
> flocks and cattle,
> male and female servants?
> 27 Now the disease of Naaman will cling to you
> and to your offspring forever.
> And he went from him, diseased as snow.

Gehazi no longer stands *before* his master (and Adonai) but near or opposite him. He has one more chance to speak the truth, but dissembles about his whereabouts, challenging the power of Elisha's knowledge. The parallels between the Naaman story and the one of Elisha and the woman of Shunem are especially prominent in this unit about Gehazi. Like the Shunammite, he *runs* after someone to receive a favor (4:22; 5:20). The same question goes back and forth between Naaman and Gehazi as between the Shunammite and Elisha, and like the Shunammite, Gehazi states that it is "shalom" (4:26; 5:21–22). For the Shunammite this was a lie; for Gehazi it is a surface truth but in reality a lie because things are far from "well" with him as he deceives Naaman and his master. In the story about the Shunammite he was ineffective and not entirely trustworthy; in this story, the negative qualities of his character—there only hinted at (see p. 190 above)—come to the surface.

Elisha accuses Gehazi with a rhetorical question: "Is it a time to *take*?"—a verb with strong resonance in the story. In their exchange, Naaman had urged Elisha to *take a gift* (lit. a "blessing"), something which Elisha, swearing "by the life of Adonai" refused: "I will not *take* it," even when Naaman urged him again to *take* it (15–16). In verse 20, where Gehazi is named "the lad of Elisha, the man of God," he declares that his master "let this Aramean off by *not taking*" and makes the decision to go after Naaman, swearing "by the life of Adonai . . . to *take* from him." Eventually, he *takes* from the hands of his lads (24) the gift Naaman urged him to *take* (23). With his inquiry, Elisha asks whether this is the moment for *taking*. The goods he mentions do not seem to fit the crime, but the intention is not so much to present a literal list as to associate Gehazi "with the worst excesses of corruption" under the monarchy (cf. 1 Sam 8:14–17).[159] Many of the stories in the Elijah and Elisha cycle depict the time as one of scarcity for common people. Elisha's presence does not represent *taking* but *giving*—opportunities for restored life and abundance of provisions. In the Naaman story, the one who *took* from Naaman's hand in the end also took from him the disease that had plagued him.

## Act V: Elisha and the War with Aram (2 Kings 6:1–8:6)

*This war, like every war, sends out a ripple of costs that finally settles on vulnerable women and resourceless lepers.*[160]

War with Aram is at the forefront of this set of narratives, with Elisha involved in diplomacy and intrigue. There is a miracle story at the beginning in the midst of his disciples (6:1–7) and at the end a reference to one of his most phenomenal acts in the private sphere with a return of the woman of Shunem (8:1–6). In between these two short episodes, war with Aram results in a temporary peace brought about by Elisha's efforts (6:8–33), and when hostilities recommence, Elisha foretells the alleviation of besieged Samaria through divine intervention (7:1–20). Although the activities of Elisha are not finished after the reappearance of the Shunammite, no other examples of supernatural interventions through active engagement on his part are recorded thenceforth.

### Act V, Scene 1: A Place to Live (2 Kings 6:1–7)

*The miracle seems both trivial and pointless.*[161]

159. Cohn, *2 Kings*, 42.
160. Brueggemann, *1 & 2 Kings*, 354.
161. Nelson, *First and Second Kings*, 184.

Three verses serve to introduce the issue of cramped quarters for Elisha's disciples, for which they themselves propose a logical solution: gathering enough beams to build a place to live in. The word *place* occurs in every sentence, forming a leading motif in the passage. There is no *place* for them where they are living *before* Elisha, who by this time evidently has a permanent dwelling, and they need more room. They propose going to the Jordan to cut logs, and on Elisha giving his consent, one of them begs him to accompany them. Clearly, the disciples are self-supportive and capable of the rough work it takes to construct a dwelling from the ground up.

The Jordan is important because of its role in the supernatural incident that follows, providing a link to the story of Naaman. As they cut down trees, one of them, perhaps the same one who spoke up earlier, identified only as "the one" (3, 5), drops the ax—identified simply by its metal, "the iron"—in the river and cries out that it was a borrowed item, a small personal catastrophe on account of its cost. Upon this outcry, Elisha throws a log in the water at the spot where the ax head sank, and the iron comes to the surface as if the wood had magnetic power. The iron appropriates the properties of wood, floating in the river. The story once again shows off Elisha's powers and bridges the distance between the natural element, wood, and the human-made one, an iron tool. "Under the holy man's power, this gap is closed by a reversal of natures."[162] A seemingly "trivial and pointless" story becomes an opening to the predicaments faced by Israel in the sequel; the iron that floats is a harbinger of a far greater display of power to come.

### Act V, Scene 2: Blindsiding the Enemy (2 Kings 6:8–23)

*A high point in the story of Elisha.*[163]

A first unit (8–14) announces hostilities between Aram and Israel, with the spotlight first on the court of the unnamed Aramean king,

---

162. Nelson, *First and Second Kings*, 185.
163. Bergen, *Elisha and the End of Prophetism*, 127.

who needs a *place* to establish a military foothold inside Israel. These plans go awry because "the man of God in Israel" counsels the king to give the place where the Arameans are lurking a wide berth. The *place*—again a key word—is kept as vague as possible; the king refers to "such and such a place" and the man of God to "this place," which turns into "the place of which the man of God spoke" in verse 10. The mysterious nature of the location heralds far greater mysteries ahead. The failure of Aram to lie in wait in a location unbeknownst to Israel happens repeatedly so that the king of Aram suspects a double agent among his servants is giving the show away each time. The servants, however, enlighten him on the matter, telling him that Elisha the prophet in Israel is acquainted with even the most private conversations of the king of Aram and tells them to his king! The enraged monarch orders them to find Elisha and dispatches horses and chariots with a strong army to surround Dothan at night.[164] The challenge to Elisha has been issued.

What takes place is indeed a spectacle of grandeur on the Israelite side, but ironically, it will be visible to very few (15–20). To highlight the irony, the episode is all about *seeing* and *not seeing*. On discovering the Aramean army in the morning, Elisha's servant cries out in alarm. Elisha responds that there is no reason to fear for "there are more with us than with them." Upon Elisha's prayer, the servant's eyes are opened and "Look! The mountain was filled with horses," and "chariots of fire" surround Elisha (17). When the army comes down, Elisha prays that it may be struck with blindness, that is, that it may *not see*. The most peculiar spectacle ensues, with Elisha leading a blind and also silent army, telling it to follow him and that he will bring them to "the man you are seeking." As soon as they arrive in Samaria, Elisha prays again that they may *see* and "Look!, they were inside Samaria!" (20).

---

164. Dothan is the place where Joseph was cast in a pit by his brothers, a story most likely familiar to the ancient audience (Gen 37:17); perhaps the narrator intends this infamous spot to raise anticipation of an impending capture of Elisha.

2 KINGS 6:21–22

21 The king of Israel said to Elisha,
  when he saw them:
  Shall I strike them, strike them down, my father?
22 He said: You will not strike them down!
  What you have captured with your sword and bow
  you may strike down.
  Put food and water before them,
  so they may eat and drink
  and go to their lord.

The king *sees* the Arameans and wants to kill them. In this exchange, the deferential tone from king to prophet is striking, as is the commanding voice of the prophet, to which the monarch responds by preparing a banquet for the prisoners of war. This incident leaves unanswered the question of Elisha's aim. Was he trying to shame the Aramean soldiers and their king?[165] Or is he hoping to achieve a détente and dissuade Aram from further warfare? Has Elisha acted correctly or too much on his own steam? Should he have let the horses and fiery chariots have their way with the Aramean soldiers in the mountains around Dothan? Is there something he does not *see*? For the time being the ploy has worked, and whether in shame or with hot coals heaped on their aggressive heads, the Arameans cease sending raids to Israel (23).

### Act V, Scene 3: The Siege of Samaria (2 Kings 6:24–33)

*The mothers and their children are being consumed by the insatiable cravings of . . . political and religious leaders.*[166]

---

165. Gina Hens-Piazza (*Nameless, Blameless, and without Shame: Two Cannibal Mothers before a King* [Collegeville, MN: Liturgical Press, 2003], 40–41) views the occasion as "a stinging blow of humiliation in an ancient cultural system of honor and shame."

166. Hens-Piazza, *Nameless, Blameless*, 83.

On the heels of the peaceful relations between Aram and Israel that close the preceding chapter follows the statement that "afterward, Ben-hadad, the king of Aram . . . went up and besieged Samaria." While a temporary peace between the two countries possibly existed for a substantial amount of time before evolving into warfare at a later date, the text avoids such a conclusion by putting the two events—abstinence from war and a ferocious pursuit of it—in close proximity, moving from one to the other in sequential verses. The siege of Samaria causes a famine, of which the horrifying consequences are illustrated by a short vignette involving a woman and the king of Israel (24–29). Food costs rise to incredible highs, and foodstuff is consumed that no one would eat at other times (25).[167] The consumption of food that is normally off-limits is exemplified by the story of the woman who accosts the king while he is walking on the city wall. She cries out for him to "help" her, and he replies that only God can help her. The means to help her, threshing floor and winepress (he assumes she needs food), are outside his reach (27). "What is the matter with you?" he asks. Her answer, as brief as it is, puts before the king the gravity and horrifying reality of common people.

Her two sentences are filled with verbs rooted in abundance: "give," "cook," and "eat"—the latter used four times. It is the object of the *giving*, *cooking*, and *eating* that unveils the excruciating truth. What she describes is an "unthinkable controversy" between herself and another woman, with whom she agreed "to eat their children together, one child after the other. They have already boiled and consumed this woman's child, but now the other woman has broken the pact and hidden her offspring."[168]

Famines arose in the ancient world on account of different causes, in Israel most often due to the absence of expected rainfall. Here the cause is war, a time when the powerbrokers of the world

---

167. Viz. the "the head of a donkey" and "pigeon dung." A donkey is an unclean animal. While pigeon dung is sometimes explained as the name of a plant (so Fox, *The Early Prophets*, 728), others take it literally as an example of the filth people will eat at a time of starvation (so Alter, *Ancient Israel*, 759n25).

168. Hens-Piazza, *Nameless, Blameless*, 42.

have decided there is no other solution than subduing the enemy by cutting off food supplies. In the modern world, war still causes famine. Many are familiar with the siege of Leningrad in the fall and winter of 1941 and the disastrous famine that followed. There are documented cases of cannibalism during that period.[169] Less known is the infamous "hunger winter" in the last months of the Second World War when more than twenty thousand people died of hunger in the Netherlands. We have read of famines in the Historical Books, but no passage has so vividly described the weight of it on ordinary people. This text echoes forth in the cry of Lamentations: "The hands of compassionate women/ have cooked their children;/ they became their food/ in the disaster of my people" (Lam 4:10). Yet the text in 2 Kings does not linger on their plight. It is not even clear what the woman whose son was consumed wants from the king. Neither is it known whether the children were already dead or if they killed the one they ate.

Because the report is so shocking, we may not pause to consider that the mother who cries out to the king has her focus on the wrong issue—on the fact that her companion reneged on their agreement rather than on the immorality of the act. She is thus a symbol of a world that has gone "out of kilter . . . an inverted world in which social relations have totally broken down."[170] The cannibalistic mothers stand in for all the victims of this war, of which they were not the cause and which they cannot bring to an end. "That the mothers agree to consume their own flesh and blood is not so much an indictment of them as villains; rather it is evidence of their own annihilation as victims."[171] The ancient

169. The siege of Leningrad claimed more than one and a half million victims—soldiers and civilians—and cases of cannibalism were documented by an arm of the Soviet Union's interior ministry after the war.

170. Stuart Lasine, "Jehoram and the Cannibal Mothers (2 Kings 6:24–33): Solomon's Judgment in an Inverted World," *JSOT* 50 (1991): 39. It is not clear if Lasine assumes that the mothers actually killed one child rather than consuming one who had already died. One might assume that at least one of the boys is still alive in view of his being hidden by his mother, but even so we cannot be sure.

171. Hens-Piazza, *Nameless, Blameless*, 94.

reader/listener may well have paused and concluded that such a fate was announced as a curse on the people who had given up loyalty to Adonai: "And you will eat the fruit of your womb/ the flesh of your sons and daughters/ given to you by Adonai your God/ in the siege and oppression/ by which your enemy will oppress you" (Deut 28:53).

The reaction of the king, tearing his clothes to reveal the sackcloth of mourning underneath, is to blame Elisha. Was he not the one who got them out of a dire situation earlier? Is he not the one who works wonders, multiplying food, raising children from the dead, caring for the hungry and distressed? Where is he now? Why is he not the one to hear the tale of the cannibal mother at this moment of gravest injury and distress? At this time when the world has turned upside down, "The king begins by declaring that only the Lord can help and then curses the man of God, whom he has every reason to believe *could* help."[172] It is not one of Elisha's shining moments as he sits in his house fearing for his life because the king holds him accountable for the disaster that has befallen them (31–32). In the end, the king stops short of his goal, and the scene ends with his words—fitting for the plight of the woman who faced him at the wall: "Look at this! Evil from Adonai!/ What more can I hope for from the Holy God?" (33).

### Act V, Scene 4: From Famine to Feast (2 Kings 7)

*The narrator approaches the critical events obliquely, looks at miracle from a distance, and compromises even the reader's usually omniscient expectations.*[173]

The king's negativity is immediately undercut by a prophetic declaration from Elisha to the effect that food will become cheap (therefore plentiful) by the next day. A reply from a royal officer calling the accuracy of this foretelling into question receives a sharp put-down

---

172. Lasine, "Jehoram and the Cannibal Mothers," 43.
173. Long, 2 *Kings*, 93.

(1–2).[174] Events that will make the restoration of the food supply possible are told first in a separate episode in great detail, filled with both serious and comical notes (3–11). The narrative introduces four new characters, all of them with a skin disease, the same *tsara'at* that afflicted Naaman of Aram (3–5). These four, probably shunned by their neighbors, are arguing at the entrance of the city gate. Reasoning that no matter what they do, go into the city or stay outside, they will die, they decide to cast their lot with the Arameans. As they arrive at the outer edge of the Aramean camp at twilight, there is no one to be seen.

Just as we are on the verge of entering the camp with the four characters, the narrator inserts the explanation for the disappearance of the enemy (6–7). Adonai had caused faulty hearing instead of seeing, and the entire camp emptied when it heard "the sound of chariots and the sound of horse, a great army" (6). The Arameans were so befuddled that they ascribed the uproar to Hittites and Egyptians (perhaps these two ethnic groups were proverbial for a threatening enemy, somewhat like "the golden horde" in a later day) and left the entire camp—including tents and animals—as it was, fleeing for their lives. The text resumes the point of view of the four men about to enter the camp.

2 Kings 7:8–9

8 Came these skin-diseased ones
   to the edge of the camp;
   they came into one tent
   and ate and drank.
   And they carried from there
   silver and gold and clothing.
   Then they went and hid it.
   They came back and went into another tent
   and carried stuff from there,

174. The officer asks mockingly if God is making "windows in the sky"—more likely a reference to manna than to rain (Long, *2 Kings*, 93). Elisha promises him that he will see it happen but will not profit from the supply of food.

then went and hid it.

9   Then they said to one another:
it is not right what we are doing today.
This is a day of good news
and we are silent.
If we wait until daylight,
our sin will find us.
Come, let us go and tell it to the palace.

After initially slowing the tempo by repeating the arrival at the camp, the text treats us to a full view of the delights enjoyed by the four outcasts. They *eat*, *drink*, and *carry*. Then they do what others have done in their circumstances: They hide the goods. These are no ordinary scoundrels, however, for they come to their senses and decide that they should not hide in silence but broadcast the good news (9). They go to the gate and cry out their findings to the gate-keepers, who pass it on to the court (10–11). Four men with a skin disease, rather than filling the role of victims in need of help, are the first ones to benefit from a saving action caused by Adonai, and subsequently they announce the good news to the city.

The king is not so quickly turned from despair to hope and is perhaps as filled with doubt about Elisha's prediction as was his officer, but a servant convinces him that there is little to lose by sending out an intelligence team to investigate (12–13). The scene that meets the team and those who follow it to the Jordan is a road full of discarded items: clothes and gear thrown away by the Arameans. The siege is lifted, and food is once again abundant and cheap (14–16). It is a good ending for the time being, although not so much for the officer who had cast doubt on Elisha's oracle. There is a stampede as people rush out of the gate for food, and they trample him so that he dies. The final paragraph spins out this ignominious end by repeating the speeches of both Elisha and the officer verbatim (7:1–2 = 7:18–19). In this way, an account of events in which disaster turned to a hopeful ending through Adonai's direct intervention ends with the words "trampled . . . and he died." There is another one still awaiting to be *trampled* in the near future when the raging storm that is Jehu will be unleashed on the land (9:33).

*Act V, Scene 5: Restoration to Life (2 Kings 8:1–6)*

*The exegetes, rather than the authors of the Old Testament, are the ones who judge a married woman to be incapable of business transactions.*[175]

We conclude this cycle, entitled "The Struggle for Life," dominated by the presence of the prophets Elijah and Elisha, with a short episode in which the woman of Shunem makes a reappearance. Its principal notion is the restoration of *life*. This restoration is argued through vocabulary, the emphasis on Elisha raising the Shunammite's son to life, and the concrete return of house and land to the woman. The opening unit refers to counsel Elisha gave to the Shunammite in the past on account of an impending seven-year famine (the one referred to in 2 Kgs 4:38?), an indication that there was ongoing contact between him and this family. She took his advice and stayed in Philistine country with her entire house.

The emphasis among the words related to her moving away is on the word "sojourn" (Hebrew *gur*; lit. to "live as a stranger"). It implies living as an outsider without rights and automatic access to means for one's livelihood, and it involves a radical change for the Shunammite, who has been used to living "among her own people" (2 Kgs 4:13) and conducting her own affairs. When the famine has ended, she returns to plead with the king for her "house and her land" (8:3). The word governing this first section (1–3) is "house," occurring in every verse. She left with "her house" (i.e., her family), lived as a stranger with "her house" (i.e., her family), and has come to have her "house" (i.e., her property) and land restored to her. The woman is the subject of seven verbs putting her at the center of the action: she *arose, did, went, sojourned, came back,* and *went out* to *implore.* Once Elisha had offered to speak on her behalf to the king—an offer she turned down (2 Kgs 4:13). Now, she herself stands before the king to plead her case. Once a destitute woman in

---

175. Aleida G. van Daalen, "Vertel mij toch het grote dat Elisha gedaan heeft," in *Amsterdamse Cahiers voor Exegese and Bijbelse Theologie 2*, ed. K. A. Deurloo, B. P. M. Hemelsoet, F. J. Hoogewoud, and R. Zuurmond (Kampen: Kok, 1981): 41, my translation.

front of Elisha cried for help (2 Kgs 4:1), now the Shunammite utters a similar cry, the cry of distress demanding justice. We do not know what has happened to her land; possibly it fell to the crown in her absence, as her turning directly to the highest office in the land for its restoration may indicate. There is no reason to assume that the woman has become widowed; her husband was never a major actor in her story, and her status makes it possible for her to take care of her own business.[176]

### 2 KINGS 8:4–5

4 Now the king was speaking to Gehazi,
   the lad of the man of God, saying:
   Tell me please of all the great things
   that Elisha has done.
5 It was when he was telling the king
   how he brought to life the dead one,
   and, Look!, the woman whose son he had brought to life
   was crying out to the king about her house and her field.
   Gehazi said: My lord King, this is the woman,
   and this is her son, whom Elisha brought to life.

It looks as if Gehazi's speaking is simultaneous with the appearance of the woman and her son and her making her plea. In this unit, the expression "bring back to life," using a form of the verb "to live," predominates, occurring three times in a few lines.[177] This same root will play a prominent role in the sequel to this short episode. The king asks the woman for verification (6), and "all that was hers" is *restored* to her, including the revenues that were due. So the Shunammite who *returned* from a foreign land is *returned* to her former status partly due to the fame of Elisha. Elisha's work is not done, but hereafter his presence will gradually diminish, and his activities will concern the centers of power at home and abroad.

176. Van Daalen, "Vertel mij toch het grote," 41.
177. The three references are the *Hif'il* form of the verb *hayah*, "to live."

# Cycle IV: The Tumult of War (2 Kings 8:7–13:25)

*Those who serve the state and the political process must always know that "there is a prophet among them."*[1]

The remainder of chapter 8 is devoted to Elisha's involvement with dynastic change in Damascus (8:7–15) and summary notices of kings in Israel and Judah (8:16–27). The last two verses, concerning war with Aram, set the scene for the introduction of Jehu, whose bloody exploits fill chapters 9 and 10. Affairs are not very different in Judah, where the queen mother Athaliah manages to ascend to the throne in a bloody coup and reign for six years (11:1–20). After her assassination, Joash of Judah rules for forty years—one of the "good" kings who undertakes elaborate temple repairs (12:1–17). During his reign, Aram encroaches on Judah, and Joash is forced to pay tribute in order to avoid the capture of Jerusalem. Aram's domination of Israel is held in check by Adonai's occasionally coming to Judah's aid, and both Israel and Judah experience a reprieve.[2] The end of the cycle reports the death of Elisha and the beginning of the reign of Jeroboam II in Israel, at which point we have reached the first half of the seventh century BCE.

---

1. Hens-Piazza, *1–2 Kings*, 285.
2. J. Maxwell Miller and John H. Hayes (*A History of Ancient Israel and Judah*, 2nd ed. [Louisville: Westminster John Knox, 2006], 327) ascribe the period of relative security for both the kingdoms to renewed Assyrian encroachment on Damascus.

## Act I: The Rise of Hazael in Aram (2 Kings 8:7–29)

*Hazael is indomitable and will not quit his campaign against Israel.*[3]

The remainder of chapter 8 turns first to the international scene with Elisha and a coup in Damascus, where an upstart replaces an ailing king—possibly by murdering him. Then the text resumes its synchronic listing of kings, closing with a joint adventure between Judah and Israel against Aram, which turns out to the disadvantage of the Israelite king, who is wounded and remains ill in Jezreel (28–29). The act thus opens and closes with kings on their sickbeds, neither of whom recovers and each of whom dies under dubious circumstances.

### Act I, Scene 1: Elisha and the King of Aram (2 Kings 8:7–15)

*Along the way the images have blurred and reformed, like one oily color mixing and dissolving into another.*[4]

The scene opens with Elisha's arrival in Damascus without further explanation for his presence in that city. One might think that relations between Israel and Aram would still be too fraught for the prophet to turn up there without risk of being molested, but the king lies ailing and is in no mood for hostilities.[5] He sends one Hazael to ask the

---

3. Brueggemann, *1 & 2 Kings*, 433.

4. Burke O. Long, *2 Kings*, FOTL 10 (Grand Rapids: Eerdmans, 1991), 105.

5. The king of Aram is named Ben-hadad in many of these narratives—at the time of King Asa of Judah and of Ahab and his successors—so that this cannot have been the same ruler and is not a reliable indicator for a specific time period. Miller and Hayes (*A History of Ancient Israel and Judah*, 297–99), allowing for the theoretical nature of their reconstruction, recap the rulers of Aram/Syria in Damascus as follows: Rezon (968–928?), Solomon's contemporary; Ben-hadad I (908–871), a contemporary of Asa and Ba'asha; Hadadezer (854–842), a contemporary of Ahab and Jehoram; Hazael, Jehu's contemporary (usurper between 845 and 841); and Ben-hadad II (821–789), a contemporary of Jehoahaz and Jehoash and probably the Ben-hadad of the Elisha stories and the battle accounts in 1 Kings 20; 22:1–38.

prophet to make inquiries of Adonai and find out if he will come back to life from his illness (7–8).[6] The phrase "come back to life" is based on the same verb that governed the unit immediately preceding this one (8:1–6), connecting the presence of Elisha to life as well as creating the (false) hope that Elisha will bring the king back to life.[7] A new life lies ahead, but not for Ben-hadad. Hazael, whose relationship to the king is not specified, is clearly the king's right-hand man, and what begins as a story about Ben-hadad turns out to be the beginning of Hazael's rise to kingship. The question about recovery is posed to Adonai through the prophet, a not uncommon example of an inquiry issued to the god of another country (cf. 2 Kgs 1:2). Moreover, Elisha's fame has spread far and wide, and he is a known expert in this area.

Hazael arrives with a stupendously large gift (forty camel loads of goods!) and poses the question to Elisha, referring to the king as "your son" and adopting appropriate humble terminology for the king-prophet relationship. He leaves out the part about inquiring of Adonai, and Elisha gives a contradictory double response to the inquiry, only one part of which relates to a divine revelation: "Go, say to him: You will live, yes live; and Adonai revealed to me that he will die, yes die" (10). Does he mean to divide what Hazael should *say* from what will actually happen? Or does he mean to imply that it is not the *illness* from which the king will die, although he will indeed die? As they stare at one another, Elisha weeps because he foresees that Hazael will wreak havoc on Israel. He claims to have received a revelation from Adonai and first declares the disastrous result of that rule. The announcement about Hazael's kingship takes place after Hazael asks "what dog would do such a thing?" Hazael returns to his master with only the message of recovery (14–15). The next day, he spreads a wet blanket on his face, and the king dies. Hazael succeeds to the kingship. Most commentators assume Hazael murdered his lord, but the narrator omits a clear statement to that effect, leaving room for doubt. The questions of how Hazael, who was apparently

6. The story is a stereotypical narrative in which a ruler who is ill inquires about the course of his illness through a prophet (cf. 2 Kings 1:2–17).

7. The verb occurs six times in 8:8–15, each time in the *Qal* form and twice with the doubling of the root (8, 9, 10, 14).

a nobody, succeeded so easily to the kingship is also left open.[8] The matter of his rise to the throne is of course a leftover item from God's charge to Elijah (1 Kgs 19:15), but we note that Elisha does not anoint Hazael. The story reflects on the reach of the authority of both Elisha and Adonai. In the future, Hazael will play the role of "external villain" as counterpart to the "internal evil, the Israelite Baalizers."[9]

### Act I, Scene 2: Kings of Judah and Israel (2 Kings 8:16–29)

*Why raise the specter of the destruction of Judah unless events are leading inevitably in that direction?*[10]

The text returns to the synchronic listing of reigns, for the first time going back to the rule of a Judean king—the same one last mentioned in 1 Kings 22:51. It thus moves back in time to the fifth year of the king of Israel—a son of Ahab called both Joram and Jehoram in the text—whom we assume to be the king in Israel for most of the period of Elisha's activity.[11] The Judean king is also named either Joram or Jehoram and is reviewed in the typical summary manner, with a report on his loyalty to Adonai and a fragment of events during his reign. Unusual for a king of Judah, he is said to have "walked in the ways of the kings of Israel" (18), although his transgression receives no further specification and is only alluded to by his relationship through marriage to "a daughter of Ahab." The identity of this woman is withheld until verse 26.

During Joram's reign in Judah, Edom, still allied with Israel and Judah in 2 Kings 3, revolts, and although Judah may have achieved a temporary victory, Edom remains in rebellion together with Libnah from that point on (20–22). Joram receives the usual death notice

---

8. An inscription of Shalmaneser refers to Hazael as "son of a nobody" (Miller and Hayes, *The History of Ancient Israel and Judah*, 208).

9. Long, *2 Kings*, 107.

10. Robert L. Cohn, *2 Kings*, Berit Olam (Collegeville, MN: Liturgical Press, 2000), 63.

11. See 2 Kgs 1:17. For a note on the naming and the possibility of the references being to the same king, see p. 167n103 above.

and is succeeded by his son Ahaziah, whom we find in Jezreel in the presence of King Jehoram of Israel at the end of the chapter. The name of his mother, Athaliah is revealed—here called a daughter of Omri, most likely with the meaning of descendant—together with the evaluation that he "walked in the ways of Ahab and did what was evil in the eyes of Adonai" (27). That his disloyalty is connected to his mother is clear from the appended note, "for he was son-in-law" to the house of Ahab. It is also because of the family connection that Ahaziah joins Jehoram of Israel in a battle with King Hazael of Aram at Ramoth Gilead, resulting in a victory for Aram and the wounding of the king of Israel. As the injured king leaves his army to recover in Jezreel, he is joined there by Ahaziah. In Jezreel are two kings, one of Israel, one of Judah, both from Ahab's house, one of whom is weakened. It sounds foreboding.

**Act II: The Rise of Jehu in Israel (2 Kings 9–10)**

*It marked the end of an era.*[12]

The anointing of Jehu, the usurper who causes the fall of the house of Ahab, was a task laid on Elijah in 1 Kings 19:16. Elijah did not fulfill this task and it falls to Elisha to oversee the rise of Jehu. Two chapters relate in grisly detail Jehu's murderous path to his rule. Jehu begins his reign in the last part of the ninth century, and four descendants will follow him without another bloody coup until the decades immediately preceding the Assyrian conquest of the North.

***Act II, Scene 1: "Tricky, Brutal and Cold"[13] (2 Kings 9)***

*A tale of conspiracy, deception, irony and murder.*[14]

---

12. Miller and Hayes, *A History of Ancient Israel and Judah*, 327.
13. Richard Nelson, *First and Second Kings*, IBC (Atlanta: John Knox, 1987), 201.
14. Cohn, *2 Kings*, 65.

While Ahaziah of Judah and Jehoram of Israel are brought together in Jezreel on account of a military crisis, Elisha commissions one of his disciples to go and find a certain Jehu, who is with the troops as a commander in Ramoth Gilead across the Jordan. Elisha's "lad" is to identify him and take him into an "inner room" to anoint him as king over Israel in the name of Adonai (1–3). So begins one of the most appalling and bloodcurdling tales of violence in the Bible. In its attention to detail of setting and dialogue, it calls to mind the heroic legends of Judges. Possibly the story was originally preserved in circles in which Jehu was considered a man of great stature whose exploits were worthy of celebration.[15] From the moment the messenger of Elisha arrives in Ramoth Gilead until Jehu is declared king, the scene is worthy of a Shakespearean play (4–13). With the prophet's lad, we view the commanders "sitting around"—perhaps rolling dice, drinking, passing the time of day—when this stranger arrives with an outlandish appearance (they will later call him a "crazy man," v. 11).

### 2 KINGS 9:4–6

4  Then went the lad,
the lad of the prophet,
to Ramoth Gilead.
5  When he got there, Look!,
the commanders of the army sitting (together).
He said: I have a word for you, commander.
Jehu said: For which one of us all?
He said: For you, commander.

6  He arose and went into the house,
and poured the flask of oil on his head

15. Marvin Sweeney (*I & II Kings: A Commentary*, OTL [Louisville: Westminster John Knox, 2007], 330) assigns the original composition of the tale of the rise of Jehu to the reign of Jeroboam II in the first half of the eighth century BCE and suggests it was later incorporated into subsequent editions of the historical material in Kings.

and said to him:
Thus says Adonai the God of Israel:
I have anointed you as king
over the people of Adonai, over Israel.

Elisha's lad identifies Jehu because he is the one who responds to his announcement of having "a word for you." We recall that the noun for "word" in Hebrew also means "something," and like Ehud before King Eglon, the messenger has *something* as well as a *word* for Jehu, albeit in Jehu's case an object to honor rather than to kill him (cf. Judg 3:18–23). The anointing must be done in secret (cf. 1 Sam 10:1; 16:3); Elisha has instructed that it be in an "inner room" (2), so that is where they go. Elisha's servant declares Jehu king, adding the words "the people of Adonai" to "Israel," and then launches into a substantial speech with echoes of words from the Elijah narratives. The purpose of Jehu's kingship will be to decimate the house of Ahab, to *cut down* from that house *all who piss against the wall*, likening its fate to that of the *house of Jeroboam*. Jezebel's fate to be eaten by dogs is mentioned separately, as it was in 1 Kings 21. Everything takes us back to Elijah's announcement to Ahab after the murder of Naboth (2 Kgs 9:8–10a = 1 Kgs 21:21–23; cf. 1 Kgs 14:10; 16:11) and is a fulfillment, via the agency of Elisha, of the tasks laid on Elijah by God at Horeb (1 Kgs 19:15–16). The elaborate speech that accompanies the anointing, not included in Elisha's instructions (9:2–3), may be a sign of an editorial hand that presents the arising of a new royal house in the Northern Kingdom as a link in a chain of doomed houses. Jehu's house will, of course, not escape the fate of Jeroboam's.[16]

It is worth noting that Elisha himself stays far from the action and has instructed his servant to "flee without delay" once the anointing is accomplished (3). The narrative has depicted Elisha as

---

16. Long, *2 Kings*, 119: "The speaker and his words in vv. 6b-10a transcend their immediate context: they transform the simple words of anointing-designation, 'I anoint you king over Israel,' into an elaborate announcement of judgment, and, at the same time, evoke much of the connective tissue belonging to the larger story of the northern monarchs."

acting on behalf of the descendant of the house of Ahab currently on the throne and, though existing in a fraught relationship, maintaining a position of authority vis-à-vis the royal house. In addition, Elisha had a role in the takeover of the Aramean throne by Hazael, at the moment one of Israel's most dangerous enemies. Proximity to Jehu, especially once he has received the divine imprimatur, is not a logical step for the prophet or his disciple in view of the dedication with which Jehu will take up his task of eradicating potential enemies.

Before he can go on the warpath, there is a second declaration of Jehu's kingship by his cronies. They are the first of a series of individuals to ask if everything is well—in Hebrew, "Is it peace?" They wonder what the "crazy man" who came around was up to, and when Jehu is pushed to reveal the truth, they put down their cloaks for him to stand on, blow the shofar, and declare him king (11–13).[17] There is a touch in this scene of both the farcical and reality, as revolutions of this sort in the Northern Kingdom often have their roots among the military, and it is natural for the troops around a commander to begin a coup (cf. 1 Kgs 15:28; 16:9). It sounds as if the original tale begins with verse 14: "Then conspired Jehu . . . against Joram "(cf. 1 Kgs 15:27; 16:9). The narrative returns to the whereabouts of the Israelite king in Jezreel on account of wounds incurred in the war with Aram (cf. 8:28–29), placing everyone in their location: Jehu with the army in Ramoth Gilead and Jehoram in Jezreel. Jehu orders his comrades to guard the city so no one will get out to tattle about a possible revolution; he wants to come at the king by surprise.

"The shofar blast and royal shout of 9:13 signal the start of a headlong race in which Jehu drives to Jezreel and on to Samaria."[18] In the section immediately following, the perspective shifts from Jezreel to Jehu and back, from the watchtower to the approaching Jehu, drawing the reader/listener into the breathless pace. First, we

17. In Kgs, blowing the shofar to announce kingship is, outside of this passage, only mentioned in connection with King Solomon (1 Kgs 1:34, 39).

18. Francisco O. Garcia-Treto, "The Fall of the House: A Carnivalesque Reading of 2 Kings 9 and 20," in *Reading Between Texts: Intertextuality and the Hebrew Bible*, ed. Danna Nolan Fewell (Louisville: Westminster John Knox, 1992), 162. Garcia-Treto points out that the verb "to ride" and the noun "chariot" occur sixteen times in chs. 9 and 20.

view Jehu pelting along in his chariot from the watchtower in Jezreel, where he is not yet recognized; then we are at his side, joined by a rider sent to meet him; finally, we move back to the watchtower where uncertainty prevails because the messengers fail to return. Each time, the phrases "Is it peace?" and "What have you to do with peace?" are exchanged between the rider sent out from the city and Jehu so that the word *shalom* echoes five times in three verses (17–19). Jehu was anointed by a "madman" (11) and drives like a "madman" (20), which is what gives him away in the end. As soon as Jehoram hears this, he heads out also, together with Ahaziah, and stops to meet Jehu "in the plot of Naboth the Jezreelite" (21). One more time the question "Is it peace?" sounds to be answered sarcastically by Jehu. Jehu shoots his lord in the back as the king turns his chariot around to flee (23–24).

Jehu's sarcastic reply calls into question any kind of peace in the face of "the whorings of Jezebel your mother and her many sorceries" (22). The "sorceries" of Jezebel are news even in a text that has consistently presented her in a negative light and sound as if they are piled on by Jehu in his effort to be as insulting as possible. With Jehoram dead, there is still Ahaziah to take care of, since he too is related to the house of Ahab through Ahab's daughter, Athaliah. In a sidebar, Jehu reminds his shield-bearer that they witnessed the curse put on Ahab in view of his dealings with Naboth (1 Kgs 21:20–24) and to throw the body of King Jehoram on Naboth's land (25–26). Again, the narrative forges a link in the chain of events as it portrays them fitting into Adonai's design through Jehu's pronouncement.

Ahaziah does not die in his chariot but, mortally wounded, flees to Megiddo, from where his servants transport his body to be buried in Jerusalem (27–28). He receives his death notice (29), but his successor is not yet announced because his death unleashes a violent uprising not to be told of until a few chapters later. Instead, the text follows Jehu to Jezreel, where Jezebel awaits him with mocking words and a haughty demeanor—her self-confidence unshaken by another upstart ruler (30–33).[19] She awaits the death of being

---

19. Nelson, *First and Second Kings*, 336: "Jezebel's question suggests that Jehu is a flash-in-the-pan who will meet a similar fate [to that of Zimri]."

thrown from the window, out of which she looks and asks of Jehu once again if all is "peace"—addressing him with the name of Zimri, the rebel who ruled only for seven days and burned down together with his house (1 Kgs 16:9–18). As she falls, her blood spatters the wall, "and he trampled on her," the use of the third masculine form of the verb leading to the conclusion that Jehu is the subject (33).[20] Then Jehu leaves her body to be further desecrated and goes in to eat and drink, piously pronouncing that all this came to pass because of the words from Elijah spoken about Jezebel (36; cf. 1 Kgs 21:23) and adding some chosen invective of his own (37).

## JEZEBEL

*Even though 2 Kgs 9.37 pronounces that no one can say, "This is Jezebel," the irony is that "This is Jezebel" is exactly what people have said, ever since this Deuteronomic proverb.*[21]

Jezebel makes more appearances in the narratives of 1 Kings than any other queen of either Israel or Judah. She emerges in the text initially as the Sidonian princess who becomes the wife of King Ahab (1 Kgs 16:31). She is the daughter of King Etbaal and a devotee of the Sidonian Baal, as devoted to her god as the Israelites are expected to be to Adonai. Royal marriages were a matter of diplomatic relationships, and it is unlikely that Jezebel had any say in the matter of her marriage to Ahab. With the initial notation on the rule of King Ahab, the narrator comments that Ahab adopted the worship of his wife and began to serve the Baal (1 Kgs 16:31). Although Jezebel is not accused outright of luring Ahab into the worship of her god, the close proximity of her name to the idolatry of Ahab causes a suspi-

---

20. Garcia-Treto ("The Fall of the House," 165) considers Jezebel's blood spattering against the wall to be an allusion to the idiom for males used in 9:8 and elsewhere: "While her blood is allusively turned into urine against the wall, her body, eaten by dogs, is literally to become dung on the ground (9:36, 37)."

21. Tina Pippin, "Jezebel Re-vamped," in *A Feminist Companion to Samuel and Kings*, ed. Athalya Brenner (Sheffield: Sheffield Academic, 1994), 205.

cion that his worship of Baal and his marriage to Jezebel are related. Not only does Jezebel follow the deity of her own people, she actively combats the adherents of Adonai: "She eliminated/destroyed the prophets of Adonai" (1 Kgs 18:4). Obadiah refers to this aggressive behavior in his conversation with Elijah (1 Kgs 18:13). She provides for large groups of Baal and Asherah personnel, according to Elijah (1 Kgs 18:19). After Elijah returns the favor in the aftermath of the contest on Mount Carmel by slaughtering the Baal prophets, Jezebel swears by the gods that Elijah will share the fate of the dead prophets by the next day. To this point, she has come to the fore in only a few sentences as a strong, devoted worshiper of Baal, aggressive and acting independently of her husband.

Her devotion turns out to be not only to her gods but also to her husband when in the next episode she concerns herself with matters of state and procures for Ahab the vineyard he desires by deceptive means and murder (1 Kgs 21:5–15). In this episode, she takes a central place as a devoted wife, a clever but also deceptive schemer, and the executioner of a plan. As others have pointed out, her actions are on a par with those of David toward Uriah.[22] Only in this episode is she a dominant character who sets events in motion and sees them to their end, with the cooperation of a group of coconspirators in Jezreel. She sounds concerned but also imperious when she speaks to her husband; she promises she will take care of things, and she does (1 Kgs 21:7).

She has been absent from the Elisha stories and her appearance during Jehu's rampage comes as a surprise. As Bergen puts it, commenting on 2 Kings 9:30, "Readers are suddenly reminded that Jezebel has been alive all through the life of Elisha."[23] Her absence

22. Tikva Frymer-Kensky, *Reading the Women of the Bible* (New York: Schocken, 2002), 212.

23. Wesley J. Bergen (*Elisha and the End of Prophetism*, JSOTSup 286 [Sheffield: Sheffield Academic, 1999], 165), who has few positive things to say about Elisha and his activities, observes that "the absence of references to Baal in the Elisha narratives is truly remarkable." It is of course possible that abuses in worship were not high on Elisha's agenda, either because there was not as much evidence of them in his time or because other matters on the national and international front became more pressing. Or it could be that

also highlights a shift in preoccupation from one prophet to the other, as Elisha is less focused on idolatry than Elijah in his dealings with the monarchy. In any case, there is Jezebel in her Sunday best, certainly not because she intends to make herself attractive to Jehu but because a person's appearance, a woman's appearance, makes her feel more powerful even if she has lost all the power she ever had, as in Jezebel's case. The manner of her death is gruesome and gruesomely described, and the heart does not grow fonder of Jehu in the face of his verbal abuse, his encouragement of physical abuse, and his pious rejoicing over the death of the queen (2 Kgs 9:36–37).

Somewhat strangely, Jezebel became the archetype of the sexually promiscuous, scheming seductress in the worlds that inherited the biblical text. She lives on in the New Testament as a woman in Thyatira who claims to be a prophet, who leads the faithful astray and lures them into immorality (Rev 2:20). As Tina Pippin reviews the imagery that clings to Jezebel in the Southern United States, she sums up the list of negative epithets: Jezebel is a woman who is "famous for her badness; vamp, vampire, temptress, femme fatale, siren, witch—a woman who takes or ruins the life of another."[24] The texts in Kings do not speak of her seducing Ahab into anything, and the activity of "whoring" ascribed to her in Jehu's taunt to her son refers to idolatry rather than the work of prostitution (2 Kgs 9:22). Here is the thing about Jezebel: As Alice Ogden Bellis observes, "Jezebel is not a model of morality, but she does not deserve the symbol of evil that she has become."[25] She deserves it no more than David or Elisha or any other person in the text who is human and set on the

---

Jehu's zeal for Adonai and his violence against the house of Ahab more than make up for the absence of the concern for Baalists in the Elisha narratives in the eyes of the compilers. Another possibility is that Elisha's activities took place in a different era than the one in which the biblical writers place it. Cohn, 2 *Kings*, 95: "These observations raise the suspicion that the Elisha stories were originally not connected to the Omride kings at all but were set later during the reign of the Jehuite kings, by which time the Baalists had been defeated."

24. For a long list of descriptive adjectives and nouns related to Jezebel in US culture, see Pippin, "Jezebel Re-vamped," 196–97.

25. Alice Ogden Bellis, *Helpmates, Harlots and Heroes: Women's Stories in the Hebrew Bible* (Louisville: Westminster John Knox, 1994), 165.

page with all his flaws. But Jezebel was an outsider and a woman, and in the period immediately following the Babylonian exile, an unfortunate byproduct of the circle-the-wagons mentality of the community in Judah was the mistrust and possible mistreatment of women who had married into the community from outside.[26] If Israel had so gone astray in the past, it could do so again, and the pointing finger went to the "woman" as it once did in the Garden of Eden story (Gen 3:12). Hens-Piazza writes, "In Jehu's political scheme and in that of the narrator of this story, Jezebel serves as the scapegoat. As an easy target, Jezebel becomes emblematic of the ills that the coup will address, an exponent of the evil that Jehu must right. It is not necessary to be innocent to be a victim."[27] For a reader today, there is no reason to make Jezebel out as better than she was, but neither is there reason to paint her in the lurid colors of the traditions that arose around her name. She was a strong woman, faithful to the religion of her ancestors, who committed grave sins according to the text, and we may do best by allowing her to have a right to her sins, to be as flawed as any other character in the Bible.

### Act II, Scene 2: Not a Single Survivor (2 Kings 10)

*Slaughter will be the price of covenant loyalty.*[28]

Jehu is by no means done slaying opponents, real and imagined. First on the agenda is the total destruction of the house of Ahab until "there remained to him not a single survivor" (11). Such efforts never quite work out to be as total as the perpetrator envisions; witness the continuation of Ahab's house through the monarchy of Judah. But one cannot say of Jehu that he is not thorough. First, he

---

26. For a discussion of a possible expulsion of women during the period of Ezra and Nehemiah, see Johanna W. H. van Wijk-Bos, *Ezra, Nehemiah, and Esther*, Westminster Bible Companion (Louisville: Westminster John Knox, 1998), 39–48.

27. Gina Hens-Piazza, *1–2 Kings*, AOTC (Nashville: Abingdon, 2006), 296.

28. Cohn, *2 Kings*, 72.

manipulates the caretakers of the sons of Ahab to deliver him their heads in baskets (1–10). Ahab, so the text has it, had seventy sons, like Gideon (Judg 8:30); and like the sons of Gideon, these seventy do not fare well under a new regime (Judg 9:1–5). Jehu taunts the governing elite and the caretakers of Ahab's sons in Samaria by inviting them to choose a new king from among Ahab's sons—to put him on the throne to become a contender for the kingship opposing Jehu (1–3). As he no doubt foresaw, this creates confusion and fear, and their response is that they will do everything he tells them to do: "We will not make a man king;/ do as is good in your eyes" (4–5). This dangerous invitation elicits from Jehu the command to deliver to him the heads of all of Ahab's sons, and so it comes to pass that Jehu receives seventy heads in baskets in Jezreel (6–7). He puts them in two heaps on display at the city gate, where he preaches a short sermon to the people going out and coming in to the effect that they are not accountable for this particular act of atrocity and that the members of the old regime are the guilty ones; in the meantime, all that has taken place has been according to the will of Adonai (8–10). The heaps of severed heads become a "public object lesson."[29] Next in line for the chopping block is anyone associated with the reign of the house of Ahab: "All his great men, his confidants, and his priests, until there remained to him not a single survivor" (11).

On his way from Jezreel to Samaria, Jehu "finds" a group of brothers of the Judean king, Ahaziah; some of these are descendants of the line of Ahab through Athaliah (2 Kgs 11:1), and Jehu has forty-two of them slaughtered after they blithely tell him who they are and that they are headed to Jezreel to visit their relatives (12–14).[30] Jehu invites a companion, one Jonadab, for the continuation of his massacres (cf. 9:25–26). Jonadab readily agrees to ride with him in his chariot to witness Jehu's "zeal for Adonai" (15–17). Once again, there is a reference

29. Long, 2 Kings, 136. Apparently, Assyrian rulers employed similar methods to display victory and ward off rebellion.

30. Beth Eqed of the Shepherds, where Jehu finds the brothers (10:12), is an uncertain location, perhaps at the southeastern edge of the Jezreel valley (Sweeney, I & II Kings, 337). The number forty-two, like the earlier seventy, is a conventional number rather than a literal one.

to Jehu's *cutting down* "all who remained to Ahab in Samaria" as he had previously done in Jezreel. A final step in the extermination process is the destruction of the "servants of Baal," which he accomplishes deceptively by pretending to be a worshiper of Baal and gathering them in Baal's temple so his guard can murder them all, making sure no one escapes (18–27). In the end, the temple of Baal is demolished and transformed into a latrine.[31] It seems a particularly heinous crime to slaughter people inside their house of worship.

An approving word from Adonai promising four descendants of Jehu to sit on Israel's throne because he has "acted well, doing what is right in my eyes according to all that was in my heart" (30) is wedged between two less complimentary comments. The first refers to the fact that Jehu destroyed the baals from Israel but continued in the sin of Jeroboam by not destroying the golden calves of Bethel and Dan (28–29). The final observation is more severe: "Jehu was not careful to walk in the Teaching of Adonai, the God of Israel, with his whole heart." The text then repeats the line about following in the sin of Jeroboam (31). Cohn writes, "By thus checking (hedging?) divine plaudits with his own appraisal, the writer is able to account both for the continuation of Jehu's line and the reduction of his territory (v. 32)."[32] Even the mixed review seems too mild for the destructive wildfire raging through Israel that was Jehu the son of Jehoshaphat the son of Nimshi.

Before Jehu, who reigned for 28 years, receives his death notice (34–36), the narrator inserts a historical comment to the effect that Israel at this time begins to lose territory, especially east of the Jordan, where Aram conquers the territory of Gilead, Gad, and Reuben as well as Manasseh (32–33).[33] It is certain that in this pe-

31. Turning an idolatrous shrine into a latrine may have been common practice for reformers of Israel and Judah's worship, as shown by an archaeological find near the city of Lachish stemming from the period of King Hezekiah in Judah, about a century after the Jehu reforms in the North. It served perhaps no practical purpose but was a symbolic desecration. See https://www.biblicalarchaeology.org/daily/news/ancient-latrine-king-hezekiahs-reforms/.

32. Cohn, *2 Kings*, 25.

33. Miller and Hayes (*A History of Ancient Israel and Judah*, 337) assign only seventeen years to Jehu's reign.

riod, the end of the ninth century BCE, "Israel and Judah fell under the shadow of more powerful states (Assyria and Damascus), and moments of national autonomy were to be the exception rather than the rule during the remainder of their respective histories."[34] From historical inscriptions we know that Jehu made an alliance with Shalmaneser III of Assyria, who occupied himself with eroding the power of Aram, but clearly the whole Transjordanian region was eventually occupied by Aram/Syria.[35]

The chapters that record the revolt of Jehu, texts that appear to present no ethical difficulties for the biblical writer and the compilers, will today certainly be read as "difficult texts." "Innocent offspring are beheaded. Those who speak honestly and come peacefully are taken alive, then slaughtered, and docile worshipers of another persuasion are herded together, double-crossed, and executed. In the process, violence is given free rein."[36] To increase the difficulty, the actions of Jehu receive God's approval (30). Challenged by such material, we become aware that all stories "carried out in the name of God summon caution."[37]

## Act III: Revolt and Reform in Judah (2 Kings 11–12)

*God does not seem to do anything or say anything.*[38]

During approximately the same period in which Jehu is slaughtering the house of Ahab in Israel, Judah for once does not experience a peaceful transition from one Davidic descendant to another. A queen mother instigates a coup and reigns in Judah for six years (842–836) while her grandson is hidden by her family and Temple personnel. When the rightful king, still a boy, ascends the throne, a

---

34. Miller and Hayes, *A History of Ancient Israel and Judah*, 327.

35. References to both Hazael of Damascus and Jehu of Israel turn up in Assyrian inscriptions. Yet Assyria itself underwent a period of instability.

36. Hens-Piazza, *1–2 Kings*, 305.

37. Hens-Piazza, *1–2 Kings*, 304.

38. Nelson, *First and Second Kings*, 212.

planned reform of worship begins to take place. During the reign of King Joash, Judah too experiences incursions from Aram.

### *Act III, Scene 1: A Queen in Judah (2 Kings 11³⁹)*

*Athaliah's slaughter takes a page from the book of Jehu—and that of virtually every other monarch in antiquity. Unlike Jehu, she is not praised for her actions.*[40]

2 Kings 11:1–3

1 When Athaliah, the mother of Ahaziah,
   saw that her son was dead,
   she arose and destroyed all the royal offspring.
2 And Jehosheba, daughter of King Joram,
   sister of Ahaziah, took Joash, the son of Ahaziah,
   and stole him away from among the sons of the king,
   who were being killed,
   him and his nurse, into the bed chamber.
   They hid him from Athaliah,
   and he was not killed.
3 And he was with her in the house of Adonai,
   hidden away for six years
   while Athaliah was ruling over the land.

Athaliah, the only queen in the annals of Judah, who ruled the land for six years, receives only a minimum of text. At her introduction, it is stated that "she saw," "she arose," and "she destroyed." She was the mother of Ahaziah, who was killed by Jehu, and likely of at least some of the other sons of Joram of Judah slain by Jehu; and upon

39. I follow the chapter divisions of the traditional Hebrew Text, in which the verse that appears as 11:21 in the NRSV and other English translations appears instead as 12:1. This verse is thus grouped with the subsequent scene.

40. Wilda C. Gafney, *Womanist Midrash: A Reintroduction to the Women of the Torah and the Throne* (Louisville: Westminster John Knox, 2017), 257.

experiencing the death of her offspring, she goes into action. Death calls forth more death in an imitation of the actions of Jehu. At the close of the short unit, it is clear that she has ruled for six years—not a negligible amount of time—but we hear nothing more about this period in terms of her reign. As Gafney notes, she cannot have killed the royal offspring singlehandedly, so she must have had support.[41] Yet of support nothing is said. Nor are there other observations about her, her associations, and her worship inclinations, which might have served a narrative well that is clearly tilted to favor the succession of little Joash, Athaliah's grandson.

Many interpreters assume she is a foreigner, a usurper, and a Baal worshiper.[42] She may have been a daughter of Jezebel, but in the text one finds only that she was a daughter of Ahab and a daughter/descendant of Omri (2 Kgs 8:26–27), which puts her firmly in an Israelite context, albeit as the descendant of a disapproved house.[43] Her name is Hebrew, with the theophoric -yahu ending: Atalyahu, perhaps meaning "Adonai is great."[44] As to Baal worship, there is no mention of it in the text, where only one line, such as "she walked in the ways of the kings of Israel" (cf. 2 Kgs 8:27), would have sufficed. It is unclear why she decides to destroy the rest of the royal offspring, of whom, in any case, there may have been only a few left after Jehu was done with them.[45] She is, however, a direct descendant of the Omride house, which the new Israelite king is determined to exterminate. Does she therefore

41. Gafney, *Womanist Midrash*, 257.

42. Sweeney (*I & II Kings*, 344) calls her a "foreigner of Phoenician descent" and ascribes to her the establishment or maintenance of a "temple to Baal in Jerusalem." Yet the narrator, who has every opportunity of doing so, omits any mention of her name in connection with Baal worship.

43. For an overview of the complex family relations and different possibilities involving marriages between the royal houses of Israel and Judah, see Reuven Chaim (Rudolph) Klein, "Queen Athaliah: The Daughter of Ahab or Omri?" *JBQ* 42 (2014): 11–20.

44. See J. J. Stamm, "Hebräische Frauennamen," in *Hebräische Wortforschung: Festschrift zum 80 Geburtstag von Walter Baumgartner*, VTSup 16 (Leiden: Brill, 1967), 335.

45. Frymer-Kensky, *Reading the Women of the Bible*, 86.

establish herself on the throne in order to hold the reins of power out of fear for her own life? Frymer-Kensky offers as one suggestion that she may have acted in imitation of Jehu in ridding the country of Baal worship,[46] while Hens-Piazza suggests that the murder of so many of her family members by Jehu had driven her to insanity.[47] Her attempt cannot be identified as a failed coup in view of the duration of her reign. Her clear failure lies in not completing the task of killing the royal offspring, since both Jehosheba, either her own daughter or the daughter of King Jehoram by a different mother, and her grandson Joash survive.[48]

So how many and whom exactly did she "destroy"? The text cites "all the royal offspring," phrasing unique to this passage and its counterpart in 2 Chronicles 22:10, using the word *zera'*, a general word for descendants not confined to males. How then did Jehosheba survive? The phrase in verse 1 sounds curiously vague, where it is usually specific (cf. 2 Kgs 10:11, 14, 17). Did Athaliah attempt to take the reins of power in her hands and kill no one at all? The writers thought it important to paint her in as negative a coloring as possible—a direct descendant of Ahab and a woman. Yet in that part of the ancient world, female rulers were not unknown (cf. 1 Kgs 10:1–13). Wil Gafney writes, "The biblical writers are silent on the seven years of peace, stability, and prosperity during Athaliah's reign. One can easily imagine that they would trumpet any instability or political or national disaster as a sign of divine disfavor. They have nothing negative to say, so they say nothing."[49] It would have been helpful to know more about the only queen who reigned in Judah instead of relegating her to a virtual footnote. She was most likely

---

46. Frymer-Kensky, *Reading the Women of the Bible*, 86.

47. Hens-Piazza, *1–2 Kings*, 307.

48. Jehosheba, according to the text "the sister of Ahaziah," could be considered his sister if she was the daughter of the same father (cf. 2 Sam 13:2). Miller and Hayes (*A History of Ancient Israel and Judah*, 349) suggest that Joash was not who the biblical writers say he was: "In view of the circumstances as described . . . one can hardly avoid wondering whether Joash might have been an impostor whom Jehoiada used to get rid of Athaliah and bring his own influence to bear on the nation."

49. Gafney, *Womanist Midrash*, 259.

not a "nice" person, but if niceness were a criterion for writing about people, the Bible might not have been composed at all.

As it is, following the note on Jehosheba's successful hiding of Joash in one of the Temple chambers (2–3), the bulk of the chapter is devoted to the counter-coup engineered by the priest Jehoiada, who puts the seven-year-old prince Joash on the throne through a carefully planned takeover of Temple and palace (4–12).[50] First, he makes a covenant with the guards so they will act on his instructions, and then he divides them so both Temple and palace are surrounded. The directions are presented in the text with a great specificity as to the location and weaponry, with the result that there are guards not only surrounding the key buildings but also the king in the Temple. It looks as if these significant structures have been well-defended during Athaliah's reign. It all takes place in such an orderly fashion, including her assassination, because affairs have been kept in order. Not surprisingly, when she sees what has transpired, she cries out, "Conspiracy, conspiracy!" They are the only words she gets to utter in the story.

Joash is anointed, given the emblems of his royalty, and proclaimed king. It is the tumult of this event that brings out Athaliah to see what is going on, and this affords the opposition the chance to seize her and bring her to the entrance of the stables, where she is killed (13–16). Jehoiada concludes a covenant to pledge king and people to the service of Adonai and king and people to one another (17). There will be only one more such covenant-making in Judah in years to come, and the covenant Jehoiada establishes heralds a renewal of the loyalty between the Davidic house and the people and a renewal of their devotion to Adonai. A celebratory destruction of the temple of Baal follows (18). The king, all of seven years old, can take "his seat on the throne of the kings" with the people rejoicing

50. Joash is one of the kings referred to in the text as either Joash or Jehoash, which will also be the case for one of the descendants of Jehu in Israel. In this volume, the longer form is used for the king of Israel and the shorter form for the king of Judah. The reason for the variation is that in Hebrew the beginning syllables *Yo* (Joash) and *Yeho* (Jehoash) each includes a reference to the sacred name of God in the Hebrew Bible. The same issue caused the variant spelling of Joram as Jehoram.

and the city at peace, a statement made during crowning and kingship only at the time of King Solomon (19–20; cf. 1 Kgs 1:40; 4:20; 8:66). The strain of the house of Omri—present also in the house of David, Athaliah being the grandmother of the new king—remains tactfully unmentioned, although Athaliah's death is recorded once more for good measure.

### Act III, Scene 2: Reform and Assault (2 Kings 12[51])

*The price for peace is high.*[52]

Joash will rule for a long time, although his actual leadership cannot have begun until a decade into his kingship.[53] His introductory note includes the synchronic reference to the Israelite king (Athaliah received no such honor) and a standard evaluation, which in his case is positive (1–3). There is, however, a negative comment added: that "the heights did not go away" and people still sacrificed there. His obituary includes his assassination by his servants, signaling that during his reign, instability beset the country, which may have led to his demise (20–22). He is buried with his ancestors and succeeded by his son, so the case is not one of a palace coup, and no mention is made of the reason for his servants to conspire against him. The major part of the chapter is devoted to repairs in the Temple, first failed (5–9)—was Joash still too young to have the work properly overseen?—and eventually successful (10–17).

The first act of importance is the order Joash gives the priests for temple renovation (5–6). Such a plan is not only important on

51. I am following the chapter divisions of the traditional Hebrew text. Consequently, verse references in 2 Kings 12 in this volume will be one number higher than most English versions.

52. Long, *2 Kings*, 159.

53. The text assigns him a forty-year rule, which we count as a conventional number rather than exact. Even so, it points to a long period. Miller and Hayes (*A History of Ancient Israel and Judah*, 336–38) tentatively assign him approximately thirty years (832–803), leaving open the possibility of a forty-year rule.

the religious level but is significant as a sign of national restoration and would thus raise the status of king and people as well as the center of worship.[54] The king's proposal relies on the priests to use the money received through both a type of individual temple tax (cf. Exod 30:11–16; Lev 27:30–33) and voluntary offerings (cf. Exod 32:1–6; 35:20–29) for the work needed. That the Temple needs repairs does not necessarily imply it is neglected; in view of its age, cracks and other flaws would have naturally appeared in the masonry. The priests are put in charge of the labor (6), not charged with doing it themselves. The plan runs aground when, in the twenty-third year of his reign, nothing has been done and Joash calls those responsible for the project to account. Because we do not know when the plan was put into effect (the text in v. 5 begins with the vague "then"), there is no telling how long this state of affairs has gone on. Whatever the case may be, at age thirty, King Joash takes the matter in hand and orders a new system, which relieves the priests from taking money or overseeing repairs (9). There is no explicit rebuke to the priests, but they clearly have not been doing their job—either because it was too onerous or because they were not willing to part with the money.

The new plan is more specific, involving a collection box, a particular sector of priestly personnel to oversee accumulating the funds on a regular basis, and the appointment of "woodworkers, masons, and stone cutters" to do the necessary labor (10–13). An explanatory note makes clear that the work does not include creating new implements for the Temple but that everything is used for repair (14–17). In addition, the overseers who pay the workers do not have to provide an accounting because they "acted in good faith" (16). One may wonder about the wisdom of the lack of accountability, but the repairs get underway, or so one assumes. A note on the completion of the work is missing. Throughout the explanation of the new process, there is a hierarchy of responsibility: The priests who guard the threshold to the Temple bring the collected money to the king's secretary and the high priest; they then count it and give it to the overseers of the work, who in turn distribute it to the appropriate personnel for the different jobs.

54. Sweeney, *I & II Kings*, 351.

Ironically, Aram is still on the rampage and lays siege to Jerusalem, which forces poor King Joash to rob the very temple he has repaired. "All the dedicated things dedicated by Jehoshaphat, Jehoram, and Ahaziah and by himself, and all the gold" he takes and hands to Hazael, who consents to leave Jerusalem for the time being (18–19). The arm of Syria has grown long indeed. It may be partly because of this event that there is unrest in the city and discontent with Joash's reign, causing his own servants to rise against him—a report that became part of his death notice (21–22). The signs for the Kingdom of Judah are not much better than they are for the North.

### Act IV: Aram and Israel (2 Kings 13)

*Even in success, the regime fails to enact the full prophetic promise.*[55]

The last chapter in this cycle reports continued assaults of Aram on Israel, which were a mark of the period during Jehu's rule (10:32–33), under the reigns of Jehoahaz and Jehoash during the last quarter of the ninth and the first years of the eighth century BCE (1–12, 22–25).[56] The second king achieves a reprieve, most likely due to Assyrian aggression that causes Aram to lose its grip on Israel for the time being.[57] Elisha comes back into the story with one last symbolic act before the report of his death (14–21).

---

55. Brueggemann, *1 & 2 Kings*, 434.

56. The confusing names continue, with the Israelite king who ruled during the last decade of the ninth and the first years of the eighth century BCE also named either Joash or Jehoash, like the Judean king who preceded him. In this volume, the Israelite king will be referred to as Jehoash. See p. 230 above.

57. For a chronology that differs from the biblical account in 2 Kings 13, see Miller and Hayes, *A History of Ancient Israel and Judah*, 338–47. They theorize that success was achieved by Jehoahaz rather than Jehoash because this "would have been a propitious time to challenge Syrian authority." By the end of the reign of Jehoash, "Israel had apparently long since regained both independence from Damascus and domination over Jerusalem" (345). For the purposes of our review, we follow the biblical story, in which the major point is relief from Syrian oppression for Israel.

*Act IV, Scene 1: Two Kings of Israel (2 Kings 13:1–13, 22–25)*

*Change is on the horizon.*[58]

The period of Jehoahaz, son of Jehu, receives the negative evaluation of Israel's kings that "he walked in the sins of Jeroboam, the son of Nevat" (1–2). The account then turns to ascribe the hostile incursions of Hazael of Aram against Israel to the "anger of Adonai" (3). This phrase and its sequel that "he delivered them into the hand of" the king of Aram is reminiscent of the period of the Judges rather than the monarchy and will occur in a similar context in Kings only one other time, in 17:20. The subsequent verses appear to be an amalgam of terminology associated with the oppression of the Israelites in Exodus as well as Judges. Jehoahaz "beseeched" Adonai, who sends a "deliverer" because he "saw the oppression of Israel because Aram oppressed them" (4–5; cf. Exod 3:9; Judg 1:34; 2:18; 3:9, 15; 4:3; 6:9; 10:12). Yet there is no true repentance in Israel, by either king or people. The verb is a plural in verse 6: *they* are *walking* in the sin of Jeroboam. The result is a pitifully small defense force left to the king of Israel (7). Soon, he receives his death notice with a reference to the "scroll of the acts of the kings of Israel" (8–9).

In this chapter, the military undertakings of Jehoash, son of Jehoahaz, receive scarcely more attention than those of his father, but he will return to the story in subsequent episodes. Here, he receives only his negative evaluation and his death notice (12–13). With his death, we reach the period of King Jeroboam II and come nearer to the halfway point of the eighth century BCE. There is more to tell about Jehoash before we get to Jeroboam, events already alluded to in his obituary, which includes a reference to a battle with Amaziah of Judah. In addition, the end of the chapter (22–25) returns to the reign of a king who is buried in the first half by noting both the oppression endured under King Jehoahaz and the compassion of Adonai.

---

58. Hens-Piazza, *1–2 Kings*, 318.

2 Kings 13:22–23

22 Hazael, the king of Aram,
oppressed Israel all the days of Jehoahaz.
23 Then Adonai had pity on them
and was compassionate.
He turned toward them
for the sake of his covenant
with Abraham, Isaac, and Jacob;
he did not wish to destroy them
and has not cast them away
from his presence until now.

God *turns toward them* although they *have not turned* from the sin of Jeroboam (6); he *does not wish to destroy them and has not cast them away.* Divine compassion extends to Israel and is made concrete in the victories of the son of King Jehoahaz, who *takes back* cities from the Aramean king, the son of the father who had *taken* them (25).

### Act IV, Scene 2: Exit Elisha (2 Kings 13:14–21)

*Like relics, his bones in death perform what his body performed in life.*[59]

With this scene, we step back into the period when Jehoash, the son of Jehoahaz, was king in Israel to the bedside of Elisha, who lies ill with the illness of which he will die (14). Next to him is King Jehoash, who weeps and cries out the same words Elisha pronounced at the departure of Elijah: "My father, my father, chariots of Israel and its horsemen!" (15; cf. 2 Kgs 2:12). The literal repetition brings to mind the prophet Elijah and the tie that binds the two prophets.[60] As is at times the case in these narratives, Elisha is on cordial terms

59. Cohn, *2 Kings*, 89.
60. It is also possible that the exclamation is a traditional saying at the impending departure of a powerful figure.

with the monarch of the era. It may be that the saying uttered by the king brings to the prophet's attention the diminished power of Israel or that he is already aware of the need for relief from Aramean domination. Two symbolic actions follow, both of which are best identified as "ritual drama that symbolizes and ensures the desired results."[61] First, the king shoots an arrow to the east, which symbolizes total victory over Aram (15–17). Then the king must strike the ground, which brings about a modification of the foretelling because the three-times-repeated action was not sufficient (18–19). Consequently, he will defeat Aram only three times rather than destroying it completely. The modification fits the reality of the rise of Aram later in the century. Then Elisha dies. Finally, by the great power of Elisha, even in death, a corpse thrown into his grave revives and rises to his feet (21). Cohn writes, "Elisha exits, but his power lives on. If Elijah's death is unique, so too is Elisha's 'afterlife.'"[62]

## Elijah and Elisha

Ancient Israel shared the phenomenon of prophecy with the rest of the ancient Mediterranean world, and we encounter it in three of the books of the Former Prophets. In its origin, it consists of "intuitive manticism or divination, soothsaying and clairvoyance" with a variety of functions.[63] It became an institutionalized office in Israel attached to political and religious centers of power. From such circles, including the ecstatic prophets we meet in the books of Samuel, individuals emerged to act independently as critics of society and the monarchy. Two prophets—foretellers, miracle workers, representing the traditional forms of prophecy but also critics of the leadership of the realm—stride through the chapters from 1 Kings

61. Sweeney, *I & II Kings*, 359.

62. Cohn, *2 Kings*, 89.

63. Rainer Albertz, *A History of Israelite Religion in the Old Testament Period*, trans. John Bowden, vol. 1, OTL (Louisville: Westminster John Knox, 1994), 151; trans. of *Religionsgeschichte Israels in alttestamenlicher Zeit* (Göttingen: Vandenhoeck & Ruprecht, 1992). For Albertz's lucid overview of the phenomenon, including the prophets Elijah and Elisha, see 151–56.

17 to the end of 2 Kings 13 and infuse the text with their power-ful presence. Even when they are not at the center of the action or when they are altogether absent from the text, their authority and charisma hover in the background.

They are the only two prophets in the Bible who function to-gether as prophet and disciple, with the disciple eventually becom-ing the successor to his master, inheriting his gifts in duplicate, sym-bolized by the mantle passing from one to the other. They are not the same person, do not perform the same tasks, and have different characteristics. Even the larger-than-life legendary tales of their undertakings convey dissimilarities in disposition and perspective. They both have their roots in the Northern Kingdom, but where Elisha receives a patronymic and known location—son of Shafat of Abel-Meholah in the central Jordan Valley, apparently a farmer by occupation—Elijah's origins are more mysterious. He comes on the scene as "the Tishbite," which conceals as much as it reveals. He is someone with roots in the land east of the Jordan, the "other" side. People may well have viewed him as a foreigner.[64] Both are referred to as "the prophet" but as often as not are identified as "the man of God." Both accomplish miracles related to food supply and both raise a boy from death. Of the two, Elijah (meaning "my God is Adonai") became a principal figure in the religious traditions, especially of Judaism, where he took on the role of peacemaker, guardian angel, settler of disputes for the Talmudic rabbis, among many other functions. He takes a central place in the ritual life of Jews and is seen as the "herald of the redemption of Israel and the precursor of the Messiah."[65] In the Christian gospels, he is a witness,

---

64. The entire line in 1 Kgs 17:1 reads, "Elijah the Tishbite from the set-tlers in Gilead," which does not refer to a known location of Tishbe. Walsh, *1 Kings*, 226: "He is from Gilead, an Israelite region east of the Jordan River, but whether he is a native of the region or an immigrant is not clear." Sweeney, *I & II Kings*, 211: "From the perspective of Ephraimite hill country, the people of the Transjordan might very well be viewed as foreigners." Elijah is called "the Tishbite" in 1 Kgs 17:1; 21:17, 28; 2 Kgs 1:3, 8; 9:36.

65. For an overview of the role and importance of Elijah in Jewish tradi-tion and contemporary ritual, see Joshua Gutmann, S. David Sperling, Moses Aberbach, Dov Noy, Bathya Bayer, Michael Stone, and H. Schauss, "Elijah,"

together with Moses, at the transfiguration of Jesus (Matt 17:1–8; Mark 9:2–8; Luke 9:28–36).

Far more than his disciple and successor, Elijah is preoccupied with idolatry and the struggle against the invasion of the worship of Adonai by other deities, specifically Baalism. He speaks for God and to God; he prays and invokes God's power both in the intimate and the public sphere. He is often found by the side of the ruling monarch, mostly Ahab, to announce dire events to come or hurl accusations about the king's sinful behavior. He is active in the company of ordinary people in two stories: his encounter with the widow of Zarephat and the event on Mount Carmel. In the course of his career, he experiences a serious crisis regarding his usefulness and appears overwhelmed by his task. In the dramatic scene on Mount Horeb, Adonai reveals to him that more work lies ahead and assigns him three specific tasks, only one of which he approximately fulfills. The other two will be undertaken by Elisha. His most spectacular moment comes at the time of his death, when rather than dying as a mere mortal, he is taken away in a storm, with the appearance of fire surrounding chariots and horses. Fire is the element that belongs to the story of Elijah. Fire from Adonai determines the outcome on Mt. Carmel, fire is present to herald the presence of God at Mt. Horeb, and fire devours the soldiers sent to fetch him by King Ahaziah.

Elisha (meaning "my God saves") is from the beginning of his career surrounded by others called "the disciples of the prophets." He may operate by himself, but in such cases he is often accompanied by a servant, Gehazi, who has his own role to play in the narratives. More than Elijah, Elisha is active among common people, meeting ordinary needs, especially for food, for healing, or for shelter. He also deals with the reigning powers of his day, and although he can be critical in his contacts with monarchs, there are times when their relations are more cordial, as in the moments leading up to his death, for example. He is in some ways a more colorful person than his predecessor, a man of quick temper perhaps, unleashing deathly power on youth who mock and dishonor him. His element is

in *Encyclopaedia Judaica*, 2nd ed., ed. Fred Skolnik and Michael Berenbaum (New York: Macmillan, 2007), 6:331–38.

water rather than fire: He divides the water of the Jordan after Elijah is taken up; his first miraculous intervention consists of throwing salt in poisonous water; he calls forth water for the armies of Israel and Judah in the desert, casts a healing substance in foul-tasting food (vegetables presumably boiled in water), sends Naaman to the Jordan to wash, and makes iron float like wood in the water of the Jordan. He fulfills the tasks left unfinished by Elijah regarding the ruling houses of Damascus and Israel, but they are completed by others on his initiative, and he remains at a distance both from the ailing Ben-hadad in Aram and from Jehu in Israel. He may speak in the name of Adonai—extensively on the occasion of creating water in the desert—and act in God's name, but his miracles are at times accomplished in his absence and do not always involve a reference to a specific divine intervention. He has no encounters with God and prays only three times, of which the very brief content is recorded only twice. His preoccupation is not with idolatry, which may point to his activity in a period following a major religious reform (see p. 221n23 above). It is worth observing how often during Elisha's engagement with monarchs the references are simply to "the king" or "the king of Israel" without further identification.

Elisha moves in a less rarefied atmosphere than Elijah, who comes out of nowhere and is rarely found indoors. In a rare sketch of outward appearance, the text provides a rough picture of Elijah's clothing and perhaps hairy exterior. The presence of hair in the Bible can be a signifier of power and authority. In contrast, we learn from the episode with the bears and the boys that Elisha is bald. Elisha travels around but finds temporary lodging with a patron and evidently has a home base from which his disciples seek to move to more spacious quarters. He is indoors at the end of his life, where King Jehoash of Israel visits him and shoots an arrow through a window. A room with a window points to housing beyond just the merely adequate. (The episode of Elisha's last days may be in keeping with the period in which the stories have their origin, Jehoash being the second of Jehu's descendants.)

The Elijah narratives provide little information about the lives of ordinary people and their needs, which come to the fore through their interactions with Elisha to a far greater degree. In the presence of Elisha, people are concerned about their livelihood, adequate food, debts, housing, and other provisions. Because the text of Kings is elsewhere centered on the monarchs, these glimpses into the life of the community are important signifiers of life in general among the population, especially of Elisha's day. With Jehoash son of Jehoahaz son of Jehu, we are entering the eighth century BCE, and the time of the prophets Amos and Hosea is not too far off. Those two will lay bare the consequences of accumulation of wealth by the few with the resulting deprivations of large groups of people and a breakdown of the more egalitarian ideals of the earlier periods. Economic oppression will be the major concern of the great prophets of the eighth century: Amos, Hosea, Micah, and Isaiah. It was easy for a small farmer to fall into debt and subsequently lose livelihood or part of the family to a creditor, as exemplified by the poor widow who appeals to Elisha for help.[66]

On top of social crises, there were the upheavals of revolution inside and hostilities from the larger world. Both Aram/Syria and the Assyrian empire looked to enlarge their empires to make use of the important trade routes that ran through Israel. In addition, there were ongoing hostilities inside the kingdoms, with Israel and Judah at odds during a large part of the period of Elijah and Elisha. Wars and revolutions do not in general benefit the lives of common people; heavy tributes to foreign powers are not solely paid for by treasures of Temple and palace, and many people must have suffered deprivation. With the disappearance of Elijah and Elisha from center stage, ordinary people and their concerns disappear also, and we return to the world of the palace in the final chapters of 2 Kings.

66. See Albertz (*A History of Israelite Religion*, 159–63) for information about the social and economic developments of the period.

# Cycle V: The Road to Collapse (2 Kings 14–17)

*The narrator, from a perspective of convinced faith, tells a sorry truth about then . . . and about now.*[1]

Four chapters document the three-quarters of a century from Jehoash of Israel and Azariah/Uzziah of Judah until the collapse of the Northern Kingdom. The chapters, as usual, review the different monarchies in an uneven way, providing very little coverage of the longest period, the relatively prosperous and calm reign of Jeroboam II (788–748), and more on the tumultuous phases preceding and following. Pressures subside and rise according to the strength or weakness of Aram and Assyria. Inside the kingdoms, hostilities break out between Israel and Judah at the beginning of the eighth century, ending with Judah paying tribute to its neighbor (ch. 14). After the brief account of the reign of Jeroboam II in the final seven verses of chapter 14, the next chapter jumps to the last decades of the Kingdom of Israel, with a succession of five revolutionary takeovers following the assassination of Zechariah, the fourth descendant of Jehu. Assyria under Tiglat-pileser III marches into Israel in 738, and a total takeover is averted only by tribute exacted from the population. Chapter 16 describes the unfortunate alliance between Syria and Israel under Rezin and Pekah, resulting in even greater jeopardy for land and people; and in 726, Shalmaneser V of Assyria begins a siege of Samaria, which falls in 722. Chapter 17, the last chapter in this cycle, offers an extensive evaluation of the reasons for Israel's fall and reviews the aftermath of the Assyrian takeover in terms of religious developments.

1. Brueggemann, *1 & 2 Kings*, 461.

## Act I: A Helper for Israel (2 Kings 14)

*The attempt by the elites in power in Israel and Judah to safeguard this power by skillful maneuvering between the great powers of their time . . . thus proved quite ruinous.*[2]

Strife between Jehoash of Israel and Amaziah of Judah was incorporated in the death notice of Jehoash in 13:12, and in chapter 14 we step back in time to get the full story of that altercation. Subsequently, the period of Jeroboam II is recapped in a very short review with a brief glimpse of his enlarging the borders of his country due to a weakened Aram and a friendship with Assyria. The text skips back and forth from Israel to Judah, and due to the long reign attributed to Azariah of Judah, we will reach the second half of the eighth century BCE by the time Zechariah, the fourth descendant of Jehu, ascends the throne in 15:8. Five bloody rebellions follow one another in Israel, with the Assyrian wolf constantly at the door of the kingdom. The last decades before the capture of Samaria witness an alliance between Aram and Israel in revolt against Assyria in the so-called Syro-Ephraimite war.

### Act I, Scene 1: The Thistle and the Cedar (2 Kings 14:1–22)

*Amaziah not only loses face, he loses the war.*[3]

We step back in time to the period of Jehoash in Israel in the last years of the ninth century BCE, when Amaziah becomes king in Judah. Amaziah's evaluation consists of "limping praise"[4]; that is to say, he did "what was right in the eyes of Adonai," but "like his father Joash he

---

2. Rainer Albertz, *A History of Israelite Religion in the Old Testament Period*, trans. John Bowden, vol. 1, OTL (Louisville: Westminster John Knox, 1994), 163; trans. of *Religionsgeschichte Israels in alttestamentlicher Zeit* (Göttingen: Vandenhoeck & Ruprecht, 1992).

3. Burke O. Long, *2 Kings*, FOTL 10 (Grand Rapids: Eerdmans, 1991), 167.

4. I take this phrase from Long, *2 Kings*, 170.

did not remove the heights," and people went on worshiping there (1–4). His first act is to take vengeance on his father's assassins, though it is noted that he avoids extending the blood feud to their offspring (5–6), as is "written in the scroll of the Teaching of Moses," an unusual reference in Kings, found elsewhere only in David's instructions to his son Solomon (1 Kgs 2:3) and in reference to King Josiah (1 Kgs 23:25). Here it is clearly a reference to the specific prescription in Deuteronomy that each person shall be responsible for their own sin (Deut 24:16). In the next breath, he achieves victory over Edom (7) and then gets above himself and challenges the king of Israel (8–10). His invitation to Jehoash for a confrontation is met with derision and a scathing short parable highlighting the difference in stature between them.

2 KINGS 14:9–10

9  Jehoash, the king of Israel, sent a message
   to Amaziah, the king of Judah, as follows:
   The thistle of the Lebanon sent a message
   to the cedar in the Lebanon as follows:
   Give your daughter to my son for a wife.
   Then there passed by a wild beast of the Lebanon
   and trampled the thistle.
10 You completely struck down Edom,
   and now your heart has lifted you.
   Enjoy your glory and stay at home!
   Why get involved in trouble
   so you will fall, and Judah with you!

In this eloquent piece of rhetoric, the references are quite clear, and the talk of wild beasts "trampling" sounds threatening in the extreme (cf. 2 Kgs 7:17, 20; 9:33). Jehoash tells his Southern colleague that he has become too big for his britches and he should cool down. The fall of a king, after all, involves his entire realm. Amaziah, probably deeply enraged by being compared to the lowly thistle, decides to go to war. As it turns out, this is an unwise move. Judah is defeated, Amaziah gets captured, and the wall of Jerusalem is breached. Amaziah has to pay heavy tribute to the king of Israel, who also exacts hostages—most likely members of the elite or the royal family. One wonders what there is left in the Temple and treasuries of the palace of gold and silver after it has been plundered so many times, as recently as the rule of Amaziah's father (2 Kgs 12:19[18]), but perhaps replenishment through taxation took place regularly. Such a constant availability of funds in the treasuries points to extra burdens being laid on the populace as soon as the stores are depleted.

The death notice of Jehoash of Israel repeats the one already given in chapter 13 (14:15–16 = 13:12–13). Evidently, Amaziah was left in place to continue as king of Judah, and he meets his end, like his father, by assassination (17–20). The subject of the clause "they conspired against him in Jerusalem" is vague, but presumably it refers to a party at the court. There may have been general unhappiness resulting from the war with Israel and the consequent deprivation and unrest. Eventually killed in Lachish, Amaziah does receive his burial in Jerusalem (14:20), but no further reference to his "acts" is provided. His successor Azariah, also called Uzziah, is "made king" by "all the people of Judah" (21), an unusual succession in Judah, once again indicating the general unrest of the period for the Southern Kingdom. Azariah will return to the narrative in the next chapter.

### Act I, Scene 2: Jeroboam II of Israel (2 Kings 14:23–29)

*This chapter jars one's growing confidence about God and how God acts. . . . God appears to dole out rewards according to what people need and not according to what they deserve.*[5]

When Jeroboam II ascends the throne in 788, the third descendant in the line of Jehu, his evaluation is the standard negative one of Israel's kings doing "what is evil in the eyes of Adonai . . . not turning from all the sins of Jeroboam, the son of Nevat" (24). On the heels of this statement follows the observation that he brought the border of Israel back to former frontiers, a fulfillment of prophetic

---

5. Gina Hens-Piazza, *1–2 Kings*, AOTC (Nashville: Abingdon, 2006), 333.

foretelling (25). Miller and Hayes write about this long period, "During much of the second half of the century of the Jehu dynasty. . ., especially during the reign of Jeroboam II (788–748), Israel enjoyed a period of national restoration and expansion."[6] Even if the statements made in the text are extravagant and hyperbolic, Jeroboam must have expanded the territory belonging to Israel. For all his success, the text of Kings allots him a scant seven verses (23–29), and two of those are devoted to the fact that the success was the work of Adonai, who sent Jeroboam as a rescuer of Israel from its distress (26–27). When his father Jehoash of Israel was on the throne, whose evaluation was no more positive than that of his son, he too was sent as a "deliverer" because Adonai "saw" the oppression with which Aram oppressed Israel (13:4–5). Once again God has "seen" the suffering and lack of a "helper" for Israel, and Jeroboam becomes the instrument for a reprieve.[7]

The long period of Jeroboam II's reign is by some also identified as one in which the divide between rich and poor became exacerbated by the formation of large estates, pushing many small farmers into debt and economic depression. Burdens of large taxation, increased during times of war, weighed far more heavily on the social stratum of the population whose survival depended on the small self-sustaining farm. "They were compelled more and more frequently to resort to loans in order to get by. This put large parts of the farming population under such direct pressure from the economically expanding upper class that on a wide front they were driven to dependence upon it and became permanently impoverished."[8] The general categories used by the prophets who fulminate against the social injustices of the period—of "the poor," the "weak," the "destitute," and the "wretched"—highlight these specific

---

6. J. Maxwell Miller and John H. Hayes, *A History of Ancient Israel and Judah*, 2nd ed. (Louisville: Westminster John Knox, 2006), 352.

7. Nelson (*First and Second Kings*, IBC [Atlanta: John Knox, 1987], 220) points to the background of liturgical language for 2 Kgs 14:26–27. In many psalms, God is called on to be the helper of the weak and powerless (see Pss 10:14; 30:11[10]; 54:6[4]; 72:12; 118:7). To have one's name wiped out is the ultimate curse in Deut (Deut 29:19[20]).

8. Albertz, *A History of Israelite Religion*, 160.

economic realities. The last decades of the reign of Jeroboam II are also the years of the activities of Amos and Hosea in the North, but their concerns are not uppermost in the minds of the writers and compilers of Kings, and we look in vain for a mention of their names or their concerns. Jeroboam dies with a death notice once more referring to his accomplishments in terms of territorial conquest, and his son Zechariah becomes king in his place (29).

## Act II: "A Depressing Succession of Rulers"[9] (2 Kings 15–16)

*The reader is left with the impression that from this point on, the problem of synchronism and chronology has gotten the better of the narrator.*[10]

The next two chapters take us at breakneck speed through the decades until conquest of Israel by Assyria can no longer be averted. At the end of chapter 15, the era of the next to last king has begun. Chapter 16 takes a long detour into Judah and the reign of Ahaz, who becomes subservient to Assyria and has a new altar built for the Temple in Jerusalem.

### Act II, Scene 1: Headlong into Disaster (2 Kings 15)

*As though a monstrous beast approaches the borders of both kingdoms.*[11]

Chapter 15 opens with the continuation of the reign of Amaziah's son Azariah in Judah, a confused synchronistic listing that will continue in the text. Of his reign we hear little except that he was an acceptable king in the manner of his father Amaziah but that like him did not remove "the heights" (1–4).[12] Stricken with a skin disease

---

9. Everett Fox, *The Early Prophets: Joshua, Judges, Samuel, and Kings* (New York: Schocken, 2014), 763.

10. Nelson, *First and Second Kings*, 221.

11. Long, *2 Kings*, 172.

12. Azariah is also called Uzziah in the text. Miller and Hayes (*A History*

of a serious nature—the *tsara'at* of Naaman and the four men who discover the camp of the Arameans deserted (2 Kgs 5:1; 7:3–10)—the king is confined to separate quarters until his death while his son Jotham administers the affairs of the kingdom.[13] Although assigned an exceptionally long reign, he is gone to his grave almost as soon as he appears (6–7). The chapter will end, as it began, with a review of a Judean king (32–38), thus framing the succession of rulers in Israel—perhaps to provide a contrast between the two kingdoms. In Israel, the slide to disaster is taking on speed; Zechariah the son of Jeroboam II reigns for only six months before he is assassinated by Shallum. He receives no death notice, as is usual for a king who is murdered, but he gets an entirely stereotypical negative evaluation, which is repeated for the next three rulers (9, 18, 24, 28).

Taking a look outside of the text at what is happening with Israel's most important neighbor, Assyria, we observe that after a period of decline in the mid-ninth century, the Neo-Assyrian Empire begins taking on renewed energy for expansion following Jeroboam's

---

*of Ancient Israel and Judah*, 337, 365) list their reconstruction of the regnal periods in Israel and Judah of the last part of the ninth and of the eighth centuries as follows:

| JUDAH | ISRAEL |
|---|---|
| Athaliah (838–833) | Jehu (839–822) |
| Joash (832–803[793]) | Jehoahaz (821-805) |
| Amaziah (802–786/774) | Jehoash (804–789) |
| Azariah/Uzziah (785–760/734) | Jeroboam II (788–748) |
| Jotham (759–744) | Zechariah and Shallum (748) |
| Ahaz (743–728) | Menahem (746–737) |
| Hezekiah (722–699) | Pekaiah (736–734) |
| | Pekah (734–731) |
| | Hoshea (730–722) |
| | Fall of Samaria 722 |

13. The affliction is ascribed to an act of God according to the traditional understanding that Adonai is the author of all things, for good or ill. The phrase for the separate housing (*bet hahofshit*) lit. means "the house of freedom," with freedom perhaps being a euphemism for confinement. The medieval Jewish scholar Rabbi David Kimhi judged the word "freedom" to refer to the king being relieved of the burdens of his office (cited in Fox, *The Early Prophets*, 769).

rule in Israel.[14] King Tiglat-pileser III (744–727) inaugurates more than a century of Assyrian domination over Southwest Asia, including the Mediterranean seaboard. While the Kingdom of Judah escapes the fate of conquest and deportation for another century and a half, it is never again truly independent of its powerful neighbor to the northeast.

There are still kingships to record, but the story is dull in its repetitive mention of evil deeds and negative evaluations, lacking any tension except that of the looming disaster. Shallum is king for only a month when he is struck down by Menachem (13–16), during whose ten-year rule Tiglat-pileser, here called Pul, has to be bribed to leave the land alone for the time being (19–20). For the first time, we hear that a tribute is exacted from the population (20). After Menahem, his son Pekaiah is king for perhaps two years before he is struck down by Pekah, the son of his commander. Only Menahem receives a burial notice; all the others are assassinated. It is in Pekah's time that the narrator stops the monotonous recital of murder to record the invasion of Tiglat-pileser into the North and the Transjordan, from which he deports the population (29). Pekah and his colleague Rezin will come back into the story in the following chapter, which deals mainly with Judah. For now, his story ends with yet another assassination, of Pekah by Hoshea, the last monarch of Israel (30–31).

As if to provide a short relief from the list of depressing rulers in Israel, the text returns to Judah, where Jotham, the son of Azariah/Uzziah, ascends the throne in 759 (32–35). He receives an approving evaluation with the usual qualifier that the heights were not removed and an approving note on his building the upper gate of the Temple in Jerusalem. His death notice, with the reference to another record as well as his burial place and successor (36, 38), surrounds

14. For a detailed overview, see Miller and Hayes, *A History of Ancient Israel and Judah*, 360–74. As they point out, the eighth century ushered in the succession of far-flung international empires: Assyria, Babylonia, Persia, Greece, and Rome. These empires affected the history of Israel, the period of restoration in Judah after the Babylonian exile, and in the religious context, Judaism and Christianity as the two offshoots of the religion of the period that created the Hebrew Bible.

the observation that Pekah of Israel and Rezin of Aram harass Judah in "those days" (37). We place the actual period of those hostilities under Jotham's successor Ahaz. It is as if the anxiety besetting the kingdoms invades the text, which anticipates troubles for Judah in the near future.

### Act II, Scene 2: Detour to Judah (2 Kings 16)

*For Ahaz, seeing is believing; one look at the altar in Damascus apparently convinces him that he must have one too.*[15]

We move to the South for the story of a part of the rule of Ahaz, the son of King Jotham. The story is not too complicated if we know some background. With Assyria now the most powerful and aggressive force in the region, Israel and Aram decide to form an alliance against it, and they try to compel Judah to become a part of their coalition in the so-called Syro-Ephraimite war. Aram and Israel have other smaller states (Phoenicia, Philistia, Moab, and Edom) on their side, which means Judah is also threatened from the south unless it decides to join the partnership.[16] In their first attempt to conquer Jerusalem, the alliance fails, which buys Ahaz time to appeal to the Assyrian king (5–9). Once again, the storehouses of the palace and the silver and gold of the Temple are plundered and sent as a bribe to Tiglat-pileser (8). The word used for the tribute is "bribe" (*shohar*) rather than "gift," a noun that may be used for tribute (1 Kgs 5:1 [4:21]; 10:25; 2 Kgs 17:3, 4). The word "bribe" always has a negative connotation (Exod 23:8; Deut 10:17; 16:19; 27:25; 1 Sam 8:3), and whether the action of Ahaz is his only way out of the predicament or not, it provides a deleterious coloring to his ploy. It may also not

---

15. Robert L. Cohn, *2 Kings*, Berit Olam (Collegeville, MN: Liturgical Press, 2000), 114.

16. The most likely meaning of Elat being "returned" to Aram by Rezin in v. 6 is that the Edomites joined the coalition. It is clear that those of Judah who lived there were expelled. Elat, in the far south, a port that was established by Solomon, was lost to Edom at some point.

have been necessary at this moment since Rezin and Pekah were headed for defeat by Assyria anyway.[17]

When Ahaz comes on the scene in verses 1–4, he receives elaborate condemnation. He is compared negatively to King David and said to walk in the ways of the kings of Israel. He engages in worse than idolatrous practices, like those of the original inhabitants of the land—possibly even child sacrifice. In addition, he himself sacrifices on the heights: on the hills and under every green tree. After the king of Assyria has taken care of the uprising on the part of Aram and Israel and conquered Damascus, Ahaz goes to meet him there and views the altar. Subsequently, the chapter is devoted to the construction and use of a new altar after the model of Damascus in Jerusalem (10–16). First, instructions are sent to the priest Uriah, who oversees the construction; then proper sacrifices are made, with the king officiating. The new altar will henceforth be the location for the regular offerings while the original bronze altar will serve as the king's as a site for private inquiry—prayer seeking God's counsel. After these arrangements, the narrative describes a further stripping of bronze from the Temple to be sent as more tribute to Assyria (17–18). The death notice of Ahaz is brief and does not list a successor (19–20).

Why was this story incorporated into the material immediately preceding the collapse of the North? After the initial negative evaluation of Ahaz, did the rest of his actions only contribute to the downslide of Judah? His vassalage to Assyria will ensure continued bondage of Judah to that empire until Assyria's fall in 621. Is the altar built after a Syrian model to replace the original one a metaphor indicating the inevitable doom of Judah? Scholars are divided in their opinion of Ahaz, but it is difficult to see anything here that is positive.[18] He begins with the most abominable practices the text ever mentions in terms of his worship and engages in active idolatry

17. See Robert Alter (*Ancient Israel: The Former Prophets: Joshua, Judges, Samuel, and Kings* [New York: Norton, 2013], 804n8). Alter judges the word "gift," as most translations render it, a mistake.

18. Nelson (*First and Second Kings*, 227) disagrees with Cohn (*2 Kings*, 112–15), who believes the narrative is highly critical of Ahaz by implication. Nelson writes, "In religious matters, then, as in foreign relations, Ahaz's reign was something of a tossup."

according to the standard of Kings by sacrificing on the "heights." He sends a "bribe" to Assyria and further strips the Temple of expensive metals, on top of the gold and silver he had contributed.[19] Without doubt, the vassalage to Assyria included a tax burden on the populace. One wonders, in view of these actions, where the funds came from to construct a new altar and whether this move, besides being potentially idolatrous, was a wise one in view of the deprivations Judah already had to suffer. It seems most likely that this chapter aims to portray a situation in Judah that anticipates a fate similar to Israel's, which is just around the corner.

### Act III: Fall and Judgment (2 Kings 17)

*All the blame for the exile of the northern kingdom is placed squarely on the Israelites' collective shoulders.*[20]

A first scene in this chapter describes the actions of the final king of Israel, Hoshea, and the eventual siege and capture of Samaria by Sargon II of Assyria with the resulting exile of Israel's inhabitants in 722 (1–6). A long explanation for this event follows in a second unit, a commentary tightly constructed on the theme of the people's rejection of God's instructions (7–23). A third scene describes the aftermath of the deportation and repopulation of Israel (24–33). Finally, the last scene comments on the situation described as one of religious syncretism, where everyone worships the god or gods of their tradition, including Adonai (34–41). There are thus two narrative sections, each of which elicits commentary.[21]

19. He orients the original bronze altar to the North, which, according to Sweeney (*I & II Kings: A Commentary*, OTL [Louisville: Westminster John Knox, 2007], 385), "symbolizes subjugation to Assyria."
20. Lyle Eslinger, *Into the Hands of the Living God*, JSOTSup 84 (Sheffield: Almond, 1984), 184. Eslinger understands the tirade against Israel, here and in Judg 2:1–23, as ironic in tone and intention.
21. For this arrangement and in-depth analysis of the chapter, see Pauline Viviano, "2 Kings 17: A Rhetorical and Form-Critical Analysis," *CBQ* 49 (1987): 548–59.

### Act III, Scene 1: The Demise of the North (2 Kings 17:1–6)

*A unit concerned with a moment, indeed the final moment, in the history of the Northern Kingdom.*[22]

This brief narrative section first describes King Hoshea, who replaced Pekah in the last violent overturning of a monarchy in the Northern Kingdom (1–4; cf. 15:30). He comes on the throne in 731 BCE and rules for nine years. His evaluation is negative mixed with faint praise; the evil he did was "not like the kings of Israel who were before him" (2). Before we can hear more about the reasons for this unusual note, the text goes on to describe aggression from the Assyrian king, Shalmaneser V, most likely to force Hoshea to pay more tribute. This in turn makes Hoshea appeal to Egypt for help and costs him his freedom. We hear no more about Hoshea—whether he lived the rest of his life in prison or if something else happened—for the story moves on to tell of the siege and capture of Samaria, a three-year-long event told in a few sentences (5–6). In 722, the curtain falls on the kingdom that was established by Jeroboam at the close of the tenth century. It survived for two centuries, all its kings continuing in the shadow of the one who "went and made . . . other gods and cast images" and who "threw" Adonai behind his back (1 Kgs 14:9). It is taken into exile, deported, dispersed in a foreign land.

### Act III, Scene 2: The Reasons Why (2 Kings 17:7–23)

*An ingrate slap in the face to the redeemer God who delivered them from Egypt.*[23]

What follows is a long explanation of the reasons for the fall of the kingdom. It shows numerous repetitions but has a clear construction, beginning with the headline in verse 7.[24]

---

22. Viviano, "2 Kings 17," 549.

23. Eslinger, *Into the Hands*, 184.

24. Declaring the text a "rambling homily" is not a fair assessment (so Nelson, *First and Second Kings*, 230).

2 KINGS 17:7

This was because the Israelites sinned
against Adonai their God,
who brought them up from the land of Egypt,
from under the hand of Pharaoh, the king of Egypt,
and they feared other gods.

The indictment is clear: The people's sin consists of *fearing* other gods than their God, the one who liberated them from bondage in Egypt. Unlike other recitals of people's transgressions against Adonai, the list of God's wondrous redeeming actions on their behalf in the past is kept to just two lines.[25] From their orientation to other deities flowed the actions they undertook as described in this first unit, which is mainly concerned with idol worship (8–12). They sacrificed to the wrong gods in the wrong places and did this in imitation of the peoples who originally inhabited the land. They did this in the face of having been told not to do so.

The next unit elaborates on this theme of information that was ignored or counteracted by recalling the warnings God provided and how these were flouted (13–17). We note that Judah is included in this indictment. Where the first unit is in the third person, referring to the people as "they," the next list of transgressions commences with the more direct "you" as it quotes divine admonitions presented by prophets and seers, repeating them in the imperatives: "Turn from your evil ways;/ keep my commandments," referring to the teaching (*torah*) already given to the ancestors and repeated through the prophets. Verse 14 cites a series of three negative actions, "they did not keep," "they made their neck hard," and "they did not trust Adonai." These transgressions are summed up in the charge of their *rejecting the covenant* God made with the ancestors and all the statutes and commandments that went with it.

---

25. Cf. Ps 78, which with its long list of the people's sinful behavior eloquently and at length describes God's gracious actions toward them.

2 Kings 17:15b

They walked after vapor and became vapor
and after the peoples around them
about whom Adonai commanded them
not to do like them.

The word here translated "vapor" in Hebrew means "breath, vanity,
nothing," a key word in the text of Ecclesiastes. The summary of this
unit that follows the accusations once again makes them concrete in
that they *made* images and an asherah and *served* Baal, the epitome
of idol worship in this period. Added to this is engagement in practices native to Canaan, outlawed for Israel, making their children *go
through the fire* and practicing *divination*.[26] On top of all this, they
did it to spite/vex Adonai.

In the third unit, the consequences of the people's behavior are
spelled out in the most severe terms (18–23). First, the announcement is made that Adonai removed the people from his presence
(lit. "his face"). Then, the rejection by Israel of Adonai has as its consequence Adonai's rejection of "all the seed of Israel" (20); Adonai
"abused them" and "gave them into the hand of plunderers" (cf. Judg
2:14). In verses 21–23, the *tearing of the kingdom* is attributed to
Israel instead of the divine initiative cited in 1 Kings 11:11, 12, 13,
31. It was Israel who *made Jeroboam king*, the one who drew all the
people into following "all the sins which he did." In the end, the dire
statement is once again made that Adonai *removed* the people from
his presence so that Israel "went into exile away from its land to Assyria until this day" (23).[27] It is hard to overstate the severity of these
denunciations, which are without equal in the Historical Books.

26. Eslinger (*Into the Hands*, 215) is correct in observing that such practices have not been mentioned before this moment in the chapters that indict
the kings of Israel. They are forbidden in the Torah (Deut 18:10, 11) and also
sternly condemned in especially the prophets shortly before and during the
exile (Isa 44:25; Jer 27:9; 29:8; Ezek 13:6, 9, 23; 21:28[23]; Cf. Mic 3:6, 7, 11)

27. The word for "Assyria" in Hebrew is *Assur* and the verb for "remove"
uses forms of the root *sur* so that the statement in verse 23 exhibits word play
on these two words.

### Act III, Scene 3: Each Nation and Its Gods (2 Kings 17:24–33)

*Deportation is a two-way street.*[28]

A brief account concerns the repopulation of the land from which the exiles have been deported (17:24–28). As Viviano has pointed out, the theme is centered on the words *fear* and *justice/customs.*[29] Because of the different peoples' lack of acquaintance with the proper way to serve Adonai, lions come out, sent by Adonai to kill them. The assumption here is that Adonai comes with the territory: "Anyone living in the land must fear him if they know what's good for them."[30] Lions have been associated with destructive divine power in these texts before (1 Kgs 13:25, 26, 28; 20:36). The unnamed reporters of the events to the Assyrian king, most likely Assyrian officials, do not know which god is offended, but they understand the destructive lions as divine tools and ascribe the reason for their presence to a lack of knowledge about the "custom of the god(s) of the land" (26). The Assyrian ruler proposes that an Israelite priest will go back as a teacher of "how to fear Adonai" (28). This is an ironic twist, since a member of the people who "did not fear" Adonai now must inform those alien to Israel's religion about how to do this right. It works, apparently, to the degree that Adonai is included in the worship of multiple deities. No more is heard about voracious lions, and everyone worships according to their own rules: "Adonai they feared, and their own gods they served" (33).

---

28. Walter Brueggemann, *1 & 2 Kings*, SHBC 8 (Macon, GA: Smyth & Helwys, 2000), 482.

29. In Hebrew, the word "to fear," used for the reverence for "other gods" in v. 7, occurs in the opening and closing of vv. 24–28. The word "justice," an important word in the Hebrew Bible (see van Wijk-Bos, *The Road to Kingship*, 72), is here more appropriately rendered "rules" or "customs" or "practices" (cf. 1 Kgs 18:28). The word always reverberates with complex echoes, even in this more concrete setting. For the observations on the ring construction of the two words, see Viviano, "2 Kings 17," 554.

30. Cohn, *2 Kings*, 120.

*Act III, Scene 4: You Shall Not Fear Other Gods*
*(2 Kings 17:34–41)*

*The objectionable practices of apostasy now become intensified.*[31]

The final commentary section is focused on the word "fear." It begins by pointing out once again that "they do not fear Adonai" (34) and ends by stating that "these peoples feared Adonai and also served their idols" (41). The impossibility of acting this way and at the same time gaining God's approval is pointed out in the rest of the unit. First, "not fearing Adonai" is the equivalent of "not acting" according to God's instruction about worshiping Adonai to the exclusion of "other gods." It was, after all, the people of Israel, "the children of Jacob," with whom God made a covenant *not to fear other gods*. This idea of *not fearing other gods* is repeated three times in the short sequence and forms the frame around the section.

2 KINGS 17:35–39

35 Adonai cut with them a covenant
and commanded them as follows:

You shall not fear other gods,
or bow down to them,
or serve them,
or call them to mind.
36 But Adonai, who brought you up
from the land of Egypt
with great strength and an outstretched arm,
him you shall fear;
to him you shall bow down and to him make sacrifice.
37 And the statutes and practices
and Teaching and the commandment
that he wrote down for you you shall keep

31. Hens-Piazza, *1–2 Kings*, 334.

to do for all time.
And you shall not fear other gods.
38 And the covenant I cut with you
you shall not forget,
and you shall not fear other gods.
39 But Adonai your God you shall fear,
and he shall deliver you from the hand of your enemies.

The frame for this address, with its repeated mention of the prohibition not to "fear other gods" in counterpoint to the commandment to "fear Adonai your God," is in the third person descriptive form, beginning and ending with the phrase "until this day" (34–35a, 41). The admonitions included in verses 35–39 are thus evidently not followed, as "they" went on mixing their worship of Adonai with the worship of other gods (41).

Chapter 17 consists of a report on the exile of the Northern Kingdom followed by a scathing indictment (the most severe of its sort found in the Former Prophets) followed by another report on the repopulation of the North and concluded with a final accusation. Whereas at first the people have abandoned Adonai, in the end they worship Adonai alongside other deities. What could be the purpose of this long tirade?

Lyle Eslinger observes that what has preceded chapter 17 does not cohere with the evaluations of chapter 17. Prior negative evaluations have always pertained to the kings rather than to the people, and Eslinger thus wants to understand the chapter as irony.[32] It may, however, not be prudent to draw such a strict boundary between the behavior of leaders and their subjects in the ancient world, or even in the world of today. The actions of leadership easily bleed over into those of the people. In Kings, the saying of Judges—"in

---

32. Eslinger, *Into the Hands*, 198. Eslinger maintains that the narrator is "conspicuously silent on the matter of Israel's behavior." This is not entirely correct; see, for example, 1 Kgs 14:15, 16 in the prophecy of Ahiyah. Also, every time the negative evaluation of a king occurs, it includes "the sin he caused Israel to sin" (1 Kgs 15:26, 30, 34; 16:2, 13, 19, 26; 22:53[52]; 2 Kgs 10:29; 13:2, 6, 11). It is true that these pronouncements are standard and do not mention specifics.

those days there was no king in Israel; everyone did as was right in their eyes"—could be turned into "in those days, there was a king in Israel; everyone did as was right in the king's eyes."

If we consider the subject of chapter 17 to be cohesive with the rest of Kings, however, a question arises regarding the intentions of the narrator since the extent of the transgressions have been pointed out repeatedly already—at least in the case of the monarchs. What did the narrator hope to achieve beyond beating a dead horse? It is striking that the text twice includes Judah in its accusations: In verse 13, prophets and seers are sent to Israel *and Judah*, and verse 19 comments that "even Judah did not keep the commandments of Adonai their God;/ they walked in the statutes that Israel made." The following verse, referring to God's rejection of "all the seed [i.e., descendants] of Israel" (20), is ambiguous as to who is intended. In the narratives preceding chapter 17, only the people of Judah sacrifice and burn incense on "the heights" or worship the asherahs (e.g., 1 Kgs 11:7; 14:23; 22:44[43]; 2 Kgs 12:4[3]; 15:4, 35), and so they fit the picture of 11–23 as much or more than the people of the Northern Kingdom.

Viviano maintains that 2 Kings 17 "actually highlights Judah's failings."[33] She also suggests that the chapter has "a paraenetic structure" in its entirety.[34] Paraenesis is speech that exhorts, attempting to move the one addressed to a different course of action or to make the right choice between two courses. Deuteronomy 30:1–20 is a good example of this type of address, as is the entire book, cast as an address by Moses to the people on the east side of the Jordan. But paraenetic speech is in the address form, which to a great degree is lacking in chapter 17. Rather, the chapter describes what has happened and what "they" have done wrong. Only the last section is, for the greater part, addressed to an audience in the second person plural (35–39), although these admonitions are set in the context of a covenant God made in the past. Taking Viviano's suggestion into account that the text is *about* Israel *to* Judah, with the major concern to convince the audience of the "ab-

---

33. Viviano, "2 Kings 17," 552.
34. Viviano, "2 Kings 17," 557–58.

solute necessity" to worship Adonai exclusively,[35] I suggest that the speech is indeed one of warning, applicable to both Judah before the Babylonian exile and the community of the restoration period in the fifth century.

## The State of the Region

Before we move on to consider the situation of Judah, a brief review of the condition in the region due to Assyrian domination should facilitate our understanding both of what has transpired and what is yet to happen with the remaining kingdom.[36] Beginning in the middle of the eighth century, two major political forces impinged on the kingdoms of Israel and Judah, with power and aggression toward Israel and Judah waxing and waning between Syria (biblical Aram) and its powerful neighbor Assyria to the east. At its largest, the Assyrian empire comprised parts of what are now Syria, Turkey, Iraq, Iran, and Egypt, as well as the entire Mediterranean seaboard. Its most powerful opponent was Egypt. Both realms sought to control the crucial trade routes, wending along the coast of ancient Israel and through lands to the east of the Jordan River. From time to time, anti-Assyrian coalitions formed, comprised of the smaller kingdoms in Israel and Judah's vicinity. A territory besieged by such a coalition might appeal to a more powerful entity for intervention— at a cost, of course (2 Kgs 16:7–9). It was evidently the practice of a large empire like Assyria to conquer and devastate a land and its cities only as a last resort or in case of open rebellion. It was more prudent to leave existing administrations in place and work with them as vassal states.

35. Viviano, "2 Kings 17," 559. I take no position on the time of composition of the chapter, viewing it as possibly composed by a Northern writer shortly before the fall of the Kingdom or by a writer of postexilic Judah, although I lean more in the direction of the latter. Both communities could be considered a ready audience to hear warnings about the dangers of idolatry and syncretism.

36. For extensive overviews of the complex history of the region and era, see Miller and Hayes, *A History of Ancient Israel and Judah*, 327–91.

For ordinary people, the constant tumult of war clearly brought about conditions of deprivation and great need, as one can tell especially from parts of the Elisha narratives. Military raids would devastate not only towns but the countryside, destroying crops and robbing people of any accumulated goods. Famines might be the result, with their obvious, horrendous consequences—people scrounging for bits of food (2 Kgs 4:38–41) and even resorting to cannibalism (2 Kgs 6:26–29). In connection with internal revolutions—the violent takeovers of royal houses—devastation did not remain confined to the royal victims listed in the biblical records. When the text records that "Jehu struck down all that remained of the house of Ahab" (2 Kgs 10:11), referring only to male descendants, their entire families as well as a number of servants must have been included. When royal princes fell, their retinues went with them. Even if we assume habitual exaggeration of numbers, the damage must have been enormous.

When situations changed and times became calmer and more prosperous, as they did under Jeroboam II in the middle of the eighth century BCE, prosperity remained confined to a small number of elite groups and individuals, creating an increased gap between rich and poor (see p. 245 above). It is for this type of injustice that prophets like Amos, Hosea, Micah, Isaiah, and later Jeremiah excoriated the people and warned them of impending doom unless they changed their ways and doings and practiced the ideals of communal life presented in the law codes—caring for widow, orphan, and stranger. This concern is not uppermost in the minds of the writers and compilers of the text of Kings. For them, the gold standard of abiding by covenant rules is to worship Adonai to the exclusion of all other deities. The theological voice that evaluates kings and their behavior, including the one dominating 2 Kings 17, is by scholars identified as Deuteronomistic. If this is the Deuteronomistic voice, meaning it coheres with the text of Deuteronomy, it is an attenuated voice that leaves out the abiding interest of that work with the well-being of orphan, widow, and stranger and the practice of justice in the land. This voice has lost the tension inherent in holding instructions for a holy life, which consist above all in protection of the weak and the stranger, together with insistence on worship of Adonai the God of Israel alone, an emphasis which on its own calls for warding off and annihilating the outsider.[37]

"The eighth century introduced what amounted to a new age of empires that lasted well into the first millennium C.E. Assyria, Babylonia, Persia, Macedonia, and Rome took their places, each in turn, as the head of major and far-flung international empires."[38] With the struggle of the kings of Israel to hold on to their small national territory in the middle to late eighth century, we have reached the height of Assyrian power, beginning with Tiglat-pileser III in 747 and lasting until the fall of its capital in 621. Despite maintaining a state of semiautonomy for a few decades, the Northern Kingdom eventually succumbed to its mighty neighbor and was punished for an attempted alliance with Egypt by total conquest and deportation and the reduction of the former kingdom to an Assyrian province. Deporting large parts of the original population and importing others into the region, a policy coherent with the picture presented in 2 Kings 17:24, had the result of crushing religious and national identity. The economic needs of the empire, as well as the political ones, dictated the particular status of a conquered area: whether it would be semiautonomous or completely under Assyrian control.

As we enter the period of Judah under Hezekiah at the end of the eighth and the beginning of the seventh century BCE, it is helpful to be aware of this political reality: Its northern neighbor is under domination in all respects by Assyria, an empire still in the course of expanding its territory. Judah existed in a state of constant vassalage to Assyria and was under constant threat of undergoing the same fate that befell Israel. The small country of Judah was faced with its immediate neighbor to the north, first

37. Legislation regarding the stranger is found throughout Deuteronomy, with its most stringent requirement in chapter 10: "And you shall love the stranger, for you were strangers in the land of Egypt" (10:19). See Johanna W. H. van Wijk-Bos, *Making Wise the Simple: The Torah in Christian Faith and Practice* (Grand Rapids: Eerdmans, 2005), 198–202.

38. Miller and Hayes, *A History of Ancient Israel and Judah*, 360.

destroyed, then settled by various people with various religions, including the worship of Adonai and no doubt of Assyrian deities. Certain segments of the population in the North may have fled to Judah ahead of the final onslaughts and brought with them their own traditions, including "some form of the royal annals, an early form of Deuteronomy and prophetical narratives such as the Elijah and Elisha stories."[39]

39. Miller and Hayes, *A History of Ancient Israel and Judah*, 390.

# Cycle VI: The Final Years (2 Kings 18–25)

*Judean history throughout the eighth and seventh centuries must be viewed . . . as the history of a small corner of the Assyrian empire.*[1]

Eight chapters conclude the history of the kings, from the last decades of the eighth until the first of the sixth century BCE, the era when Judah is the only remaining kingdom in the land. This period of more than a century is reviewed in the usual uneven way, with the greatest amount of text devoted to Hezekiah (chs. 18–20) and Josiah (22:1–23:30), both of them reformer kings. In between these two, the dreadful and long reign of Manasseh and the short rule of Amon together take up only twenty-six verses (21:1–26). Divine judgment announcing the eventual collapse of Judah arrives during the reign of Manasseh (21:10–15); and following the death of Josiah (609 BCE), the writing is on the wall. After a period of great turmoil and a succession of puppet kings, Jerusalem falls to the Babylonians in two separate attacks in 597 and 586 BCE, respectively under Kings Jehoiachin and Zedekiah. The narratives focused on Hezekiah and Josiah are marked by lively description and verbal exchange, but the text devolves into description only from the end of chapter 23 through chapter 25.

The turbulent history of the period between 722 and 586 is one in which the dominating power in the region is for a while still Assyria, to which Hezekiah is forced to pay tribute, although King

---

1. J. Maxwell Miller and John H. Hayes, *A History of Ancient Israel and Judah*, 2nd ed. (Louisville: Westminster John Knox, 2006), 360.

Sennacherib, for his own reasons, leaves Jerusalem untouched. As such empires do, the Assyrian empire eventually exhausted itself with too many battles on too many different fronts, and its southern neighbor Babylonia, already a threat at the time of King Hezekiah, eventually conquered Assyria under King Nabopolassar, with the fall of Nineveh occurring in 612. Nabopolassar's successor, Nebuchadnezzar, is in charge during the fall of Judah. Throughout the period, Egypt is also a force to be reckoned with, at times subject and at times hostile to the Assyrian empire, but also in alliance with it. During Josiah's reign in the last half of the seventh century, Judah is most likely subject to Egypt, which exercises control over the monarchial succession subsequent to Josiah's death (23:33–37).

### Act I: King Hezekiah of Judah (2 Kings 18–20)

*Hezekiah's reign had . . . its moments of glory and hope but also its tragedies and calamities.*[2]

Hezekiah is introduced in extravagant, complimentary terms but suffers under the onslaughts of the Assyrian king, who sends his officials to instill fear in Hezekiah, the Judean officials, and the people of Judah. The Hezekiah narrative is characterized by speech throughout, creating vivid portraits of Assyrian and Judean representatives, beginning with a long speech by an Assyrian delegate. Over against the ambassadors from Assyria are placed Hezekiah and especially the prophet Isaiah, who counteracts the words of the messengers sent by Sennacherib on two occasions. One of Isaiah's pronouncements arrives in classic Hebrew poetic form, a unique feature in the book of Kings. The last scene depicts Hezekiah's illness and healing, including a miraculous sign as a guarantee of his cure. The prophet Isaiah is deeply engaged in these events, and he prophesies the eventual doom of Judah and the royal house.

2. Miller and Hayes, *A History of Ancient Israel and Judah*, 421.

### Act I, Scene 1: A Righteous King (2 Kings 18:1–16)

*A consummate reformer who forged a new epoch in Judah's history.*[3]

Hezekiah ascends the throne around the time of the fall of Samaria. In his introduction, he receives the highest accolades assigned to one of Judah's kings yet (1–8). Not only does he do "what was right in the eyes of Adonai" just like his ancestor David, but the phrase "only he did not remove the heights"—so often a part of preceding appraisals, even of faithful kings—is missing here, turned instead into "It was he who removed the heights" (4). A few other specifics of his reforming zeal follow, capped by an unusually effusive assessment of his faith in Adonai.

2 KINGS 18:5–6

5   In Adonai, the God of Israel, he put his trust;
    neither after him nor before him
    was there anyone like him of the kings of Judah.
6   He clung to Adonai and did not turn away from him
    and kept his commandments,
    which Adonai commanded Moses.

The concept of *trust* will play a central role in the speech from the Assyrian official in the next scene. Hezekiah's "clinging" to Adonai and not "turning away" stand in contrast to the kings of Israel, who did the opposite as they "clung to the sins of Jeroboam" and "did not turn away from it" (3:3), as well as to King Solomon, who "clung" to those in his household who worshiped gods other than the God of Israel (1 Kgs 11:2). Unusually, the lines refer to commandments that go back to Moses, an allusion that in Kings occurs only a few times. Moses appears three times in the opening scene of this chapter (4, 6, 12), and in addition to exalting Hezekiah as unique among the kings of Judah, these references create a connection between Hezekiah and this unparalleled servant of God.[4]

---

3. Burke O. Long, *2 Kings*, FOTL 10 (Grand Rapids: Eerdmans, 1991), 195.
4. The crushing of the bronze serpent (*nehushtan*), which had become

Hezekiah is reported successful not only in the religious arena but also in the political one. The text notes his "rebellion" against Assyria, apparently by extending his rule to the coast (perhaps in a moment when Assyria was occupied elsewhere), striking down Gaza and its territories (7–8). This success was significant in that it gave Judah access to the important coastal area and its trade route. The verb "rebel" of verse 7 does not draw on the usual root for this action in Kings but uses a word that will be repeated by the Assyrian official against Hezekiah (20), and it occurs only twice more in Kings in the last desperate days of the kingdom (24:1, 20). To set all of Hezekiah's undertakings in sharp contrast to the downfall of the Northern Kingdom, the next four verses repeat the overview of the capture of Samaria and its king and the exile of Israel (9–12; cf. 17:5–6).

Whether in reaction to the rebellion of Hezekiah or for other reasons—the text does not inform us—in the next breath, Sennacherib of Assyria marches through Judah, capturing its cities, causing Hezekiah to sue for peace (13–16).[5] Sennacherib, who has come as far as Lachish, south of Jerusalem on the other side of the hill country, demands a large tribute so that Hezekiah has to collect "all the silver" of the Temple and the palace, besides stripping the doorposts of the Temple that he himself had overlaid. It is the usual thing to do in such a situation. Temple and royal treasury have been depleted for such purposes from as long ago as the time of Rehoboam, who thus kept Pharaoh Sheshonq (the biblical Shishak) from besieging Jerusalem (1 Kgs 14:26), and as recently as when Hezekiah's father Ahaz asked Tiglat-pileser for help (16:7–8). Usually, it works, but not this time. Perhaps the total does not quite amount to what the Assyrian king has demanded. The text ominously neglects to men-

---

an object of worship, refers to Moses also (Num 21:4–9). For the "crushing" of the bronze serpent (2 Kgs 18:4), the narrator uses the same verb for the action of Moses on the golden calf (Deut 9:21). The word *nehushtan* appears to be a combination of the words for "bronze" (*nehoshet*) and "snake" (*nahash*). In the Babylonian Talmud, the rabbis argue about the continued existence of this object and the importance of not clinging to traditions just for the sake of them. In the end they suggest that Hezekiah's ancestors left him something by "which to distinguish himself" (b. Chullin 7a).

5. A version of 2 Kgs 18:13–20:19 can be found in Isa 36–39.

tion the success of Hezekiah's endeavor to keep the Assyrian army away from Jerusalem.

### Act I, Scene 2: Agents Confront Agents (2 Kings 18:17–19:13)

*The Spirit of God roams in the spaces of disbelief or wavering faith.*[6]

Instead of a promise of peace and a return of Sennacherib to Assyria, three Assyrian agents arrive at the walls of Jerusalem, accompanied by a great army, and take a stand at a location from which they can be heard on the wall, the place where the three agents of King Hezekiah face their opponents (18:17–18).[7] "Like a description of a shoot-out in a Western movie, the scene depicts the two opposing sides facing each other."[8] In this case, the opposing parties use words rather than guns. The three from Assyria are each named by their titles; they are officials of some sort, one of them the chief cup-bearer—that is, the Rabsakeh, the spokesperson for the king of Assyria. Hezekiah's delegation consists of the overseer of the palace, a scribe, and a secretary (18:18). The Rabsakeh addresses the absent king in the name of his lord, the king of Assyria, and launches a glorious piece of oratory resonating with rhetorical questions, taunts, threats, and boasts (18:19–25). Such speeches were a method of psychological warfare, a valuable tool to instill fear in one's opponents and break their will to fight. The central issue of Rabsakeh's speech concerns trust. It is the issue to which he makes double reference in his opening line: "What is this trust with which you trust?" (18:19).[9]

6. Gina Hens-Piazza, *1–2 Kings*, AOTC (Nashville: Abingdon, 2006), 367.
7. The location, "the conduit of the upper pool which is on the main road to Fuller's field," is open to debate. Marvin Sweeney (*I & II Kings: A Commentary*, OTL [Louisville: Westminster John Knox, 2007], 414–15) understands it as the Kidron valley, which "forms a natural roadway at the eastern side of the city" and "a convenient site from which the Rab Shakeh's words could be heard . . . by the men guarding the eastern wall of the city."
8. Robert L. Cohn, *2 Kings*, 129.
9. Everett Fox, *The Early Prophets: Joshua, Judges, Samuel, and Kings* (New York: Schocken, 2014), 793: "What is this reliance on which you rely?"

The major part of the oration is addressed to Hezekiah personally, who should know better than to put trust in that broken reed, Egypt, which will not supply him with the needed forces to withstand Assyria (18:19–21, 23–24). A short part addresses the entire people, who are mocked for putting their trust in their God (18:22). In this context, he refers to the removal of the "heights and altars" that made it mandatory to worship in Jerusalem, tapping into a possible discontent with this reform among the population. Surely, they are not so foolish as to put their trust in a god who demands worship in one specific place only! Returning his focus once again to Hezekiah, he wagers Hezekiah, who stupidly trusts in Egypt's capacity to help him, that he cannot provide 2,000 riders if the king of Assyria gives him 2,000 horses. For good measure, he punctures a hole in the king's trust in Adonai, for Sennacherib, he says, is only acting on Adonai's orders (18:25). No military ally will come to Hezekiah and his people's aid; nor will trust in their God bring deliverance. Egypt is of no use, and Adonai has switched sides.[10]

The Assyrian is not done because one of Hezekiah's ambassadors provides a new opening for him by urging him to speak not in Hebrew but in Aramaic, the common language of high officialdom in that time and place, so that other people who are listening on the wall will not be able to understand him (18:26). Their motivation is left unstated, and we can only guess at it. They may worry about provocation resulting in a popular assault on the agents of Sennacherib, which could unleash the fury of the entire army, or they may have concerns about popular loyalty toward Hezekiah. Whichever the case may be, their request meets with vociferous disdain. Now, the Rabsakeh turns to the people, first stating that surely everyone there, officials and common people, will together be in the same boat as victims of a siege or a total conquest. Then he continues to speak more loudly in Hebrew, warning them to not let Hezekiah *deceive* them by making them *trust* in Adonai. "Let not Hezekiah

---

10. As Nelson (*First and Second Kings*, IBC [Atlanta: John Knox, 1987], 238) points out, the observation that Sennacherib could be acting at the behest of Israel's God is supported by the arguments against Samaria in vv. 9–12 of this chapter.

deceive you"; "let Hezekiah not make you trust"; "do not listen to Hezekiah" (18:29, 30, 31). Each time the Rabsakeh refers to his own lord as "the great king of Assyria" while he mentions Hezekiah without his title. He urges the people to make a deal (lit. a "blessing") and see how well their life will turn out.

> 2 KINGS 18:31–32
>
> 31 Do not listen to Hezekiah,
>     for thus says the king of Assyria:
>     Make me a blessing-gift and come out to me![11]
>     And eat, each, of their own vine and fig tree,
>     and drink, each, water from their own well.
> 32 Until I come and take you
>     to a land like your own land,
>     a land of corn and wine,
>     a land of bread and vineyards,
>     a land of olives and honey.[12]
>     And you will live and not die.
>     Do not heed Hezekiah,
>     for he leads you astray by saying:
>     Adonai will deliver us.

Instead of taunts and derision, the people get admonitions and commands. Trust in Hezekiah, who commands trust in Adonai, is a bad idea. They should instead rely on the great king of Assyria. So have all conquerors in history announced their intentions for improvement and peace to their victims, the falsity of which is always evident by the violence they perpetrate. To the list of rhetorical questions regarding divine power's effectiveness in the face of Assyria's might with which he ends his tirade (18:33–35), he could have

---

11. The word "blessing" can be used for a gift of appeasement, something to smooth the way, like Jacob's gift to Esau at their reunion (Gen 33:11), Abigail's gift to David (1 Sam 25:27), and David's gift to the elders of Judah (1 Sam 30:26).

12. The description of the "good land" is a kind of parody of Deut 8:7–9 (Nelson, *First and Second Kings*, 238).

added, "Has any conqueror ever in any land improved the lives of the peoples they destroyed?" This is what the people, who respond to the speech with silence only, may think. Hezekiah's agents, on the other hand, go to their lord in mourning (18:36–37).

Hezekiah, who is as disturbed as his ambassadors are, sends them to Isaiah not for a consultation or prediction but for a prayer (19:1–4). His somber words concern only disaster and uncertain words about the possibility of punishment on Assyria for the taunt issued to "the living God." It sounds as if the solid faith and trust of Hezekiah is indeed shaken. He refers to the day as one of "disaster, chastisement, and shame" (19:3). He no longer counts on a future in which deliverance is a possibility and asks only that Isaiah "lift up a prayer for the remnant that is left," as if the population is already destroyed and there are only a few survivors.[13] The prophet returns a promise of hope, but his words are clothed in mystery, referring to a "breath" or "spirit"—a "rumor" that will make the Assyrian monarch turn around to be killed in his own land (19:6–7).

There is some obscurity in the next lines as the Rabsakeh goes back to the king of Assyria and the main army, now at Libnah, a little north of Lachish, but there is a renewed message from the Assyrian king, this time by letter (19:8–13).[14] The letter revisits the theme of useless reliance on deities to provide relief from occupation and devastation. It mentions a number of nations who no longer have kings and whose gods did not help them: "Did they bring deliverance for them, the gods of the nations whom my ancestors destroyed?" (19:12). The main point is to counsel Hezekiah not to put trust in the God of Israel, an issue more eloquently presented to the people by the Rabsakeh in the previous episode.[15]

13. The word "remnant" is especially at home in the text of the prophet Isaiah (Isa 14:30; 37:4, 32).

14. There is a reference to a rumor heard by Sennacherib about "Tirkahah the king of Cush" who "has come out to fight against you" (19:9), but Tirkahah was not on the throne in 701, the time when these events take place. It may be an anachronistic reference to a difficulty experienced by Assyria from Ethiopia and Egypt—although perhaps not in this period.

15. The countries mentioned in the letter were conquered by Assyria in previous centuries (Sweeney, *I & II Kings*, 417).

### Act I, Scene 3: A Prayer and a Prophecy (2 Kings 19:14–37)

*Sennacherib . . . grows to the legendary size of the brash, overreaching blasphemer.*[16]

Tension still persists as the siege continues and no relief arrives. We find Hezekiah with the letters sent by Sennacherib and, after reading them, taking them to the Temple, where he spreads them out before Adonai (14).[17] Before he appeals to God, he brings the evidence of what is transpiring. His prayer is traditional, moving from praise of God's greatness and power to an urgent request for God "to hear" and "see" the taunting words of Sennacherib to a description of the woes created by Assyria and a plea to "deliver" (15–19). The point of the saving act is that the whole world will know that other peoples' gods are only wood and stone, but only Adonai is the true God. Once again, the contest is as much between gods as between humans (cf. 1 Kgs 18:39). It turns out that Hezekiah needed to *see/hear* the threat with his own eyes and ears before he is moved to approach God with his request. Before, he asked Isaiah to pray; at this point, he uses his own voice to plead with God. Not many of the kings in the book of Kings are reported as praying. Solomon's prayers are referred to at the dedication of the Temple (1 Kgs 8:28, 54; 9:3), but there is no mention of other kings engaged in prayer.[18]

Unasked, Isaiah has a second message for Hezekiah; it arrives in poetic form as a response to his prayer and functions as a retort to the taunting speech of the Rabsakeh and Sennacherib's letters, and in its turn it taunts the mighty conqueror with rhetorical questions (21–28).

---

16. Long, *2 Kings*, 226.

17. The narrator states that Hezekiah "read the letters" (the word is plural and there may have been more than one tablet or papyrus with different directives and information). For the parallel passage, see Isa 37:14–20.

18. The list of references to official prayers in Long (*2 Kings*, 226) includes from Kings only the prayers of Solomon in 1 Kings 3 and 8.

2 Kings 19:21b–22

21b She despises, she mocks you,
    virgin daughter Zion;
    behind you she wags her head,
    daughter Jerusalem.
22 Whom did you taunt and revile?
    Against whom raised your voice?
    You lifted on high your eyes
    against the Holy One of Israel!

The poem is a combination of an apostrophe and a persona poem, addressed to the king of Assyria and assuming different voices in a series of strophes. First, the voice of Zion/Jerusalem takes on the mocking tone of the Assyrian king and his messengers against them. The language is at home among prayers where the individual describes contempt and mockery from others (see Pss 31:18–19[17–18]; 119:22; 123:3, 4). "Wagging the head" is stereotypical language for the haughty attitude that sharpens the suffering of the faithful (Pss 22:8[7]; 109:25; Lam 2:15). "Taunting" occurs in this chapter in verses 4 and 16 besides 22 and 23. It is standard language in the Psalms for the one who feels alone and surrounded by hostility (Pss 42:11[10]; 44:17[16]; 102:9[8]; 119:42), for God who taunts adversaries (Ps 57:4[3]), and for the unbeliever who challenges God (Pss 74:10; 79:12; 89:52[51]). It is joined in verse 22 by the rare verb *gadaf* ("revile" or "blaspheme"; see Ps 44:17[16]), creating the sound-rhyme *herafta wegidafta*. The *ah* sounds in the first line (*bazah lekha laʿagah lekha betulat bat tsion*, v. 21) re-create the "ha ha" of mocking laughter. To lift the eyes and raise the voice are signs of haughtiness (Pss 18:28[27]; 131:1), and the Rabsakeh proclaimed his challenge in a "loud voice" (2 Kgs 18:28). He may have thought his tone and words were addressed to the king, the officials, and the people of Israel, but actually the real target was the God of Israel. The stress rhythm of the lines is taut, mostly with three accents to the colon, so that the accusations rain down in sharp staccato.

The second strophe (23–24) takes on the persona and the voice of the Assyrian king, picking up the word "taunt" again. All of strophe 2 is presumed braggadocio in the first person on the part of

Sennacherib, who thinks that he can not only destroy cities and lands but become the master of nature, the *heights in the reaches of Lebanon, the tops of its cedars* (23). The boastful voice repeats the first-person pronoun: *I* do this and *I* do that.

The final stanzas are in the voice of Adonai. Against this overweening pride the Deity puts forth the fact that all Sennacherib thought to have achieved—ruined cities, terrorized inhabitants becoming powerless as dried-up herbage—was in fact the doing of Adonai: "I have done it, have brought it about" (25). The language of the first lines of the third strophe (25–26)—of "have you not heard?" and "I have done it," of *shaping* and *bringing about*—is at home in the poetry of Second Isaiah (Isa 43:1, 7, 10, 21; 44:2, 9, 10, 12, 21; 45:11, 18; 46:11). The conceptual world is postexilic, emphasizing on the one hand the power and might of the God of Israel and on the other God's willingness to save, both of which were subject to doubt in the aftermath of the devastating losses during the Babylonian exile.

Finally, there is nothing about Sennacherib that is not known to Adonai. The notes of Psalm 139 are heard in the statement "your sitting and your going out and coming in I know" (27; cf. Ps 139:2–3). These are ordinary actions, which cannot be said of the "raging" of Sennacherib. God not only *knows* Sennacherib's movements but has *heard* his carrying on "against me" (27). The climax and resolution of the poem arrive in the last verse with the threat of "a hook through your nose and bridle on your mouth" to send him home (28). The references to the hook and bridle evoke the image of victims of Assyrian warfare led through the Assyrian capital by ropes and a hook in the nose. It is as eloquent a put-down of the mighty power of Assur as one could hope to hear.

The promises added by Isaiah of abundant crops and survivors of Judah who will thrive almost come as an anticlimax after the poetry that precedes it, but they make concrete what is only metaphorically present in the poetry (29–34). Especially verse 32 makes abundantly clear what will happen: The king of Assyria *will not enter, will not shoot, will not besiege,* and *will not cast up a siege mound.* Rather he will *go back.* The phrase "he will not enter" encloses the lack of hostile action and the positive action of return (32, 33). The counterpart of the threatened *hook* and *bridle* for Assyria of verse 28 is the *deliverance of the city* brought about by Adonai.

The episode ends in a miracle, with the entire camp of the Assyrian army a heap of corpses in the morning so that Sennacherib indeed turns around and goes back to Nineveh, where he is promptly assassinated by his own sons (35–37). According to Sennacherib's own account, he did devastate Judah and besiege Jerusalem in 701 BCE. But he did not claim to have captured it or its king or to have forced Hezekiah from his throne. Probably the Assyrians had their hands full with fending off the Babylonian threat by Merodach-baladan, with whom Hezekiah was in alliance.[19] This partnership will become evident in the second half of the next chapter.

### *Act I, Scene 4: The Healing of Hezekiah (2 Kings 20:1–11[20])*

*The transcendent joins with the mundane.*[21]

2 KINGS 20:1–3

1 In those days Hezekiah became ill
to the point of death,
and came to him Isaiah, the son of Amoz,
the prophet, and said to him:
Thus says Adonai:
Put your house in order,
for you will die and not live.
2 He turned his face to the wall
and prayed to Adonai, saying:
3 Please, Adonai, remember that I walked before you
in truth and with a whole heart
and did what is good in your eyes.
And Hezekiah wept loudly.

---

19. Sweeney, *I & II Kings*, 412–13.
20. See the parallel story in Isa 38:1–8. The story in Kings lacks the thanksgiving prayer of Hezekiah in Isa 38:9–20.
21. Long, *2 Kings*, 239.

"In those days" is an imprecise time indicator, but to go by the promise from Isaiah that the city will be delivered, it must mean that the siege of Jerusalem is ongoing and has not been relieved. We have witnessed prophets' involvements in Israel and Aram with kings or their offspring suffering from a deathly illness (1 Kgs 14:1–17; 2 Kgs 1:2–18; 8:7–15), but so far have not seen it in Judah. Before Isaiah's entrance into the story, prophetic presence in Judah has not been mentioned after the appearance of Ahiyah during Solomon's reign (1 Kgs 11:29–39). Two hundred years later, the prophet Isaiah is asked by King Hezekiah to pray for the people of Jerusalem in view of the threatening and insulting words of the Rabsakeh of Assyria (19:2–4). In response, Isaiah promises a retreat by the Assyrians. The second time, Hezekiah prays, facing Adonai with threatening letters from Sennacherib, and Isaiah sends a promise of deliverance for the city without being solicited (19:20–34). In this episode, Isaiah comes unbidden to Hezekiah's side, the first time we find them in each other's presence, to tell him the bad news that his illness is fatal—a message he brings as a word from God.

Hezekiah's response is to turn his face to the wall and pray (3). The absence of prayer in the face of illness on the part of monarchs has been striking so that once again the uniqueness of this king is highlighted. Hezekiah's prayer is brief and consists merely of a plea for Adonai to remember his devotion. The plea for God "to remember" is language familiar from the Psalms. The believer may pray for God to *remember* divine compassion (Ps 25:6) or, conversely, *to forget* or *not to remember* sins (Pss 25:7; 79:8). The appeal to one's own righteousness and to deeds that meet God's approval is unusual. There is also a notable absence of a request for healing. Overcome by grief, Hezekiah can only weep.

The open ear and eyes of God, to which the king once called in the face of the Assyrian threat to his people (19:16), notice the suffering of the king, and Isaiah is still in the palace precinct when he receives word to go back and bring a promise not only of healing for Hezekiah but also of deliverance for the city (4–6; 20:6b = 19:34). "The fate of Hezekiah, the ideal king, is bound up with that of Jerusalem, the ideal city."[22] Yet the healing of the illness is not

---

22. Long, *2 Kings*, 238.

accomplished merely by a miraculous intervention; human action is needed through the application of a compress of fig cakes (7).[23] The unit describing this activity of Isaiah as medicine man can be viewed as an extension of the healing process in which Hezekiah also asks for a sign that he will indeed recover. Asking for signs does not carry a negative connotation in the biblical story, and on this occasion the process is especially interesting because the king gets to choose the manner of the sign (8–11; cf. Judg 6:36–40). Long writes, "The transcendent joins with the mundane; God needs human powers focused on earthly matters to affect the events of royal history."[24] The purpose of the story is thus not to put Hezekiah in a bad light but rather to underline his loyalty to Adonai, who responds in kind.

### Act I, Scene 5: Portents of Exile (2 Kings 20:12–21)

*The dynasty is on artificial life support.*[25]

The next incident begins with "at that time," leading to the assumption that what follows takes place in the context of Hezekiah's illness and recovery. The king of Babylon sends messages and a present in light of the report about the king's illness.[26] In response, Hezekiah shows the Babylonian ambassadors everything he has in his treasury, "silver, gold, and spices, precious oil and his armory, and everything found in his storerooms"(13). Isaiah learns what has gone on and questions Hezekiah closely about the men's origins and what they saw (14–15). Hezekiah responds that they saw everything: "There was nothing I did not show them in my storerooms" (15). This *seeing* of *everything* may not have been as innocent as it sounds, and in

---

23. Figs are well-known for their nutritional value, but softened with water and flattened, they can also be used as a poultice to counteract pain and inflammation.

24. Long, 2 *Kings*, 239.

25. Cohn, 2 *Kings*, 145.

26. The name of the Babylonian king in 20:12 is Berodach-baladan, known usually as Merodach-baladan, a ruler at the end of the eighth century who created serious difficulties for the Assyrian empire.

fact may have amounted more to an inspection in light of the future plans of the Babylonians.[27] It may be that Hezekiah is admitting to engagement in an alliance with Babylonia.

In any case, the admission from the king elicits a word about the future exile of Judah. Although Isaiah's words do not include a charge or accuse Hezekiah of a lack of faith, verses 17–18 ring with the word *taken*. Everything the messengers from Merodach-baladan have seen will be *taken*; the *nothing* Hezekiah "did not show them" (lit. "did not let them see") turns into "*nothing* will be left." Descendants of Hezekiah will be among the ones *taken*, becoming servants in the *palace of the king of Babylon*. The possibility of entering into an alliance with Babylon apparently goes counter to the total trust demanded of the king in the help of Israel's God, which has now been promised to him three times (19:6–7, 34; 20:6).[28] Yet the narrative is silent about this possibility and leaves inferences up to the reader/listener. Hezekiah's reaction to the prophecy is approving, the reason (which we know through access to his thoughts) being that nothing, after all, will happen during his lifetime (19). It is recognizably human, characterized by the idea of the floodwaters not reaching one's doorstep quite yet—and who knows what may happen to change the direction of things?

The death notice of Hezekiah follows directly upon this prophecy of doom and includes mention of the great engineering feat accomplished under his reign of connecting the Gihon spring through a tunnel to a pool inside Jerusalem's walls.[29] One of Judah's most

27. Long, *2 Kings*, 243: "It may be that Hezekiah's 'heeding' and 'showing' imply that command of resources willingly or unwillingly . . . has passed from a vanquished or compliant state (Judah) to a dominant power (Babylon)."

28. Jeremy Schipper ("Hezekiah, Manasseh, and Dynastic or Transgenerational Punishment," in *Soundings in Kings: Perspectives and Methods in Contemporary Scholarship*, ed. Mark Leuchter and Klaus-Peter Adam [Minneapolis: Fortress, 2010], 81–105, 86–87) argues that it goes counter to Zion theology for Judah's kings to seek foreign alliances.

29. The so-called Siloam Stone is the archaeological artifact that preserves the memory of the workers hewing the tunnel encountering one another from either end. The words on the stone are among the oldest testimonies to a Hebrew text. Today it is preserved in a museum in Istanbul and reads

lauded kings has gone to his grave, and the bell announcing the end of the small kingdom has tolled.[30]

## Act II: From Manasseh to Amon (2 Kings 21)

*The worst king ever.*[31]

One chapter serves to cover the next half century and more (698–640 BCE) during the reign of Manasseh and his son Amon, both of them with negative evaluations. During the long reign of Manasseh, prophecies by undesignated individuals announce the impending demise of Judah and Jerusalem. His son Amon follows in his father's footsteps and reigns only two years before he is assassinated. The voices of these two kings are not heard in the description; only the prophetic words of looming disaster reverberate in this section.

### Act II, Scene 1: Manasseh of Judah (2 Kings 21:1–18)

*The youthful Manasseh inherited a reduced and war-torn Judean state.*[32]

---

as follows: "And this was the manner of the boring through. While the workers were wielding the pick, each one toward his co-worker, and while there was still three cubits to be bored through, [there could be heard] the sound of each worker calling to his co-worker, for there was a fissure in the rock to the right and to the left. And on the day of the boring through, the workers struck, each to meet his co-worker, pick against pick. And then the waters from the spring [Gihon] flowed to the pool for twelve hundred cubits. And a hundred cubits was the height in the rock above the head of the workers" (Miller and Hayes, *A History of Ancient Israel and Judah*, 409).

30. Miller and Hayes (*A History of Ancient Israel and Judah*, 410–21) argue that according to archaeological evidence and nonbiblical texts, Hezekiah engaged in elaborate military planning and fortification. The Siloam tunnel was a part of his program to enable Jerusalem to withstand a prolonged siege.

31. Nelson, *First and Second Kings*, 247.

32. Miller and Hayes, *A History of Ancient Israel and Judah*, 422. Miller and Hayes observe that the devastation of Judah in the day of Sennacherib

Apparently, Judah played no role on the international scene during the long reign of Manasseh—55 years according to the text—perhaps partly due to the fact that the storm of Assyrian aggression had abated while Assyria faced "troublemakers" from different sides. Neither is anything of local importance to Judah or Jerusalem reported in the chapter, which consists for a great part of a recital of Manasseh's condemnable actions. He is an apostate king who "did what was evil in the eyes of Adonai" (1–6). Everything his father, Hezekiah, did, he undoes. Not only does he erect altars to Baal and make an asherah, he builds altars to the "host of heaven" in the Temple. Perhaps in some of these respects, Assyrian influence made itself felt, Judah being a vassal state of Assyria during the entire timespan. The Assyrian goddess Ishtar was considered to be the "queen of heaven," and Assyria worshiped astral deities.[33] Yet the practices of which Manasseh is accused are "the abominations" of the original inhabitants of Canaan, not those of neighboring peoples. It is especially of altar building to the wrong gods and in the wrong places that he is guilty (3–5). From the conflict between forces of strict loyalism to Adonai and the more accommodating policies of the monarchy arises the condemning voice of the loyalists against Manasseh. Once again, there is the charge of "passing his son through the fire" (cf. 16:3). The list of transgressions is long and detailed, serving to lay a strong foundation for the disaster prophecy to follow.

A second unit contrasts Manasseh's idolatrous actions with the desire of Adonai to have a house for his name (7–9); idols are now present in Adonai's house! (7). God's promise to Israel of a permanent foothold is subject to the condition of "guarding" the Teaching (*torah*) of Moses. Verse 9 announces that Manasseh has dragged the people along in his wrongdoing:

---

must have been "enormous." Disruption of populations and ravaged land were from now on a part of the landscape. Assyrian texts refer to Manasseh as "king of the city of Judah," implying he ruled over a city-state kingdom.

33. For arguments against Assyrian influence in the temple cult during this time, see William S. Morrow, "Were There Neo-Assyrian Influences in Manasseh's Temple? Comparative Evidence from Tel-Miqne/Ekron," *CBQ* 75 (2013): 53–73.

2 KINGS 21:9

They did not listen
and Manasseh led them astray
to do greater evil than the peoples
Adonai destroyed before the Israelites.

The word "destroyed" in the last line of this accusation echoes forth into the next unit with its prophetic announcement: "Then spoke Adonai" (10). Everything that will happen to Judah is "because" of the "greater evil" that Manasseh has done (11) and in the end "because" of "the evil they have done" (15), moving the subject from the singular king to the plural people. These two phrases enclose the announcement of the "evil" Adonai will bring on Jerusalem and Judah. A message of disaster that will cause the "ears to ring" (12) can be found also in 1 Samuel 3:11 regarding the house of Eli and in Jeremiah 19:3 regarding the calamity about to befall Jerusalem. The king with his kingdom and the city will be treated like Ahab and Samaria. They will be wiped out like a bowl—cleaned and turned upside down (13). This last threat, the "turning upside down" (*hafakh*), alludes to the destruction of Sodom and Gomorra (Gen 19:21, 25, 29); it is the proverbial image of devastation (Lam 4:6; 5:2; Amos 4:11; Jonah 3:4). The charge is once again that the transgressions of the people have "provoked" Adonai—the same relentless indictment leveled at the kings of the North (1 Kgs 14:9, 15; 15:30; 16:2, 7, 13, 26, 33; 21:22; 22:54[53]) and eventually against its people (2 Kgs 17:11, 17). Earlier hints at the transgressions of Judah and its eventual fate come to full flower in this section (cf. 2 Kgs 8:19; 17:13, 19–20; 20:17–18). The mirror of guilt and responsibility, the effect of a king's actions on the population, is held up during the reign of three kings in the last century of Judah's existence as a kingdom—most extensively in this chapter (cf. 20:17–18; 22:16–17; 23:26–27).

One other sin of Manasseh gets mention following this judgment on the entire city and land: Manasseh shed "much innocent blood," filling Jerusalem with it (16). The shedding of innocent blood deserves attention in light of the paucity of statements about royal transgressions in the social sphere in Kings. Shedding "innocent blood" is cited in Jeremiah as a specific sin of the royal house of its time (Jer 22:17; cf. Deut 19:10; 21:8; 27:25). Although specifics of Manasseh's crimes in this area are lacking, the gist is clearly that he disregarded judicial process; certainly in Jeremiah, the notion of shedding blood or innocent blood is connected to an absence of justice and to oppression of the fatherless, the widow and the stranger (Jer 7:6).[34]

Even Manasseh's death notice varies from the standard statement accompanying the demise of a king in that it refers to the scroll in which is written "all the sin that he sinned" rather than the "rest of his deeds" (17). Yet there is no record of Manasseh meeting with any kind of adversity as a consequence of his sins; he is buried with his ancestors in a garden (18).

### Act II, Scene 2: Amon of Judah (2 Kings 21:19–26)

*Like father like son.*

In the very brief account of Amon, who succeeds Manasseh and reigns for only two years, the references to his father stand out (19–22): "He did what was evil . . . as had done Manasseh his father; he walked in all the ways his father walked, served the idols his father served." Hardly any more need be said, and hardly any more is said—except the redundant statement that he "abandoned Adonai"—before he is set upon and killed by "the people of the land" who make little Josiah, all of eight years old, king in his stead (24). Yet like his father, Amon does not bear the consequences of his apostasy in terms of a divine verdict. He too is buried in the garden (26). We found "the people of the land" earlier, in 2 Kings 11, where they rejoiced in the crowning of King Joash of Judah and participated in the overthrow of Athaliah and the destruction of idols (11:14, 18–20). We note that on this occasion there is also a king who is clearly not yet able to take the reins of his rule in his hands, as was the case with his ancestor Joash. The phrase points to common folk rather than the elite. The poor among them are the ones left behind after the first deportation to Babylon (24:14).

34. Nelson, *First and Second Kings*, 249.

The purpose of inserting the summary notices about both Manasseh and Amon must be to highlight the nature of their apostasy and thus provide a more complete message of future destruction than the one given at the time of King Hezekiah (20:17–18). As Marvin Sweeney points out, "Our narratives struggle with a theological question: why was Jerusalem destroyed?"[35] We are not to forget that following Queen Athaliah, all the kings on the throne of Judah are descendants of Omri's house.

## Act III: "The Best King Ever"[36] (2 Kings 22:1–23:30)

*Even Josiah's demonstrable righteousness and repentance does not reverse the divine decree.*[37]

Two chapters focus on the reforms of the young King Josiah, beginning when he is twenty-six years old. Repairs of the Temple are followed by the central role of a document found in the sanctuary, brought to the attention of the king and authenticated by the prophet Huldah. Subsequently, the king pledges himself and the people in complete loyalty to Adonai, and purification of the worship in Jerusalem and Judah commences. The second chapter depicts Josiah continuing his efforts of reform in the former Northern Kingdom. His reign of thirty-one years is cut short by his death in battle at Megiddo. Throughout, Josiah is held up as the ideal king, although his exemplary behavior will not stave off the doom of Judah and Jerusalem.

With Josiah, we enter the last half of the seventh century and the last decades of the domination of the region by Assyria, a period for which we are especially informed by the Babylonian Chronicles

---

35. Sweeney, *I & II Kings*, 427. Both Kgs and Chr (see 2 Chr 33:1–20) wrestle with the question of theodicy, and both choose to "assign responsibility for the destruction of Jerusalem on the people, either Manasseh or the generation of the Babylonian conquest" (428).

36. Nelson, *First and Second Kings*, 252.

37. Sweeney, *I & II Kings*, 440.

from the reigns of Nabopolassar (625–605 BCE) and Nebuchadnezzar (604–566 BCE). In Assyria, there was civil strife between 627
and 623 as it faced consistent threats from semi-nomadic peoples,
such as the Scythians and Medes. Medians and Babylonians formed
an alliance to capture Assyria's capital Nineveh in 612 BCE, and the
Assyrian empire came to an end in the last decade of the century.[38]
Egypt operated in partnership with Assyria against Babylon during
this time and exercised control over much of the Mediterranean
seaboard, including Judah. Miller and Hayes surmise that Josiah was
under Egyptian dominance throughout his reign.[39]

### Act III, Scene 1: The Last Great Hope of Judah (2 Kings 22)

*Huldah is a link, a triangulation point between herself, the words of the
Book, and the world around her.*[40]

The major events of this scene can be summarized as follows: Once
King Josiah has reached maturity, he sets Temple repairs in motion,
during which the high priest finds a scroll which the king's scribe
reads to him. The king reacts strongly to what he has heard and
sends a delegation to inquire of Adonai, for which the group approaches the prophet Huldah, who verifies that the scroll is indeed
God's word of judgment. The reactions of Josiah to the word brought
back to him by the delegation are described in the next scene.

The introduction reveals Josiah's age, the name of his mother,
and the rightness of his actions in the eyes of Adonai (1–2).[41] "He

---

38. In the Hebrew Bible, the book of Nahum reflects on this event.

39. For a historical overview of the period, see Miller and Hayes, *A History of Ancient Israel and Judah,* 441–54.

40. Tikva Frymer-Kensky, *Reading the Women of the Bible* (New York:
Schocken, 2002), 326.

41. The text puts a gap of eighteen years between vv. 2 and 3, leaving
one to surmise the identity of the regency for the child of eight. It could have
been his mother Yedidah, who is mentioned with her antecedents, perhaps
pointing to her importance. But the text hurries on to the major events of the
period of Josiah's reign.

walked in all the way of David his ancestor and did not turn to the right or the left." The phrase about not turning *to the right or the left* is rare in Kings and picks up on instructions from Deuteronomy, where both people and king are obligated to follow the Teaching of Moses (Deut 17:11, 20; cf. 28:14). In addition, it draws a direct line from Josiah to Joshua, who was required not to turn *to the right or the left* (Josh 1:7). The long arc of the narrative thus stretches from the beginning of the enterprise of entering the land to the end of the story, just before the land is lost. Josiah, like his great-great-great-grandfather Joash, undertakes Temple repairs. The elaborate instructions on how the money is to be dealt with (3–7) hark back to similar endeavors by Joash (12:10–16), repeating the phrase that there is to be no accounting because the overseers and workers are assumed to "act in good faith" (7). This background story lays down a false trail; the real event is not Temple repairs but something else entirely, which the next unit describes.

The central issue of the episode concerns "the writing of the Teaching" found by High Priest Hilkiah in the Temple and passed from him to Scribe Shafan, who brings it before the king.[42] This writing, a document, is passed up the chain, ending before the Deity.[43] In Deuteronomy, there is a writing or scroll with the words of the Teaching that Moses orders to be put *next to* the Ark of the Covenant as a witness (Deut 31:24–26), a copy of which is to be kept,

---

42. The word "scroll" or "writing" needs to be maintained rather than transposed with the modern word "book." Books, also with sacred text, did not appear on the scene until the first century CE. The container of the text makes a difference. Although it is generally assumed by scholars that the texts of the first five books of the Bible, the Torah, were put in the order they are today at an early date on one scroll, the other biblical "books" were only placed in a certain order with the invention of the codex (i.e., the book). In the Hebrew text of vv. 8–13, the Hebrew consonants for "scroll" (*sefer*) occur every time there is a reference to the scribe (*sofer*). Verses 8-10 read, "High Priest Hilkiah said to *Sofer* Shafan: A *sefer* of the Torah I have found. . . . *Sofer* Shafan came to the king. . . . Then *Sofer* Shafan said to the king: A *sefer* gave to me Hilkiah."

43. From v. 3, it appears that Shafan has greater authority than Hilkiah, as he is the one to command Hilkiah to begin the work of collecting the funds for Temple repair.

studied, and followed by the king (Deut 17:18–19). Similar wording is used for the Teaching to which Joshua is answerable (Josh 1:8). At the outset of Kings, David admonishes his son to abide by "what is written in the Teaching of Moses." References to this document can thus be found elsewhere and lay down a trail through the biblical narratives. Joshua is said to have *written* in "a scroll of the Teaching of God" (Josh 24:26). What is unique here is that there is no such action, no writing or copying, but instead "finding." The key word is not *writing* but *reading what is written* (8, 10, 13) and responding to it. Much scholarship has been devoted to *what* was in this writing, as well as to its origin. Was it a core of Deuteronomy and indeed *found* at the time of King Josiah, or was it constructed during his time? These are questions of great interest, but they may cause us to overlook the pivotal moment at which a *written document is authenticated as the word of God*. While there are hints and other traces of this step, for example in the writing of the stone tablets, there is no other moment in the Bible quite like this. It is one huge step on the road to an acceptance of a *text* contained in a document as the center around which a community of faith will find its identity and focus; a text by which it will measure its conduct—in other words, a canon.[44]

The steps taken in this process are precisely described in this chapter (8–10). First, there is the moment of Hilkiah's handing the scroll to Shafan, who *reads* it (8) and brings word to the king (9–10). The word he brings, as reported in verse 9, concerns first the issue of the finances; only after that does he mention "a writing" that "Hilkiah the priest gave to me." Holding back the moment of this revelation increases the tension around this object, first mentioned in Hilkiah's word to Shafan ("A writing of the Teaching I found").

44. Another such moment is to be found in Nehemiah 8:1–3, where Ezra brings "the scroll of the Teaching of Moses" and reads it before the gathered community in Jerusalem. For a thorough discussion of references to the "scroll of the Teaching of Moses," see G. J. Venema, *Reading Scripture in the Old Testament*, trans. Ch. E. Smit, OTS 48 (Leiden: Brill, 2003); trans. of *Schriftuurlijke Verhalen in het Oude Testament* (Delft: Eburon, 2000). An earlier step on this road is reportedly the assent of the people to the reading by Moses at the covenant-making in Exod 24:7.

These two lines—Hilkiah's and Shafan's—form the frame around the action in verses 8–10. Shafan then *reads* the writing to the king.[45]

The king's dramatic reaction is to tear his clothes, a sign of deep mourning, and to give an order for five individuals to go make inquiry of Adonai.

### 2 KINGS 22:13

Go, inquire of Adonai
on my behalf and on behalf of the people
and on behalf of all Judah
about the words of this writing that was found.
For great is the wrath of Adonai
that is kindled against us
because our ancestors did not listen
to the words of this writing,
by doing what is written about us.

The phrase "the words of this writing" refers back to "the words of the writing of the Teaching" (11) and is repeated twice as "the words of this writing" in what follows. The command to "inquire of Adonai" usually implies seeking the counsel of a prophet. That the king understands the words he has heard is made clear by his asking counsel not only for himself but for the entire community. He thinks as responsible leaders should of the well-being of his people. He does not further specify what the inquiry should entail, but it is clear that he wants to know if this is indeed a word of Adonai, because he understands God's wrath to be aroused because "the ancestors" did not "listen . . . by doing," and he is concerned that God's anger will burst forth in his time.

Without delay, the royal delegation goes to Huldah, the prophet. Their names are mentioned twice (12, 14) underlining the high standing of the individuals involved. The high priest, the scribe (a person with great administrative responsibility), the scribe's son Ahikam,

---

45. Possibly what is intended here are Deut 28–29 with their spelled-out consequences of following and not following this teaching.

and one of the king's personal attendants all go on the mission, along with one Akbor.[46] We note that the king did not *send* them to *her* as is frequently assumed. He sends them to *Adonai*, and they go to *Huldah, the prophet* (14). The text does not remark on the fact that they do not go to a male prophet—not to Jeremiah, the most famous prophet of this time (at least to a later reader)—but to a woman. Women prophets are mentioned in the text and may have been far more ubiquitous than explicit mention in the narratives leads one to assume (see also 2 Kgs 4:1–7; p. 179 above). It is in any case so unremarkable that it does not receive comment. Huldah is introduced by her family context—her husband (who has a high position at the court) together with his father and grandfather—and the location where she lives in Jerusalem.[47] Why does the royal delegation seek her out? She may live close to the palace, or perhaps she is more readily available than Jeremiah or is as well-known in her day. The men *speak* with her rather than *reading* the writing to her (14), and she will refer to "the scroll the king of Judah has read" (16).

2 KINGS 22:15–17

15  She said to them:
  Thus says Adonai the God of Israel:
  Say to the man who sent you to me:
16  Thus says Adonai:

---

46. Akbor is identified only as the son of Micaiah, a name that occurs in Neh 12:35, 41 as one belonging to the priestly ranks, while Akbor himself reappears in Jeremiah as the father of a member of a delegation sent to Egypt by King Jehoiakim (Jer 26:22); the same man, Elnatan son of Akbor, is counted among the princes in another passage (Jer 36:12).

47. That the text makes no big deal of the consultation with a female prophet does not mean it received no comment from the rabbis, who surmised that Huldah as a woman would give a more compassionate interpretation of the harsh Deuteronomic predictions (b. Meg 14b as cited in Leila Leah Bronner, *From Eve to Esther: Rabbinic Reconstructions of Biblical Women* [Louisville: Westminster John Knox, 1994], 175). Leila Bronner also points out the rabbis look favorably on Huldah's public role and her position as an instructor of the law.

Look!, I am bringing evil on this place
and on its inhabitants—
all the words of the writing
that the king of Judah has read.
17 Because they abandoned me
and burned incense to other gods
to vex me by all the works of their hands,
my wrath will be kindled against this place
and it will not go out.

Her first words, "thus says Adonai," identify her pronouncement as a prophetic word, a fact reinforced by the repetition in verse 16. She names Josiah as "the man who sent you to me" rather than "the king," an indication that she views him as important only as the recipient of her message, which comes directly from the highest authority, the Deity, through her agency. Josiah spoke of the "wrath of Adonai that is kindled against us" because of the refusal of the ancestors to listen (13); Huldah's first words are exactly the same as the report of the prophecy in the days of Manasseh, with "this place and . . . its inhabitants" replacing "Jerusalem and Judah" (16; cf. 21:12). Because of their consistent apostasy, it will be just as it is written in the writing.[48] From the ancestors, Huldah's prophecy brings the accusation home to "this place and . . . its inhabitants." The term "this place" is at home in the prophecies of Jeremiah as a stand-in for Jerusalem/Zion or the Temple.[49]

Huldah adds a word specific to the king that accounts for his reaction to the words of the writing (18–20). In the main, because Josiah "listened," Adonai has listened and will not bring the evil about during Josiah's lifetime. "Your eyes will not see the evil that I am bringing on this place" (20). The declaration that Josiah will go to

48. "Burning incense" on "the heights" or to "other gods" is a consistent refrain in Kgs, even under kings loyal to Adonai in Judah (1 Kgs 11:33; 22:44[43]; 2 Kgs 12:4[3]; 14:4; 15:4, 35; 17:11; cf. Jer 1:16). On the whole, the phrasing is very close to that of Jer 19:3–4.

49. "This place" is found in Jeremiah's well-known "Temple Sermon" and in numerous other locations. Half of the occurrences of the term are in Jeremiah.

his grave "in peace" is not related to the manner of his death, which will not be peaceful, but to a delay of the disasters to befall Jerusalem so that they will not happen during his lifetime.

### Act III, Scene 2: Cleaning House (2 Kings 23:1–30)

*Josiah is the ideal monarch who corrects problems introduced by earlier monarchs.*[50]

We can divide chapter 23 into four units. First, the king calls the people together for a reading of the discovered writing and a pledge of renewed loyalty to Adonai (1–3). A second unit describes in detail the removal and destruction of all that reeks of idolatry in the Temple, in Jerusalem, and in their immediate environs (4–14). Heading to the north, the third unit describes a similar series of actions against Bethel and Samaria, concluding with a Passover in Jerusalem (15–23). A final unit (24–30) recaps the actions of cultic cleansing and once again praises Josiah, although the wrath of Adonai is not moved toward compassion on Jerusalem and Judah by the king's exemplary behavior. Josiah is killed unexpectedly at Megiddo in 610, and his son Jehoahaz succeeds him. The scene is mostly descriptive, in contrast to the previous scene. Josiah's voice is heard only once, as he discovers the grave of the prophet from the time of Jeroboam (17–18).

After hearing the report of the delegation that met with Huldah (22:20), Josiah goes into action. He calls together a large group of people, elders, leaders, inhabitants of Jerusalem, priests and prophets, "all the people from small to great." To "all of these" he reads "all the words of the writing of the covenant found in the house of Adonai" (23:2).

2 Kings 23:3

The king stood at the pillar
and concluded the covenant before Adonai
to follow Adonai and to keep his commandments,

---

50. Sweeney, *I & II Kings*, 441.

his statutes, and his ordinances
with all his heart and all his soul,
to maintain the words of this covenant
that were written in this writing.
And all the people stood by[51] the covenant.

The words of the writing give rise to a pledge of loyalty to Adonai on Josiah's initiative, resounding with Deuteronomic phrasing. This is not a covenant "renewal," as it is often identified, in the sense that it repeats the actions of the covenant concluded at Sinai (Exod 24:3–8), which is described as an initiative taken by God and executed by Moses. The word "covenant" is used here in the sense of a solemn pledge, linking it to the actions of Joshua (Josh 24:25–27) and of Jehoiada, the priest under King Joash (2 Kgs 11:17–18). The pledge is made "before" (i.e., in the presence of) "Adonai" to act in specific ways. The pledge of commitment involves first of all an obligation in terms of worship—as usual the center of attention in Kings—so that the actions of cultic cleansing logically follow the oath taking.

The activities begin with the priests removing vessels used in the service of Baal, Asherah, and the "host of heaven." These are burned outside with the ashes carried farther away (4). Then Josiah becomes the subject of the action (5–14). Although he cannot have accomplished these things singlehandedly, such is the impression created by the text: "He put an end to," "he brought," "he burned," "he crushed," "he threw," "he demolished," "he brought back," "he desecrated" (5–10). The list goes on and on. Without doubt, we need to envision a large group of people participating and engaging in violent destruction of objects and living beings. The details bring to mind the iconoclasm that raged in the northern countries of Europe during the Protestant Reformation.[52]

51. This phrasing keeps the repetition of the verb "to stand" intact, meaning the people entered into the covenant.

52. In the Low Countries, the purification of church buildings in the middle of the sixteenth century took on the violent forms of smashing statues, destroying paintings and other artistic works, and feeding of the elements of the Eucharist to goats and dogs. The Reformers of that era considered the church to be polluted by idolatry—a pollution of which the church was

From Jerusalem, Josiah moves to the north to include the altar at Bethel and the high place there in the act of purification (14–20). It is highly unlikely that this activity could have taken place as told in a region that at this time was an Assyrian province, but the narrator is not as much interested in realism as in the description of the total destruction that happens everywhere, even in places where it could not have happened. In the midst of the action, there is a pause, and we stop to watch with Josiah as he discerns a grave different from the ones he has already desecrated and is informed that this is the place where the "man of God" is buried who prophesied everything that Josiah has just executed (16–18; 1 Kgs 13:1–32). Josiah thus comes as the fulfillment of a prophecy made three centuries earlier. He moves on to Samaria, where he slaughters the priests and burns their bones on the heights where they had exercised their profession (cf. 1 Kgs 13:2). The entire effort is concluded by a Passover in Jerusalem, a celebration the likes of which "was not held from the days of the Judges who judged Israel and in all the days of the kings of Israel and the kings of Judah" (22). Indeed, the last time a Passover celebration was mentioned was in Joshua, following the crossing of the Jordan River into the land (Josh 5:10–11), again connecting the figures of Joshua and Josiah.

To conclude the complete removal of all things and people unholy, Josiah burns the mediums (cf. 1 Sam 28:7), soothsayers, and idols—including household idols, which we found in Saul's household (1 Sam 19:13, 16) but do not encounter in Kings. The short section ends with renewed praise for Josiah using a phrase from Deuteronomy that occurs only in these two places in the Hebrew Bible: He has turned to God with "all his heart and all his soul and all his strength" (25; Deut 6:5). The accolade that there was no one like him *before* or after him is a variation on the same prerogative assigned to Hezekiah (2 Kgs 18:5). Since Josiah follows Hezekiah, it will not do to take the expression too literally. Descending to more realistic ground, the narrator comments that the prophecy

cleansed with the enthusiastic participation of the population. See Johanna W. H. van Wijk-Bos, *Reformed and Feminist: A Challenge to the Church* (Louisville: Westminster John Knox, 1991), 29–31.

of Jerusalem's destruction stands. Josiah may have *turned* to God, but God did not *turn* from the decision to reject Judah and the chosen city (26–27).

Josiah's end comes as a letdown after all the praise heaped upon him. Between the reference to another record of his deeds and his burial notice, the incident that caused his death is noted (28–30). He went to meet Pharaoh Neco and "he killed him at Megiddo." It is possible that Josiah decided to throw his lot in with Babylon, in rebellion against Egypt, at this time, but nothing is clear. The text in verse 29 creates confusion with its undefined personal pronouns, although it sounds as if Neco kills Josiah. Josiah's servants carry his body home, and he is buried there "in his grave" rather than "with his ancestors" (23:30). The succession is evidently either not regulated or there is unhappiness with the rightful heir, because the "people of the land" step in once again and declare Josiah's son Jehoahaz king.

### Act IV: Dissolution (2 Kings 23:31–25:30)

*The narrative approaches its sorry end.*[53]

With Josiah's death in 609 BCE we are a little more than a decade away from the first capture of Jerusalem under King Nebuchadnezzar of Babylon. Egypt still has control of the region but with gradually diminishing power. Eventually, Egypt is decisively defeated by Nebuchadnezzar at the battle of Carchemish in 605, and Judah moves from Egyptian to Babylonian domination; kingship in Judah endures from then on at the behest of the Babylonian ruler. Nearly every king until the final capture of Jerusalem rebels against Babylon according to the record in Kings. Rebellions cause the empire to exact punishment, and Jerusalem is besieged and captured twice, with two deportations as a result. The first siege in 597 causes the exile of King Jehoiachin to Babylon, where he surfaces at the end of the last chapter. The second siege, in 586 during King Zedekiah's

---

53. Brueggemann, *1 & 2 Kings*, 567.

rule, brings about a more total devastation of Jerusalem and another deportation. With the exile of King Zedekiah, the rule of the house of David comes to an end.

### Act IV, Scene 1: From Jerusalem to Babylon (2 Kings 23:31–24:20)

*As it turned out it was the Egyptian Pharaoh, not 'the people of the land,' who had the last say.*[54]

The end of chapter 23 records the ascension of Jehoahaz to the throne and his very brief reign—three months before he is taken into captivity by the Egyptian Pharaoh, first in a region of Syria before eventually being transported to Egypt, where he dies (23:31–34). The extreme brevity of his rule does not prevent the narrator from issuing a negative judgment: "He did what was evil in the eyes of Adonai" (23:32), a judgment passed three more times, on every one of these last kings of Judah (23:37; 24:9, 19). Pharaoh Neco puts in place another son of Josiah, Jehoiakim, who pays tribute, which he exacts from the population, to Egypt (23:35).[55] "The people of the land" are in the end the ones who must pay the price for subjugation. While there is no clarity in the text on either Josiah's political allegiance or that of his sons and we have no information from sources outside of the Bible, it looks as if resistance to the yoke of Egypt began under King Josiah and persists into the next generation. The reason for the imprisonment of Jehoahaz may have been that he was a known sympathizer with his father's cause. In any case, Jehoiakim shows no signs of resistance to Egypt. His reign lasts from 609–598, a period during which the balance of power over Judah shifts decisively in the direction of Babylon under the rule of King Nebuchadnezzar.

Babylonia defeated Egypt in 605 at the battle of Carchemish, and Nebuchadnezzar became master in the region that includes the

---

54. Miller and Hayes, *A History of Ancient Israel and Judah*, 461.

55. To go by the ages of the two sons of Josiah, Jehoiakim is the older by two years (cf. 23:31, 36). It may be that he was the logical successor and that "the people of the land" had preferred his younger brother.

Kingdom of Judah. Egypt no longer dominated the kingdom, but that did not mean that its existence and power were out of the picture. There were factions in Judah that agitated for an alliance with Egypt while others held that a policy of submission to Babylonia would be the best course of action. Notably, the prophet Jeremiah advocates against a partnership with Egypt and consistently speaks of ruin to arrive from Babylon (Jer 42:13–44:30; 46:2–26; 20:4–6; 21:2–10). The judgment of Jehoiakim's rule is the same as that of his brother's: "He did what was evil in the eyes of Adonai like all that his ancestors did" (37)

Three years after Jehoiakim comes under the thumb of Babylon, he foments rebellion. This gives Nebuchadnezzar a reason to set upon Judah using nations to the north and east of Judah: bands of Chaldeans, Arameans, and Moabites, which is to say Babylonian and auxiliary forces (24:1–2). The attacks are, however, not said to originate from Babylon but from Adonai.

2 KINGS 24:3–4

3  Surely by command of Adonai
   this happened to Judah
   to remove them from his sight
   on account of the sins of Manasseh,
   according to all he did
4  and also the innocent blood he shed,
   filling Jerusalem with innocent blood;
   Adonai was not willing to forgive.

The same word of judgment will reappear in verse 20 of this chapter during the reign of King Zedekiah, reaffirming that all is happening under the guidance and according to the will of Israel's God. The increasing threats to the continued existence of the kingdom and Jerusalem of course call into question the continued allegiance of Adonai not only to the royal house but to the land and its people, as well as to Jerusalem (see p. 300 below). Either Israel's God is not powerful enough to save it or does not care enough. In Kings, the narrator opts firmly for an affirmation of God's power over God's compassion.

Jehoiakim goes to his grave in relative peace, the last king of Judah to do so, and his son Jehoyachin succeeds him. In an aside, the narrative reports that Egypt is staying put because of Babylonian aggression (24:7). The harassment of Judah by bands of marauders has apparently not been to Nebuchadnezzar's satisfaction, for he besieges Jerusalem in the year of the new king's ascension to the throne so that, like his predecessor Jehoahaz, Jehoiachin gets only three months to reign (one would think it not quite enough time to do "what was evil in the eyes of Adonai" as the narrative judges in v. 9) before the siege begins and he capitulates to the invader (24:8–12). The verse that reports his submission indicates a large group of Jehoyachin's people—family and servants—who will accompany a large part of the population into exile (24:12–14). The exile, anticipated in the Former Prophets at the birth of Eli's grandchild (1 Sam 4:21–22), is becoming a reality.[56] Not everyone leaves with this first deportation; "the poor people of the land" remain. In the hill country especially, it would be difficult to round up every last soul, so a remnant stays behind.

2 KINGS 24:15–17

15 He exiled Jehoyachin in Babylon;
   and the mother of the king
   and the wives of the king,
   the eunuchs, and the citizenry of the land
   he made to go into exile from Jerusalem to Babylon.
16 Also, all of the soldiers of the army,
   seven thousand of them,
   and of metalworkers and smiths a thousand,
   all the strong heroes who wage war;
   and the king of Babylon exiled them to Babylon.
17 The king of Babylon made Mattaniah,
   his uncle, king in his place,
   and changed his name to Zedekiah.

---

56. The number 10,000 recorded in 24:14 is most likely unrealistic, with the number 3,023, reported in Jer 52:28, coming closer to the truth.

The fivefold repetition of the name Babylon (*bavel*) could not make more clear who is in charge. The name of the puppet king put in place by Nebuchadnezzar, Zedekiah, connects the sacred name of God with righteousness in Hebrew—ironic because he too "did what was evil in the eyes of Adonai." Following this statement is another word of judgment regarding the "wrath of Adonai" that is causing these disasters to happen (24:18–20). Further, tacked on to the notice about the duration of his kingship and his evaluation is the observation that he "rebelled against the king of Babylon." He will be the last descendant of David to sit on the throne of Judah.

### Act IV, Scene 2: The End (2 Kings 25)

*An inventory of plundered sancta, a verbal witness to what was and is, for the author, no more.*[57]

The rebellion of Zedekiah announced at the end of the last chapter apparently takes place in Zedekiah's ninth year and results in a renewed assault on Jerusalem. The second siege lasts two years, causing famine in the city (1–3). When a breach is made in the city wall, a part of the Judean army flees with the king, but they are overtaken near Jericho, and Zedekiah is taken to Riblah as Jehoahaz was (4–6). Zedekiah, his sons slaughtered before his "eyes" while he can still see and then blinded after this spectacle, is brought in shackles to Babylon (7). About him there is no further word in the text.

A second unit (8–12) details the sacking of Jerusalem and the burning down of the Temple, the palace, and the houses under commander Nebuzaradan. The wall of Jerusalem is torn down and the "rest of the people, the remainder of the city" is taken into exile. This time as well there are those left behind, the "poor of the land," who are put in charge of crop production, "vintners and farmers"—a situation that may have improved their lot. The looting of all the precious metals that could be found in the Temple, gold and copper, is cataloged in detail (13–17). The narrative reports the breaking

---

57. Cohn, 2 *Kings*, 169.

up of materials for the sake of taking the metal (cf. Jer 52:17–23).[58] Subsequently, seventy-two people are taken—twelve belonging to the service of the Temple and the court along with sixty "people of the land"—and executed in Riblah, where Zedekiah met his fate. The final sentence in this unit—"Judah went into exile from its land"—repeats the fate of Israel (17:23).

Over those left behind in the land, Nebuchadnezzar appoints Gedaliah, perhaps as a kind of governor (22–25). He is said to be related to Shafan through his son Ahikam, both of whom were members of the delegation consulting with the prophet Huldah in 22:12, 14. He is presumably a person of standing in the royal administration. Gedaliah counsels the army commanders to consent to the rule of the Babylonian king, but one of them, a descendant of the royal house, is apparently of a different mind. He kills Gedaliah and a group of Judeans and Babylonians with him. The killing of a group of people indicates that more than one individual is involved in the coup, and the assassination is likely a protest against Babylonian domination. The same group may be indicated with "all the people," who in the next verse flee to Egypt out of fear of reprisals from Babylon (26).[59]

The closing unit of Kings recounts the fate of King Jehoiachin, who was taken into exile during the first assault on Jerusalem in 597 BCE. He surfaces thirty-seven years later in Babylon in the first year of the next Babylonian ruler. This king, in the Bible called Evil-Merodach,[60] rules for only one or two years before he is killed in a revolution. At his ascension, he extends hospitality to the former king of Judah and allows him to eat at his table.

---

58. 2 Chr 36:18 notes the taking of utensils and other implements from the Temple intact, which coheres with the report in Ezra 1:7. Both the stripping of metal and the taking of entire implements may have occurred.

59. For a more extensive version of these events, see Jeremiah 40–41. A self-imposed exile to Egypt serves to explain the presence there of a community of Jews in the centuries following.

60. *Evil-Merodach*, the Hebrew name for the Babylonian King Amel-Marduk, does not carry implications of wickedness despite including a homonym of the English word "evil."

2 KINGS 25:28–30

28 He spoke kindly to him
  and gave him a royal seat at his side in Babylon.
29 He changed his prison clothes,
  and he ate food always in his presence,
  all the days of his life.
30 And his allowance was a continuous allowance
  given to him from the king
  day after day,
  all the days of his life.

All of these actions are gracious, and it is possible to read in this turn of events for the last descendant of David's house a tentatively hopeful note. Robert Alter writes "This concluding image . . . seeks to intimate a hopeful possibility of future restoration: a Davidic king is recognized as king, even in captivity, and is given a daily provision appropriate to his royal status."[61] On the other hand, in view of the fact that Jehoiachin must have been in his fifties at the time and the imminent demise of the Babylonian king is around the corner, one may wonder how long "all the days of his life" on either his part or that of his benefactor were to last. Eating a bite of bread at the house of a superior brings to mind also the prophecy regarding a descendant of Eli who will beg for a bite to eat following the collapse of Eli's house (1 Sam 2:36) as well as one of the last offspring of the house of Saul, the "man from nowhere" whose house would go nowhere, eating bread at David's table (2 Sam 9); such is the man from the

---

61. Robert Alter, *Ancient Israel: The Former Prophets: Joshua, Judges, Samuel, and Kings* (New York: Norton, 2013), 852n30. So also Cohn, *2 Kings*, 73: "The special food provisions offered to Jehoiakin 'all the days of his life' (v. 30) point ever so subtly to hope for the future beyond destruction." Such comments overlook the thirty-seven years of imprisonment that preceded the provisions and the complete dependency of this descendant of the house of David, who is still robbed of his freedom in exile far from his home and whose fate hangs on the goodwill of the Babylonian ruler. More realistically, Hens-Piazza (*1–2 Kings*, 401) calls the verses that end the book of Kings a "frayed thread of hope."

prison house who, notwithstanding his title, is in exile far from his kingdom and whose descendants will not sit on any throne.

## HOPE FOR THE FUTURE

In Joshua, Judges, Samuel, and Kings, we have read about a people's beginning filled with hope, a descent into chaos at the end of the first period of its existence, a new beginning and new potential with the establishment of a monarchy in fits and starts—revising the possibilities embedded in this adventure along the way—and an end that constitutes a complete collapse of its dreams. It will continue as a small group of people in exile, with an even smaller group left behind in the land of their dreams and another group back in Egypt, from which they once were liberated.

As with any history written by its subjects, the narrative has its heroes and villains, but the heroes after Joshua are all flawed. When Samuel warned the people about kingship, he spoke of all the *taking* the king they desired would do (1 Sam 8:10–18). He should have added that kingship would cost them their land and that their rejection of God would result in God's rejection of them (2 Kgs 17:15, 20; 23:27). The book of Kings is a cycle of one king after another damaging the people's relationship with Adonai. The few exceptions to this situation are not able to prevent the disaster that will overcome them. Kings is, in truth, a remarkable record of failure—failure of loyalty to Adonai, failure of exercising just administration, failure of political stability. A lamentation over the fate of land and people is not to be found in Kings. To hear that voice, we must go to the prophet Jeremiah.

### JEREMIAH 8:20–23

20 The harvest is past,
    ended is summer,
    and we, we are not saved!
21 Because of the breach of my people
    I am broken, dressed in mourning;

horror has seized me.
22 Is there no balm in Gilead?
   Is there no physician there?
   Why has it not come,
   healing for my poor people?
23 Oh, that my head were water
   and my eye a fountain of tears;
   then I would weep day and night
   for the slain of my poor people.

Kings only utters the voice of judgment and a detailed description of destruction. Brueggemann writes, "The telling is . . . so that the massiveness and the brutality can sink in, from shovels to snuffers, everything, all, everyone, everybody, no mercy, no compassion, no exception. Only Babylon now. . . . Mercy is just beyond the reach of our narrative that gives no hint of mercy."[62] Of course, the kingdom is portrayed in its downward spiral as an explanation and instruction for the generations to come—how it happened that Ezra can say that "today we are slaves" (Neh 9:36). The loss of land, city, and Temple is ascribed to the power of God, but the responsibility is put squarely on the shoulders of monarchs and people. One lesson for the future is that hope does not reside in kingship. Where then is hope to be found?

Only a generation after Jehoiachin is taken from his prison to eat at the king of Babylon's table, a new empire will have arisen in Babylon's place, and a new situation will have come about in which an exiled community returns to its homeland to rebuild what they can, even under duress and the imposition of foreign rule. There will be a slow awakening to the fact that even without a land and without a sanctuary where Adonai alone can be worshiped, there is something around which this particular community, with new ups and downs, falling and getting up, will preserve its identity and its devotion: the written text of which the core was validated under Josiah by the prophet Huldah. If the locus of biblical Israel's utopian

---

62. Walter Brueggemann, *1 & 2 Kings*, SHBC 8 (Macon, GA: Smyth & Helwys, 2000), 598–99.

vision was initially the land promised to the ancestors as a place for the people of God's covenant to be God's people—a vision in due course concentrated on the city chosen by Adonai, Zion/Jerusalem—the locus of the restored community becomes the words of a written text. The text with all its contradictory voices, all its embedded arguments—debates which the rabbis will continue in the centuries to come—becomes the core around which the community will continue to form and reform itself as a community of faith. It will be the river to feed new communities of faith while the descendants of the exiles continue to flourish for many centuries without a land, without a central sanctuary, with the words of the text as abiding testimony to the humility and grace of a God who condescends to revelation in the human word. The fall of Judah and Jerusalem and the disappearance of the monarchy is an end indeed, but then again, this too is "the end of the beginning."

# *Appendix: Hebrew Words in This Volume*

Throughout this book, Hebrew words are transliterated in italics. When reading these words, observe the following:

> *a* is always as in f<u>a</u>ther, not as in d<u>a</u>d.
>
> *e* generally as in m<u>e</u>t, sometimes a light sound as in <u>a</u>bout, rendered by ʾ.
>
> *i* generally as in fl<u>ee</u>t, sometimes as i in k<u>i</u>ss.
>
> *o* is always as in b<u>o</u>ne, not as in g<u>o</u>t.
>
> *u* is always as in r<u>u</u>ler, not as in r<u>u</u>n.
>
> *ey* as in pr<u>ay</u>.
>
> *g* is always hard as in <u>g</u>old.

Hebrew has no syllables that contain two vowels. If an a word is spelled with two consecutive vowels, it is pronounced with two syllables: Baal = bah-<u>al</u>.

Each word below is followed by a phonetic pronunciation to provide further help articulating the Hebrew words. Stressed syllables are underlined. They occur generally at the end of the word, but not always. Pronunciation of /*ch*/ or /*kh*/ is always as in Ba<u>ch</u>; Hebrew has no /*ch*/ as in <u>ch</u>eese.

## Abbreviations

> adj. = adjective
>
> n. = noun
>
> n.comb. = nouns in combination
>
> pr. = pronoun
>
> pr.n. = proper noun
>
> prep. = preposition
>
> v. = verb

*adon* (ah-dohn) n.—lord, 124, 155n83

*af hu* (af hoo) part. + pr.—even he, 171n110

*al* (ahl) prep.—upon, against, over, 28

*am* (ahm) n.—people, 88, 89

*asherah* (ah-shay-<u>rah</u>) n.—sacred pole, the goddess Asherah, 108–10, 115, 155, 221, 254, 279, 290

*awon* (ah-<u>vohn</u>) n.—offense, guilt, punishment, 120n12, 13

Baal (bah-<u>al</u>) n.— Baal (deity), master, 89, 112, 115, 122–23, 125, 127–28, 130–31, 134, 152, 155, 162, 164–66, 176, 220–21, 225, 228–30, 254, 289, 290

*be'alim* (b'-ah-<u>leem</u>) n.—baals, idols, masters, 126n22

*ba'ar* (bah-<u>ar</u>) v.—burn, sweep away, 102n37

*bedam* (b'-<u>dahm</u>) prep. + n.—in blood, 27

*beney* (b'-<u>nay</u>) n.—sons, children, descendants, disciples, 40n53, 149, 172, 179n127

*beney beliya'al* (b'-nay b'-lee-yah-<u>al</u>) n.comb.—scoundrels, worthless men, 149

*beney hannevi'im* (b'-nay ha-n'-vee-<u>eem</u>) n.comb.—disciples of the prophets, 172n112, 179n127

*bet hahosfshit* (bayt hah-chof-sheet) n.comb.—the house of freedom/ confinement, 247n13

*dam* (dahm) n.—blood, 27

*el* (el) prep.—to, near, by, opposite, 198n158

El (el) pr.n.—El the deity at the head of the Canaanite pantheon, 33n35

*elohim* (eh-loh-<u>heem</u>) n.—god, gods, 66

*esh* (aysh) n.—fire, 166

*esh min hashamayim* (aysh min ha-shah-<u>mah</u>-yeem)—fire from heaven / the sky, 166

*eyn* (ayn) n.—well, eye, 18, 23n17

Eyn Rogel (ayn <u>ro</u>-gel) n.comb.—well of the scout/spy, 18, 23n17

*gadaf* (gah-<u>dahf</u>) v.—revile, blaspheme, 272

*gazar* (gah-<u>zahr</u>) v.—cut, hew, 38

*ger* (gayr) n.—stranger, 121n14

*geva'ot* (g'-vah-<u>oht</u>) n.—heights, 33n34

*gevir* (g'-<u>veer</u>) n.—master, 107

*gevirah* (g'-vee-<u>rah</u>) n.—mistress, woman of high rank, 107

*gur* (goor) v.—sojourn, live as a stranger, 121n14, 188n137, 209

*hafakh* (hah-<u>fahch</u>) v.—overturn, 280

*hannevi'im* (ha-n'–vee-<u>eem</u>) n.—the prophets, 172n112, 179n127

*harag* (hah-<u>rahg</u>) v.—slay, 125n17

*haratsahta vegam yarashta* (hah-rah-tsahch-tah v'-gam yah-rahsh-<u>tah</u>)— have you killed and also taken possession?, 152n77

*hashamayim* (hah-shah-mah-<u>yeem</u>) n.—the sky, the heavens, 166
*hassoferet* (hah-soh-<u>feh</u>-ret) n.—the female scribe, 40n53
*hata'* (chah-<u>tah</u>) v.—miss the mark, fall short, sin, 20n10
*hayah* (chah-<u>yah</u>) v.—live, 210n177
*hazaq* (chah-<u>zahk</u>) v.—seize, take hold, 189n138
*heder* (<u>cheh</u>-der) n.— (private) chamber, 20n9
*hesed* (<u>cheh</u>-sed) n.—kindness, devotion, 33, 144
*hinneh* (hin-nay) v.—look! 124, 142
*hokhmah* (<u>chohch</u>-mah) n.—wisdom, 76

*ish* (eesh) n.—(a) man, 166
*ish ha'elohim* (eesh hah-eh-loh-<u>heem</u>) n.comb.—man of (the) god, 166

*kavad* (kah-<u>vahd</u>) v.—be heavy, 77
*kaved* (kah-<u>vayd</u>) adj.—heavy, weighty, 77

*lepanaw* (l'-pah-nahf) prep.—before him, 193
*lifney* (lif-<u>nay</u>) prep.—in the presence of, before, 193, 198n158
*lishnayim qera'im* (lish-<u>nah</u>-yeem k'-rah-<u>eem</u>) n.comb.—in two pieces, 171n109

*ma'og* (mah-<u>ohg</u>) n.—a baked thing, 119n9
*mas* (mahs) n.—forced labor, 31, 40, 46, 72n119
*mashal* (mah-<u>shal</u>) n.—proverb, saying, 61n98
*metsora* (m'-tsoh-rah) n.—skin disease, 194
*mifletset* (mif-<u>leh</u>-tset) n.—abominable image, 109
*min* (min) prep.—from, 166
*mishkan* (meesh-<u>kahn</u>) n.—dwelling, 48
*mut* (moot) v.—die, 125n17

*naga* (nah-<u>gah</u>) v.—touch, strike, 134
*nahalah* (nah-chah-<u>lah</u>) n.—inheritance, 148n68
*nahash* (nah-<u>chash</u>) n.—snake, 265n4
*nasa'* (nah-<u>sah</u>) v.—carry, 16n4
*navelah* (nah-v'-<u>lah</u>) n.—folly, wicked error, 96
*nefesh* (<u>neh</u>-fesh) n.—life, soul, being, 121, 186
*nehoshet* (n'-<u>cho</u>-shet) adj.—bronze, 265n4
*nehustan* (n'-choosh-<u>tahn</u>) pr.n.—name for the image of the bronze serpent, 265n4
*ner* (nayr) n.—lamp, light, 74n125
*neshamah* (n'-shah-<u>mah</u>) n.—life-breath, 121
*nevelah* (n'-vay-<u>lah</u>) n.—corpse, 96

*pesel* (<u>peh</u>-sel) n.—hewn image, 46

*qum* (koom) v.—arise! 151
*qum red* (koom rayd) v.—arise, go down! 151

*qum resh* (koom raysh) v.—arise, take possession! 151

*rahamim* (rah-chah-<u>meem</u>) n.—compassion, 39n47

*rahav* (rah-<u>chahv</u>) v.—be wide, broad, 88

*rahum* (rah-<u>choom</u>) adj.—compassionate, 39n47

*red* (rayd) v.—go down! 151

*rehem* (<u>reh</u>-chem) n.—womb, 39n47

*resh* (raysh) v.—take possession! 151

*ruah* (<u>roo</u>-ahch) n.—spirit, breath, 65

*satan* (sah-<u>tahn</u>) n.—accuser, tester, 71n117

*sefer* (<u>say</u>-fer) n.—scroll, 284n42

*sevel* (<u>say</u>-vel) n.—service, labor, 72n119

*shakhan* (shah-<u>khan</u>) v.—dwell, 47

*shalom* (shah-<u>lohm</u>) n.—wholeness, peace, 186n135, 199, 219

*shamayim* (shah-<u>mah</u>-yeem) n.—heavens, sky, 166

*sharat* (shah-<u>raht</u>) v.—serve, 17

*shelomo* (sh'-loh-<u>moh</u>) pr.n.—Solomon, 66, 78n130

*shenehem* (sh'-<u>nay</u>-hem) n.—the two of them, 171n109

*sheninah* (sh'-nee-<u>nah</u>) n.—taunt, 61n98

*shema* (shay-mah) n.—report, 66

Sheol (sh'-ohl) pr.n.—world of shades after death, Sheol, 26, 27, 76

*shofar* (shoh-<u>fahr</u>) n.—shofar, 22, 23, 218

*shohar* (shoh-<u>chahr</u>) n.—bribe, 249

*shuv* (shoov) v.—return, 90, 94

*sofer* (soh-fayr) n.—male scribe, 284n42

*soferet* (soh-<u>feh</u>-ret) n.—female scribe, 40n53

*sur* (soor) v.—turn aside, 189, 254n27

*tahar* (tah-<u>har</u>) v.—be (ritually) clean, 197

*taval* (tah-<u>val</u>) v.—dip, 197

*torah* (toh-<u>rah</u>) n.—instruction, teaching, 51, 59, 123, 159, 253, 279

*tsaraat* (tsa-<u>rah</u>-aht) n.—skin disease, 195n150, 207, 247

*ugah* (oo-<u>gah</u>) n.—cake, 119n9

*vayhi* (vay-<u>hee</u>) v.—there was, 98n30

*vayhi ish* (vay-<u>hee</u> eesh)—there was a man, 98n30

*vayhi ish ehad* (vay-<u>hee</u> eesh eh-<u>chahd</u>)—there was a certain man, 98n30

*yashav* (yah-<u>shahv</u>) v.—stay, live, sit, 47n71, 55n87

*yeladim* (y'-lah-<u>deem</u>) n.—lads, youngsters, 86, 87

*zera* (<u>zeh</u>-rah) n.—seed, descendants, 229

*zonah* (zoh-<u>nah</u>) n.—whore, 35n38, 37

# Bibliography

## Books

Albertz, Rainer. *A History of Israelite Religion in the Old Testament Period.* Translated by John Bowden. Vol. 1, *From the Beginnings to the End of the Monarchy.* Louisville: Westmister John Knox, 1994. Translation of *Religionsgeschichte Israels in alttestamentlicher Zeit.* Göttingen: Vandenhoeck & Ruprecht, 1992.

Alter, Robert. *Ancient Israel: The Former Prophets: Joshua, Judges, Samuel, and Kings.* New York: W. W. Norton, 2013.

———. *The Art of Biblical Narrative.* New York: Basic Books, 1981.

———. *The Art of Biblical Poetry.* New York: Basic Books, 1985.

———. *The David Story: A Translation with Commentary of 1 and 2 Samuel.* New York: Norton, 1999.

Amit, Yairah. *Hidden Polemics in Biblical Narrative.* BibInt 25. Leiden: Brill, 2000.

———. *History and Ideology: An Introduction to Historiography in the Hebrew Bible.* Sheffield: Sheffield Academic, 1999.

Bellis, Alice Ogden. *Helpmates, Harlots and Heroes: Women's Stories in the Hebrew Bible.* Louisville: Westminster John Knox, 1994.

Bellis, Alice Ogden, and Joel Kaminsky, eds. *Jews, Christians, and the Theology of the Hebrew Scriptures.* Atlanta: Society of Biblical Literature, 2000.

Bergen, Wesley J. *Elisha and the End of Prophetism.* JSOTSup 286. Sheffield: Sheffield Academic, 1999.

Brenner, Athalya, ed. *A Feminist Companion to Samuel and Kings.* Sheffield: Sheffield Academic, 1994.

Bronner, Leila Leah. *From Eve to Esther: Rabbinic Reconstructions of Biblical Women.* Louisville: Westminster John Knox, 1994.

Brueggemann, Walter. *1 & 2 Kings.* SHBC 8. Macon, GA: Smyth and Helwys, 2000.

Buber, Martin, and Franz Rosenzweig. *Bücher der Geschichte: Verdeutscht von Martin Buber gemeinsam mit Franz Rosenzweig.* Cologne: Jakob Hegner, 1965.

Carr, E. H. *What Is History?* 40th anniv. ed. Basingstoke, UK: Palgrave, 2001.

Cohn, Robert L. *2 Kings.* Berit Olam. Collegeville, MN: Liturgical Press, 2000.

Collins, John J., T. M. Lemos, and Saul M. Olyan, eds. *Worship, Women and War: Essays in Honor of Susan Niditch.* Providence, RI: Brown University Press, 2015.

Coogan, Michael, ed. *The Oxford History of the Biblical World.* New York: Oxford University Press, 1998.

Dijk-Hemmes, Fokkelien van. *The Double Voice of Her Desire: Texts by Fokkelien van Dijk-Hemmes.* Ed. J. Bekkenkamp and F. Dröes. Leiden: Deo, 2004.

Eslinger, Lyle. *Into the Hands of the Living God.* JSOTSup 84. Sheffield: Almond, 1984.

Fewell, Danna Nolan, ed. *Reading Between Texts: Intertextuality and the Hebrew Bible.* Louisville: Westminster John Knox, 1992.

Fewell, Danna Nolan, and David M. Gunn. *Gender, Power, and Promise: The Subject of the Bible's First Story.* Nashville: Abingdon, 1993.

Fokkelman, J. P. *King David.* Vol. 1 of *Narrative Art and Poetry in the Books of Samuel.* Assen: Van Gorcum, 1981.

Fokkelman, J. P., and Wim Weren, eds. *De Bijbel Literair: Opbouw en Gedachtegang van de Bijbelse Geschriften en hun Onderlinge Relaties.* Zoetermeer: Meinema, 2005.

Fox, Everett. *The Early Prophets.* New York: Schocken, 2014.

_____. *The Five Books of Moses: A New Translation with Introductions, Commentary, and Notes.* New York: Schocken, 1995.

Fretheim, Terence E. *First and Second Kings.* Westminster Bible Companion. Louisville: Westminster John Knox, 1999.

Frymer-Kensky, Tikva. *In the Wake of the Goddesses: Women, Culture and the Biblical Transformation of Pagan Myth.* New York: Macmillan, 1992.

_____. *Reading the Women of the Bible:* New York: Schocken 2002.

Gafney, Wilda C. *Daughters of Miriam: Women Prophets in Ancient Israel.* Minneapolis: Fortress, 2008.

_____. *Womanist Midrash: A Reintroduction to the Women of the Torah and the Throne.* Louisville: Westminster John Knox, 2017.

Goldingay, John. *1 and 2 Kings for Everyone.* Louisville: Westminster John Knox, 2011.

Gravett, Sandra L., Karla Bohmbach, F. V. Greifenhagen, and Donald C. Polaski, eds. *An Introduction to the Hebrew Bible: A Thematic Approach.* Louisville: Westminster John Knox, 2008.

Gur-Klein, Thalia. *Sexual Hospitality in the Hebrew Bible: Patronymic, Metronymic, Legitimate and Illegitimate Relations in the Bible.* London: Routledge, 2014.

Habel, Norman C. *The Land Is Mine.* Minneapolis: Fortress, 1995.

Hartmann, Benedikt, Ernst Jenni, E. Y. Kutscher, Victor Maag, I. L. Seeligmann, and Rudolf Smend. *Hebräische Wortforschung: Festschrift zum 80 Geburtstag von Walter Baumgartner.* VTSup 16. Leiden: Brill, 1967.

Hayes, John H., and Paul K. Hooker. *A New Chronology for the Kings of Israel and Judah and Its Implications for Biblical History and Literature.* Atlanta: John Knox, 1988.

Hens-Piazza, Gina. *1–2 Kings.* Nashville: Abingdon, 2006.

_____. *Nameless, Blameless, and Without Shame: Two Cannibal Mothers Before a King.* Collegeville, MN: Liturgical Press, 2003.

Hornsby, Teresa J., and Ken Stone, eds. *Bible Trouble: Queer Reading at the Boundaries of Biblical Scholarship.* Atlanta: Society of Biblical Literature, 2011.

Hurowitz, Victor (Avigdon). *I Have Built You an Exalted House: Temple Building in the Bible in Light of Mesopotamian and Northwest Semitic Writings.* JSOTSup 115. Sheffield: Sheffield Academic, 1992.

Isserlin, B. S. J. *The Israelites.* Minneapolis: Fortress, 2001.

Knoppers, Gary N., and J. Gordon McConville, eds. *Reconsidering Israel and Judah: Recent Studies on the Deuteronomistic History.* Winona Lake, IN: Eisenbrauns, 2000.

Lapsley, Jacqueline E. *Whispering the Word: Hearing Women's Stories in the Old Testament.* Louisville: Westminster John Knox, 2005.

Lehnhart, Bernhard. *Prophet und König im Nordreich Israel: Studien zur sogenannten vorklassischen Prophetie im Nordreich Israel anhand der Samuel-, Elija- und Elischa- Überlieferungen.* Leiden: Brill, 2003.

Leuchter, Mark, and Klaus-Peter Adam, eds. *Soundings in Kings: Perspectives and Methods in Contemporary Scholarship.* Minneapolis: Fortress, 2010.

Long, Burke O. *2 Kings.* FOTL 10. Grand Rapids: Eerdmans, 1991.

McKenzie, Steven L., and Stephen R. Haynes, eds. *To Each Its Own Meaning: An Introduction to Biblical Criticisms and Their Application.* Louisville: Westminster John Knox, 1999.

Meyers, Carol. *Discovering Eve: Ancient Israelite Women in Context.* Oxford: Oxford University Press, 1988.

_____. *Rediscovering Eve: Ancient Israelite Women in Context.* Oxford: Oxford University Press, 2011.

Miller, J. Maxwell, and John H. Hayes. *A History of Ancient Israel and Judah.* 2nd ed. Louisville: Westminster John Knox, 2006.

Moore, Megan Bishop, and Brad E. Kelle. *Biblical History and Israel's Past:*

*The Changing Study of the Bible and History*. Grand Rapids: Eerdmans, 2011.

Nelson, Richard D. *First and Second Kings*. Int. Atlanta: John Knox, 1987.

Niditch, Susan. *War in the Hebrew Bible: A Study in the Ethics of Violence*. Oxford: Oxford University Press, 1993.

Rost, Leonhard. *The Succession to the Throne of David*. Translated by Michael D. Rutter and David M. Gunn. Sheffield: Almond Press, 1982.

Russell, Stephen. *The King and the Land: A Geography of Royal Power in the Biblical World*. Oxford: Oxford University Press, 2017.

Schottroff, Luise, and Marie-Theres Wacher, eds. *Feminist Biblical Interpretation: A Compendium of Critical Commentary on the Books of the Bible and Related Literature*. Translated by Lisa E. Dahill. Grand Rapids: Eerdmans, 2012. Translation of *Kompendium Feministische Bibelauslegung*. Gütersloh: Gütersloher Verlagungshaus, 1999.

Schulz, Kathryn. *Being Wrong: Adventures in the Margin of Error*. New York: Harper Collins, 2010.

Schwartz, Regina M. *The Curse of Cain: The Violent Legacy of Monotheism*. Chicago: University of Chicago Press, 1997.

Seibert, Eric A. *Subversive Scribes and the Solomonic Narrative: A Rereading of 1 Kings 1–11*. London: T&T Clark, 2006.

Sweeney, Marvin A. *1 & II Kings: A Commentary*. OTL. Louisville: Westminster John Knox, 2007.

Terrien, Samuel. *The Elusive Presence: Toward a New Biblical Theology*. San Francisco: Harper & Row, 1978.

Trible, Phyllis. *God and the Rhetoric of Sexuality*. Philadelphia: Fortress, 1978.

Venema, G. J. *Reading Scripture in the Old Testament*. Translation by Ch. E. Smit. Leiden: Brill, 2003. Translation of *Schriftuurlijke Verhalen in het Oude Testament*. Delft: Eburon, 2000.

Walsh, Jerome T. *1 Kings*. Berit Olam. Collegeville, MN: Liturgical Press, 1996.

_____. *Ahab: The Construction of a King*. Collegeville, MN: Liturgical Press, 2006.

Wijk-Bos, Johanna W. H. van. *The End of the Beginning: Joshua & Judges*. A People and a Land 1. Grand Rapids: Eerdmans, 2019.

_____. *Ezra, Nehemiah, and Esther*. Westminster Bible Companion. Louisville: Westminster John Knox, 1998.

_____. *Making Wise the Simple: The Torah in Christian Faith and Practice*. Grand Rapids: Eerdmans, 2005.

_____. *Reformed and Feminist: A Challenge to the Church*. Louisville: Westminster John Knox, 1991.

_____. *The Road to Kingship: 1–2 Samuel*. A People and a Land 2. Grand Rapids: Eerdmans, 2020.

Würthwein, Ernst. *Das Erste Buch der Könige: Kapitel 1–16*. ATD 11.1. Göttingen: Vandenhoeck & Ruprecht, 1977.

———. *Die Bücher der Könige: 1 Kön. 17 – 2 Kön. 25*. ATD 11.2. Göttingen: Vandenhoeck & Ruprecht, 1984.

## Articles and Chapters

Amit, Yairah. "A Prophet Tested: Elisha, the Great Woman of Shunem, and the Story's Double Message." *BibInt* 11 (2003): 279–94.

Bellis, Alice Ogden. "The Queen of Sheba: A Gender-Sensitive Reading." *JRT* 51 (1994–1995): 17–28.

Ben-Barak, Zafrira. "The Status and Right of the Gebira." Pages 170–85 in *A Feminist Companion to Samuel and Kings*. Edited by Athalya Brenner. Sheffield: Sheffield Academic, 1994.

Bodner, Keith. "The Locutions of 1 Kings 22:29: A New Proposal." *JBL* 122 (2003): 533–46.

Burnside, Jonathan. "Flight of the Fugitives: Rethinking the Relationship between Biblical Law (Exodus 21:12–14) and the Davidic Succession Narrative (1 Kings 1–2)." *JBL* 129 (2010): 418–31.

Davis, Ellen F. "Losing a Friend: The Loss of the Old Testament to the Church." Pages 83–94 in *Jews, Christians and the Theology of the Hebrew Scriptures*. Edited by Alice Ogden Bellis and Joel Kaminsky. Atlanta: Scholars Press, 2000.

Dijk-Hemmes, Fokkelien van. "De grote vrouw uit Sunem en de man Gods: Een tweeledige interpretatie van 2 Koningen 4:8-37." *Mara. Tijdschrift voor feminisme en theologie* 2 (1989): 45–53.

Dozeman, Thomas B. "The Way of the Man of God from Judah: True and False Prophecy in the Pre-Deuteronomic Legend of 1 Kings 13." *CBQ* 44 (1982): 379–93.

Fewell, Danna Nolan. "Feminist Criticism." Pages 268–82 in *To Each Its Own Meaning: An Introduction to Biblical Criticisms and Their Application*. Edited by Steven L. McKenzie and Stephen R. Haynes. Louisville: Westminster John Knox, 1999.

Fokkelman, J. P. "Algemene Inleiding: Oog in Oog Met De Tekst Zelf." Pages 7–32 in *De Bijbel Literair: Opbouw en Gedachtegang van de Bijbelse Geschriften en hun Onderlinge Relaties*. Edited by J. P. Fokkelman and Wim Weren. Zoetermeer: Meinema, 2003.

Fox, Nili. "Royal Officials and Court Families: A New Look at the ילדים (*yĕlādîm*) in 1 Kings 12." *BA* 59 (1996): 225–32.

Garcia-Treto, Francisco O. "The Fall of the House: A Carnivalesque Reading of 2 Kings 9 and 20." Pages 153–71 in *Reading Between Texts: Intertextuality and the Hebrew Bible*. Edited by Danna Nolan Fewell. Louisville: Westminster John Knox, 1992.

Gilmayr-Bucher, Susanne. "She Came to Test Him with Hard Questions: Foreign Women and Their View on Israel." *BibInt* 15 (2007): 135–50.

Gilmour, Garth. "An Iron Age II Pictorial Inscription from Jerusalem." *PEQ* 141 (2009): 87–103.

Glover, Neil. "Elijah versus the Narrative of Elijah: The Contest between the Prophet and the Word." *JSOT* 30 (2006): 449–62.

Hadjiev, Tchavadar. "Elijah's Alleged Megalomania: Reading Strategies for Composite Texts, with 1 Kings 19 as an Example." *JSOT* 39 (2015): 433–49.

Hays, J. Daniel. "Has the Narrator Come to Praise Solomon or to Bury Him? Narrative Subtlety in 1 Kings 1–11. *JSOT* 28 (2003): 149–74.

Hepner, Gershon. "Three's a Crowd at Shunem: Elisha's Misconduct with the Shunamite Reflects a Polemic against Prophetism." *ZAW* 1 (2010): 387–400.

Jobling, David. "Forced Labor: Solomon's Golden Age and the Art of Literary Representation." *Semeia* 54 (1991): 59–76.

Kim, Jean Kyoung. "Reading and Retelling Naaman's Story (2 Kings 5)." *JSOT* 30 (2005): 49–61.

Klein, Reuven Chaim (Rudolph). "Queen Athaliah: The Daughter of Ahab or Omri?" *JBQ* 42 (2014): 11–20.

Kitz, Anne-Marie. "Naboth's Vineyard after Mari and Amarna." *JBL* 134 (2015): 529–45.

Lasine, Stuart. "Jehoram and the Cannibal Mothers (2 Kings 6:24–33): Solomon's Judgment in an Inverted World." *JSOT* 50 (1991): 27–53.

———. "Reading Jeroboam's Intentions: Intertextuality, Rhetoric, and History in 1 Kings 12." Pages 133–52 in *Reading Between Texts: Intertextuality and the Hebrew Bible*. Edited by Danna Nolan Fewell. Louisville: Westminster John Knox, 1992.

———. "The Riddle of Solomon's Judgment and the Riddle of Human Nature in the Hebrew Bible." *JSOT* 45 (1989): 61–86.

Lemos, Tracy M. "Were Israelite Women Chattel? Shedding Light on an Old Question." Pages 227–43 in *Worship, Women and War: Essays in Honor of Susan Niditch*. Edited by John J. Collins, T. M. Lemos, and Saul M. Olyan. Providence, RI: Brown University Press, 2015.

Long, Burke O. "Historical Narrative and the Fictionalizing Imagination." *VT* 35 (1985): 405–16.

Mead, James K. "Kings and Prophets, Donkeys and Lions: Dramatic Shape and Deuteronomistic Rhetoric in 1 Kings XIII." *VT* 49 (1999): 191–205.

Moberly, R. W. L. "Does God Lie to His Prophets? The Story of Micaiah ben Imlah as a Test Case." *HTR* 96 (2003): 1–23.

Morrow, William S. "Were There Neo-Assyrian Influences in Manasseh's Temple? Comparative Evidence from Tel-Miqne/Ekron." *CBQ* 75 (2013): 53–73.

Muntean, Fritz. "Asherah: Goddess of the Israelites." *Pomegranate* 5 1998: 36–47.

O'Connor, Michael Patrick. "The Biblical Notion of the City." Pages 18–39 in *Construction of Space II: The Biblical City and Other Imagined Spaces.* Edited by Jon Berquist and Claudia V. Camp. London: T&T Clark, 2008.

Olanisebe, Samson O. "Laws of Tzara'at in Leviticus 13–14 and Medical Leprosy Compared." *JBQ* 42 (2014): 121–27.

Olley, John W. "Yнwн and His Zealous Prophet: The Presentation of Elijah in 1 and 2 Kings." *JSOT* 80 (1998): 25–51.

Provan, Iain. "Why Barzillai of Gilead (1 Kings 2:7)? Narrative Art and the Hermeneutics of Suspicion in 1 Kings 1–2." *TynBul* 46 (1995): 103–16.

Rand, Herbert. "Pronunciation: A Key to Meaning: 1 Kings 3:16–28." *JBQ* 24 (1997): 246–50.

Roi, Micha. "1 Kings 19: A 'Departure Journey' Story." *JSOT* 37 (2012): 25–44.

Russell, Stephen C. "Ideologies of Attachment in the Story of Naboth's Vineyard." *BTB* 44 (2014): 29–39.

Sawyer, John F. A. "A Note on the Etymology of Tsara'at." *VT* 26 (1976): 241–45.

Schipper, Jeremy. "Hezekiah, Manasseh, and Dynastic or Transgenerational Punishment." Pages 81–105 in *Soundings in Kings: Perspectives and Methods in Contemporary Scholarship.* Edited by Mark Leuchter and Klaus-Peter Adam. Minneapolis: Fortress, 2010.

Seow, Leon. "The Syro-Palestinian Context of Solomon's Dream." *HTR* 77 (1984): 141–52.

Shields, Mary E. "Subverting a Man of God, Elevating a Woman: Role and Power Reversals in 2 Kings 4." *JSOT* 58 (1923): 56–69.

Siebert-Hommes, Jopie. "The Widow of Zarephath and the Great Woman of Shunem: A Comparative Analysis of Two Stories." Pages 98–114 in *Samuel and Kings.* Edited by Athalya Brenner. A Feminist Companion to the Bible, second series. Sheffield: Sheffield Academic, 2000.

Spanier, Ktziah. "The Queen Mother in the Judean Royal Court: Maacah—A Case Study." Pages 186–95 in *A Feminist Companion to Samuel and Kings.* Edited by Athalya Brenner. Sheffield: Sheffield Academic, 1994.

Stamm, J. J. "Hebräische Frauennamen." Pages 301–39 in *Hebräische Wortforschung: Festschrift zum 80 Geburtstag von Walter Baumgartner.* Edited by Benedikt Hartmann, Ernst Jenni, E. Y. Kutscher, Victor Maag, I. L. Seeligmann, and Rudolf Smend. VTSup 16. Leiden: Brill, 1967.

Viviano, Pauline. "2 Kings 17: A Rhetorical and Form-Critical Analysis." *CBQ* 49 (1987): 548–59.

Van Winkle, D. W. "1 Kings XII 25–XIII 34: Jeroboam's Cultic Innovations and the Man of God from Judah." *VT* 46 (1996): 101–114.

_____. "1 Kings XIII: True and False Prophecy." *VT* 29 (1989): 31–43.

Walsh, Jerome T. "The Contexts of 1 Kings XIII." *VT* 39 (1989): 355–70.

Wijk-Bos, Johanna W. H. van. "Writing on the Water: The Ineffable Name of God." Pages 45–59 in *Jews, Christians, and the Theology of the Hebrew Scriptures*. Edited by Alice Ogden Bellis and Joel Kaminsky. Atlanta: Society of Biblical Literature, 2000.

Wolde, Ellen van. "Who Guides Whom? Embeddedness and Perspective in Biblical Hebrew and in 1 Kings 3:16–28." *JBL* 114 (1995): 623–42.

# Author Index

# Subject Index

# Scripture Index